Transformed in Christ

Princeton Theological Monograph Series

K. C. Hanson, Charles M. Collier, D. Christopher Spinks,
and Robin Parry, Series Editors

Recent volumes in the series:

Susan Marie Smith
*Christian Ritualizing and the Baptismal Process:
Liturgical Explorations toward a Realized Baptismal Ecclesiology*

James L. Papandrea
Novatian of Rome and the Culmination of Pre-Nicene Orthodoxy

Aliou Cissé Niang
*Text, Image, and Christians in the Graeco-Roman World:
A Festschrift in Honor of David Lee Balch*

Sara M. Koenig
Isn't This Bathsheba?: A Study in Characterization

Gale Heide
*Timeless Truth in the Hands of History:
A Short History of System in Theology*

Atsuyoshi Fujiwara
*Theology of Culture in a Japanese Context:
A Believers' Church Perspective*

Koo Dong Yun
*The Holy Spirit and Ch'i (Qi):
A Chiological Approach to Pneumatology*

Stanley S. MacLean
*Resurrection, Apocalypse, and the Kingdom of Christ:
The Eschatology of Thomas F. Torrance*

Transformed in Christ

Christology and the Christian Life in John Chrysostom

Ashish J. Naidu

☙PICKWICK *Publications* • Eugene, Oregon

TRANSFORMED IN CHRIST
Christology and the Christian Life in John Chrysostom

Princeton Theological Monograph Series 188

Copyright © 2012 Ashish J. Naidu. All rights reserved. Except for brief quotations in critical publications or reviews, no part of this book may be reproduced in any manner without prior written permission from the publisher. Write: Permissions, Wipf and Stock Publishers, 199 W. 8th Ave., Suite 3, Eugene, OR 97401.

Pickwick Publications
An Imprint of Wipf and Stock Publishers
199 W. 8th Ave., Suite 3
Eugene, OR 97401

www.wipfandstock.com

ISBN 13: 978-1-61097-490-5

Cataloguing-in-Publication data:

Naidu, Ashish J.

    Transformed in Christ : christology and the Christian life in John Chrysostom / Ashish J. Naidu.

    xvi + 276 pp. ; 23 cm. Includes bibliographical references and index(es).

    Princeton Theological Monograph Series 188

    ISBN 13: 978-1-61097-490-5

    1. John Chrysostom, Saint, d. 407—Contributions in Christology. 2. Jesus Christ—History of doctrines—Early church, ca. 30–600. I. Series. II. Title.

BT198 .N35 2012

Manufactured in the U.S.A.

For

Sabita and Sharon

Contents

Acknowledgments / ix

Abbreviations / xi

Introduction / xiii

1. Historical Context and Background / 1
2. Reading and Interpretation of the Scriptures in the Early Church / 18
3. The Doctrine of Christ in Chrysostom's Homilies on the Gospel of John / 83
4. The Doctrine of Christ in Chrysostom's Homilies on Hebrews / 168

Conclusion / 247

Bibliography / 261

Subject Index / 273

Acknowledgments

THE PREPARATION OF THIS MONOGRAPH WAS FACILITATED BY A HOST of individuals to whom I owe a debt of gratitude. I would like to thank Professor Iain R. Torrance for his remarkable supervision in the initial stages of my research at the University of Aberdeen, which led me to investigate the relationship between Christology and the Christian life in John Chrysostom. Many thanks are due to Dr. Ian A. McFarland for his outstanding guidance in the later stages of my research, which enabled me to refine my thinking on the topic. I am also indebted to the late Professor David F. Wright, who served as the external examiner of my dissertation and recommended it for publication.

I would like to recognize a group of postgraduates (a.k.a. "The DAWGS"), whose camaraderie made my experience in Scotland a memorable one. The fond memories and the many seasons of prayerful fellowship with them shall be cherished. I am deeply grateful for their friendship, which Augustine prized as "cocta fervore parilium studiorum" (matured by our passion for like studies). Many thanks are due to Peter and Eleanor Dickson, the Hilton church family (Aberdeen), Donnie and Janet Macrae, and the Church of Scotland family (Gairloch) for their fervent prayers and gracious hospitality.

The present form of the monograph owes much to the generosity of my friends and colleagues at Talbot School of Theology, Biola University. I owe a debt of gratitude to my deans, Drs. Dennis Dirks and Michael Wilkins, and to department chair Dr. Henry Holloman for granting me a research leave that eventually resulted in this publication. I wish to acknowledge my students, both past and present, whose poignant questions continue to remind me of the relevance of the consensual voice of the historic Christian faith. I hope that this book will serve as a credible piece of scholarship both for the academy and the church. Special thanks are also due to my former student and teaching assistant, Matthew Wilcoxen, who diligently proofread the revised manuscript and offered detailed suggestions for refining it. I also wish to express my heart-felt appreciation to the efficient and professional staff at Wipf & Stock, particularly to Robin Parry, Charlie Collier, Jim Tedrick, Jacob Martin, Christian Amondson, and Patrick Harrison.

My sincere gratitude is extended to my parents, Dan and Meena, for their generosity and prayers over all these years. Finally, on a personal note, I am profoundly grateful to my dearest wife, Sabita, and daughter, Sharon, for their unwavering love, patience, and support, without which this project could not have been completed. To them this work is affectionately dedicated.

Soli Deo Gloria,
Ashish J. Naidu
Talbot School of Theology
Biola University
La Mirada, CA

Abbreviations

ACW	Ancient Christian Writers
ANF	Ante-Nicene Fathers
CCSG	Corpus Christianorum, Series Graeca
CCSL	Corpus Christianorum, Series Latina
CSCO	Corpus Scriptorum Christianorum Orientalium
FOC	Fathers of the Church
GCS	Die Grieschischen Christlichen Schriftsteller
NPNF	Nicene and Post-Nicene Fathers, First Series
PG	Patrologia Cursus Completus, Series Graeca
PL	Patrologia Cursus Completus, Series Latina
Pusey	*Sancti Patris nostri Cyrilli Archiepiscopi Alexandrini in D. Joannis Evangelium*
SC	Sources Chrétiennes

Introduction

ALTHOUGH JOHN CHRYSOSTOM'S REPUTATION AS ONE OF THE EARLY church's distinguished preachers is undisputed, his christological thought has been a matter of debate among patristic scholars. Nearly all of the previous studies of Chrysostom's Christology have failed to meaningfully locate this doctrinal content in the nexus of the church's faith. By contrast, this study affirms that the doctrine of the person of Christ cannot be considered apart from Chrysostom's understanding of the Christian life. Chrysostom's picture of Christ is pastoral and paraenetic in nature, and thus inseparable from the life of faith in the ecclesiastical context.

Having been ordained in Antioch as a priest in AD 386, and subsequently as the bishop of Constantinople in 398, Chrysostom's ecclesiastical career flourished at a time when Nicea and Constantinople were past events. The Council of Ephesus would not be held until some two and a half decades after Chrysostom's death in 407, and the Council of Chalcedon another two decades after Ephesus. The ecumenical pronouncements at the Council of Constantinople in 381 reasserted the Nicene Symbol, underscoring the consubstantiality of Christ with the Father (against Arianism), insisting on his full humanity and divinity (against Apollinarianism), while maintaining the distinction of persons in the Trinity (against Sabellianism). The question of the relation between the human and divine natures of Christ had not yet been raised at this point in the history of the church. The ensuing fifth-century Nestorian and Eutychian controversies—which led, respectively, to the Councils of Ephesus (431) and Chalcedon (451)—and the questions concerning the union of the two natures, whether it was prosopic or hypostatic, were yet to appear on the horizon. Thus Chrysostom exercised his ministerial duties at a period in church history when there was relative calm on the conciliar front.

Chrysostom addressed Christians first as a priest in Antioch and subsequently as a bishop in Constantinople, two historic cities in the

Christian East, and therefore his exegetical homilies are a valuable source of information for understanding the relationship between doctrine and practice in patristic thought. A cursory reading of Chrysostom's exegetical oeuvre betrays the fact that pastoral concerns govern his preaching, and that his doctrinal thought is inseparably bound to the life of faith and the church's worship. Scholarly readings of Chrysostom's Christology have hardly considered the intimate relationship that existed between doctrine and praxis in patristic theology in general, and in Chrysostom's theology in particular. Isolating Chrysostom's doctrinal thought from his paraenetic thought leads to an etiolated representation of his christological picture. Chrysostom's Christology is not theoretical or speculative in outlook; rather, it is pastoral in nature. Any evaluation of patristic positions on christological questions must take into consideration the relationship between doctrine and the context of exposition. Within this conceptual framework, Chrysostom's exegetical commentaries on John's Gospel and the Epistle to the Hebrews are examined in order to formulate his picture of Christ as it relates to the Christian life.

The present study is divided into four chapters. The first chapter is a brief survey of Chrysostom's life and times. This chapter is mainly biographical in nature and contextualizes Chrysostom's ecclesiastical career both as a priest in Antioch and as a bishop in Constantinople. The second chapter examines Chrysostom's place as an exegete with reference to the so-called Alexandrian and Antiochene schools of interpretation. This chapter surveys how the Alexandrian and Antiochene fathers read and appropriated the Scriptures, and examines Chrysostom's reading and interpretation of Scripture in this context. The study of patristic exegesis from both "schools" highlights the point that Alexandria and Antioch shared a common platform and goal: the church and the Christian edification of its audience. It will be suggested that the Alexandrian and Antiochene "schools" are better viewed as two corresponding traditions that operated within the early church and approximated the central idea of Christ in their unique ways, spiritually and practically. I underscore the point that the intimate relationship between doctrine and application, theory and praxis, is most apparent in Chrysostom's exegesis.

The third and fourth chapters investigate Chrysostom's exegesis of John's Gospel and of Hebrews, highlighting Chrysostom's use of images and formulating his christological picture as it emerges in his exposition. In these two chapters, Chrysostom's christological thought is examined by way of a threefold structure: the ontological considerations, the sacramental mediation, and the practical outworking. The third chapter surveys Chrysostom's exegesis of John's Gospel and discusses his Christology from three perspectives that correspond with the threefold analytical structure. The first perspective, which is labeled as a *Christology of Restoration*, examines Chrysostom's incarnational thought and its soteriological implications. Here Chrysostom's view of the ontology of the incarnation as it relates to his soteriology is discussed. The second perspective, called a *Christology of Participation*, investigates Chrysostom's sacramental thought with particular reference to his understanding of the Eucharist, underscoring the participatory character of his theology. The third perspective, a *Practical Christology*, examines the praxeological aspects of Chrysostom's christological thought with reference to the life of faith and virtue.

In keeping with the threefold analytical structure, the fourth chapter investigates Chrysostom's exegesis of Hebrews from three perspectives as well. The first, a *Christology of Identification*, considers Chrysostom's view of the ontological continuity of the Logos-Son in his incarnate and ascended existence, addressing the soteriological significance of the reality of Christ's human experience. The second perspective, called a *Christology of Mediation*, explores the relationship between the sacramental and sacerdotal aspects of Chrysostom's theology as they relate to the person of Christ. The final perspective, termed a *Christology of Grace*, examines the relationship between the christological and charitological dimensions of Chrysostom's theology as they pertain to the Christian life.

My study of Chrysostom's exegesis of John's Gospel and of Hebrews will demonstrate that his christological picture is unitive in character and paraenetic in its outlook: the idea of Logos-Son as the single subject in Christ has sacramental and praxeological implications. The christological portrait that emerges in Chrysostom's preaching is a depiction of the personal continuity of the Logos-Son in Christ; his sacramental presence in the church, the body of Christ; and his transforming work in the Christian to the likeness of Christ. In summary, it will be shown that Chrysostom's understanding of the Christian life is the outworking of his unitive Christology.

The existence of a voluminous number of manuscripts of Chrysostom's works attests to his popular reception in the church; this broad reception is also probably the reason why no complete critical edition of his works has yet been compiled.[1] The Greek text by Migne is the Benedictine edition produced under Montfaucon (13 vols., 1718–38; revised 1834–40).[2] Critical editions of a limited collection of Chrysostom's treatises can be found in *Sources chrétiennes*.[3] Besides the dated English translations of Chrysostom's works, which include his exegetical homilies and commentaries in the *Nicene and Post-Nicene Fathers* (*NPNF*) first series, recently updated translations of his homilies, treatises, and commentaries may be found in the *Fathers of the Church* (*FOC*) series.[4] In the absence of critical editions of Chrysostom's commentaries on John's Gospel and Hebrews, the Greek text that is used in this work is from the *PG* series, volume 59 (John's Gospel) and volume 63 (Hebrews). The English citations are from updated translations where they apply. Due to the lack of an updated English translation of Chrysostom's homilies on Hebrews, the *NPNF* translation (volume 14), with minor modifications, is used. The citations for the homilies on John's Gospel are from the *FOC* series (volumes 33 and 41).[5]

---

1. Baur notes that there may be around two thousand manuscripts in the catalogues of the libraries of Europe and in Jerusalem. See Baur, *S. Jean Chrysostome et ses oeuvres dans l'histoire littéraire*. Young has estimated that the number is likely to be in the region of three to four thousand. Young, *From Nicea to Chalcedon*, 157. For a comprehensive list of Chrysostom's writings, see Geerard, *Clavis Patrum Graecorum*. The mammoth task of cataloging manuscripts and distinguishing the authentic texts from the spurious has been made in the recent past. See Aubineau, *Codices Chrysostomici Graeci I: Britanniae et Hiberniae*; Carter, *Codices Chrysostomici Graeci II: Germaniae*; and Aldama, *Repertorium pseudochrysostomicum*.

2. *Patrologiae corpus completum. Series Graeca*. 47–64.

3. These volumes contain both the critical edition of the Greek text and a modern French translation.

4. *NPNF First Series*, 9–14. Recent English translations include Chrysostom, *Homilies on Genesis*, trans. Hill, *FOC* 74, 82, 87; Chrysostom, *Commentary on the Psalms*, trans. Hill, *FOC* 1–2.

5. Chrysostom, *Commentary on Saint John the Apostle and Evangelist*, trans. Goggin, *FOC* 33, 41.

1

Historical Context and Background

Early Life and Training

JOHN, BETTER KNOWN BY HIS TITLE *CHRYSOSTOMOS*—OR GOLDEN Mouth—was born in Antioch circa AD 349.[1] Having spent his early years as a student of rhetoric, philosophy, and the Bible, he was ordained as a deacon in 381, and then as a priest five years later. Chrysostom subsequently became the bishop of Constantinople in 398. The Seleucids founded Antioch, a Greek-speaking city in the province of Syria, in 300 BC. A sparkling city on the banks of the river Orontes, it was known for its culture and architecture.[2] The city also happened to be the residence of the Roman governor of Syria, the *comes orientis*. The chief military officer of the Eastern provinces, the *magister militum per orientem*, also made his headquarters there. By ancient standards the city was large, but smaller than Rome; it was roughly the same size as Constantinople and Alexandria, with a population somewhere between 150,000 and 300,000 inhabitants.[3] It was to some extent cosmopolitan, with Greek as its common language, although peasants in the surrounding countryside spoke Syriac. The higher social strata of the city consisted of a large number of professional men: lawyers, teachers of rhetoric, high-ranking civil ser-

---

1. The title was applied for the first time in the "constitution" of Pope Vigilius in the year 553 on account of his extraordinary oratorical skills. For an exhaustive overview of John Chrysostom's biographical account, see Kelly, *Golden Mouth*; Baur, *John Chrysostom and His Time*; Wilken, *John Chrysostom and the Jews*.

2. By the fourth century the city was thoroughly Hellenized in language, education, civic organization, art, architecture, and in its tastes and prejudice. See Wilken, *John Chrysostom and the Jews*, 4.

3. Liebeschuetz, *Antioch*, 92–100.

vants, and the higher clergy.[4] The social milieu of Antioch was filled out by shopkeepers, craftsmen, workers of the land, and traders. The majority of its inhabitants were Christian, besides pagans and Jews.[5]

The second half of the fourth century witnessed much change in the political, ecclesiastical, and theological landscape. Julian, who was named Caesar in 355, became the emperor of the East after the death of his uncle Constantius. In an edict, he announced religious freedom for pagans and called on the pagans to reopen the temples and restore the worship of old gods. The bishops who were exiled by Constantius were given permission to return to their respective sees. At one particular juncture in the mid-360s, there were three bishops in Antioch: Meletius (the Nicene bishop, who also enjoyed support from factions of the Arian party and who would eventually ordain John as lector); Euzoius, the Arian bishop; and another Nicene bishop named Paulinus. For a brief period after 375 there was also a fourth bishop who headed another party founded by Apollinarius.[6] Chrysostom was familiar with life in a divided community of Jews, pagans, Manichaeans, Arians, Apollinarians, and Nicene Christians. Amidst these rivalries, Chrysostom would surpass several key individuals to become one of the outstanding figures of the Eastern Church. Augustine, his slightly younger Western contemporary, described him as *eruditus et erudiens* in the Catholic faith and esteemed him as a distinguished witness and defender of the faith, placing him among the most celebrated learned men and saints.[7]

Although Chrysostom spoke very little about himself in his works, he is one of the few ecclesiastical figures of the fourth century whose life has been well documented. Several ancient biographers and panegyrists have left a wealth of information about his early life, ecclesiastical career, and exile and death, in addition to detailing his legendary rhetorical skills, which eventually earned him the title of Golden Mouth.[8]

---

4. Wilken, *John Chrysostom and the Jews*, 4.

5. Liebeschuetz, *Antioch*, 224. The city council enjoyed a Christian majority, who recalled with pride that the Apostles Peter and Paul had both worked at Antioch and that according to Acts 11:26, it was there that believers had first been called Christians. Kelly, *Golden Mouth*, 2.

6. Wilken, *John Chrysostom and the Jews*, 12–13.

7. Augustine, *Contra Julianum*, 1.6.22, cited in Baur, *John Chrysostom and His Time*, 1:365.

8. For a list of ancient biographers whose works are extant, see Baur, *John Chrysostom and His Time*, 1:xxi–xxii. See also Kelly, *Golden Mouth*, 291–95. Among the ancient bi-

John was born into a well-to-do family. His father, Secundus, was a civil servant in the bureau of the *magister milium per orientem* (secretariat of the commander-in-chief). His mother, Anthusa, was widowed at the age of twenty, when he was an infant. She did not choose to marry a second time; instead, she devoted herself to raising John and his slightly older sister. John reminisces about the tender loving care his mother extended towards him as a child in his well-known *De Sacerdotio* (*On the Priesthood*). Not much is known about his childhood, but he certainly would have attended elementary school, where reading, writing, and basic arithmetic skills were taught. His exceptional intellectual skills may have been noticed early on, for John does not seem to have attended the higher schools of education in Antioch. He studied rhetoric under the well-known rhetorician Libanius, and philosophy under Andragathius. On the linguistic front, Chrysostom spoke only Greek—he never learned Syriac, the language that was spoken in the countryside. Neither does he seem to have learned Hebrew, as he depends entirely on the Greek translations of the Old Testament for his exegesis.[9] Chrysostom graduated under the tutelage of Libanius and like his fellow students may have planned to join the civil service in the *Sacra Scrinia* (the branch of the government that was responsible for drafting official edicts).[10] However, at some point following his graduation, he became deeply interested in the religious life and dedicated himself to studying the Scriptures.[11] He seems to have been influenced by the pro-Nicene bishop Miletius, who eventually baptized him. Chrysostom later joined the *askētērion*, a seminary led by Diodore and Carterius, where theology and exegesis

---

ographers, Palladius' biography is considered to be a reliable authority on Chrysostom's life, especially during his years in Constantinople as bishop. A friend and supporter of Chrysostom, Palladius wrote his account around 408, shortly after Chrysostom's death. See Palladius, *Dialogue on the Life of St. John Chrysostom*. Socrates, a fourth-century historian, also recorded events pertaining to the life and times of Chrysostom. See Socrates, *Historia Ecclesiastica*, 6:2–23; 7:27, 45. Sozomen, a fifth-century historian, relied on Socrates and incorporated biographical information from other sources. His account of Chrysostom's life can be found in Sozomen, *Historia Ecclesiastica*, 8:2–24, 26 and 28. English translations of Socrates and Sozomen can be found in vol. 2 of *NPNF*. In addition to Baur and Kelly, other English biographies of Chrysostom include: Attwater, *Saints of the East*; Macgilvray, *John of the Golden Mouth*; Neander, *The Life of John Chrysostom*; Puech, *Saint John Chrysostom*; Stephens, *Saint Chrysostom*.

9. Baur, *John Chrysostom and His Time*, 1:97.
10. Wilken, *John Chrysostom and the Jews*, 5.
11. Palladius, *Dialogue on the Life of St. John Chrysostom*, 5:18.

were taught. Theodore, later to become the bishop of Mopsuestia, and Maximus, later the bishop of Seleucia, were fellow students of Diodore along with Chrysostom. According to Palladius, John was appointed to the position of an official reader or lector around 371.[12] This position was the lowest order in the Eastern Church, just below that of a deacon.

Shortly after John was appointed as lector, he decided to dedicate himself to the monastic lifestyle, commonly known *askēsis*, which involved the exercise of self-denial, moral discipline, mortification of the flesh, prayer, and the study of the Bible.[13] The monastic movement, which had its beginnings in Egypt, had spread throughout the Roman world, particularly the East, including Syria. Within a short period of time the Syrian monks rivaled those of the Egyptians. The stature of Syrian monasticism is evidenced by the fact that Jerome chose Syria over Egypt for monastic training.[14] This monastic lifestyle seemed to have attracted many Christians and became an ideal for those wishing to disengage from worldly pursuits. Chrysostom's decision to join the eremitic monks did not go unchallenged; his mother, who could not bear losing her only son to the monastic life, pleaded with him not to abandon her.[15] Shortly after Anthusa's death, John joined the monks and spent four years under the guidance of a Syrian ascetic in the mountains surrounding Antioch. Chrysostom spent two additional years retreating to a cave where he denied himself sleep by continually standing and memorized the Scriptures by heart. The extreme rigor of this ascetic lifestyle permanently damaged Chrysostom's stomach and kidneys.[16] Driven by failing health, he returned to Antioch and resumed his duties as a lector. Baur suggests that Chrysostom's *A King and the Monk Compared* and the letter *To Theodore When He Fell Away*, in addition to other short ascetic treatises, were probably composed during his monastic period. Kelly, however, contends that this would not have been possible, given

---

12. Kelly, *Golden Mouth*, 24. Cf. Neander, *Life of John Chrysostom*, 14–15.

13. Mayer and Allen, *John Chrysostom*, 3. Stephens notes, "He [John] was irresistibly gravitated towards that kind of life which his friend Basil had already adopted, a life of retirement, contemplation and pious study—'the philosophy' of Christianity, as it was called at that time." Stephens, *Saint Chrysostom*, 26.

14. Wilken, *John Chrysostom and the Jews*, 8.

15. Chysostom, *De Sacerdotio*, 1.5 (PG 47.625). English translation by Stephens, *NPNF* 9:33f. For an updated translation see Neville, *Six Books on the Priesthood*.

16. Palladius, *Dialogue on the Life of St. John Chrysostom*, 5.

the rigorous regimen in the *askētērion*.[17] After the death of Valens circa 378, his nephew Gratian (who favored the Nicenes) issued a decree permitting the return of all exiled bishops and proclaiming freedom of worship. Miletius, who was exiled earlier during the reign of Valens, returned to Antioch and resumed his duties as the lawful bishop of the city and installed Chrysostom as a deacon.[18]

Ecclesiastical Career

Chrysostom served as a deacon for five years before he was ordained to the priesthood by the bishop Flavian in 386. Flavian was installed as the bishop of Antioch after Miletius, who died while presiding over the Council of Constantinople in 381. It was during these years as a deacon, and subsequently as a priest in Antioch, that John's fame as an eloquent preacher and expositor spread far and wide. Discussing his articulate preaching, Baur observes, "Chrysostom is the only one among the Greek Fathers of the church who was, as it were, baptized twice. He went through life under the name John; he is known to posterity as Chrysostom, the Golden-mouth, and this name he earned in the pulpit. Nothing that he accomplished as an exegete, as an author or as a bishop brought him this distinction, but what he accomplished as a preacher."[19] The fame Chrysostom won through preaching is evident in the fact that his published sermons led Jerome to accord him a place in the *Viri Illustres* in 392, mentioning his literary activity and esteeming him as a theological writer. Antioch, therefore, would become the city where Chrysostom spent most of his theological and ecclesiastical career: five years as a deacon and twelve years as a priest. After Antioch, he spent approximately five and a half years as the bishop of Constantinople before his ecclesiastical career came to an abrupt end.

Chrysostom as Deacon and Priest at Antioch

Formerly a prominent Hellenistic city, Antioch was a busy center in the Roman world. Trade routes from different directions that connected the Far East to the Mediterranean world converged at Antioch. This feature

17. See Baur, *John Chrysostom and His Time*, 1:115; cf. Kelly, *Golden Mouth*, 20, 31.
18. Kelly, *Golden Mouth*, 36; cf. Baur, *John Chrysostom and His Time*, 1:141–43.
19. Baur, *John Chrysostom and His Time*, 1:206.

attracted buyers and traders from the surrounding rural areas. It had an eclectic mix of people from different social backgrounds, who enjoyed a pleasurable lifestyle and frequented the theatres, baths, the hippodrome, and the circus. As far as its means permitted, the church in Antioch placed a high degree of importance on supporting the poor and needy. Regular worship services were conducted in at least two churches: the Old (*Palaia*) Church and the Great Church (the episcopal church).[20]

After the death of Miletius in 381, Flavian installed Chrysostom as a deacon. Chrysostom's duties included preparation of the sacred vessels (the elements of the Eucharist), making sure the unbaptized left the church before the mass, charitable duties to the poor, and occasionally assisting the officiating priest at the eucharistic service. And although deacons were not allowed to preach, they often taught the catechumens. His role as an instructor spurred Chrysostom's literary career, and some of his earlier works are attributed to this period: *De s. Babyla Contra Iulianum et Gentiles* (PG 50.533–72); *Adversus Iudaeos et Gentiles Demonstratio quod Christus sit Deus* (PG 48.813–38); *De Compunctione* (PG 47.393–432); *Ad Stageirios* (PG 47.423–94); *De Virginitate* (PG 48.533–96); *Ad Viduam Iuniorem* and *De non Iterando Coniugio* (PG 48.599–620); *Adversus Oppugnatores Vitae Monasticae* (PG 47.319–86).[21]

Most scholars assign Chrysostom's well-known work *De Sacerdotio* (*On the Priesthood*) to the period during his retreat to the mountains with the eremitic monks, but Socrates assigns it to his diaconate.[22] Baur and Kelly challenge the veracity of this position and suggest that it was probably composed during his term as a priest, sometime after 386 and before 392. The reason: Jerome noted that he had read this work by Chrysostom in his *De Viris Illustribus*, which appeared in the year 392.

Bishop Flavian saw the obvious potential in John and ordained him to the priesthood in the year 386. John preached extensively during his term as a priest, and over nine hundred sermons, most of which are attributable to this period, survive. It is generally maintained that Chrysostom's sermons were taken down by stenographers and, in some

---

20. Baur, *John Chrysostom and His Time*, 1:159. Cf. Mayer and Allen, *John Chrysostom*, 17.

21. For an exhaustive listing, see Baur, *John Chrysostom and His Time*, 1:153–74, and Kelly, *Golden Mouth*, 36–54.

22. Socrates, *Historia Ecclesiastica*, 6.2.

cases, revised before he published them himself.²³ He often preached extemporaneously without notes, to the amazement of his listeners.

As a priest, his duties included assisting the bishop and celebrating the Eucharist. The main function of the priest, however, was preaching and instructing the people on Sundays, feast days, and other occasions.²⁴ Although one cannot ascertain where he may have preached (whether in the Old Church or the Great Church), Kelly maintains that as Flavian's aide, John may have preached in whichever church the bishop visited during his tenure, an assumption that has been contested.²⁵

One of the first series of sermons Chrysostom ever preached was from the book of Genesis. In the fall of 386, he preached a series called *De Incomprehensibili Dei Natura* (*On the Incomprehensible Nature of God*).²⁶ These homilies were preached against the Anomeans or the Neo-Arians, a radical group of Arians associated with the figure of Aëtius and his disciple Eunomius (subsequently the bishop of Cyzicus), who gained notoriety during the 340s and 350s. It was this faction, albeit in its decline in the late 380s and 390s, that Chrysostom polemically engaged from his pulpit. The Neo-Arians maintained that God is essentially simple and one; He is ἀγέννητος (unbegotten or ungenerated) and not produced, therefore no being γέννητος (begotten or generated) can be God. A being that is begotten must be ἀνόμοιος (dissimilar or unlike) in essence. They rejected the ὁμοούσιος (*homoousios*) of the Nicene party and the ὁμοιούσιος (*homoiousios*) of the followers of Basil of Ancyra and adhered to the teachings of Arius in regard to the dissimilarity of the essence of the Son. On the one hand, they concurred with the Arian teaching on the distinction of essence between the Father, Son, and the Holy Spirit—a conviction that sprang from their apprehension of the Sabellian denial of the distinct identities in the Godhead. On the other hand, they were critics of Arius in that they denied that the Son was elevated to a divine status through God's prior knowledge of his moral obedience. Furthermore, they maintained that the Father's essence was unknown to the Son (or anybody, for that matter), thereby denying the

23. Ibid., 6.4. See Kelly, *Golden Mouth*, 57.
24. Baur, *John Chrysostom and His Time*, 1:184.
25. Mayer and Allen, *John Chrysostom*, 6–7.
26. *PG* 48. For English translation, see the translation by Paul W. Harkins: Chrysostom, *On the Incomprehensible Nature of God*, vol. 72 in the Fathers of the Church series. The first ten homilies were delivered in Antioch, whereas homilies 11 and 12 were delivered in Constantinople.

reality of revelation, an idea that contradicted their epistemology: the possibility of the knowledge of God in his essence. Chrysostom mounted a frontal attack on their doctrine in this series of homilies (and also in his exposition on the prologue to John's Gospel with regard to the consubstantiality of Christ), arguing from different texts that God's nature is beyond human comprehension, for even angels cannot comprehend his essence; only the Son (who is consubstantial with the Father) and the Spirit (who is divine) have complete knowledge of the Father. After backing his arguments from different biblical texts, Chrysostom reminds his listeners that humans cannot comprehend the real essence of the sky above their head, nor even their own soul, let alone God in his essence.

In Lent of 387, a year after Chrysostom was ordained to the priesthood, his pastoral mettle would be put to the test. In his treatise *On the Priesthood*, he remarks that the caliber of a steersman cannot be determined while the ship is in the harbor. The title of excellent steersman can only be applied to a pilot who is able to guide his ship to safety in the midst of a stormy sea.[27] Chrysostom would do precisely this as he exhorted and comforted his nervous and panic-stricken congregation at Antioch after the riot of the statues.[28] The emperor Theodosius had imposed a heavy tax on the citizens of Antioch, which resulted in a riot and the destruction of the imperial statues, an incident that would make it into the history textbooks of antiquity. The populace, in vehement protest against this levy, pulled from their pedestals the golden statues of the emperor, his deceased wife Flacilla, and his son Arcadius, and dragged them through the streets. They even attacked the governor's residence and vandalized the public baths. This insurrection by the citizens of Antioch would end in much tragedy. The rioters were flogged—and some were executed, including children. In subsequent trials others were rounded up and arrested, which prompted many to flee from the city. Antioch came to a complete standstill as businesses, theatres, baths, and the marketplaces were shut down. Consequently, the churches were well attended, as people sought to find comfort and refuge there. Bishop Flavian, then an octogenarian, decided to travel to the capital, Constantinople, to meet the emperor and personally intercede on behalf of the people of Antioch. Chrysostom, meanwhile, comforted the citi-

---

27. Chrysostom, *On the Priesthood* 6:6–7, NPNF 9:77.

28. For an exhaustive historical account of the event, see van de Paverd, *St. John Chrysostom, the Homilies on the Statues*, 15–159.

zens through his preaching. His optimism regarding Flavian's personal journey to the capital can be seen in the following remarks: "I tell you God will not suffer the errand to be fruitless. The very sight of the venerable Bishop will dispose the Emperor to mercy. This is the holy season. In such a season Flavian will show the emperor the blessedness of forgiving sins, for this is the season when we remember how Christ died for the sins of the world."[29] Flavian procured a pardon from the emperor and returned to the city shortly before Easter with the good news. On Easter Sunday, Chrysostom preached a sermon that reverberated with a tone of gratitude and thanksgiving, paying great tribute to the bishop, who took it upon himself to travel to the capital in inclement weather—as well as leaving his sister on her deathbed—in order to obtain a pardon from the emperor.[30]

It was during Chrysostom's years as a priest in Antioch (386–397), Kelly believes, that he probably composed his best-known work, *On the Priesthood*. Moreover, during this decade Chrysostom produced the following works: *De Inani Gloria et de Educandis* (SC 188) (English translation in Laistner[31]); a series of commentaries on Genesis (*PG* 53) and Psalms (*PG* 55.39–498); and four homilies on Isaiah 6 (*PG* 56.107–19; 129–42). His systematic expositions on the New Testament from this period include ninety homilies on Matthew (*PG* 57–58); eighty-eight on John (*PG* 59); thirty-two on Romans (*PG* 60.391–682); fourteen on 1 Corinthians (*PG* 61.11–382); thirty on 2 Corinthians (*PG* 61.381–610); six on Galatians (*PG* 61.611–82); eighteen on 1 Timothy (*PG* 62.501–660); ten on 2 Timothy (*PG* 62.559–662); six on Titus (*PG* 62.663–700) and twenty-four on Ephesians (*PG* 62.9–174).

Baur is of the opinion that the homilies on the epistle to the Colossians, 1 and 2 Thessalonians, Acts, Philemon, Philippians, and Hebrews are of Constantinopolitan provenance, and were produced during his episcopate.[32] The scholarly community is divided on the issue of the provenance of these homilies, especially the Constantinopolitan provenance of Colossians, Philippians, and Hebrews. Although the consensus posits that they belong to the period when Chrysostom was in his episcopal office, it has been convincingly argued that these series of homilies in fact

---

29. Chrysostom, *On the Statues* 2:39, cited in Payne, *The Holy Fire*, 228–29.
30. Chrysostom, *On the Statues* 21, NPNF 9:482f.
31. Laistner, *Christianity and Pagan Culture in the Later Roman Empire*, 85–122.
32. Baur, *John Chrysostom and His Time*, 2:93–94.

contain material from both Antioch and Constantinople.³³ Chrysostom seems to have been very productive and successful as a priest at Antioch, and his reputation spread far and swiftly enough that even Augustine, his contemporary in the West, could quote him.³⁴ Those in high ecclesiastical echelons knew he was the heir apparent to the throne of the bishop of Constantinople. This abrupt promotion would soon take place when bishop Nectarius (who succeeded Gregory of Nazianzus) of Constantinople died on September 26, 397.

Chrysostom as the Bishop of Constantinople

After the death of Theodosius I in 395, his son Arcadius assumed the throne in the East. Historians maintain that Arcadius was swayed by stronger personalities than his own, especially individuals like the imperial eunuch, Eutropius, who shrewdly managed to rise above the ranks of a common chamberlain to a position of influence in the capital. The office of the bishop of Constantinople was a very powerful one, and much coveted. The bishop of the capital had considerable influence and was in constant communication with the emperor, the court, and the highest officials. Other bishops in the empire were under the jurisdiction of the bishop of Constantinople. The bishop would attend all official court ceremonies, perform royal weddings and baptisms, and wielded great influence in the empire.³⁵

The vacant episcopate of the capital caught the attention of Cyril's uncle Theophilus, the controversial bishop of Alexandria, who saw a golden opportunity to install a priest from his see, one named Isidore. Eutropius, however, had other plans; he had his eye on John, the priest at Antioch. He convinced the people and the clergy of Constantinople to install John as the bishop. John had no knowledge of what was transpiring in the capital. In October 397, he received a summons to meet the *comes orientis* (count of the East), Asterius, at the martyrium near the city gate—and before Chrysostom realized what was happening, he was transported off to Constantinople. In February 398, a number of bishops were invited at the capital to install John to the episcopate. Theophilus, the rival bishop of the see of Alexandria, was invited to pre-

---

33. Allen and Mayer, "Thirty-Four Homilies on Hebrews," 309–48.
34. Quasten, *Patrology*, 3:429.
35. Baur, *John Chrysostom and His Time*, 2:2.

side over the synod. He furiously tried to oppose the decision to install Chrysostom as the bishop of Constantinople, vying instead for his candidate, Isidore. Eutropius had come prepared for all contingencies; he threatened Theophilus that if he did not proceed as instructed, he was going to be tried, for many Alexandrian bishops had made complaints against him in writing. Theophilus acquiesced and reluctantly consecrated Chrysostom as the bishop of one of the most significant sees in the East, Constantinople.[36]

The city of Constantinople was built by Constantine in AD 330 and became the eastern capital of the Roman Empire. Constantinople was a coastal city and was slightly larger than Antioch. It was surrounded by water on three sides. The city was bound by the Sea of Marmara to the south and by an inlet known as the Golden Horn to the northeast. In contrast to Antioch, where the roads from Egypt, Asia Minor, and the Far East converged, Constantinople was a well-known port, and the destination of sea routes from Egypt and the Black Sea. As the imperial capital of the East, it was an important junction that connected Asia Minor and the Far East to Rome and other regions in the West.[37] Here, Chrysostom would begin to undertake his duties as the bishop and work in close proximity with the emperor and his court. There were four churches in the capital: the Great Church; the *Hagia Eirene* (Holy Peace) Church, also called the Old Church (*Palaia*, probably the venue of the council of 381); the Church of the Holy Apostles; and another church built by Theodosius I in 391.[38] Constantinople, like Antioch, had a mixed populace. In addition to the natives, there were Egyptians, Armenians, Syrians, Goths, and other ethnic groups from Asia Minor who belonged to different theological persuasions. The Neo-Arians were a conspicuous presence in the city, as they had their own churches and even organized nocturnal processions at certain times of the year, which in turn were rivaled by Chrysostom and his group. As the bishop of Constantinople, Chrysostom led a busy life. In addition to his episcopal duties, he trav-

---

36. There seems to be a discrepancy regarding the dates of Chrysostom's consecration as the bishop of Constantinople. Both Baur and Kelly agree with Socrates' date of February 26, 398 (*Historia Ecclesiastica* 6.2). Kelly correctly points out that the lapse of five months since the death of Nectarius and the consecration of John has never been satisfactorily explained. Kelly, *Golden Mouth*, 106. Cf. Baur, *John Chrysostom and His Time*, 2:6–14.

37. Mayer and Allen, *John Chrysostom*, 10–11.

38. Kelly, *Golden Mouth*, 108.

eled to other sees to ordain clergy, sent missionaries to neighboring provinces (especially to the Goths), and also founded hospitals.[39]

As a preacher, Chrysostom was admired in the city and his services were well attended. It was his insistence on high moral standards, not only among the clergy but also among the lay people, which would eventually sour and sever his cordial relations with the imperial family. It was this conflict that ultimately led to his short tenure as the bishop of Constantinople. Chrysostom imposed high standards of conduct on his clergy, and insisted on living a simple lifestyle himself. He cut down on unnecessary expenses and reduced the episcopal budget. He vehemently opposed the common practice of *suneisaktoi*, where unmarried virgins lived with and governed the household affairs of monks and priests.[40] As in Antioch, he continued to preach against extravagant living and attendance at the theatre, the circus, and the races. His sermons were filled with exhortations to his listeners to lead simple, holy, and moral lives.[41] In a community divided between the wealthy and the poor, he continually advocated generosity.

In the year 399, Eutropius was overthrown and, fearing for his life, he found refuge in the church. Chrysostom made use of this opportunity to preach against pride, excessive material possessions, and the fleeting nature of power. His ornate rhetoric can be seen in the way he makes use of the situation to communicate his displeasure of these vices:

> Vanity of vanities, all is vanity... Where are now the brilliant surroundings of your consulship? Where are the gleaming torches? ...Where is the applause that greeted you in the city? ... they are gone—all gone: a wind has blown upon the tree shattering down all its leaves, and showing it to us quite bare, and shaken from its very root; for so great was the violence of its blast, that it has given a shock to the fibres of the tree and threatens to tear it up from the roots ... Was I not continually telling you that wealth was a runaway? But you would not heed me. Did I not tell you that it was an unthankful servant? But you would not be persuaded. Behold actual experience has now proved that it is not only a runaway, and ungrateful servant, but also a murderous one, for it is this which has caused you now to fear and tremble ... Have you seen the insignificance of human affairs? Have you seen the frailty of power? Have you seen the wealth

---

39. Liebeschuetz, *Antioch*, 168–71.
40. Clark, "John Chrysostom and the Subintroductae," 171–85.
41. Young, *From Nicea to Chalcedon*, 147.

that I have always called a runaway and not a runaway only, but also a murderer. For it not only deserts those who possess it, but also slaughters them; for when one pays court to it then most of all does it betray him.⁴²

Eutopius' life was spared, but only for a short time. After a few months, he was stripped of his power, his property was confiscated, and he was tried and executed in Chalcedon.⁴³ Chrysostom's rigorous standards of moral life and his constant allusions to conforming one's life to a certain code of conduct did not go well with many. This was especially so with two deacons who were expelled because they were found guilty of adultery and murder.⁴⁴ Theophilus would later have them present at a synod as the chief accusers of Chrysostom in order to depose and exile him on disciplinary grounds.

The controversy reached its zenith after Theophilus, in alliance with the empress Eudoxia (who now harbored ill feelings against Chrysostom because of hostile tale-bearers), would accuse him of baseless charges at the Synod of the Oak, and ultimately depose him. It all began with the controversy of the tall brothers, a group of Egyptian monks who were accused of Origenism and consequently excommunicated and driven out of Egypt and Palestine by Theophilus. The monks were headed by four brothers—Dioscorus, Ammonius, Eusebius, and Euthymius—who sought Chrysostom's help. Though Chrysostom received them and promised to help them, he did not let them receive communion. The tall brothers found an audience with the emperor and voiced their complaints against Theophilus. In the fall of 403, the bishop of Alexandria was summoned to Constantinople to answer charges brought against him by the Egyptian monks.

Meanwhile, Severian, the bishop of Gabala, who substituted for Chrysostom during his absence, was establishing and securing a position for himself at the imperial court. This ambitious homilist was not well received by Chrysostom's archdeacon, Serapion, and a rivalry soon ensued. When Theophilus arrived in Constantinople with his entourage of monks, an anti-Chrysostom sentiment was already brewing at the palace, especially with the empress, who was informed that Chrysostom

---

42. Chrysostom, *On Eutropius*, 1:1–3, NPNF 9:249–52.
43. Kelly, *Golden Mouth*, 150.
44. Palladius, *Dialogue on the Life of St. John Chrysostom*, 8:27.

was slandering her in his sermons (particularly when he delivered the homily *On Vainglory*).

Chrysostom was asked to preside over the issue of the tall brothers by the emperor; he refused, for he probably did not want to interfere with matters that pertained to the see of Alexandria. It was during this delicate interval that the tables were turned and Theophilus himself, who was summoned to answer charges in Constantinople, saw an opportunity to depose Chrysostom—the very candidate he was forced to ordain a few years earlier. Theophilus garnered all the support that he could from clergy who disliked Chrysostom, particularly from the two deacons whom Chrysostom had expelled and from Serapion, who also accused him of wrongdoing.

Theophilus held a synod on the outskirts of the city (the aforementioned Synod of the Oak) and summoned Chrysostom to appear. Chrysostom sent word to the synod that he would be willing to appear if his enemies were removed from the group. Theophilus disregarded John's request and began the proceedings in his absence, reaching a decision to depose him on the charges of refusing to appear at the synod. The emperor supported the decision, and Chrysostom was stripped of his office. The citizens of Constantinople voiced their opinion by demonstrating against the decision of the synod. Not wanting a riot to ensue on his account, John surrendered himself to the authorities. He was taken to the harbor and put on a boat headed for Praenetos, a port between Helenopolis and Nicomedia.[45]

In a strange turn of events, Chrysostom was recalled by the superstitious empress due to a mishap interpreted as a bad omen. He returned to Constantinople and resumed his duties as the bishop for about seven months, from October 403 to Easter 404. During this time he also had the emperor convene another synod to nullify the charges that were brought against him at the Synod of the Oak. Chrysostom's return to the capital would be short-lived, however, as he would be exiled for good in June 404.

Life in Exile and Death

Two months after his return, Chrysostom would have another skirmish with the empress Eudoxia, and this time his enemies would prevail.

---

45. Kelly, *Golden Mouth*, 232.

According to Socrates and Sozomen, Chrysostom complained about the raucous celebrations that were being held to honor the dedication of Eudoxia's silver statues, which were erected in close proximity to the church.[46] Word quickly spread to the empress that John was alluding to her excesses in his sermons; this infuriated her afresh, and she moved to curtail his authority as a bishop, prohibiting him from officiating at the Easter services. Although Chrysostom was allowed to reside in his official residence, he was barred from performing his episcopal duties at the Great Church. Baptismal services normally held during Easter at the Great Church were moved to another location; these celebrations ended in bloodshed, as soldiers who were sent to disrupt the services clashed with John's allies. It was not until two months later, in June 404, that the opposition finally convinced the emperor Arcadius to issue a decree that would send Chrysostom to his second and final exile to Cucusos in Armenia.

Little is known about Chrysostom's time in exile. During this period he wrote a series of letters to Olympias, a deaconess.[47] These letters describe some of his experiences during his exile, detailing his ailing health, inactivity, and lack of sleep:

> For the winter which has become more than commonly severe, brought on a storm of internal disorder even more distressing, and during the last two months I have been no better than one dead, nay worse. For I had just enough life to be sensible of the horrors which encircled me and day and dawn and noon were all one night to me as I spent all my time closely confined to my bed, and in spite of endless contrivances I could not shake off the pernicious effects of the cold; but although I kept a fire burning, and endured a most unpleasant amount of smoke and remained cooped up in one chamber, covered with any quantity of wraps, and not daring to set a foot outside the threshold I underwent extreme sufferings, perpetual vomiting supervening on headache, loss of appetite, and constant sleeplessness.[48]

During his exile he was occasionally visited by admirers, who journeyed all the way from Antioch and other Syrian cities to see him. He seems to

---

46. Socrates, *Historia Ecclesiastica*, 6:18. Cf. Sozomen, *Historia Ecclesiastica*, 8:20.

47. See PG 52. English translation of the seventeen extant letters can be found in NPNF 9:287–304. Critical edition in the volume edited by A. M. Malingrey: Chrysostom, *Sur l'incomprehesibilité de Dieu*, vol. 13 in the Sources Chrétiennes series.

48. *Letters of St. Chrysostom to Olympias*, NPNF 9:297.

have been instrumental in organizing outreaches to different groups of people, and Sozomen reports that he had ample funds at his disposal for such projects. It is reported that at one point he even secured the release of several people who were taken into slavery by the Isaurians.[49] The increasing flurry of activity, and the news of the visits from his friends, eventually caught the attention of his enemies in Constantinople. In the summer of 407, a military party arrived from Constantinople with orders to dispatch him to Pityus, a remote location at the foot of the Caucasus Mountains. By this time Chrysostom was weakened by years of illness and his health had deteriorated. He was escorted on foot over difficult terrain, but his frail health and condition allowed him to walk only as far as Comana. The following day, Chrysostom, exhausted from the journey, begged the soldiers to delay the journey until later, but they refused. His physical condition would not allow him to reach Pityus; he collapsed on the way and was brought back to Comana, where he died on September 14, 407, at the age of fifty-eight.[50] In the year 438, the emperor Theodosius II, the son of Arcadius and Eudoxia, transferred the remains of Chrysostom from Comana to the Church of the Holy Apostles in Constantinople. They remained there until the first capture and sack of the city by the crusaders in 1204 and were subsequently transferred to St. Peter's Basilica in Rome. After eight hundred years, in November 2004, the remains of the two former bishops, Gregory of Nazianzus and John Chrysostom, were returned to the Greek Patriarchate in Istanbul.[51]

Chrysostom's advanced training under the pagan rhetorician Libanius, and his years of theological training under Diodore, contributed greatly to his fame both as a preacher and an exegete. During his time at the *askētērion* he committed the New Testament to memory, and his keen mind enabled him to quote verses with great ease in his sermons.[52] Rhetorical devices evident in his preaching are consistent

---

49. Sozomen, *Historia Ecclesiastica*, 8:27.

50. Kelly, *Golden Mouth*, 272–85.

51. I am grateful to the ecumenical patriarch Bartholomew's staff at the Greek Patriarchate for an insightful discussion pertaining to the ministries of Gregory and Chrysostom in Constantinople, and a personal tour of the church premises on my visit to Istanbul in the summer of 2010.

52. Chrysostom's six hundred homilies contain about eighteen thousand Scripture citations; of these, about seven thousand are from the Old Testament, and eleven thousand from the New Testament. Baur, *John Chrysostom and His Time*, 1:316.

with examples found in ancient handbooks.⁵³ Chrysostom's skillful use of metaphors, mostly drawn from athletics, the military, the sea, pastoral life, and medicine, reflect the fact that he was a gifted orator.⁵⁴ Sozomen points out that when Libanius was asked whom he would want to become his successor, he replied, "John, if the Christians had not stolen him."⁵⁵ Chrysostom's homilies, considered as prime examples of late fourth-century Christian oratory, are replete with poignant verbal images. His levelheaded interpretation of Scripture is characteristic of the tradition to which he belonged.⁵⁶ Commenting on Chrysostom's homiletical skills, Young observes:

> If his style and methods of sermon construction fail to appeal to our taste, they were nevertheless the most effective method of communication in his time; it is no wonder that his great collections of exegetical sermons are carefully preserved and regularly read in the Greek-speaking church. His brilliant use of sophisticated conventions with flexibility and originality is hardly matched elsewhere; nor is his remarkable grasp of the Christian message as it spoke to his own day . . . In spite of the fact that he unavoidably speaks the language of the past and his works read as topical for an age long gone, his vivid imagery, together with his love and understanding of the Bible and of the erring hearts of men, gives his work an abiding quality and relevance. Christianity is not simply a set of disputed doctrines, but a way of life, and Chrysostom never lets this be forgotten.⁵⁷

Consequently, it is not surprising that it was John's reputation as an orator, preacher, and teacher that eventually earned him his well-deserved sobriquet *Chrysostomos* (Golden Mouth) and a place of honor as one of only four doctors among the Greek fathers in the Eastern tradition.

---

53. Mitchell, *Heavenly Trumpet*, 22–28. Cf. Baur, *John Chrysostom and His Time*, 1:223.

54. Wilken, *John Chrysostom and the Jews*, 106–12. See also Ameriger, *Stylistic Influence of the Second Sophistic on the Panegyrical Sermons of St. John Chrysostom*. Cf. Sawhill, "Use of Athletic Metaphors in the Biblical Homilies of St. John Chrysostom."

55. *Historia Ecclesiastica*, 8.2.

56. Pelikan, *Preaching of John Chrysostom*, 13.

57. Young, *From Nicea to Chalcedon*, 158.

2

Reading and Interpretation of the Scriptures in the Early Church

Introduction

The purpose of this chapter is threefold: to survey how the Alexandrian and the Antiochene fathers read and appropriated the Scriptures; to consider John Chrysostom's exegetical efforts in this context; and ultimately to investigate the relationship between scriptural usage and church life.[1] The present study explores the functional relationship between exegesis and spiritual life in the early church, as this was a vital concern of the fathers: "the modern divorce between biblical exegesis and systematic theology, or indeed between biblical exegesis and *praxis* would have been unthinkable in the days of the fathers."[2] Most of John Chrysostom's exegesis was performed in a churchly context and is best understood when considered in that milieu. When his exegetical oeuvre is isolated from its proper framework, bifurcating the expository from the praxeological, one may underestimate his skills as did Simonetti, who contends, "He is of less interest to us from the specifically exegetical standpoint, since the

---

1. There have been several studies on the history of patristic scriptural interpretation; the classic study is Farrar, *History of Interpretation*. Other introductions and aids to patristic interpretation of the Scriptures, include: von Harnack, *Bible Reading in the Early Church*; Lampe and Woolcombe, *Essays on Typology*; Daniélou, *From Shadows to Reality*; Hanson, *Tradition in the Early Church*; Hanson, *Allegory and Event*; Grant and Tracy, *Short History of the Interpretation of the Bible*; Ackroyd and Evans, *Cambridge History of the Bible*; Froehlich, *Biblical Interpretation in the Early Church*; Trigg, *Biblical Interpretation*; Kugel and Greer, *Early Biblical Interpretation*; Ramsey, *Beginning to Read the Fathers*; Simonetti, *Biblical Interpretation in the Early Church*; Torrance, *Divine Meaning*; Young, *Biblical Exegesis and the Formation of Christian Culture*.

2. Young, *Biblical Exegesis and the Formation of Christian Culture*, 4.

primary objective of his rhetorical output was to draw out of the text a lesson to educate, warn, or edify his listeners, rather than to illustrate the text for its own sake."[3] This chapter will demonstrate that Chrysostom's exegesis is cohesive, textual, and balanced compared to that of his peers, and reflects a modification of the Antiochene hermeneutical tendencies in a direction which is broadly consonant with the Alexandrian tradition. He was primarily a scriptural theologian with pastoral concerns, whose efforts yielded a wealth of teaching that was both dogmatic and practical. His biblical interpretation, which was primarily pastoral in nature, masterfully blends doctrine with spirituality. It has been rightly suggested that the exegesis of the fathers is "intimately and unselfconsciously bound to ecclesiastical life and its norms and needs."[4]

Patristic scholars sometimes use the terms *hermeneutics* and *exegesis* interchangeably.[5] In this chapter, a distinction between the aforementioned terms will be made, being cognizant of the fact that they are closely related. The former will be used to refer to patristic methods, principles, or rules of interpretation; and the latter will be employed to refer to the explication of the meaning of the text. Hermeneutics is a broader term that often subsumes various aspects of exegesis; therefore, exegesis is usually considered as an integral part of hermeneutics. Froehlich appropriately delineates the relationship between patristic hermeneutics, the theological framework in which the biblical writings were interpreted, and the methodology employed in understanding them. He maintains that

> Patristic hermeneutics concerns itself with the developing principles and rules for a proper understanding of the Bible in the early Christian church. The principles reflect the theological framework in which the biblical writings were interpreted by different groups and individuals at various times; . . . The *rules* reflect the methodology by which the language of biblical revelation was scrutinized so that it would yield insight into God's *oikonomia* and its ramifications for the life of the community . . . Rules and principles are intimately related . . . they show [selections from the volume] how biblical language determined theology and, on the other, how theological presuppositions shaped the reading of the Bible. It was in the hermeneutical circle of biblical text,

---

3. Simonetti, *Biblical Interpretation*, 74.
4. Gorday, *Principles of Patristic Exegesis*, 32.
5. Grant and Tracy, *Short History*, 4.

tradition, and interpretation that Christian theology as a whole took shape.⁶

Some scholars tend to exaggerate the differences between the Alexandrian and the Antiochene traditions and thus fail to see their common concerns, which were often pastoral in nature. The view that theological convictions informed patristic exegesis, which in turn led to different interpretations is strongly argued by Greer: "theology shapes exegesis in the sense that it determines the questions asked of the text . . . the role of theology is not only decisive in shaping exegetical results, it is of great importance in the formulation of exegetical methods."⁷ But Greer tends to overemphasize this "correlation," for he tries to juxtapose the two schools based on their differences, failing to take into consideration their common understanding of the central biblical message of God's redemptive plan in Christ, which was applied in the context of worship for the edification of the recipients. The exegetical differences between the two schools, reflected to some extent their theological presuppositions, though this supposed antithesis often tends to be overstated and too sharply contrasted. However, Bromiley makes a balanced observation in this regard, "In presentation of patristic hermeneutics attention is often focused so sharply on the inner differences that the strong element of agreed understanding, while not, of course, denied, does not receive its proper due. Yet a cursory acquaintance with the fathers quickly reveals that for all the exegetical variations, they undoubtedly shared the same basic understanding."⁸ The theological and christological presuppositions, which functioned as an overarching framework for the patristic exegetical infrastructure were derived from Scripture itself, and this operative relationship should not be undermined.⁹ On the one hand, it is clear that the fathers worked with certain presuppositions that governed

---

6. Froehlich, *Biblical Interpretation in the Early Church*, 1.

7. Greer, *Captain of Our Salvation*, 5.

8. See Bromiley, "The Church Fathers and Holy Scripture," in Carson and Woodbridge, *Scripture and Truth*, 212.

9. Torrance illustrates this relationship from the hermeneutics of Athanasius by showing how christological and soteriological concerns were decisive, not by bringing an independent notion to bear upon the Scriptures, but by deriving the overarching framework from Scripture itself. Torrance observes, "Athanasius' doctrine of the *Logos* arises out of the exegesis of the Scriptures, although at the same time it affects the doctrine of Scripture and determines its proper and regular interpretation." See Torrance, *Divine Meaning*, 230.

their exegesis and, on the other hand, the Scriptures were regarded as a canon and guide for all interpretation. Therefore, as Grillmeier argues, a careful study of this "hermeneutical circle" is warranted: "the study of the use and understanding of Scripture would be of the greatest significance for the whole of Patristic christology."[10] Certain patristic interpretations might seem novel from a modern critical perspective,[11] but the appropriation and application of the christological message of Scripture was central to their endeavors:

> They [the fathers] knew what was their aim in handling Scripture ... It was to discover, and to preach and teach, the burden, the purport, the drift, the central message of the Bible. This is explicitly admitted by several Christian writers. Irenaeus describes this as the hypothesis of the Scriptures, Tertullian as the *ratio*, Athanasius as the *skopos*. They were aware that their treatment of details may be open to question ... But they realise that what matters is, what the Bible comes to, where the main weight of its evidence lies, in what direction its thought thrusts.[12]

Variant interpretations on secondary matters aside, the consensual faith of the church functioned as an epistemic grid, which saw a spiritual unity in the biblical narrative. Whether one belonged to the Alexandrian or the Antiochene tradition the Scriptures were the final court of arbitration; it did not matter how the case was argued—literally or non-literally—it was all done to make clear the central message in the light of the church's faith.

For the fathers, the Old Testament and the New Testament together constituted the Scriptures; their message was considered harmonious and complementary, for the same Spirit inspired them. Jesus read and interpreted the Old Testament as prophesying and testifying to him and passed this on to his disciples, who in turn handed this method of reading and interpretation to the early church. Consequently, the fathers read the Old Testament as a prefiguration of the coming Messiah. The New Testament was understood as the inauguration of a new age with

---

10. Grillmeier, *Christ in Christian Tradition*, 1:34. See also Sellers, *Two Ancient Christologies*, 243.

11. E.g., the reference to Abraham's circumcision of the 318 males in his household is said to symbolize Jesus and the cross, because the number 318 written in Greek contains the first two letters in Jesus' name and the letter *tau* resembles a cross. See Barnabas, *Epistle* 9.

12. Ackroyd and Evans, *Cambridge History of the Bible*, 452.

the coming of Christ in God's purposeful economy. Furthermore, the unity and harmony of both Testaments attested to a divine teleology and provided the conceptual framework for a systematic understanding of the Scriptures: the God of the Old Testament is the God of the New Testament. Highlighting this patristic consensus on the coherence of the Scriptures, Gorday observes:

> The biblical writings do possess for patristic exegetes a real and vital wholeness. This wholeness proceeds from the fact that for the fathers the Old and New Testaments together are "Scripture," i.e. the authoritative body of writings on the basis of which theology can be synthesized and comprehensively stated. This wholeness proceeds from the obviously churchly context in which the fathers work and is reflected in the 'patterns' or all embracing structures which they find in Scripture and which come to expression in the summary or creedal statements which clearly became normative for the catholic church.[13]

A careful study of the central role of Scripture in ecclesiastical life is in order if one wants to understand the *raison d'être* of patristic exegesis. As a guide for doctrine, a text for liturgy, and a resource for the devotional life, the canon of Scripture was vital to the life of the early church. The authority of the Scriptures was for the fathers the bedrock on which the edifice of all interpretation was built. Therefore it would have been inconceivable to bifurcate biblical authority and interpretation from life in the church. As Bromiley rightly concludes: "As the Word of God given by the Spirit of God, Scripture had for the Fathers the status of primary authority in the life, teaching, and mission of the church. Deriving from God and enshrining the truth of God it had indeed the authority of God Himself. This applied to the Old Testament in its virtue of its prophetic testimony to the Christ who was still to come. It applied to the New Testament in the virtue of its apostolic witness to the Christ who had already come in fulfillment of the promises."[14] These common presuppositions, which saw a harmony between the messages of the two Testaments (the coherence of which was brought by Christ), enabled them to develop hermeneutical approaches that conclusively reflect the interconnections between reading, interpretation, and application.

---

13. Gorday, *Principles of Patristic Exegesis*, 35.

14. Bromiley, "The Church Fathers and Holy Scripture," in Carson and Woodbridge, *Scripture and Truth*, 207.

The Fathers and Scripture

The Jewish Scriptures, consisting of the Law, the Prophets, and the Writings, essentially became the Scriptures of the early believers because Jesus and the apostles had referred to them as such. The Old Testament was read from the perspective of Christ's life and ministry because he taught his disciples that the Scriptures testified of him (Luke 24:26–27; John 5:39–40). The early church, in one sense, inherited the Old Testament from Judaism through Jesus and his disciples. The Greek translation of the Old Testament (Septuagint), which included additional writings (Apocrypha), became the most widely known version as the church expanded beyond the borders of Palestine.[15] Although a few Antiochenes like Theodoret and Chrysostom quoted the Apocrypha for its edificatory value, some Eastern fathers like Melito of Sardis, Athanasius, Cyril of Jerusalem, and John of Damascus refused to recognize the authority of the Apocrypha and contended that only the original Hebrew core constituted the true canon. Hilary, Rufinus, and Jerome in the West preferred to restrict the canon to the Hebrew works, from which alone, they maintained, the church derived its authoritative teaching. Augustine, however, held to the broader position, which was eventually recognized by a synod held at Carthage in 397; the Roman endorsement was added by Innocent I in a letter dated 405. This position went unchallenged until the Reformation, and Reformers sided with elements of the early church and Jerome, recognizing the Hebrew works and rejecting the Apocrypha. The Council of Trent, on the other hand, endorsed the larger canon, which is also recognized by modern Roman Catholicism.

Although the New Testament canon did not exist in its present form in the early church, the corpus of writings by the apostles (the gospels and the epistles) were eventually recognized as being authentic. By the end of the second century one finds writings of the New Testament being treated as Scripture and authoritative enough to be placed alongside the Old Testament. Second Clement, Justin Martyr, Irenaeus, Clement of Alexandria, and Tertullian recognized the authority of the main New Testament books.[16]

---

15. Lamarche, "The Septuagint," in Blowers, *Bible in Greek Christian Antiquity*, 16–29.

16. See 2 Clement 2.4; Justin Martyr, *Dialogue with Trypho*, 49.5 (PL 6.882f.); Irenaeus accorded the same authority to the gospels as he did to the Old Testament, *Against Heresies*, 4.9.1 (PG 7.996) cf. 3.11.7–8 (PG 7.884–85); Clement of Alexandria

In response to the Jewish opposition and to Gnostic attempts to employ the early church writings to serve their ends, Justin Martyr's (ca. 100–165) typological interpretation, with its roots in Palestinian Judaism, surfaced in the latter part of the second century.[17] Arguing against Jewish critics, he maintained that the Old Testament clearly predicted and prefigured events concerning Christ in detail: his virgin birth, his ministry, his suffering, his death, and his resurrection. The types of the cross were of particular interest to him; he found them in the figure of Moses praying in the battleground against Amalek (Exod 17:10–11) or in the horns of the wild ox (Deut 33:17). Justin held that the types of the cross were to be found in every stick, wood, and tree mentioned in the Bible.[18] Arguing against the Gnostics, he insisted on the harmony of the two Testaments. Typological interpretation owes its development to the conviction that there is a harmony between the Old Testament and the New, and that the message of the Old Testament pointed to and is superseded by the New. As Daniélou has conclusively argued, typology was well employed in response to both Jewish and Gnostic opposition in the early church.[19] Torrance correctly observes that the use of typology reflected deep connections between the Gospel and the ancient history. It was a significant exegetical and apologetic tool employed, "against gnostic and Marcionite attempts to cut it away from its historical sources and its ground in the fulfillment in space and time of God's creative and redemptive acts."[20] Further, Torrance adds that according to Justin, the clues to understanding the Scriptures are to be found in the distinction (not contradiction) between the two covenants and two advents. The first refers to the old law with its rituals made with historical Israel, and the second refers to the new and eternal covenant inaugurated in Jesus Christ who enlightens all who come to him. In Justin's view, the old covenant already carries within it the promise of the new and points ahead to it; this implies that many Old Testament statements have a double

---

uses the phrase "the new testament" in *Pedagogue*, 1.7.59 (*PG* 8.321).

17. Grant and Tracy, *Short History*, 42. For a lucid and exhaustive account of the intricacies of Gnosticism in the early church, see Torrance, *Divine Meaning*, 15–39.

18. See *Dialogue* 86; 90–91 (*PL* 6.680; 689–92).

19. Daniélou, *From Shadows to Reality*, 1–7.

20. Justin Martyr, *Apology*, 1.26; 56; 58.

meaning or a predictive sense which are made clear and revealed in the New.[21]

Irenaeus and Tertullian

Following Justin Martyr, Irenaeus (ca. 130–200) and Tertullian (ca. 155–255) opposed the Gnostics by emphasizing the fact that true biblical interpretation was entrusted to the church through Christ and his apostles. The centrality of Christ, the wholeness of Scripture, and the endorsement of apostolic teaching together shaped their hermeneutical approach.[22] Kelly remarks that "for both of them Christ himself was the ultimate source of Christian doctrine, being the truth, the Word by whom the Father had been revealed; but he entrusted this revelation to his apostles, and it was through them alone that knowledge of it could be obtained."[23] While Grant called Irenaeus the father of authoritative exegesis in the church, Greer credits him with establishing the first overall framework for dealing with the Christian Bible.[24] Irenaeus claimed that the Gnostics exploited the Scripture to their own advantage by appealing to an alleged secret apostolic tradition for which they had exclusive access.[25] In response to these esoteric interpretations Irenaeus proposed an interpretation according to a summary of the apostolic tradition and succession, taught in churches.[26] This was called *the rule of faith* or *the rule of truth*, the two phrases often being used interchangeably.[27] Irenaeus is one of the earliest writers to appeal to individual texts and books from both the Old Testament and the New Testament to explicate the rule. This became a gauge for the interpretation of Scripture, for only in the church could the Scripture be properly interpreted: "If Irenaeus wants to prove the truth of a doctrine materially, he turns to Scripture, because therein the teaching of the apostles is objectively accessible, proof from tradition and from Scripture serve one and the same end: to identify the teaching

---

21. *Dialogue* 2.4; 24.1; 67.9
22. Irenaeus, *Against Heresies*, 3.12.2 (PG 7.893).
23. Kelly, *Early Christian Doctrines*, 36
24. Grant and Tracy, *A Short History*, 50. Cf. Kugel and Greer, *Early Biblical Interpretation*, 155–76.
25. Irenaeus, *Against Heresies*, 3.2.1 (PG 7.846).
26. Ibid., 3.1–5 (PG 7.843–60).
27. Ibid., 2.9.1 (PG 7.738); 27:1–3 (PG 7.802–3); 3.4.1f. (PG 7.855).

of the church as the original apostolic teaching. The first establishes that the teaching of the church is the apostolic teaching and the second, what this apostolic teaching is."[28] Irenaeus likens Gnostic misinterpretations of Scripture to taking an artful mosaic of the image of a king and turning it into an image of a fox.[29] Christ, Irenaeus maintained, brought perfection to all that was announced by the prophets; the apostles transmitted this message and the church receives, protects, and communicates it.[30] Commenting on Christ's claim that the Scriptures testify of him (John 5:39), Irenaeus inquires, "How therefore did the Scriptures testify of Him, unless they were from one and the same Father instructing men beforehand as to the advent of His Son, and foretelling the salvation brought in by Him?" He then proceeds to give an answer of how Christ was prefigured throughout the writings of the Old Testament, even in the writings of Moses:

> The Son of God is implanted everywhere throughout his [Moses'] writings: at one time, indeed, speaking with Abraham, when about to eat with him; at another time with Noah, giving to him the dimensions [of the ark]; at another; inquiring after Adam; at another, bringing down judgment upon the Sodomites; and again, when He becomes visible, and directs Jacob on his journey, and speaks with Moses from the bush. And it would be endless to recount [the occasions] upon which the Son of God is shown forth by Moses. Of the day of His passion, too, he was not ignorant; but foretold Him, after a figurative manner, by the name given to the Passover; and at that very festival, which had been proclaimed such a long time previously by Moses, did our Lord suffer, thus fulfilling the Passover.[31]

The centrality of Christ in the Scriptures, the apostolic tradition, and the church's sole authority in scriptural interpretation are the salient features of Irenaeus's thought. Any interpretation of Scripture performed outside the bounds of the apostolic church and its canon, in his view, was a misguided enterprise.[32]

---

28. Hanson, *Tradition in the Early Church*, 109.
29. Irenaeus, *Against Heresies*, 1.8.1 (PG 7.519); 1.9.4 (PG 7.543).
30. Irenaeus, preface to *Against Heresies* 5 (PG 7.1119).
31. Ibid., 4.10.1 (PG 7.999–1000).
32. See Jourjon, "Irenaeus's Reading of the Bible," in Blowers, *The Bible in Greek Christian Antiquity*, 105–10.

Tertullian, following the lead of Irenaeus, argued that the rule was a fixed form—unshakeable and irreformable, identical with the totality of the revelation of God, and prior to any heretical teachings of the Gnostics.[33] Furthermore, he argued that the church possessed the true teaching of Christ and hence the true interpretation as well: "only the churches which stand in succession of the apostles possess the teaching of Christ where it will appear that the truth of Christian discipline and faith are found, there also will be the true Scriptures, the true interpretations and all the true Christian traditions."[34] Tertullian's fundamental assumptions can be summarized thus: Jesus Christ came to preach the truth of revelation, next he entrusted this teaching to the apostles, and finally the apostles transmitted it to the apostolic churches which were founded by them. Therefore only the churches, which stand in succession to the apostles, possessed the true teaching of Christ.[35] For Tertullian the main issue was not interpretation but the very right to use the Scriptures by those "outside" the church.[36] Grant condenses Tertullian's principal arguments on the sole right of the church to interpret Scripture thus: the first one is called *Praescriptio veritatis*, which states that the prescription of truth points to the unity of doctrine between the apostles and the apostolic churches, and that these churches possess the truth vis-à-vis the heretics who disagree among themselves. Secondly, there is the *Praescriptio principalitatis*, which states that the truth is prior to variations from it. As in the parable of the wheat and tares, where the wheat was sown before the devil brought in the tares, so in the church the pure truth was sown before the devil brought in false teaching. It is in the church where the truth is preserved. Finally, there is the *Praescriptio proprietatis*, which states that the Scriptures belonged to the church through inheritance from the apostles long before the heretics thought of using them.[37] In short, for Tertullian the unity of doctrine, the initial deposit of truth in the apostolic church, and the church's first possession of it, formed a hermeneutic bulwark against the Gnostic claims to authoritative biblical interpretations.

---

33. Osborn, "Reason and Rule of Faith in the Second Century AD," in Williams, *Making of Orthodoxy*, 40–61.

34. Tertullian, *Prescription Against Heretics*, 19 and 20.1. (*CCSL* 1:201).

35. Ibid., 20f. (*CCSL* 1.201f). Cf. Grant and Tracy, *Short History*, 75.

36. Tertullian, *Prescription Against Heretics*, 14.1–2 (*CCSL* 1.198).

37. Ibid., 35–40.

Irenaeus and Tertullian contended that the illegitimate usage of Scripture led to serious misinterpretation and misrepresentation of the rule of faith. Both appealed to the church's tradition for an authoritative interpretation and contended that if one wished to interpret Scripture one had to be consistent with the rule of faith and the tradition of the church. Marcion's decision to excise the whole of the Old Testament and all of the New Testament, apart from Luke and the ten epistles of Paul, was strongly opposed by Irenaeus and Tertullian.[38] They both defended the canonicity of the four Gospels, and Tertullian added his attestation to the thirteen epistles of Paul, Acts, Hebrews, 1 John, and Revelation.[39] In the midst of this debate the rise of a working canon and the making of the rule of faith provided hermeneutical boundaries within which typological and christological interpretations could be employed.

Emergence of the Two Traditions of Interpretation: Alexandria and Antioch

The Alexandrian School and Some of Its Representatives

Stereotyping the Alexandrian and Antiochene schools of biblical interpretation as non-literal and literal is not en vogue in current scholarship. As Young correctly observes, the traditional categories of "literal," "typological," and "allegorical" are inadequate to describe the differences between the schools, adding, "Nor is the Antiochene reaction against Alexandrian allegory correctly described as an appeal to the 'literal' or 'historical' meaning."[40] This is primarily because of the recognition of two facts. First, a simplified hermeneutical distinction made between the Alexandrian and the Antiochene biblical interpretations does not hold true under careful scrutiny, as fathers from both traditions crossed the boundaries of their respective classifications. For example, Origen did not deny the historical aspects of most texts, nor did Antiochenes like Diodore, Chrysostom, or Theodore always adhere to just the literal

---

38. Marcion, in Tertullian's opinion, was using a knife and not a pen in deciding the canonicity of the books in question. See *Prescription Against Heretics*, 40 (*CCSL* 1.220).

39. Irenaeus, *Against Heresies*, 3.11.8 (*PG* 7.885f.); Marcion, 4–5, cited in Bromiley, "The Church Fathers and Holy Scripture," in Carson and Woodbridge, *Scripture and Truth*, 201.

40. Young, *Biblical Exegesis and the Formation of Christian Culture*, 2.

sense of the Scriptures. Second, as Simonetti has maintained, there were differences in the institutional structures as well: the establishment at Alexandria was more like a scholastic institution with a succession of connected teachers organized and supervised by the local bishop, whereas at Antioch different individual exegetes and theologians tutored and supervised their own students (e.g., John Chrysostom and Theodore of Mopsuestia were under the tutelage of Diodore). Farrar preferred to classify the Antiochene school as a theological tendency rather than an organized institution.[41] Simonetti concurs with him, "The group was closely united within itself, less by student-teacher relationships than by a common stamp of theology and exegesis."[42] The usage of the term "school" or "tradition" in this context will refer to clearly exhibited hermeneutical and exegetical tendencies that were peculiar to Alexandria or Antioch.

Eusebius mentions a certain Pantaenus who distinguished himself as a scholar and eventually became the leader of the catechetical school at Alexandria.[43] It was with Clement of Alexandria (ca. 150–215) that the one can detect the hermeneutical technique defined by a stress on a non-literal or allegorical interpretation, which is usually associated with Alexandria. This method of interpretation was seen as a means of conveying the truth through symbolical language, a legacy from Platonism. The Jewish community in Alexandria, in an attempt to prove that their faith was indeed consistent with the highest aspirations of Hellenic philosophy, had already adopted this approach. This was done to demonstrate that the content of the Scriptures was similar or identical to the most enlightened Greek philosophy. Philo, an Alexandrian Jew, was a good example of this as he sought to blend the insights of Judaism and Greek philosophy to demonstrate that the former is not very different from the latter. Wolfson observes that Philo was greatly influenced by Greek philosophical, rhetorical, and hemeneutical devices. Similar to the midrashic interpretations of the rabbis of Palestinian Judaism, he proposed a non-literal method of interpretation to discover in Scripture the hidden teachings of philosophy.[44] Philo's hermeneutical approach was designed to make the teachings of Judaism acceptable to the Greek mind. His primary endeavor, as Grant notes, was apologetic, "in his mind many

---

41. Farrar, *History of Interpretation*, 212.
42. Simonetti, *Biblical Interpretation*, 67. Cf. Farrar, *History of Interpretation*, 212ff.
43. Eusebius, *Ecclesiastical History*, 5.10 (GCS 2.450f).
44. Wolfson, *Philosophy of the Church Fathers*, 29f.

insights of Judaism, properly understood, do not differ from the highest insights of Greek philosophy."[45]

Clement of Alexandria

Influenced by Philo's hermeneutic, Clement of Alexandria (ca. 160–215) held that every text had more than one meaning, a deeper meaning beyond the literal sense. This was to be gleaned through allegorical interpretation: "Finding the deeper meaning is thus the process by which God gradually, by means of parable and metaphor, leads those to whom God would reveal himself from the sensible to the intelligible world."[46] He spoke of the Old Testament as speaking of the coming of Christ figuratively in "mysteries" and in "parables," and therefore argued that it should be interpreted in the light of this future fulfillment.[47] The Scripture is regarded as the actual voice of the divine Logos and every word and syllable has meaning, though this is not immediately obvious.[48] He held that the divine Logos teaches, guides, and instructs humanity. "Our Instructor is the holy God Jesus, the Word, who is the guide to all humanity. The living God himself in our Instructor."[49] Clement believed that the Scriptures contain enigmatic utterances, which conceal the deeper meaning in symbolic language together with allegories and metaphors—and all this is placed under the rubric, mystical interpretation.[50] Against the Gnostics, he argued that Scripture must be treated as a single testament, as it has come to humanity by one God, through one Lord.

Clement was the first Christian author to deal with principles of biblical interpretation in a definitive way. He contended that no biblical text is to be interpreted as saying anything inappropriate about God or conflicting with the rest of the Scriptures.[51] In contrast to Tertullian, who argued against the use of philosophy in theology, Clement maintained

---

45. Grant and Tracy, *Short History*, 53. "[B]y a process of interpretation which made plentiful use of philosophical concepts and terminology, especially Platonic and Stoic, he was able to introduce to the Greek mind a religious perspective which had been quite foreign to it." Simonetti, *Biblical Interpretation*, 7.

46. Clement, *Stromateis*, 6.15.126. (*PG* 9.349).

47. Ibid., 6.15.129 (*PG*, 9.353); 4.21.134, (*PG* 8.1345).

48. Clement, *Protrepticus*, 9.82.84 (*PG* 8.192ff.); *Stromateis*, 4.25.160 (*PG* 8.1372).

49. Clement, *Paedagogus*, 1.7 (*PG* 8.316).

50. Clement, *Stromateis*, 5.6.32 (*PG* 9.56); 5.4.21 (*PG* 9.41); 5.6.37 (*PG* 9.64).

51. Ibid., 7.16.96 (*PG* 9.533).

that God gave philosophy to the Greeks as a way of preparing them for the coming of Christ, similar to the way he gave the Law to the Jews. Clement opines, "Thus until the coming of the Lord, philosophy was necessary to the Greeks for righteousness. And now it assists those who come to faith by way of demonstration, as a kind of preparatory training for true religion . . . philosophy was given to the Greeks immediately and directly, until such time as the Lord should call the Greeks. For philosophy acted as a schoolmaster, to bring the Greeks to Christ, just as the Law brought the Hebrews to God. Thus philosophy was by way of preparation, which prepared the way for its perfection in Christ."[52] Although Clement and Tertullian disagreed on the role of philosophy in theology, both affirmed that the rule of faith should be the guiding principle in biblical interpretation. "Those are slothful who, having it in their power to provide the fitting proofs for the Divine Scriptures from the Scriptures themselves, nevertheless select what is exclusively favorable to their own pleasures; and those are ambitious who, of set purpose, explain away by other words beliefs handed down by the blessed apostles and teachers, and thus oppose divine tradition with human doctrines in order to establish their heresy."[53] Furthermore, Clement describes the rule of the church as truth in contrast to philosophy and heresy, which leads back to the words and works of Jesus and on to true *gnosis*. This rule of the church is both the saving revelation of Christ and ultimate reality. It is Christ, the first principle who speaks through the prophets and the apostles. The rule of the church ultimately points to him through the agreement and harmony of the Law, the Prophets, and the Gospels.[54]

Clement makes an interesting connection between faith and knowledge. He maintains that faith is the *sine qua non* of knowledge.[55] Torrance suggests that the clue to understanding Clement's thought is his penchant for the statement from Isaiah 7:9 (LXX): "if you will not believe, you will not understand." Faith, according to Clement, is grounded in rational judgment available to all who believe. Reason acts as a tool of persuasion, therefore human knowledge and philosophy should be employed in the inquiry of divine revelation.[56] Reflecting the Platonic dichotomy

52. Ibid., 1.5.28 (*PG* 8.717).
53. Clement, *Stromateis*, 7.16.96 (*PG* 9.533).
54. Ibid., 6.15.125f (*PG*, 9.349f).
55. Ibid., 2.4.12–14 (*PG* 8.944–45).
56. Ibid., 1.1.8.2 (*PG* 8.693); 2.4.12.1 (*PG* 8.944f). See also Torrance, *Divine Meaning*, 130–31.

between the intelligible and the sensible realms, Clement makes a corresponding distinction between the senses of Scripture—the literal and the non-literal. This suggests that there is an obvious meaning of the letter, which is open to all, while the hidden meaning is accessible only to a few who practice discipline, love, and contemplation.[57] Clement, like Philo, compares the literal sense of Scripture to the body, with the implication that the non-literal sense is analogous to the soul. He notes, "some look at the body of Scriptures, the expressions and names . . . while others see through the inner meanings and what is signified by the names."[58] The truth is hidden in the Scriptures to provoke inquiry and not to give occasion for blasphemy or misunderstanding when things are said that are beyond comprehension.[59] Although Clement did not provide a systematic or consistent account of his hermeneutical principles, it is clear he relied heavily on Philo's techniques of interpretation.[60] Overall, one can classify his method of interpretation into two categories: literal and non-literal.

With Clement of Alexandria one encounters an allegorical interpretation that is highly ramified. Although his interpretation of most of the Old Testament is christological, he also makes ready use of the mystical interpretation of numeric symbolism and the etymology of Hebrew names. Hatch comments on the influence of Greek ideas on Christian exegesis and argues that the reason for doing so rested on the assumption that religious truth was concealed in symbol. He avers, "The habit of trying to find an *arrière pensée* beneath a man's actual words had become so inveterate, that all great writers without distinction were treated as writers of riddles . . . It tended to become a fixed idea in the minds of many men that religious truth especially must be wrapped up in symbol, and that symbol must contain religious truth."[61] For example, Clement allegorizes Noah's ark into moral qualities, so the wood, for instance, stands for firmness, and the dimensions of the ark denote various mysteries. Interestingly, he makes no reference to baptism this context.[62] Among Old Testament characters, Abraham represents faith; Sarah, wisdom;

---

57. Clement, *Stromateis*, 1.9.43–45 (PG 8.740–41); 1.28.176–79 (PG 8.921–25); cited in Torrance, *Divine Meaning*, 160–61.

58. Ibid., 6.15.132 (PG 9.357).

59. Ibid., 6.15.129 (PG 9.353).

60. Wolfson, *Philosophy of the Church Fathers*, 53f.

61. Hatch, *Influence of Greek Ideas on Christianity*, 65.

62. Clement, *Stromateis*, 6.2.84 (PG 9.305).

and Hagar, pagan culture. The fact that Sarah gives birth to Isaac denotes the contribution of Greek philosophy to the progress of true wisdom.[63] Abraham's lifting up his eyes on the third day (Gen 22:4f.) and seeing the place which God had appointed is interpreted to mean that on the first day he attained to the sight of what is fair, on the second day to the best desires of the soul, and on the third to an insight into spiritual things.[64]

Illustrating the wholeness of Scripture, Clement speaks of the ecclesiastical symphony of the two choirs of the Old and New Testaments, employing a musical metaphor to explain their unity.[65] The dialectic between the Law and the Gospel was not a problem, as the same Instructor provided both, not just to Israel and the church, but also to all humanity.[66] He was also the first among the fathers explicitly to use the term *testament* to refer to the two parts of the Bible.[67] Schaff offers a balanced appraisal of Clement of Alexandria:

> Clement was the father of the Alexandrian Christian philosophy. He united thorough biblical and Hellenic learning with genius and speculative thought. He rose, in many points, far above the prejudices of his age, to more free and spiritual views. His system, however, is not a unit, but a confused eclectic mixture of true Christian elements, with many foreign Stoic, Platonic, and Philonic ingredients. His writings are full of repetition, and quite lacking in clear, fixed method. He throws out suggestive and often profound thoughts in fragments, or purposely veils them, especially in the Stromata, in a mysterious darkness, to conceal them from the esoteric multitude, and to stimulate the study of the initiated or philosophical Christians. He shows here an affinity with the heathen mystery cultus, and the Gnostic arcana. His extended knowledge of Grecian literature and rich quotations from the lost works of poets, philosophers and historians, give him importance also in investigations regarding classical antiquity.[68]

---

63. Ibid., 1.5.30–31 (*PG* 8.721–24).
64. Ibid., 5.52.
65. Clement, *Stromateis*, 6.11.88 (*PG* 9.309).
66. Ibid., 1.21 (*PG* 8.819ff.).
67. Ibid., 2.6.29 (*PG* 8.964).
68. Schaff, *History of the Christian Church*, 499.

Origen

It was Origen (ca. 185–254), Clement's student and successor, who would eventually become one of the most influential patristic exegetes from the Alexandrian tradition.[69] Daniélou notes that as "a master of the catechetical school, he laid the foundations of scientific Bible study and carried the spiritual exegesis of the Scriptures to the highest pitch."[70] Although Origen's extant works comprise by far the largest body of work by a single author from the first three centuries, they are nonetheless only a small fraction of his output.[71] Origen had a very high view of the Scriptures: "the holy books are not the compilations of men, but were written and have reached us as a result of the inspiration of the Holy Spirit by the will of the Father of all through Jesus Christ."[72] This view of the divine origin of the Bible, coupled with the fact that Origen trained as a grammarian, led him on a quest for a proper text of the Scriptures. He secured a copy of the Greek translation of the Hebrew three-columned Bible that was in use in the synagogues at Alexandria. This codex placed translations by Jewish scholars Aquila and Symmachus next to the standard Greek translation. Such a tool was indispensable for someone seeking to compare the Septuagint with other translations of the Hebrew. Origen then proceeded to add two other versions (LXX and Theodotion) in parallel columns to the existing translations. The resulting work was a manuscript, which contained the entire Old Testament written out five times. This enabled anyone consulting it to notice at a glance where the Septuagint differed from the other translations and from the Hebrew original. He also used critical signs (which were standard critical marks developed by the Alexandrian textual critics of the second century BC) to mark words that were either absent or added in the standard. This work known from its four Greek versions was called the *Tetrapla*. Origen later supplemented the *Tetrapla* with two additional translations; this work with six versions of the Bible next to the translated Hebrew was known as the *Hexapla*. The eye for critical detail set Origen apart as the father of textual criticism in the early church and marked a milestone in

---

69. Eusebius, *Ecclesiastical History*, 6ff. (GCS 2.518ff.).
70. Daniélou, *Origen*, 131.
71. Trigg, *Biblical Interpretation*, 23.
72. Origen, *De Principiis*, 4.2.9 (GCS 5.318f). For an overview of Origen's understanding of inspiration, see Hanson, *Allegory and Event*, 187–209.

biblical scholarship. This work remained at Caesarea in Palestine where it was consulted by a number of scholars including the church historian Eusebius, and Jerome, who produced the Vulgate. The *Hexapla* unfortunately did not survive the Arab conquest, being either lost or destroyed.[73]

Origen's exegetical works can be divided into three classes: *Scholia*, *Commentaries*, and *Homilies*. The *Scholia* were collections of explanations and short notes on difficult and selected passages, all of which have been lost. The *Homilies* were sermons preached at Caesarea towards the end of his life: sixteen homilies on Genesis, thirteen on Exodus, sixteen on Leviticus, twenty-eight on Numbers, twenty-eight on Joshua, nine on Judges, and nine on Psalms, all extant in the Latin translations of Rufinus. Jerome translated twenty-five homilies on Isaiah, fourteen on Ezekiel, twenty on Jeremiah, and thirty-nine on Luke. Origen also wrote several commentaries on the Old and New Testaments, some of which are now lost. His extant commentaries include those on the Psalms, the Song of Songs, the Gospels of Matthew and John, and the Epistle to the Romans.[74]

Origen's procedure of biblical interpretation can be found in the first three chapters of book four of his treatise *First Principles*, translated into Latin by Rufinus as *De Principiis*. He begins by establishing the divine inspiration of the Scriptures and then proceeds to demonstrate that the spiritual sense of the Scriptures can only be understood if one looks beneath the mere literal expression of the Bible. Origen believed that the fulfillment of prophecies from the Old Testament and the widespread appeal of Christianity within the ancient world proved the divine origin of the Scriptures. Christ, the Word of God, speaks throughout the biblical narrative, and this is established by the fact that the teachings of the Christian faith were spread far and wide with amazing effectiveness.[75]

Origen maintained a twofold purpose of the Spirit in Scripture. He argued that, on one hand, it was the Spirit's scope (*skopos*) to enlighten the apostles and prophets to become partakers of the divine counsel revealed in the incarnation. The doctrines concerning God and the mediatory work of Jesus Christ in relation to humanity were of primary importance. On the other hand, it was the scope of the Spirit to conceal

---

73. Eusebius, *Ecclesiastical History*, 6.16f (*GCS* 2.554ff.); cf. Schaff, *History of the Christian Church*, 503ff.; Trigg, *Origen*, 82–86.

74. Daniélou, *Origen*, xii–xiii. Cf. Schaff, *History of the Christian Church*, 507.

75. Origen, *De Principiis*, Preface, 1 (*GCS* 5.7ff.).

these doctrines in such a way as to provoke inquiry, and in the process point to the spiritual truths contained therein.[76]

Ultimately it is the coherence or the unity of doctrine in the Scriptures that was the principal scope of the Spirit.[77] Origen held that whenever the Bible appears irrelevant it is likely because the inner sense has not been grasped. If this spiritual sense is not apparent on the surface it must be understood symbolically. The trouble in comprehending the Scriptures lies in the fact that their deeper spiritual meaning is hidden under the literal expression.[78] The literal meaning should not be discarded; though it does not represent the ultimate goal of Scripture, it is the starting point. To stop here would be to repeat the errors of the Jews and Gnostics: the former limited their understanding of the Scriptures to the mere observance of the Law and failed to recognize the Messiah, while the latter read the anthropomorphisms of the Old Testament literally and thus failed to see that the God of the Old Testament was indeed the Father of Jesus Christ.[79] Against both positions, Origen contends that the difficulty in understanding may indeed be the intention of the Holy Spirit to prevent deep truths from being readily accessible to those who are not worthy, or perhaps, unappreciative of them.[80] Since the words of the Bible were inspired by the Holy Spirit, its teachings were divine as well.[81] Like Clement, Origen affirmed the unity of both Testaments and maintained that the whole of Scripture is but one single instrument of God, flawless and harmonious in its message.[82] All teaching in Scripture, in Origen's view, must be understood in the light of the Bible's overarching christological framework.

Origen asserted that the Scripture contains three levels or divisions of meaning, corresponding to the Pauline division of a human person (1 Thess 5:23) into body (*sōma*), soul (*psychē*), and spirit (*pneuma*).[83]

76. Ibid., 4.1.7–9 (GCS 5.318–20).
77. Ibid., 4.2.7 (GCS 5.318).
78. Ibid., 3.6.1 (GCS 5.279f), 4.1.6 (GCS 5.352), 4.2.8 (GCS 5.301).
79. Ibid., 4.2.1 (GCS 5.305–6).
80. Ibid., 4.2.7 (GCS 5.318).
81. Ibid., 4.1.7 (GCS 5.302–3).
82. Origen, *Commentary on Matthew* 2 (PG 13. 832).
83. Hanson observes that Origen based this hermeneutic on a mistranslation of Proverbs 22:20 from the LXX, which should actually read, "Have I not written unto thee excellent things," but is wrongly rendered, "Have I not written unto thee in a triple way," *De Principiis*, 4.2.45. See Hanson, *Allegory and Event*, 235.

The literal sense corresponds with the physical, the moral with the emotional, and the allegorical with the spiritual.[84] Torjesen convincingly argues that Origen did not intend to use this principle for every verse, since it cannot be sustained from his exegesis: "the traditional identification of the body, soul, and spirit of Scripture in Origen with three separate and self-contained senses of the same text—the literal, the moral, and the mystical senses—cannot be supported from specific textual arguments."[85] Moreover, Torjesen notes that in Origen's view, Scripture contains the three distinct levels of teaching corresponding to the different maturity levels of those within the church. This hermeneutic is not addressed to the individual reader; rather, it is aimed at the teacher who must interpret the Scriptures for the congregation. Furthermore, Origen categorizes the congregation of all believers into three groups that represent the three phases through which a soul passes on its way to perfection, attributing to each group different spiritual capabilities. Therefore the three different ways of reading the text can be described as three different levels of teaching. The first level, the body, is the unexegeted text read in the liturgical service of the church; the second level, the soul, is generally edifying and meant for those who have advanced beyond the letter but are not ready for the mysteries; and the third level, the spirit, are the mysteries reserved for the perfect.[86]

In contrast to Clement, Origen compares the work of the exegete to a farmer; as a seed produces more or less fruit in proportion to the diligence of the farmer and the quality of the soil, so the mysteries of the Scriptures are uncovered in proportion to the application and the capacity of the exegete.[87] He was the first to use the term *anagōge* (leading or raising up) exegetically. In his usage it is substantially similar to allegory, though it later came to be associated with a specifically "anagogical" or "vertical" allegory in which earthly realities are seen as symbols of heavenly ones (viz., Jerusalem, Israel, the Tribes, and surrounding nations are types of spiritual realities that are in heaven). This is in contrast to a "horizontal" allegory in which events, characters, and things in the Old

84. Origen, *De Principiis*, 4.2.4 (GCS 5.312).

85. Torjesen, *Hermeneutical Procedure and Theological Method in Origen's Exegesis*, 35–43.

86. Ibid., 40–41.

87. Origen, *Homily in Exodus* 1:1, cited in Simonetti, *Biblical Interpretation in the Early Church*, 43.

Testament were *types* of the New.[88] Origen's anagogical interpretation became the hallmark for all spiritual interpretation in later years. Froehlich rightly concludes that, "Origen's biblical writings had an immense impact on later theology. While his own commentaries did not strictly follow the theory of a threefold sense, his understanding of *anagōgē* as the movement upward from the bodily level to a spiritual sense gave a firm rationale to Christian allegorization."[89]

Origen's interpretation of the Scriptures was done in a churchly context where his teachings were geared towards the nurture of the Christian life. The practical Christian life was viewed in terms of the gradual transformation and restoration of the soul to its original image. Torjesen has identified three stages in Origen's theory of the restoration of the soul: purification from sin, knowledge of the Logos, and the final stage of perfection. Sin is seen as the fleshly image that is corrupted; it is something that retards the soul's growth toward perfection and must be changed. Sin is not understood in forensic terms as something that requires forgiveness; rather, it is transformation that ultimately solves the problem of sin.[90] Origen uses disease as a metaphor for sin and conversely speaks of salvation as a metaphor for the process of restoration that involves progressive knowledge: from the knowledge of the incarnate Christ, to knowledge of the preexistent Logos, to knowledge of the Father. It begins with the knowledge of Christ's humanity, progresses to the knowledge of Christ's divinity, and finally culminates in what Origen describes as *theoria et intellectus dei* or an intimate, face-to-face knowledge of God.[91]

Thus the exposition of the Scriptures in the church is seen as central to the process of soul transformation. Since the Scriptures are inspired, they have a spiritual or a deeper meaning beyond the literal text and are best understood by the prayerful reader. Many of Origen's homilies either begin or end with a request for divine help in understand-

---

88. Origen, *De Principiis*, 4.3.6 (GCS 5.331). Wolfson, *Philosophy of the Church Fathers*, 63–64; see also Simonetti, *Biblical Interpretation*, 46.

89. Froehlich, *Biblical Interpretation*, 18.

90. Origen, *Homily in Jeremiah* 2.1, cf. *Homily in Joshua* 14.1, cited in Torjesen, *Hermeneutical Procedure and Theological Method*, 77–78.

91. Origen, *Homily in Luke* 1.4; *Homily in Numbers* 37.3; *Homily in John* 6.46. Origen employs different metaphors to explain this moment of consummation in *De Principiis* (1.3.8, GCS 5.60). See Torjesen, *Hermeneutical Procedure and Theological Method in Origen's Exegesis*, 83–84.

ing the Scriptures. Origen exhorts his student Gregory to knock on the Scriptures' closed doors so that they can be opened. That is, he asks him to seek the hidden meaning of the Scriptures through prayer, quoting the words of Christ (Matt 7:7), who not only said, "Knock and it will be opened to you, seek and you will find" but also added, "ask and it will be given to you."[92] For Origen, reading and understanding the Scriptures, in the context of faith, is ultimately the gift of God's grace. As such, it is rightly performed only in the context of the church's worship. One cannot really fathom the depth of the Scriptures and understand their ultimate function outside of the ecclesial setting.

According to Origen, the reader encounters Christ in the "flesh" of the text: Christ, the Word according to the flesh (κατὰ σάρκα), appears in the Bible according to the letter (κατὰ τὸ γράμμα).[93] For Origen the goal of reading the Bible is to "understand in a worthy manner the word which is stored up in the earthen treasures of paltry language." This hidden treasure is not available to just anyone, but only the spiritual person who can say with Paul, "we have the mind of Christ, that we may know the things which have been given to us by God."[94] Unlike Irenaeus or Clement, Origen is not consistent in his application of the rule of faith in his exegesis. Grant notes that he "relies far more on individual scholarship and intelligence than on any consensus of opinion. Like other Alexandrians he is a somewhat self-conscious intellectual."[95] The hermeneutic that searches for a meaning beyond the literal sense, common also to Clement, maintains that deeper meanings from the text are to be gleaned through allegorical interpretation. The ability to isolate this meaning was seen as a mark of spiritual maturity.[96]

It was with Clement and Origen that the non-literal method of interpretation reached its zenith. This facilitated their appropriation of the Old Testament message by giving it a christological interpretation, and it enabled them to expurgate elements in Scripture that were considered morally offensive. Further, it also equipped them to demon-

---

92. Origen, *Letter to Gregory* 4 (*Origenis Philocalia* 13), 67. See Heine, "Reading the Bible with Origen," in Blowers, *Bible in Greek Christian Antiquity*, 144.

93. Origen, *Commentary on Matthew*, 15.3 (PG 13.1257).

94. Origen, *Commentary on John* 1.24 and 1 Cor 2:12, 16, as cited in Heine, "Reading the Bible with Origen," in Blowers, *Bible in Greek Christian Antiquity*, 139.

95. Grant and Tracy, *Short History*, 60.

96. Clement, *Stromateis*, 6.25 (PG 9.240B); cf. Origen, *De Principiis*, 4.2 (GCS 5.305ff.).

strate to the pagans that the Scriptures contained teachings consistent with the deepest insights of Greek philosophy. Origen's influence on the development of biblical interpretation in the early Greek and Latin church was profound. Many patristic scholars and exegetes after him, to some extent and with reservations, emulated and applied his non-literal hermeneutic in their own biblical interpretation. Origen's student Dionysius ("the Great," d. ca. 264) succeeded him as the catechist at the school and subsequently became the bishop of Alexandria. Athanasius, the defender of Nicene orthodoxy trained in the Alexandrian tradition, was also influenced by Origen's interpretation of the Scriptures. Torrance notes that, although Athanasius did not dichotomize the sensible and intelligible worlds like Origen, he did inherit the tendency for a non-literal interpretation consistent with the teachings of Scripture.[97] At the same time, Athanasius commences an era where capricious allegorical hermeneutics were kept in check by the overarching theological framework of Nicea. The same can be said of the Cappadocians, who inherited from Athanasius a theological hermeneutic that was also consistent with the Nicene orthodoxy. Basil, Gregory of Nazianzus, and Gregory of Nyssa were indirectly influenced by Origen through his pupil, Gregory Thaumaturgus ("the Wonderworker"). Basil and Gregory of Nazianzus collected an anthology of Origen's writings on various exegetical subjects in a book titled *Philocalia*, while Gregory of Nyssa employed Origen's anagogical or mystical interpretation in its purest form in his work *Life of Moses* (see *PG* 44.297–430). Didymus the Blind (fourth century), renowned for his memory, also followed Origen's allegorical exegesis closely. As the teacher of Rufinus and Jerome, he was partly responsible for the transmission of Origen's methods to the larger Christian world.

Cyril of Alexandria

Cyril's (ca. 375–444) reputation as a passionate defender of what he believed to be true is legendary. He accompanied his uncle Theophilus to the Synod of the Oak in 402, which deposed John Chrysostom, then the bishop of Constantinople, on disciplinary grounds. Though reticent at first, after succeeding his uncle as the bishop of Alexandria, Cyril eventually restored Chrysostom's name to the diptychs (official lists of those

---

97. For an informative and exhaustive discussion on the hermeneutical methodology of Athanasius, see Torrance, *Divine Meaning*, 229–88.

who were commemorated by the church) in 417.[98] As a formidable opponent of different factions and schismatics in Alexandria, he came to be regarded as a champion of orthodoxy in the christological debates of the fifth century.

Cyril spent most of his time as a systematic expositor of Scripture before getting involved in the debates. As Wilken has pointed out, Cyril was primarily an exegete before he became known as a christological thinker. "His part in the Christological controversies of the fifth century has assured Cyril of Alexandria a prominent place in histories of Christian thought. But there is another Cyril who has been neglected. It is Cyril the exegete, a man whose mind and soul were shaped by the rhythms of biblical narrative and thought."[99] Before the eruption of the Nestorian controversy in 428, the largest body of Cyril's writings was primarily exegetical. His extant works that precede 428 include two commentaries on the Pentateuch, a commentary on the book of Isaiah (in five books), a commentary on the minor prophets, commentaries on the Gospels of Luke (160 homilies preserved in Syriac) and John (in twelve books), and several fragments on the Old and New Testaments and a series of paschal homilies which frequently include exegetical material.[100]

Kerrigan has observed that writing two hundred years after Origen, Cyril generally speaks of two senses of Scripture, the literal and the spiritual, and never uses Origen's concept of the moral sense. Consistent with the dualistic Alexandrian framework of interpretation, Cyril avers, "hence those who wish to explain the thoughts which are thus subtle and enigmatic and broad of meaning should inspect them carefully with the eye of the mind and expound both the accurate and literal signification and the spiritual sense, so that the readers may acquire knowledge of what is really useful and the explanation of the meaning of the text be lacking in nothing."[101] Cyril's affinity for the spiritual sense and its significance in understanding the deeper meaning of the passage can also be clearly seen in the following remarks: "Let nobody complain, if

98. See *Catholic Encyclopedia*, online ed., s.v. "Cyril of Alexandria." See also Campenhausen, *Fathers of the Greek Church*, 158–70; Young, *From Nicea to Chalcedon*, 240–65; McGuckin, *St. Cyril of Alexandria*, 1–17.

99. Wilken, *Judaism and the Early Christian Mind*, ix.

100. For a listing of his exegetical works, including an extensive listing of all his works, see Quasten, *Patrology* 3:119ff.

101. Cyril, *Glaphyra* (PG 70. 9), as translated and cited in Kerrigan, *St. Cyril of Alexandria*, 32.

everything contained in the literal sense is not explained. For frequently the spiritual sense is hidden in the superfluities of the literal sense, it is like those fragrant flowers of a garden that are clothed all around externally with superfluous leaves; the removal of the latter permits one to find naked what is most delectable and useful." On the need to look for the meaning beyond the externalities of the letter, Cyril observes further, "The language of the holy prophets is deep and it creeps through the hidden and inner path. Accordingly one should not think that the external surface of the letter represents the truth. One must seek rather the meaning buried in the letter."[102] The spiritual sense is a central component of Cyril's exegesis on which he bases his understanding of the united message of the Old and New Testaments.

Another aspect of Cyril's exegesis is the principle called the "scope" (*skopos*), which denotes the purpose of the writer, the overall message of a book or text of Scripture, and which contains both the literal and spiritual senses.[103] Although Alexandrian scholars commonly used this term, Cyril probably inherited it from Athanasius' exegesis. In one of his letters he cites a passage verbatim from *Contra Arianos*, where Athanasius explicitly uses the term to describe the twofold scope of the statements of Scripture, consonant with the divine and the human natures of Christ.[104] The frequency with which Cyril invokes this concept is itself an indication that he regarded it as an important hermeneutical principle.[105]

Like other patristic exegetes who preceded him, Cyril believed in the unity or harmony of both the Old and the New Testaments.[106] The

102. Cyril, *Glaphya* (PG 69.137) and *Commentary on Isaiah* (PG 70, 565), cited in Kerrigan, *St. Cyril of Alexandria*, 111.

103. See *Prologue to Micah* (Pusey 1:599, 5ff.) and *Prologue to Nahum* (Pusey 2:2, 1ff.), cited in Kerrigan, *St. Cyril of Alexandria*, 88. For a listing of the ways σκοπός was used among the fathers, see Lampe, *Patristic Greek Lexicon*.

104. Athanasius, *Contra Arianos* 3:29 (PG 26.352), as cited in Torrance, *Divine Meaning*, 239. This text was quoted verbatim by Cyril in his letter to the Egyptian monks in *Epistola I ad monachos Aegypti*, 4 (PG 77.13). See also Kerrigan, *St. Cyril of Alexandria*, 88–94.

105 Kerrigan, *St. Cyril of Alexandria*, 94.

106. Cyril remarks, "the New Testament is sister to and closely related to the Mosaic oracles; indeed it is composed of the selfsame elements. We can show that the 'life in Christ' is not remote from conduct in accordance with the law, provided that the ancient ordinances are given a spiritual sense," *Glaphyra in Genesium* (PG 68.137), as translated and cited in Kerrigan, *St. Cyril of Alexandria*, 134. Kerrigan's monograph has been the definitive study on Cyril's OT hermeneutic. Wilken's insightful discussion on the formulation of Cyril's early Christology in response to Judaism, before the Nestorian

Law and the Prophets foreshadowed Christ and ultimately their message was fulfilled in him.[107] Cyril's understanding of Christ as the fulfillment of the Law is clearly demonstrated in his response to the emperor Julian, who employed Jewish arguments against Christians to convict them of inconsistency, charging that they retained the Law but did not observe it. Cyril contends, "For we take it as axiomatic that Christ is the fullness of the Law and prophets, and we are right in doing so. Is not the fullness of the truth not appropriately perceived through obscure riddles? How could there be any doubt of it? Therefore the transition from things hidden in shadows to the truth is not a rejection of the Law given by Moses, but it makes its actual meaning all the more clear. Thus we say that the Law is termed eternal; it is not abrogated in the least in our practices of rational worship. Christ comes, not to release us from the Law and the Prophets but, as he himself said, to complete them." [108] Similarly in his commentary on the Gospel of John, Cyril emphasizes how the coming of Jesus transformed the types and shadows of the Old Testament into spiritual truths, thus bringing coherence to its message as it is fulfilled in the New. Since Jesus has come the "type shall be transferred to truth and the shadow of the law to spiritual worship."[109] The fact that Cyril titled his commentary on the Pentateuch *Adoration and Worship in Spirit and in Truth* to some degree explains his presumption that the Old Testament found its true interpretation in Christ. It also attests the fact that, for him, the Jewish way of life is replaced by a new way inaugurated by the Messiah.[110] Wilken has observed that Cyril's interpretation of John 4:24 gives us a clue to his conception of how worshiping in "spirit and in truth" takes the place of Jewish law and how the types are transformed into truth. There are two ideas that signify the importance of this text in Cyril's thought: the transformation of Judaism by the coming of Christ and the new way of life as distinguished by worship in spirit and in truth.

---

controversy, is complemented by Welch's study on Cyril's early christological and eucharistic thought. See Welch, *Christology and Eucharist in the Early Thought of Cyril of Alexandria*.

107 Cyril, *De adoratione et cultu in spiritu et veritate* (PG 68.140).

108. Cyril, *Contra Julianum* 10 (PG 76.994), as translated and cited in Trigg, *Message of the Fathers*, 28.

109. Cyril, *Commentary on John* 4:23–25 (Pusey, 1:283, 19–21), as cited in Wilken, *Judaism and the Early Christian Mind*.

110. Cyril, *Glaphyra* I (PG 69:13), as cited in Wilken, *Judaism and the Early Christian Mind*, 84.

Wilken notes that the term for transformation (*metaskeuazō*), is one of several words frequently employed by Cyril to describe the transformation of the Old Testament types into truth revealed in Christ. Cyril remarks, "Emmanuel is the firstfruits of the creation which was being remade into newness," and those who are united to him, "have been transformed to the newness of the evangelical way of life." In the same vein of thought elsewhere he adds, "Our Lord Jesus Christ transformed the things which were in types into truth."[111] The Christian faith represents the transformation of Judaism in and through Christ, and reflects a way of life characterized by worshiping God in spirit and in truth in distinction to arid ritualism.[112] For Cyril, the new way of life in Christ is contrasted with the old way of life under the Law: "through the evangelical teaching the true worshipper, the spiritual man, shall be led to a way of life well pleasing to the Father," and "worship in shadows is cast off and the things in types have been taken away, leading us to righteousness in Christ and teaching us to be remade in the evangelical way of life which only is pleasing to God . . . for God is spirit and those who worship him must worship him in spirit and in truth."[113]

Another related exegetical motif in Cyril is that of the second Adam, or the Adam-Christ typology, taken from Paul's parallelism in Romans 5 and 1 Corinthians 15. Christ, as the second Adam, is seen as consubstantial with humanity: whatever happens to Christ inevitably affects all those who are united with him. For Cyril, the typology of the second Adam is a way of talking of Christ as man: "for in him the commonality of human nature rises up to his person; for this reason he was named the last Adam giving richly to the common nature of all things what belongs to joy and glory, even as the first Adam gave what belongs to corruption and dejection." Commenting on this parallelism elsewhere, Cyril writes, "We became diseased through the disobedience of the first Adam and his curse, but we have become rich through the obedience of the second

---

111. Cyril, *De Adoratione*, 17 (PG 68.109); *Commentary on Isaiah*, 60:4–7 (PG 70:1325); *De Adoratione*, 2 (PG 68:213), as cited in Wilken, *Judaism and the Early Christian Mind*, 74.

112. *Contra Julianum* 10 (PG 76.994–95), as cited in Trigg, *Message of the Fathers*, 29–30.

113. Cyril, *Commentary on John*, 4:23–25 (Pusey, 1:284, 21–23), as cited in Wilken, *Judaism and the Early Christian Mind*, 75. Cf. *Commentary on Isaiah* 43:25–26, as cited in Wilken, *Judaism and the Early Christian Mind*, 76.

and his blessings."[114] Adam is seen as our representative. The first Adam sinned and the second Adam redeemed; the former transmitted death, while the latter through his resurrection, gives life. Like Athanasius, Cyril sees the death of Christ as the beginning of a new way for sinful humanity; Christ is the heavenly man, the Word from God, whose victory over death makes possible the restoration of sinners.

The Pauline concept of "new creation" (2 Cor 5:17) is another motif that one encounters in Cyril's exegesis. Wilken has observed that Athanasius uses this text in only three places, whereas Cyril cites it frequently in his commentary on John, Isaiah, and Micah. In his exegesis of Isaiah 42 he employs this motif in connection with explaining the tension between Judaism and Christianity, so that the new creation that Paul mentions is equivalent to the "new covenant" promised in Jeremiah: "I say new for it [the covenant] is remaking man to newness of holy life and through the evangelical way of life he is esteemed and appears as a true worshipper. For it is written that God is a spirit and must be worshiped in spirit and truth."[115] The same parallelism is found in his commentary on John 13:34 where Moses is equated with the Law, imperfection, and inferiority to Christ and correspondingly, Christ is equated with the new covenant, the renewal of the old, victory over death, and the second Adam.[116] Furthermore, in Micah 4:3-4 he views the absence of war as a foreshadowing of the new creation in Christ, for all will be completely changed into a new order of things.[117] The types and shadows of the old covenant find their fulfillment in the new covenant through the renewal that is brought about by Jesus Christ.

The new creation motif, along with the Adam-Christ typology and the idea of the transformation of Judaism by Christ, form a cohesive theological scope through which Cyril reads and interprets Scripture. Cyril's scriptural interpretation was done with a view to edify the faithful in a sacramental community of worship. With Cyril one encounters a much soberer form of biblical exegesis when compared to his predeces-

---

114. Cyril, *Commentary on John*, 1:14 (Pusey, 1:141, 6–11); 6:52 (Pusey, 1:520, 25–27). Cf. Athanasius' typology, which runs along similar lines, where Christ is the heavenly man because he was victorious over death. *Oratio Contra Arianos* 1:44. See Wilken, *Judaism and the Early Christian Mind*, 93–118.

115. Cyril, *Commentary on Isaiah*, 42:9–10 (PG 70.857–60), cited in Wilken, *Judaism and the Early Christian Mind*, 174.

116. Cyril, *Commentary on John*, 13:34 (Pusey, 2:384).

117. Cyril, *Commentary on Micah*, 4:3–4 (Pusey, 1:662).

sors like Origen, who held that all of Scripture has a deeper, non-literal meaning. Cyril's exegesis demonstrates both moderation and balance in the spiritual interpretation of the Scriptures. It is only occasionally that Cyril resorts to allegorical interpretations in his commentaries and homilies on the New Testament. For instance, in his commentary on John the five barley loaves in the feeding of the five thousand (John 6:9) represent the Pentateuch, the five books of the Law. They do not offer proper nourishment if consumed "literally." The two fish, on the other hand, represent the evangelical and apostolic preaching and provide better nourishment.[118] In connection with interpreting parables, Cyril suggested that not all parts of the parables of Christ should be interpreted allegorically, since to do so would obscure their meaning.[119] The parable of the Prodigal Son is simply interpreted as God's mercy towards sinners.[120] The two denarii in the parable of the Good Samaritan represent the two Testaments.[121] In Christ's discourse on the coming Kingdom of God in Luke 17:20ff., those who are on the rooftops represent people of high standing and those lying in bed represent people who live for pleasure.[122] Zacchaeus, who sees Christ from the top of the sycamore tree (Luke 19:4), represents those who come to him raising themselves above the passions of the world.[123] Commenting on Cyril's exegetical skills, Simonetti rightly concludes, "A more attentive study of Cyril's commentary (mainly the Old Testament, and one might argue the New Testament as well) reveals two characteristics which are closely linked: the literal interpretation is highly developed, much more so than any other Alexandrian exegete, the spiritual level is frequently missing altogether, and in these cases the literal interpretation is either accompanied only by the moral interpretation or it is on its own."[124]

The christological-soteriological exegesis of the Scriptures in the Alexandrian tradition reaches its peak in works of Cyril. The Bible is the story of one man, Adam, who was responsible for the sin and corruption of the human race, and of the second Adam, Christ, who transforms and

---

118. Cyril, *Commentary on John*, 6:9, (PG 73.609).
119. Cyril, *Homilies on Luke*, 16:1ff. (PG 72.809f.).
120. Ibid., 15:11ff. (PG 72.807).
121. Ibid., 10:25f. (PG 72.681).
122. Ibid., 17:20f. (PG 72.844–45).
123. Ibid., 19:1ff. (PG 72.865).
124. Simonetti, *Biblical Interpretation*, 81.

restores humanity into a new creation. It has rightly been observed that the second Adam concept was for Cyril an essential exegetical principle, through which he read and understood the Scriptures. It not only undergirded his understanding of redemption but also expressed some of the central ideas of his Christology.[125]

The Antiochene School and Some of Its Representatives

The allegorical interpretation of the Scriptures, which was the hallmark of the Alexandrian school, was not without its critics among the proponents of the rival school of Antioch. It experienced much opposition within the church. For even as early as the third century an Egyptian bishop named Nepos wrote a treatise entitled *Refutation of the Allegorists*. It has been suggested that even a scholar like Jerome eventually learned to respect the literal meaning of Scripture and turned from allegorization, indicating that wherever the influence of the synagogue was felt the interpretation of Scripture tended toward literalism.[126] This assumption may be contested as there was also a very influential Jewish community at Alexandria, but the hermeneutic practiced there largely tended to be non-literal or spiritual in nature. The reason therefore may not simply be the influence of the synagogue, but also the influence of different philosophical and rhetorical traditions with differing affinities. The Alexandrian school clearly exhibited philosophical leanings with its two-pronged approach, mirroring the Platonic bifurcation between the aesthetic and the sensible worlds. Although Lampe's suggestion that "the conception of Scripture as a single vast volume of oracles and riddles, as a huge book of secret puzzles to which the reader has to find clues, is the foundation of allegorical exegesis,"[127] might be too general a classification for those exegetes who practiced allegory, it does shed light on the fact that the fundamental presupposition behind all allegorizing is the idea that the text had meaning beyond the literal sense. The Antiochene proclivity for the literal dimensions of semantics, philology, and history betrayed its Aristotelian influence prevalent in the rhetorical schools of

---

125. See Welch, *Christology and Eucharist in the Early Thought of Cyril of Alexandria*, 148–60. See also Wilken, *Judaism and the Early Christian Mind*, 225.

126. Grant and Tracy, *Short History*, 63

127. See Lampe and Woolcombe, *Essays on Typology*, 31. Cf. Hatch, *Influence of Greek Ideas on Christianity*, 65.

that day.[128] Quasten surmises that the diversity in the methods of the two schools reflected the diversity of philosophical influences on the mental faculties of the exegetes in Alexandria and Antioch. "Alexandria's idealism and speculative bent owed inspiration to Plato, Antioch's realism and empiricism to Aristotle; the former inclined to mysticism, the latter to rationalism."[129] Echoing a similar idea, Froehlich maintains that the differences between Alexandria and Antioch "reflect more the methodological emphases and priorities of the schools than soteriological principles."[130] Schäublin suggests that the Antiochene exegesis may not necessarily be a reaction to Alexandrian excesses, but instead a normal outcome of the philological training of the rhetorical schools.[131] Young, contrasting the two different approaches, concurs with Schäublin's conclusion: "Symbolic allegory was characteristic of a philosophical approach to literature; the rival rhetorical approach sought to derive moral principles, useful instruction and ethical models from their study of literature. This approach, I suggest, informed Antiochene exegesis of the Bible with its reaction to Origenist Allegory."[132] Although one can oversimplify the differences between the two schools based on the bifurcation of influences and approaches, it is a general observation that the Alexandrian hermeneutic preferred a non-literal, spiritual interpretation in keeping with its philosophical influences. The Antiochene hermeneutic generally tended to be literal, and to some extent philological, in its approach. Its moral and ethical exegesis betrays the rhetorical influences of Aristotelianism. Nash, commenting on the philosophical influence on Antiochene exegesis, remarks:

> Aristotle's logical works gave an organon and demanded a system . . . A system calls for a central thought. When the central thought comes into the foreground, the things that in the mind

---

128. Froehlich observes, "There can be little doubt that the hermeneutical theories of the Antiochene school were aimed at the excesses of Alexandrian spiritualism. Careful textual criticism, philological and historical studies, and the cultivation of classical rhetoric had been the hallmark of the pagan schools in the city. Christian exegetes followed in the same path." Froehlich, *Biblical Interpretation*, 20.

129. Quasten, *Patrology*, 2:122.

130. Froehlich, *Biblical Interpretation*, 20.

131. Schäublin, *Untersuchungen zu Methode und Herkunft der antiochenischen Exegese*, 37f. Cf. Simonetti, *Biblical Interpretation*, 59.

132. Young, "Rhetorical Schools and Their Influence on Patristic Exegesis," in Williams, *Making of Orthodoxy*, 183–84.

are mixed up with it fall into the background. This, I take it, was the function of the Aristotelian logic and rhetoric in the exegesis of Antioch. It provided an apparatus for clear and systematic self-expression. In that self-expression the art of typology became self-conscious. Deeper influence it did not have. It did not at all change the essential texture of thought in the Syrian church. It gave the church the power to write clearly, and a sense for the value of definitions. The church's genius did the rest.[133]

Chrysostom and Theodore, both of whom studied under Libanius in the rhetorical school of Antioch, were probably also instructed in Aristotelian logic and rhetoric. The systematic trend in their exegesis, with its emphasis on the logical flow of thought, philology, and close attention to the text coupled with the stress on observable facts, reflects these influences to some extent. It must be noted that these influences were not entrenched in their theology to the point of assimilating it with everything Aristotelian. As Wallace-Hadrill has correctly noted, "It is only in a general sense that the Christian writers of Antioch can be called Aristotelian. The sense in which the term is admissible is that which credits them with an Aristotelian frame of mind or outlook, and is probably true of many of them even when they had little knowledge of Aristotle's work and joined the chorus of patristic condemnation of many of his philosophical tenets."[134] Chrysostom, like other Antiochenes, had little respect for the teachings of the philosophers and often criticized their assumptions. Coleman-Norton aptly demonstrates this fact, remarking, "One need not read far in the works of this most voluminous writer of the Greek Christian Fathers to discover the low opinion which he has of Greek philosophy. In one place St. Chrysostom calls it τριωβολιμαῖος [worthless] (*PG* 62.153)."[135] Chrysostom did not seem to spare even Plato and Aristotle in his homilies and derides their thought as foolishness in comparison to the doctrine of the Scriptures and the teachings of the church.[136]

Although the differing exegetical practices of Alexandria and Antioch betray varying influences on the technical level, one would be remiss to compartmentalize them on this assumption alone, while failing to look at the underlying concern that was common to both schools. All

---

133. Nash, "Exegesis of the School of Antioch," 35.
134. Wallace-Hadrill, *Christian Antioch*, 96.
135. Coleman-Norton, "St. Chrysostom and the Greek Philosophers," 305.
136. Ibid., 307–10.

patristic exegesis was done for the sake of application in an ecclesiastical context of worship, reverence, and spirituality. The different exegetical routes, whether allegorical, typological, moral or spiritual, led to a common destination: the application. It is imperative to keep this issue in the foreground, as scholarly readings often tend to highlight the influences that led to hermeneutical differences. Although these concerns are legitimate, they are not exhaustive, as they do not underscore the context in which such exegesis was carried out. Furthermore, to contrast the two schools based on their hermeneutic methods of literal and non-literal interpretation is to oversimplify the issues involved.

It is indeed difficult to classify the two traditions based on the aforementioned formula, because both schools employed typology as a hermeneutical device in their exegesis. The Alexandrian school, with its affinity for the spiritual sense, was more interested in what lay beyond the mere letter, whereas the Antiochene school preferred to pay attention to both the letter and the historical situation wherever applicable; yet the use of typology was common to both. Typology, in one sense therefore, was an exegetical bridge, a common hermeneutical practice that connected the two schools. Quasten illustrates it in the following way:

> Still between the two [Alexandria and Antioch] there was no absolute opposition; there was even broad agreement on an entire traditional exegesis; but special emphasis fell on distinct points of view. For Origen discovers types not just in certain episodes, but in every detail of the inspired word. Each line is filled with mystery. On the other hand Antioch made it a fundamental principle to see figures of Christ just occasionally, not always, in the Old Testament. Where the resemblance was marked and the analogy clear, only there would it admit a foreshadowing of the Saviour. Types were the exception, not the rule; the incarnation was everywhere prepared, but not everywhere prefigured.[137]

We shall now turn to some of the main representatives of the Antiochene school. Modern scholars credit Lucian of Antioch (ca. 240–315) with being one of the school's earliest representatives, although Antiochene tendencies can be seen in the exposition of Genesis by Theophilus of Antioch (ca. 180).[138] Born in Samosata and trained in

---

137. Quasten, *Patrology*, 2:122

138. His apologetical work *Ad Autolycum*, which antedates the work of Irenaeus and Tertullian, pays close attention to the literal meaning of the individual words of the texts

theology at Edessa and Caesarea, Lucian eventually became a priest. Not much is known about Lucian except that he had several pupils, one of whom was Arius. It is likely that he had a working knowledge of Hebrew, since he made a critical revision of the Septuagint text, showing an affinity for a literal and a grammatical exegesis.[139] This recension of Lucian became the standard text of the Greek-speaking church and was used by Diodore, Theodore, and Chrysostom in their exegetical works. Baur notes that the text form of the New Testament used by Chrysostom goes back to Lucian as well.[140] Neither Eusebius nor Sozomen mention much about his life except that he was a presbyter and was martyred.[141] Lucian may not have been a prolific writer, as there seems to be no mention of his works, except by Jerome, who refers to his *Small Treatise on Faith*.[142] In the Antiochene case, whenever a teacher appeared pupils came together for instruction and a new school developed, unlike the catechetical school of Alexandria, which had a succession of formally employed teachers. Therefore an unbroken historical connection cannot be established between the school of Lucian and that of Diodore (d. ca. 390), who was active in the final decades of the fourth century.

Diodore of Tarsus

Diodore is considered to be one of the key representatives of Antiochene exegesis. He lived in a monastic community (*askētērion*) near Antioch and eventually became the bishop of Tarsus in 378. The question whether Lucian or Diodore founded the Antiochene school is debated among scholars. Some maintained that it was the former, while others contend that it was the latter.[143] However, it was under Diodore's supervision and instruction that Chrysostom and Theodore, the two most well known Antiochene representatives, blossomed as exegetes. Diodore was a copious writer who left numerous doctrinal and polemical works and several

---

without any allusions to an allegorical interpretation. See *Ad Autolychus* 2ff., ET in *ANF* 2:97f.

139. Wallace-Hadrill, *Christian Antioch*, 30.

140. Baur, *John Chrysostom and His Time*, 1:317–18.

141. Eusebius, *Ecclesiastical History*, 8.13, 9.6; Sozomen, *Ecclesiastical History*, 3.5.

142. Jerome, *De Viris Illustribus* 77, cited in Quaten, *Patrology* 2:142.

143. Farrar, *History of Interpretation*, 212; Quasten, *Patrology*, 2:121, 142. Simonetti concurs with Farrar; see *Biblical Interpretation*, 68.

scriptural commentaries that survive only in fragments.[144] Altaner notes that Diodore's scriptural commentaries were "of a historical-grammatical exegetical bent that were distinctly opposed to the allegorical exegesis of the Alexandrians. According to the testimony of Theodore Lector in Suidas he commented on all the books of the O.T. as well as the Gospels, Acts, Romans and 1 John of the N.T."[145] Quasten maintained that Diodore was highly esteemed as a pillar of orthodoxy during his lifetime, but was later accused and condemned of heresy as the originator of Nestorianism. He was blamed for this heresy because he happened to be the teacher of Theodore, whose pupil was Nestorius.[146] Diodore was condemned approximately a century *post mortem*.[147]

It is highly probable that Diodore delineated his hermeneutical principles in his treatise *On the Difference Between Theōria and Allegoria*, which is now lost. Socrates' assertion that Diodore avoided allegory and insisted on the literal sense is exemplified by the exegesis in the remaining fragments of the latter's works, especially the *Commentary on Psalms*, which is attributed to him.[148] In this work Diodore contends that allegory undermines history, but *theōria* takes history seriously and is its foundation:

> We will not shrink from the truth but will expound it according to the historical substance (*historia*) and the plain sense (*lexis*). At the same time, we will not disparage anagogy and the higher *theōria*. For history is not opposed to *theōria*. On the contrary, it proves to be the foundation and the basis of the higher senses. One thing to be watched, however: *theōria* must never be understood as doing away with the underlying sense; it would then be no longer *theōria* but allegory. For wherever anything else is

---

144. Bardenhewer, *Patrology*, 317. See also Quasten, *Patrology*, 3:398f. for a listing of Diodore's works.

145. Altaner, *Patrology*, 369. Mariès, according to Altaner, holds that it is likely that fragments of Diodore's unedited *Commentary of Psalms* has been preserved under the name of Bishop Anastasius III of Nicaea.

146. Quasten, *Patrology*, 3:397.

147. Altaner mentions that Diodore was condemned at a synod in Antioch, *Patrology*, 369, whereas Quasten notes that he was condemned by a synod in Constantinople more than a hundred years after his death, *Patrology*, 3:94.

148. Socrates, *Ecclesiastical History*, 6.3. For fragments on Diodore's Prologue to the Psalm commentary and the Preface to the Psalm commentary, see *CCSG* 6; ET in Froehlich, *Biblical Interpretation*, 82–94.

said apart from the foundational sense, we have not *theōria* but allegory.[149]

He then goes on to comment that Paul did not seek to undermine history when he used the term allegory in Galatians 4:28, nor was he ignorant of the term *theōria*. Characteristic of the Antiochene suspicion of allegory, Diodore actually advocates that Paul's use of allegory here must be understood as *theōria*, taking the historical context into consideration. He offers a caveat that when one tries to impose allegory on to the text, without considering its literal and historical meaning, the author's intention is misunderstood. Diodore cautions:

> Even the Apostle did not discard history at any point although he could introduce *theōria* and call it allegory [cf. Gal. 4:28]. He was not ignorant of the term but was teaching us that, if the term "allegory" is judged by its conceptual content, it must be taken in the sense of *theōria*, not violating in any way the nature of the historical substance. But those who pretend to "improve" Scripture and who are wise in their own conceit have introduced allegory because they are careless about the historical substance, or they simply abuse it. They follow not the apostle's intention but their own vain imagination, forcing the reader to take one thing for another.[150]

In contrast to allegory, *theōria* is a complex term with a range of meanings: seeing, beholding, consideration, investigation, intellectual perception, and spiritual contemplation. Its exegetical use, however, suggests it was used of visions of prophets and apostles, and also to denote the spiritual sense of Scripture. It was employed by Cyril to denote the spiritual sense, where its chief object was to show Christ foreshadowed in the Old Testament. Lampe describes it as a "technical term for the spiritual sense of Scripture," usually employed by the Antiochenes in opposition to fanciful allegory."[151] *Theōria* therefore could mean the disposition of the mind, intellectual perception, and the spiritual insight, which enabled prophets to receive their vision.[152] Baur explains it thus: "By theory the Antiochenes understood in general the objectively real

---

149. Diodore, Prologue to the *Commentary on the Psalms*, as translated by Froehlich, *Biblical Interpretation*, 85–86.

150. Ibid.

151. Lampe, *Patristic Greek Lexicon*, s.v. "θεωρία."

152. Vaccari, "'Teoria' Esegetica Antiochena," 94–101.

higher sense, yielded by the historical-grammatical text, as sought after by the inspired writers themselves. To this also belonged the moral application lying in the action. With the Prophets, theory meant especially the typical messianic prophecies, in which 'theory' is to be understood, not in opposition to the literal sense, but in the direct historical sense of the prophecies."[153] This hermeneutical device was used by the Antiochenes (mainly by Diodore) to denote a higher sense, a spiritual meaning of a text without abrogating the historical framework. Simonetti describes Diodore's usage of it in the following way, "Diodorus juxtaposes allegory and *theoria*, so that, for him, while allegory weakens and abuses the letter of the text, *theoria* recognises a higher level of meaning which overlies the literal, without deleting or weakening it."[154] Diodore prefers to use *theōria* as a term that not only sheds light on the plain sense but also takes into account the true intention of the author, as it seeks to understand the spiritual meaning of the passage through proper contemplation.

Froehlich notes that *theōria* in Diodore's usage should not be equated with a typology of promise and fulfillment. Also, the terminology of type and antitype is missing in his writings.[155] It is apparent that although Diodore does not employ such terms he does advocate a sort of comparison similar to typology in his *Psalms Prologue*. He contends that *historia* ("a pure account of an actual event of the past") and *theōria* complement each other when a proper comparison is made between characters, events, and objects of the Old and New Testament. For instance, Diodore argues:

> We may compare, for example, Cain and Abel to the Jewish synagogue and the church; we may attempt to show that like Cain's sacrifice the Jewish synagogue was rejected, while the offerings of the church are being well received as was Abel's offering at that time; we may interpret the unblemished sacrificial lamb required by the Law as the Lord. This method neither sets aside history nor repudiates *theōria*. Rather, as a realistic, middle-of-the-road approach which takes into account both history and *theōria*, it frees us, on one hand, from a Hellenism which says one thing for another and introduces foreign subject matter; on the other hand, it does not yield to Judaism and choke us by forcing us to treat the literal meaning of the text as the only one worthy of at-

---

153. Baur, *Chrysostom and His time*, 1:319.
154. Simonetti, *Biblical Interpretation*, 68.
155. Froehlich, *Biblical Interpretation*, 21.

tention and honor, while not allowing the exploration of a higher sense beyond the letter also.[156]

Scripture, for Diodore and the rest of the fathers, was an inspired account of God's revelation in that it "teaches what is useful, exposes what is sinful, corrects what is deficient, and thus it completes the perfect human being."[157] Diodore claims that the Psalter cannot be fully appreciated by merely "chanting the psalms," but by appropriating them as one lives out the situation of the psalmist. The psalms are, to some degree, tailored formulations of concerns and prayers that one can make use of in approaching God and in expressing one's sentiments: "Thus, when our souls find in the psalms the most ready formulation of the concerns they wish to bring before God, they recognize them as a wonderfully appropriate remedy. For the Holy Spirit anticipated all kinds of human situations, setting forth through the most blessed David the proper words for our sufferings through which the afflicted may find healing."[158] Diodore continues by saying that even though the psalms are an excellent way to express one's concerns to God, they should not be chanted without grasping the "logical coherence of the words," but sung "from the depth of their mind, not from shallow sentiments or just with the tip of their tongues."[159]

In typical Antiochene style where close attention is paid to the wording, content, and flow of the argument, Diodore explains the general overview of the subject matter of the Psalter, dividing the book into two categories: ethical and doctrinal. Further, he subdivides the ethical category into psalms that "correct the moral behavior of the individual, others of the Jewish people only, still others of all human beings in general."[160] Not neglecting the historical aspects that relate to the individual psalms, he mentions a variety of events that surround their composition, like Israel's sojourn in Egypt, the wilderness journey, and the Babylonian captivity among others.[161]

---

156. Diodore, Prologue to the *Commentary on the Psalms*, as translated by Froehlich, *Biblical Interpretation*, 86.
157. Ibid., 82.
158. Ibid., 82–83.
159. Ibid., 83.
160. Ibid.
161. Ibid., 84.

Diodore contends that the psalms are not arranged in chronological order, stating that "[n]umerous psalms will provide evidence of this, most strikingly a comparison of the inscription of Psalm 3, 'A Psalm of David when he fled from the face of his son Absalom,' with the inscription of Psalm 143, 'A song against Goliath.'"[162] Diodore concludes that it is common knowledge that the Goliath episode occurred much earlier than the events concerning Absalom. The cause for this displacement of the psalms, he argues, was that the book was lost during the Babylonian captivity and it was only in the time of Ezra that it was rediscovered in fragments and then reassembled in the order that they were found. Diodore deduces, "Hence, even the inscriptions are mostly incorrect; more often that not, the collectors tried to guess the context of the psalms they found but did not treat them according to a scholarly method."[163] It is clear that Diodore was careful to take the historical aspect or context of the passage (or text) into account; he understood *theōria* to complement *historia* because he held that the former does not violate the latter. There can be no *theōria* without *historia*; the latter, Diodore believed is the foundation for the former, which is understood as a higher sense or as spiritual insight. Making a similar point in his *Preface to the Commentary on Psalms* 118 he states that, "In any approach to holy Scripture, the literal reading of the text reveals some truths while the discovery of other truths requires the application of *theōria* . . . the interpreter must classify and determine each figurative expression with care and precision so that the reader can see what is history and what is *theōria*, and draw his conclusions accordingly."[164]

Diodore's philological interests are clearly exhibited in his exegesis, reflecting the Antiochene penchant for grammatical analysis, which was viewed as a useful tool in biblical interpretation. He seemed keen on unpacking the hermeneutical devices for his readers so they could identify which parts needed to be read literally (or historically), and which parts should be interpreted non-literally. The end result of this labor is not just interpretation but also appropriation and application of the Psalms. Interpretation and application are not mutually exclusive in Diodore's hermeneutics.

162. Ibid., 85.
163. Ibid.
164. Diodore, Preface to the *Commentary on Psalms*, 118, as translated by Froehlich, *Biblical Interpretation*, 87.

For instance, Diodore opines that Psalm 29, spoken by the inspired writer "hyperbolically," actually applies to a real historical situation in the future—namely, to Hezekiah's prayer for deliverance. "In predicting future events, the prophets adapted their words both to the time in which they were speaking and to later times. Their words sounded hyperbolic in their contemporary setting but were entirely fitting and consistent at the time when the prophecies were fulfilled."[165] For Diodore, this Psalm applied to Hezekiah as a prayer of deliverance from illness and from the threat of war from the Assyrians (2 Kgs 19–20):

> Now these words did fit Hezekiah when he was delivered from his ills; but they also fit all human beings when they obtain the promised resurrection. For at that moment it will be timely for everyone to say to God what Hezekiah said: "I will extol you, O Lord, for you have protected me and have not let my foes rejoice over me." In Hezekiah's case, the foes were the Assyrians and those who rejoiced over his illness; the primary foes of all human beings are physical sufferings, death itself, and the devil, the whole range of experiences connected with mortality.[166]

After explaining how similar statements in the psalm apply not only to Hezekiah but also to the reader, Diodore remarks, "One will find more or less all utterances of the saints to be of this kind when one observes how they are made to fit the events of their own time but are also adapted to the events of the future. For this is the grace of the Spirit who gives eternal and imperishable gifts to human beings; I am speaking of divine words which are capable of being adapted to every moment in time, down to the final perfection of human beings."[167]

According to Diodore, the teaching of the Scriptures has to be applied to the life of the reader, which in itself presumes that the reading of the Scripture was intended to shape one's spiritual life in the context the church. Perhaps O'Keefe's critique that Diodore's exegesis "tends to sever the interpretation of the Old Testament from the life of the church" might be lopsided, as there seems to be room in his interpretation for the spiritual sense of Old Testament texts which can apply to the Christian's life.[168]

165. Ibid.
166. Ibid., 90–91.
167. Ibid.
168. O'Keefe, "Letter that Killeth," 83–104.

As a representative of the Antiochene school, Diodore displays a reluctance for non-literal interpretation—be it figurative, symbolical, or allegorical—that is not somehow connected with either the historical situation or the context of the passage. His interests in historical and philological aspects of the text betray the rhetorical influences commonly seen in Antiochene exegesis. In Diodore's exegesis one notices a cogent interpretation that follows the flow of thought, wording, and argument of the passage, paying close attention to the overall theme of a particular context. The idea of "theorizing" the message to make it spiritually applicable by appropriating its "proper" meaning through spiritual insight is a key feature in his exegesis. Diodore was keen on juxtaposing *theōria* with *allegoria* to the point that he even suggests that Paul actually meant *theōria* and not allegory in Galatians 4:28. Diodore's method of interpretation, with its emphasis on literal, historical, and philological aspects would significantly influence his two famous pupils, Theodore and Chrysostom.

Theodore of Mopsuestia

Theodore (ca. 350–428) was ordained to the priesthood in 383 by Flavian, the same bishop who would ordain John Chrysostom to the priesthood in 386. As I have noted previously, both Theodore and Chrysostom were fellow students of the pagan rhetorician Libanius before they decided to employ their skills in the service of the church. Theodore subsequently became the bishop of Mopsuestia in Cilicia, while Chrysostom later became the bishop of Constantinople. Like the sobriquet "Chrysostom" (Golden Mouth), given to John by posterity because of his eloquence, Theodore was called "the interpreter" because of his distinguished hermeneutical skills. As Wiles suggests, "Where Chrysostom is essentially the preacher who makes use of the work of biblical interpretation, Theodore is first and foremost biblical scholar and commentator."[169] Because Theodore was connected with Nestorius, and was condemned at the Fifth General Council in 553, most of his exegetical works were destroyed. His four commentaries that are extant are: the *Commentary on the Psalms*[170] (only the first 81 Psalms survive, partly in Greek and Latin), *Commentary on*

---

169. Wiles, "Theodore of Mopsuestia as Representative of the Antiochene School," 490.

170. Devreesse, *Le commentaire de Théodore de Mopsueste sur les Psaumes*.

the Minor Prophets (*PG* 66), *Commentary on the Gospel of John*[171] (in a Syriac and Latin translation), and the *Commentary on the Minor Epistles of Paul*[172] (in a fifth-century Latin translation). Theodore did not recognize Chronicles, Ezra, the book of Job, and the Song of Songs in the Old Testament as being canonical, and in regard to the New Testament he limits himself to the canon of Antioch, which seemingly did not contain 2 and 3 John, 2 Peter, Jude, and Revelation. According to Wiles, he never quotes from James, 1 Peter, or 1 John either.[173] He considered Job to be a historical figure and a model of patience and endurance, but the author of the book of Job, he held, was a learned pagan Edomite who, for selfish reasons, imposed dialogical speeches on to historical figures in the manner of Greek tragedians. The Song of Songs, according to him, was written for the occasion of Solomon's marriage to his Egyptian wife, and Theodore rejects a spiritual interpretation of it.

The *Commentary on the Psalms* was written when Theodore was in his youth. In this work he usually begins with the historical situation of the psalm, which he is about to expound. Like Diodore, he does not believe that the inscriptions at the beginning of each psalm are authentic, unless corroborated by the content of the psalm. Unlike his teacher, who held that different historical situations determined the composition of the psalms, Theodore insists that David was the author of all the psalms and that the Psalms should be read as the words of David. The historical setting of most of the psalms, he contends, belonged to the time of David. He maintained that Psalms 6, 13 and 38, speak of the occasion of David's adultery with Bathsheba. According to Theodore, Psalms 3, 22, and 70 refer to Absalom's revolt. Theodore was convinced from the internal evidence that some psalms refer to historical events of a later date. Thus he contends that despite its title Psalm 51 could not refer to the Bathsheba incident because the words in verse 18, "Rebuild the walls of Jerusalem," prove that it cannot refer to David's era, but to the time of the exile. Theodore also maintained that Psalm 72 referred to Solomon, and like Diodore he held that quite a few psalms pointed to the time of the Maccabees. He remarked that David spoke prophetically in the person of

---

171. Vosté, *Theodori Mopsuestini Commentarius in Evangelium Johannis Apostoli*, *CSCO* 115–16 (Syriac series 4:3).

172. Swete, *Theodori Episcopi Mopsuesteni in epistolas B. Pauli commentarii*, 2 vols.

173. Wiles, "Theodore of Mopsuestia as Representative of the Antiochene School," 494. Cf. Greer, *Captain of Our Salvation*, 225.

those who would experience these events in the future. Therefore David's expressions of confession, supplication, or thanksgiving provide inspiration and guidance, helping those in future generations to appropriate them at the opportune time.[174] Grant notes that Theodore was the most individualistic interpreter of the Antiochene tradition and observes that he makes a distinction between those prophecies that are genuinely messianic and those that are entirely historical. Theodore, maintains that only four psalms refer to Christ: Psalms 2, 8, 45, and 110.[175] Theodore rejected that Psalms 22 and 69 could refer to Christ's passion. He held that the final words of Psalm 22, "On account of my transgressions," should not be attributed to Christ, but rather to David as an acknowledgment of the latter's sin. The Psalm therefore must be a prayer of David at the time of his son Absalom's revolt. Psalm 69, according to Theodore, refers to the troubles of the Maccabean age; the application to Christ therefore is secondary, even though words from this psalm appear on the lips of Jesus in the Gospel accounts. Theodore contended that the New Testament writers altered and adopted the words from these psalms to describe the events surrounding Christ and hence the application to Christ is consequential. However, the only direct prophecy relating to Christ can be found in Ps 16:10, "you will not abandon my soul to Hades, nor let your holy one see corruption."[176] For Theodore, the psalms had a context, and the verses cannot be applied to situations arbitrarily. Individual verses in the psalms could not be taken as messianic prophecies if the rest of the psalm contradicted such a conclusion. The primary context of the Psalms pertained to David's life, as in the words, "My God, my God, why hast thou forsaken me?" Although employed by Christ on the cross to express his anguish the words should be understood primarily as a reference to David's lament over Absalom.

Theodore maintained a similar hermeneutic in his *Commentary on the Minor Prophets*: he believed each prophet was preaching a message to a particular people in a particular context. Simonetti rightly observes that, "Theodore prefaces his commentary on each of the minor prophets, and even on individual psalms, with an introduction fixing its historical setting, and general features precisely, and he develops his commentary

---

174. Wiles, "Theodore of Mopsuestia as Representative of the Antiochene School," 499.

175. Grant and Tracy, *Short History*, 66.

176. Ibid., 500–501; cf. Young, *From Nicea to Chalcedon*, 204.

entirely in line with these programmatic prefaces."[177] He was keen on expounding the historical situation surrounding the prophecies in the Minor Prophets, namely the precarious situation of doom, the impending judgment if the message was rejected, and the promise of hope for those who heeded the message. He taught that Hosea, Joel, Amos, and Micah were concerned with the impending fall of the northern kingdom and the threat of Assyria. The prophecies of Obadiah, Jonah, Nahum, Zephaniah and Habakkuk refer to various occasions following the eighth century, whereas Haggai and Zechariah prophesied at the return from exile, and Malachi in the period following the exile.[178] Theodore did posit that the words of the prophets pointed to Christ but only in a secondary sense as shadows and prefigurations, because the prophets did not receive the full revelation before the time of Christ. Their message had a specific reference to the particular time and situation and this must be considered in interpretation. He maintained that one Spirit inspired all scriptural writers and enabled them in accordance with the present or contemporary need.[179] Theodore's view of inspiration takes into account the specific reference to the context of the inspired writer and yet recognizes that the message could point to the future. He maintained that the contemporary aim should be preserved and expounded in all exegesis: "For this reason, however, most of what appears in the Old Testament is dispensed in this manner, so that what appears might furnish the greatest help to those living at the time and yet hold a certain reminder of things to be demonstrated clearly only later."[180]

Theodore recognized "types" but did so cautiously, especially regarding Christ. Commenting on Theodore's reticence in adducing a christological interpretation of Old Testament texts, Simonetti correctly observes, "Theodore has reduced the presence of Christ in the Old Testament to the barest necessary minimum."[181] Theodore drew a parallel between Jonah's three days in the belly of the whale and Christ's three days in the tomb. He goes even further, and takes the whole story

---

177. Simonetti, *Biblical Interpretation*, 71; cf. Theodore, *Commentary on Zechariah*, 10 (*PG* 66.534ff.).

178. Wiles, "Theodore of Mopsuestia as Representative of the Antiochene School," 502.

179. Theodore, *Commentary on Nahum* (*PG* 66.401ff.).

180. Ibid., *Commentary on Jonah* (*PG* 66.320), as translated and cited in Greer, *Captain of Our Salvation*, 226.

181. Simonetti, *Biblical Interpretation*, 70.

of Jonah, not just the incident of the three days in the whale's belly, and makes a parallel with Christ's ministry. Just as God miraculously effected the conversion of the Gentile nation through Jonah, so through Christ he effected the conversion of the Gentiles. For Theodore, if there was no *mimēsis* or genuine correspondence between an Old Testament event and a New Testament situation, then a "type" cannot be posited.[182] Only insofar as the type imitates its fulfillment can it become a foreshadowing of Christ. Therefore he admitted no indiscriminate use of typology. Remarking on Theodore's skill as a commentator of the Old Testament, Wiles writes, "Theodore's commentaries on the Old Testament show him as a scholar capable of acute historical observation. But they show him also as more than that. We see him developing there a general theory of remarkable complexity, ingenuity and originality which would be able to contain his historical insights and his sense of the religious purpose of the prophetic writings within a single scheme of an unfolding historical purpose of God."[183]

The New Testament, for Theodore, contained the whole truth of Christian doctrine, and his tendency was to emphasize the newness thereof. In his exegesis of the New Testament, as in his approach to the Old Testament, one notices close attention to historical detail, chronology, clarification of obscurities, philological interest in the text, as well as attention to the sequence of the argument. In his *Commentary on the Gospel of John*, Theodore was diffident in positing a Christian interpretation to the faith of the disciples, as the Holy Spirit was not received until after Pentecost. For example, Theodore says that when Nathaniel greets Jesus as "Son of God" at the beginning of the Gospel (1:46) he meant no more than the Jewish connotation "Messiah;" he cannot have understood and meant it in the Christian sense, as the second Person of the Trinity. Further, even Thomas' exclamation at Jesus after his resurrection, "My Lord and my God" (20:28), could just have been the cry of gratitude and praise of God and not a recognition of Christ's full divinity. This straightforward and literal kind of exegesis, coupled with his involvement with Nestorius and his refusal to recognize the canonicity of some of the biblical books, did not place him in good stead at the Second Council

---

182. Theodore, *Commentary on Jonah* (PG 66.317ff.).

183. Wiles, "Theodore of Mopsuestia as Representative of the Antiochene School," 504.

of Constantinople in 553.[184] His commentaries on the minor epistles of Paul give a glimpse of his skill as an exegete who seems to be more comfortable interpreting Pauline epistles, as opposed to the Johannine material with its affinity for the spiritual. His concern for grounding the texts in their context, maintaining the *historia* of events, and a dislike for *allegoria* can be seen in his comments on Galatians 4:22–31 where Paul's usage of the term "allegory" became a license for some Alexandrian exegetes to practice an interpretation that was improperly grounded in the literal meaning of the text.

> There are people who take great pains to twist the senses of the divine Scriptures and make everything written therein serve their own ends. They dream up some silly fables in their own heads and give their folly the name of allegory. They (mis)use the apostle's term as a blank authorization to abolish all meanings of divine Scripture. They make it a point to use the same expression as the apostle, "by way of allegory," but fail to understand the great difference between that which they say and what the apostle says here. For the apostle neither does away with history nor elaborates on events that happened long ago. Rather, he states the events just as they happened and then applies the historical account of what occurred there to his own understanding. For instance, he says at one point: "She corresponds to the present Jerusalem" [v. 25], and at another: "Just as at that time he who was born according to the flesh persecuted him who was born according to the Spirit" [v. 29]. Paul gives history priority over all other considerations, Otherwise, he would not say that Hagar "corresponds to the present Jerusalem," thus acknowledging that Jerusalem does exist now. He also would not use the term "just as" if he was referring to a person he thought did not exist.[185]

According to Theodore, when Paul speaks of Hagar and Sarah he is using an analogy to speak of justification. He says that Ishmael was born according to the order of nature, while Isaac was born according to grace. He does this to demonstrate that justification that comes from Christ is far better, as it is acquired by grace. Hagar is seen as one giving birth in the natural order, representing justification through the Law, whereas Sarah is seen as one giving birth against hope, representing justification

---

184. Theodore, *Commentary on John*, 1:49; 20:28, cited in Wiles, "Theodore of Mopsuestia as Representative of the Antiochene School," 504.

185. Theodore, *Commentary on Galatians*, 4:22–31, as translated in Froehlich, *Biblical Interpretation*, 96.

by grace. Theodore concludes that any "spiritual" interpretations, which cannot be grounded in history are foolishness and like "dreams in the night." Critiquing this sort of interpretation, he writes:

> "spiritual interpretation" is the name they like to give to their folly—they claim that Adam is not Adam, paradise is not paradise, the serpent not the serpent. I should like to tell them this: If they make history serve their own ends, they will have no history left. But if this is what they do, let them tell us how they can answer questions such as these: Who was created the first human being? How did his disobedience come about? How was our death sentence introduced? Now, if they have gleaned their answers from Scriptures, then, their so-called allegory is unmasked as being foolishness, for it proves superfluous throughout.[186]

Further, he adds that if the historicity of the events is undermined, for instance, as in the case of the events in the earlier account of Adam and his disobedience in Genesis, the very reason for the incarnation is also in question:

> Also, I shall not even mention that if they are correct, not even the reason for the events surrounding Christ's coming will be clear. The apostle says that Christ canceled Adam's disobedience and annulled the death sentence. What were those events in the distant past to which he refers, and where did they take place, if the historical account relating them does not signify real events but something else, as those people maintain? What room is left for the apostle's words, "but I fear lest, as the serpent seduced Eve" [2 Cor. 11:3], if there was no serpent, no Eve, nor any seduction elsewhere involving Adam? In many instances the apostle clearly uses the historical account of the ancient writers as the truth and nothing but the truth. The only valid interpretation is that which is grounded in its context, respecting the historicity of the events, and then making a comparison.[187]

Paul, according to Theodore was concerned with the historical realities of the events he is comparing and that the Scriptures indeed are an account of God's acts grounded in history. Hagar represents the old covenant, Sarah the new covenant, and Christ in Theodore's view inaugurates a new age in which God's gracious purposes are realized. Theodore's hermeneutic can be described as wooden and very literal and

---

186. Ibid., 97.
187. Ibid.

hence his exegesis tends to be more discrete and descriptive, in keeping with his advice: "For as we understand it, the task of the commentator is this, namely, to explain the phrases which are difficult to the majority; the preacher, on the other hand, considering the things which are clear, must also speak of these. To the latter, superfluous words are sometimes useful; the commentator, however, must give one exposition and speak concisely."[188] He keeps typology to a bare minimum and is cautious in explicating the *theōria* from a passage unless it is grounded on *historia*.

In a noteworthy article, Hay illustrates how Theodore and Chrysostom interpret the Gospel of John on the basis of their respective Antiochene christological frameworks.[189] According to Theodore, the phrase "And the Word became flesh" (John 1:14a) means that the Word came in a man (as in a specific human being). This is in contrast to Chrysostom, who maintains that the phrase means the Word assumed "true flesh." Chrysostom employs the terms "flesh" or "economy" to designate the humanity of Christ. Hay observes the following principle in Theodore and Chrysostom's exegesis of the Gospel of John: "Wherever statements are attributed to Christ in the Gospel, Theodore refers them directly to the Assumed Man unless it is clear—as in the anti-Arian texts—that they refer to the eternity or consubstantiality of the Word; while Chrysostom attributes them directly to the Eternal Son, unless there is question of physical sufferings or emotions which he attributes to the flesh."[190] Following this pattern Hay notes that Theodore attributes Christ's actions to the Assumed Man on several occasions, including among others the Good Shepherd of John 10, the prayer of Christ at the tomb of Lazarus, and the last supper. In the same passages Chrysostom speaks of Christ as one divine agent, the eternal Son, who through the example of his condescension instructs his disciples how to pray, fast, and humble themselves. In the final analysis, Hay concludes that though both Theodore and Chrysostom belonged to the same exegetical tradition, they did not belong to the same christological tradition, as their interpretations of christological texts were "far apart." The similarities

188. Theodore, *Commentary on the Gospel of John*, in Vosté, *Theodori Mopsuestini Commentarius in Evangelium Johannis Apostoli* (*CSCO* 115–16), 2, as cited by Hay, "Antiochene Exegesis and Christology of Theodore of Mopsuestia and John Chrysostom," 11.

189. Hay, "Antiochene Exegesis and Christology of Theodore of Mopsuestia and John Chrysostom," 10–23.

190. Ibid., 17.

in their exegesis were: a commitment to literal interpretation, a hermeneutic informed by the church's faith and the Nicene Creed, and a common anti-Arian exegetical strategy. The reason, according to Hay, why Theodore handled the christological texts differently from Chrysostom is the threat of Apollinarianism, which denied the existence of a rational soul in Christ. Hay maintains that Theodore was one of the principal opponents of Apollinaris and developed his teaching of the "Assumed Man" in conscious reaction to it, but incorrectly concludes that Chrysostom never seriously came to grips with this heresy, perhaps because his early training did not equip him with answers to it.[191]

Theodore's Christology was indeed a development of Diodore's and was forged in the fires of the anti-Arian and anti-Apollinarian debates. He refused to accept that the Word was the subject of Christ's activity; instead he viewed the "Assumed Man" as the subject. For Theodore, the Word was the "Son of God" and the "Assumed Man" was adopted and united with the Word, therefore the "Assumed Man" made a way for all humanity to share in this honor.

As an exegete Theodore was skillful and concise, not ornate and eloquent like his fellow pupil Chrysostom. His exegesis was as literal as possible, and typology was employed with great care. His understanding of inspiration meant that every word of Scripture must be considered with discretion, including the linguistic, philological, and grammatical aspects. The Old Testament was seen as a historical landscape dotted with God's redeeming and gracious acts, pointing to the age or dispensation of Christ. The emphasis on the historical setting of the Law and the Prophets meant that God indeed acted and worked in the way that the Scriptures record and are not fantasies or "dreams in the night." The literal interpretation, therefore, takes precedence over allegorical interpretation in Theodore's exegesis, as it remains true to the *historia* of the Scriptures. The *theōria*, or the spiritual meaning always takes *historia* seriously and hence there cannot be *theōria* without *historia*. The message of the Old Testament is the foundation for the New Testament and finds its perfect fulfillment in Christ, who is its *skopos*. Further, since the God of the Old Testament is also the God of the New there is unity and harmony in the message of the two Testaments:

> Since one and the same God, the Lord and the Maker of all, is the God of both the Old and the New Testaments, He dispensed

---

191. Ibid., 21–23.

the former and the latter with one aim (σκοπός) in view. Of old He determined that the restoration should appear, and He demonstrated its beginning in the economy of the Lord Christ. And He thought it necessary for us to exist first in this life, I mean the present, and then later to be transferred to the other life, through the resurrection of the dead, in order that we might better know through comparison the greatness of the good things we shall receive. And then, so that this might be evident and lest it should be thought that He was forming a new plan and decree for us, in many and various ways He gave men hints concerning the coming of the Lord Christ with the result that all the Jews expected this afar off.[192]

Although Theodore was very rigid in his acceptance of typology in the Old Testament, and was reticent to give a christological interpretation to many Old Testament texts (including the Psalms that had been traditionally been read christologically), he nevertheless maintained that such texts had a secondary or an extended application to Christ. Theodore's main weakness was the inflexibility of his literal interpretation, which was generally descriptive in character, and tended to blind him to theological subtleties in the different genres of Scripture.

John Chrysostom

We now turn to our final representative in the Antiochene tradition. John Chrysostom was not only an eloquent preacher but also an able exegete. Like his contemporaries in the early church, Chrysostom had a very high view of the Scriptures and their authority. He regarded the Bible as the inspired account of God's infallible revelation through which the Holy Spirit speaks.[193] The Old and the New Testaments together are viewed as an organic whole on account of the unity of their message.[194] He maintained that when the Scriptures are read the voice of God is heard.[195] In keeping with his ornate rhetoric Chrysostom employs striking images when speaking of the Bible. The hearing of the Word being read in church is akin to hearing the "Apostolic voice, a trumpet

---

192. Theodore, *Commentary on Jonah* (PG 66.317), as translated and cited in Greer, *Captain of Our Salvation*, 229.

193. Chrysostom, *Commentary on the Psalms* 4 (PG 55. 57); *Commentary on Isaiah* 1 (PG 56.14); *Commentary on the Psalms* 45; Homily 2, in *Genesis*, section 2 (PG 53.28).

194. Chrysostom, *Commentary on the Psalms* 4, translated by Hill, 1:68 (PG 55.57).

195. Chrysostom, Homily 19, in *Acts of the Apostles* (PG 60.150f).

from heaven, and a spiritual lyre" arousing one's spirit and soothing one's soul. The reading of the Scriptures is likened to a stroll through a meadow dotted with fragrant flowers and fruit;[196] it leads the soul to the inmost sanctuary, cleansing and purifying it, as it communes with God;[197] it is a strong defense against sin;[198] and strengthens one's faith.[199] Further, the Scripture is likened to a deep sea that hides priceless pearls in its depths;[200] it is like a precious stone, a diamond that reflects divine light;[201] and a treasury of medicine, which contains the means of healing for all.[202] Chrysostom often stressed that individuals should not just read the Scriptures but also study them earnestly; he even admonished his hearers to read in advance the passage that was going to be expounded in church, as he often preached *lectio continua*.[203] No other father of the church emphasized the personal need for the laity to read the Word of God, as did John Chrysostom. The inspiration of the Scriptures and their authority to govern life were two persistent motifs in his preaching. Commenting on this recurring theme in Chrysostom's preaching, von Harnack avers:

> St. Chrysostom, a truly great man, contends with all the power of heart and will, and devotes every resource of oratory to the establishing of one simple and strict ideal for all Christians. In this contest no weapon seems to him to be more powerful than the Bible. In the midst of a great metropolis filled with Christians who were Christians only in name, he never wearies in his endeavor to plant the Bible in the home, in firm conviction that, if he can only establish regular reading of the Scriptures in the family and among individuals, he is thus laying a solid foundation for a truly Christian life.[204]

Chrysostom often insisted that the Scriptures should be studied with great diligence and care. One of his favorite metaphors for the Bible

---

196. Chrysostom, Homily 1, *On the Statues*, sections 1–2, *NPNF* 9:331 (*PG* 49.16–18).
197. Chrysostom, Homily 3, *De Lazaro*, section 3 (*PG* 48.995).
198. Chrysostom, Homily 1, *De David et Saul*, section 7 (*PG* 54.686).
199. Chrysostom, *Commentary on the Psalms*, 3.1 (*PG* 55.36).
200. Chrysostom, Homily 6, *De Lazaro*, section 8 (*PG* 48.1040).
201. Chrysostom, Homily 14, in *Genesis*, section 1 (*PG* 53.111).
202. Chrysostom, Homily 37, in *John*, *FOC* 33:359 (*PG* 59.207).

203. For an informative discussion on the use of the Bible in the liturgy of the early church, see Ackroyd, and Evans, *The Cambridge History of the Bible*, 1:563–86.

204. Von Harnack, *Bible Reading in the Early Church*, 117.

is that of a gold mine: just as every particle of gold is gathered with great care, the reader likewise must pay attention to every word contained therein. Words and sentences are likened to precious pearls: it is not their size, but the beauty of their nature that determines their value:

> Let us not therefore listen carelessly; since even they who roast the metallic earth when they have thrown it into the furnace, not only take up masses of gold, but also collect small particles with the utmost care. Inasmuch, then, as we likewise have to roast the gold drawn from the Apostolic mines, not by casting it into the furnace, but by depositing it in the thoughts of your souls; not lighting an earthly flame, but kindling the fire of the Spirit, let us collect the little particles with diligence. For if the saying is brief, yet its virtue is great. For pearls too have their proper market, not owing to the size of the substance, but the beauty of their nature. Even so is it with the reading of the divine Scriptures; for worldly instruction rolls forth its trifles in abundance, and deluges its hearers with a torrent of vain babblings, but dismisses them empty-handed, and without having gathered any profit great or small. Not so however is it with the grace of the Spirit, but, on the contrary, by means of small sentences, it implants divine wisdom in all who give heed, and one sentence often times affords to those who receive it a sufficient source of provision for the whole journey of life.[205]

The admonition for the personal study of the Scriptures was a frequent theme in his sermon introductions. He maintained that the aim or scope of the Scripture ultimately was the spiritual reformation of the faithful.[206] Chrysostom never shirks from the idea of stressing that it was incumbent on his listeners to cultivate the habit of careful reading of Scripture in order to know and live out its message. On one occasion he remarked that just as any individual who seeks to learn navigation, or carpentry, or anything else, must first learn the principles of the art, so too must

---

205. Chrysostom, Homily 1, *On the Statues*, section 3, *NPNF* 9:332 (*PG* 49.18f.). Elsewhere, employing a similar metaphor, Chrysostom remarks, "If any one unpractised in the art undertake to work a mine, he will get no gold, but confounding all aimlessly and together, will undergo a labor unprofitable and pernicious; so also they who understand not the method of Holy Scripture, nor search out its peculiarities and laws, but go over all its points carelessly and in one manner, will mix the gold with earth, and never discover the treasure which is laid up in it." Homily 40, in *John*, *FOC* 33:403 (*PG* 59.229).

206. Chrysostom, *Synopsis* (ΠΡΟΘΕΩΡΙΑ) (*PG* 56.313).

one who wants to comprehend the message of the Scriptures—for the reading of Scripture "is a science that needs much wakeful attention."[207]

Central to the Scripture is the account of God's economic plan of redemption in Christ. Divine condescension in the incarnation was viewed as a paradigm for divine pedagogy: God conformed to human limitations in order to communicate his message.[208] In his classic study, Chase cogently captures the significance of Chrysostom's frequent usage of the term *sunkatabasis*, which he employed for condescension: "The great principle expressed by the word συγκατάβασις is of deep and wide application. As in the historical Incarnation the Eternal Word became flesh, so in the Bible the glory of God veils itself in the fleshly garment of human thought and human language."[209] Commenting on this unique contribution to patristic thinking on Scripture, Hill notes, "his [Chrysostom's] ease with this basic insight would seem to have claim as Chrysostom's most original contribution to the thinking of the Fathers on Scripture—not in the sense that the Scriptures had never before been presented from the viewpoint of the Incarnation, but that in this deeply theological concept of Scripture Chrysostom's independence of the contemporary influences is most manifest."[210] This incarnational understanding of Scripture contours his hermeneutical approach. Therefore, according to Chrysostom, the Word of God needs to be studied with much precision (*akribeia*). Divine revelation imposes on the reader the responsibility of meticulousness in eliciting an interpretation:

> Do you see the precision of the teaching? Do you see the extent of the considerateness the Lord shows to our human condition? How could we have learnt these things so precisely if he in his great and ineffable love had not deigned to teach humanity by

---

207. Chrysostom, Homily 8, in *Hebrews*, section 10, *NPNF* 9:407 (*PG* 63.73).

208. Chrysostom, Homily 3, in *Titus*, section 2, (*PG* 62. 678); Homily 18, in *Genesis*, section 3 (53.152); Homily 26, in *Matthew*, section 39 (51.36).

209. Chase, *Chrysostom*, 42. For a brief account of the usage of the principle of divine condescension in both Christian and Jewish traditions, see Dreyfus, "Divine Condescence as a Hermeneutic Principle of the Old Testament in Jewish and Christian Tradition," 74–86. Dreyfus correctly observes that the teachings and doctrines of the Old Testament, which were superseded or augmented by the ones in the New Testament, were often described in terms of divine condescension, (e.g., permission to divorce, sacrifices, the Old Law, anthropomorphisms, other moral issues, etc.). This principle was especially practiced in the Antiochene school, as the Alexandrian school tended to explain away these issues through the use of allegory.

210. Hill, "St. John Chrysostom and the Incarnation of the Word in Scripture," 34–38.

the author's tongue, so that we might know the order of created things, the power of the Creator, and how his word took effect, and his utterance blessed them with sustenance and the way of life? . . . For this reason, the blessed Moses, inspired by the divine Spirit, teaches us with such precision, so that we may not fall into the same errors as they did, but come to know the sequence of created things, and how each was created. If God had not had such concern for our welfare and directed the tongue of the author in this way, it would have been sufficient to say, "God made heaven and earth, the sea and all living creatures," and not mention the order of the days, nor whether a thing was made first or later.[211]

Thus, since God's Word demands great reverence and care, all details—names, particular phrases, and individual words, are to be studied with much diligence.[212]

Hill observes that there are three reasons behind Chrysostom's strong emphasis on exegetical precision with regard to the Scriptures: clarity of teaching, promotion of the reader and listener's salvation, and refutation of other people's aberrant interpretations Scripture.[213] The careful study of Scripture, Chrysostom would hasten to add, also offers the Christian divine wisdom on practical matters.[214] In his introduction to Chrysostom's *Commentary on the Psalms*, Hill comments on Chrysostom's usage of this hermeneutic principle: "It is not a principle that he and his school light upon by chance: it is a consequence of their acceptance of the deeper theological principle of incarnation, in both the historical Jesus and the biblical Word. For Chrysostom precision (ἀκρίβεια) is both a characteristic of the biblical text and an obligation on the biblical commentator."[215]

Chrysostom, like Athanasius and Cyril, employed the term *skopos* to take into consideration the aim, purport, or meaning of the inspired writer. "Just as a building which has no foundation is sound, so too Scripture is utterly profitless, if one fails to investigate its *skopos*."[216] Chrysostom admonishes his congregation to look at the overarching

211. Chrysostom, Homily 7, in *Genesis* (PG 53.64–65).
212. Chrysostom, Homily 18, in *Genesis,* (PG 53.154).
213. Hill, "Akribeia," 32–36.
214. Chrysostom, Homily 1, *On the Statues*, section 3, NPNF 9:332 (PG 49.19–20).
215. Hill, "Introduction," in Chrysostom, *Commentary on the Psalms*, 1:24.
216. Chrysostom, *Commentary on Psalm 3* (PG 55.35).

framework of the given passage and study it with diligence. When one does not take the purport of the author into account, the interpretation inevitably results in the obfuscation of the truth.[217] Learning to interpret the Scriptures carefully and arriving at an exegesis that is in keeping with the author's overall purpose is of utmost importance for Chrysostom.

Furthermore, Chrysostom asserts that there are texts in Scripture whose senses are multi-leveled and require different hermeneutical approaches. Some are to be understood literally, while others are to be interpreted spiritually. It is imperative to consider the fuller sense (*theōria*), as well as the literal and historical senses, in order to understand the underlying meaning:

> In some things, you see, it is possible to find a fuller sense, whereas others should be understood only at face value—for example, "In the beginning God made heaven and earth." Other statements, by contrast, are to be taken differently from the surface meaning—for example, "spend your time with the hart you love, with the filly that has won your favor," and "Let those things be yours alone, and let no stranger share them with you, your well is for you to drink from." I mean, if you take this saying as it occurs and do not depart from the surface meaning but stay at that level, it reflects little humanity, the counsel to share water with no one. The sense, however, is to do with one's wife . . . This is true of this verse, too, while in other places we must take the words as we find them, and the meaning arising from them, like this example, "As Moses lifted up the serpent." We must accept that this happened—it did happen, in fact—and what meaning comes from it, namely, a type of Christ.[218]

Chrysostom was cautious when interpreting figurative language and imagery. His commentary on the Psalms shows him to be a versatile exegete and more flexible than Theodore in interpreting lyrical material. There are striking similarities between Chrysostom and his mentor Diodore in the interpretation of the Psalter. Just as Diodore explains how the in-

---

217. Chrysostom, *Commentary on Galatians* 1.17, NPNF 13:11–12 (PG 61.629). Arguing along similar lines in his exegesis of Roman 7, Chrysostom invokes this principle of understanding the *skopos* of Paul and the point the apostle is making in that particular context in order to avoid misinterpretation: "You see, that if we do not receive his words with proper discretion, and keep looking to the object (σκοπός) of the Apostle, countless incongruities will follow?" Homily 13, *Romans*, section 1, NPNF 11:428 (PG 60.508).

218. Chrysostom, *Commentary on the Psalms*, 9:8, trans. by Hill, 1:185 (PG 55.126).

spired writer in Psalm 29 speaks "hyperbolically" about future events, or even speaks in the person of a historical character like Hezekiah, so does Chrysostom in his exposition of Psalm 44. "While it is the inspired author who recites the psalm, he recites not in his own person but in the person of the Maccabees, describing and foretelling what would happen at that time. The inspired authors are like that, you see: they span all times, the past, the present, the future."[219] But unlike Diodore and Theodore who held that the titles of psalms were perhaps a later addition, Chrysostom does not hint or allude to such a view.

In contrast to Theodore's reserved approach to typology, Chrysostom was not reticent in employing typology wherever he saw a hint, sketch, or a model in the Old Testament, which prefigured Christ. Chrysostom recognized "types" in the Scriptures and maintained that "types" and figures pointed forward to the reality. Nevertheless, these types were inferior to the reality. He illustrates the relation between, "type" and "truth" from the field of art, likening a type to an artist's incomplete sketch and the truth to the full portrait: "The type is given the name of the truth until the truth is about to come; but when the truth has come, the name is no longer used. Similarly in painting: an artist sketches a king, but until the colors are applied he is not called a king; and when they are put on the type is hidden by the truth and is not visible; and then we say, 'Behold the King.'"[220] He acknowledged that Noah was a type of Christ, and the ark a type of the church; the dove represented the Holy Spirit, while the olive leaf stood for the goodness or the kindness of God.[221] Further, Chrysostom maintained that Joshua was a type of Jesus;[222] Jacob's flight into Egypt was a type of Jesus' flight into Egypt;[223] the dove sent out of the ark was a type of the dove which appeared at Christ's baptism;[224] Jonah's three days in the whale was a type of Christ's three days in the tomb;[225] the manna in the desert was a type of spiritual food that Christ offers;[226]

---

219. Chrysostom, *Commentary on Psalm* 44:1 (LXX 43), translated by Hill, 1:231(*PG* 55.167f.).

220. Ibid., Homily 10, in *Philippians*, *NPNF* 13:231 (*PG* 62.257).

221. Chrysostom, Homily 6, in *De Lazario Concio*, section 6 (*PG* 48.1037).

222. Chrysostom, Homily 2, in *Matthew*, section 4, *NPNF* 10:10 (*PG* 57.26).

223. Chrysostom, Homily 8, in *Matthew*, section 4, *NPNF* 10:52 (*PG* 57.84).

224. Chrysostom, Homily 12, in *Matthew*, section 3, *NPNF* 10:77 (*PG* 57.203f).

225. Chrysostom, Homily 48, in *Matthew*, section 2, *NPNF* 10:273–74 (*PG* 57.458).

226. Chrysostom, Homily 46, in *John*, *FOC* 33:465 (*PG* 59.259).

the translation of Enoch and the taking up of Elijah were types of the resurrection of Christ;[227] and, finally, Isaac bearing the wood for sacrifice prefigured the cross.[228] Commenting on this event in Genesis, where Abraham was asked to sacrifice his son Isaac, Chrysostom employs the common patristic typology paradigm of shadow and reality, explaining:

> All this, however, happened as a type of the Cross. Hence Christ too said to the Jews, "Your father Abraham rejoiced in anticipation of seeing my day; he saw it and was delighted." How did he see it if he lived so long before? In type, in shadow: just as in our text the sheep was offered for the world. You see, it was necessary that the truth be sketched out ahead of time in shadow. Notice, I ask you, dearly beloved, how everything was prefigured in shadow: an only-begotten son in that case, an only-begotten in this; dearly loved in that case, dearly loved in this ... Up to this point there is shadow, but now the truth of things is shown to be more excellent ... Do you see the superiority of the truth? Do you see what shadow is, on the one hand, and truth, on the other?[229]

For Chrysostom, Christ was the ultimate fulfillment of the Old Testament types. Paraphrasing the words of Christ, from John 8:31–32 Chrysostom notes, "'You shall know the truth,' that is, 'shall know Me, for I am the truth. All the Jewish matters were types, but you shall know the truth from Me, and it shall free you from your sins.'"[230] The types pointed forward to the new economy inaugurated by, and fulfilled in, Christ, "For the types like patterns anticipated and sketched beforehand the dispensations which should be accomplished under the new covenant, and Christ came and fulfilled them." Further, he goes on to cite a couple of examples from the Old Testament to show how Christ himself fulfilled these prophecies in action, showing the relation between type and truth:

> What then is a type? "Take ye a lamb for an house, and kill it, and do as he commanded and ordained." (Ex. 12:3.) But it is not so with Christ. He doth not command this to be done, but Himself becomes It, by offering Himself a Sacrifice and Oblation to His father. See how the type was "given by Moses," but the "Truth came by Jesus Christ." (Ex. 17:12.) Again, when the Amalekites warred in Mount Sinai, the hands of Moses were supported, be-

---

227. Chrysostom, Homily 5, in *Colossians*, NPNF 13:283 (PG 62.336).
228. Chrysostom, Homily 55, in *John*, FOC 41:81 (PG 59.459).
229. Chrysostom, Homily 47, in *Genesis*, section 14, FOC 87:21–22. (PG 54.428–30).
230. Chrysostom, Homily 54, in *John*, FOC 41:65 (PG 59.297).

ing stayed up by Aaron and Hur standing on either side of him (Ex. 17:12); but when Christ came, He of Himself stretched forth His hands upon the Cross. Hast thou observed how the type "was given," but "the Truth came"? Again, the Law said, "Cursed is every one that continues not in all things that are written in this book." (Deut. 27.26, LXX.) But what says grace? "Come unto Me, all ye that labor and are heavy laden, and I will give you rest" (Matt. 11:28); and Paul, "Christ hath redeemed us from the curse of the Law, being made a curse for us." (Gal. 3:13.)[231]

Types in Chrysostom's understanding served a didactic function in the overarching framework of God's progressive revelation. As Woollcombe has suggested, "Typology, considered as a method of exegesis, may be defined as the establishment of historical connexions between certain events, persons or things in the Old Testament and similar events, persons or things in the New Testament."[232] Types in the Old Testament were shadows, hints, figures, and outlines of what God was going to accomplish in the new covenant fulfilled by Christ himself. The Jewish rituals, matters, and events found their true meaning in Christ. Chrysostom's exegesis of the Old Testament was intensely christological. The types and figures pointed to the coming messiah and the redemption of humanity through his incarnation, passion, resurrection and ascension. God intentionally placed these types as milestones in the inspired landscape of the Old Testament to prefigure all that he would accomplish in sending Christ.

Unlike Antiochene exegetes Diodore and Theodore, whose rigid adherence to a literal hermeneutic is legendary, Chrysostom was "hermeneutically" flexible in recognizing and attributing a non-literal interpretation to a text or passage when the context demanded one. Obermann's contention that Chrysostom actually rejects allegory does not take into account the fact that Chrysostom did in fact employ this hermeneutical method in certain instances.[233] Furthermore, Chrysostom recognized metaphorical and figurative language in the Scriptures and was comfortable interpreting them as such. Chrysostom maintained that the song of the vineyard in Isa 2:5–6 was an extended metaphor of God's attempt to bring Judah to righteousness and obedience. If the context suggested such

231. Chrysostom, Homily 14, in *John*, FOC 33:138–139 (PG 59.95–96).
232. Woollcombe, "The Biblical Origins and Patristic Development of Typology," in Lampe and Woollcombe, *Essays on Typology*, 39.
233. Oberman, *Forerunners of the Reformation*, 282.

an interpretation, he employed it. He held that there is a rule in Scripture that whenever it demands an allegory an interpretation is also provided, adding, "We are not irresponsible exponents of the laws on this matter, but we may only apply the system of allegorical interpretation when we are following the mind of Scripture."[234] On the other hand, when he felt that the context did not support an allegorical or a non-literal interpretation, he took great pains to make sure it was not misunderstood as such. Chrysostom's concern was that when things are understood allegorically without being anchored in history, the importance of the situation is undermined and the events lose their interpretive significance. God was actively involved in history and historical events in the divine economy convey meaning and underscore his redemptive purposes.

Typical of the general Antiochene reluctance for allegorical interpretation, Chrysostom on one particular occasion even disagrees with Paul's use of the term *allegory* in Galatians 4:24. Here Paul explicitly employs this term to describe the two covenants represented by Hagar and Sarah. Chrysostom, like Diodore, was careful not to undermine the historical aspect in the interpretation of this particular verse, but he admits that the history concerning the events here points to something beyond the immediate meaning. Although Diodore maintained that Paul's usage of the term should be understood in its fuller sense or *theōria*, Chrysostom understood it as a type. Both stressed that the history of the situation should be taken into account in order to understand what Paul was trying to convey. Chrysostom opines, "Contrary to usage, he calls a type an allegory; his meaning is as follows: this history not only declares that which appears on the face of it, but announces somewhat farther, whence it is called an allegory. And what hath it announced? No less than all the things now present."[235] In keeping with the Antiochene tradition, the historical detail and significance of the text is usually not sacrificed for the sake of a non-literal interpretation.

As a representative of the Antiochene tradition of interpretation, Chrysostom preferred a literal approach in most cases but was aware of the fact that there were certain expressions in Scripture which, when interpreted literally, may not make much sense and hence need to be understood in a spiritual or fuller sense. Chrysostom understood "Proverbs" as

---

234. Chrysostom, *Commentary on Isaiah* 5.3 (PG 56.60), as translated and cited in Chase, *Chrysostom*, 61.

235. Chrysostom, *Commentary on Galatians* 4.24, NPNF 13:34 (PG 62.662).

"wise sayings, as riddles, which bear one meaning on the surface, but in a figure suggest something quite different . . . they are dark words, which appear so plain that the reader is annoyed by their lack of meaning and suggestiveness, but which, when they are examined, reveal the thought which lurks in them."[236] In wrestling with interpretation, he contoured his hermeneutic approach to different genres of Scripture, especially poetic and lyrical material, without embarking on fanciful excursions into allegory. Schaff correctly observes that "Chrysostom recognizes allegorizing in theory, but seldom uses it in practice and then more by way of rhetorical ornament and in deference to custom."[237] Vawter's across-the-board suggestion that the fathers generally managed to confuse allegory with typology and "mixed the two together rather thoroughly" might not be completely true when it comes to Chrysostom. As we have seen, the latter distinguished between allegory and typology.[238] Expressions in Scripture, which had a meaning underlying the literal sense, or were intended by the author to have a deeper meaning, were interpreted allegorically. Chrysostom's allegorical interpretations, in most instances, were sustained with scriptural support and, if the context suggested, the historical meaning was taken into consideration as well. Typology functioned as an "exegetical" bridge—a means to connect prefigurations of persons, events, and things in the Old Testament with their fulfillment in the New.

Chrysostom's canon of the Old Testament was the Syrian canon of the Peshitta, which included the Apocrypha. The books that get a passing mention are Judges, Chronicles, Tobias, and Esther. Like Theodore, Chrysostom considered Ecclesiastes, Isaiah, and Daniel as authentic; he never mentions the Song of Solomon. Chrysostom seems very versatile in comparing the different texts, besides the Septuagint available to him in his commentary on the Psalms.[239] His New Testament canon did not contain Revelation, 2 Peter, 2 and 3 John, or Jude.[240] This bears a resemblance to the New Testament canon of Antioch that goes back to the recension of Lucian. This text, as noted earlier, became the official text in

---

236. Chrysostom, *Synopsis* (PG 56.370), as translated and cited in Chase, *Chrysostom*, 76.

237. Schaff, Prolegomena, chapter 13, *NPNF* 9:18.

238. Vawter, *Biblical Inspiration*, 31.

239. See Hill, "Introduction," 1:6–8.

240. Chrysostom, *Synopsis* (ΠΡΟΘΕΩΡΙΑ) (PG 56.318).

Antioch, as Diodore, Chrysostom, and Theodore made use of it in their exegetical works.[241]

Chrysostom could not conceive of interpreting the Scriptures in a manner divorced from the church's needs. In his view, interpretation and application were not mutually exclusive. His exegesis was performed in an ecclesiastical context and this is clearly reflected in his homilies and commentaries. The interpretation of Scripture severed from the devotional life would have been unthinkable, meaningless even.

The recurring themes in Chrysostom's exegesis were both pastoral and paraenetic in nature; he applied the biblical insight to the practical Christian life as he admonished his congregation to read God's Word for themselves and live according to its message. God's love (*philanthropia*) is most graciously portrayed in the Scriptures both in his actions towards his people, and in his promises, which were actualized in Christ. These truths can be gleaned by those who study them with great care (*akribeia*).

The scope of the Holy Scripture is to reform. Therefore, its message needs to be engraved on the hearts of all believers. Superficial reading will not suffice—it has to be applied and lived out. At one point in his homilies on the Gospel of John Chrysostom chides his hearers that they would rather play with draughts and dice than read some Christian book. He underscores the silliness of some in the congregation who possess fine books (portions of the Bible) inscribed in golden letters that are put away in nice bookcases never to be read for personal edification, contending, "And what gain, tell me is this? The Scriptures were not given for this only, that we might have them in books, but that we might engrave them on our hearts. For this kind of possession, the keeping of the commandments merely in letter, belongs to the Jewish ambition; but to us the Law was not so given at all, but in the fleshly tables of our hearts . . . Sanctify then your soul, sanctify your body, by having these ever in your heart, and on your tongue." [242]

Chrysostom's admonition to his hearers that they engrave the message of the Scriptures on their hearts springs from a deep personal conviction. He not only memorized vast portions of Scripture, but also cited them from memory in his homilies and commentaries. According to Baur, Chrysostom's treatises and six hundred sermons (approximately)

---

241. Baur, *John Chrysostom and His Time*, 1:317–18; Chase, *Chrysostom*, 79f.; Schaff, Prolegomena in *NPNF* 9:19. See also Hill, "Introduction," 1:6.

242. Chrysostom, Homily 32, in *John*, FOC 33:319 (PG 59.187).

contain no less than eighteen thousand Scripture citations: seven thousand from the Old Testament and eleven thousand from the New.[243]

Characteristically Antiochene, Chrysostom's exegesis follows the development of the thought in the text, sometimes point by point, ultimately leading to a practical application. His exegesis was textual and philological in nature; an approach that was contoured by the literal-grammatical hermeneutic common to the school which he represented. He recognized the fact that different genres of Scripture called for different interpretative principles. Figurative expressions, metaphors, and imagery were interpreted as such. So was typology. As an Antiochene exegete his ideology constrained his usage of allegory. He resisted the idea of carelessly attributing allegorical interpretations to a text or a passage that would either negate the scope of the author or the context. Yet he was willing to allegorize as long as the history or the actuality of the event (if there was one) was not undermined. Some texts had to be interpreted literally, some non-literally, while still others conveyed a meaning both on the literal level and non-literal level. In other instances one had to consider the fuller or the spiritual meaning to comprehend the message. His exegesis was more christological than any other Antiochene exegete; the types prefigured in the Old Testament—pointers to the coming messiah—were all fulfilled in the life and ministry of Christ.

Chrysostom's hermeneutic premise, that Scripture interprets itself, eventually became the hallmark of the Reformers. As the Word of God enfleshed in human language, veiling the glory of God, the Scriptures required great reverence both on the part of the reader and the interpreter. According to Chrysostom, when the Scriptures were read the voice of God is heard, and thus they are not to be taken lightly. The text must be studied carefully and thoroughly: every principle, precept, and concept has to be extracted with great care and delight. The Bible is the foundation on which the edifice of the Christian life stands, so much prayer and vigilance is required in its study and appropriation.[244] Besides providing the faithful with godly wisdom, the meticulous reading and application of Scripture in the context of worship was vital for spiritual transformation and personal edification.

---

243. See Baur, *Chrysostom and His Time*, 1:316.
244. Chrysostom, Homily 21, in *John*, section 1, *NPNF* 14:72 (PG 59.127).

Conclusion

The Scriptures were central to the life of the early church, as is apparent from the teaching of the fathers. As a guide to liturgy, they played an essential part in the worship of the church; as a manual for catechism, they functioned as a resource to formulate creedal statements; as a text for preaching, they provided the preacher with the lesson; and as an authoritative body of writing, they governed all ecclesiastical polity. The reading and interpretation of Scripture was undertaken within the sacramental context of communal worship. As early as the second century Irenaeus and Tertullian asserted that all interpretation of Scripture must be performed under the auspices of the church. The "rule of faith," which was understood as the distillation of the apostolic teachings, became a yardstick and a guiding principle for scriptural interpretation aimed against false teachings. The Scriptures belonged to the church, were inherited from the apostles, and they can only be properly interpreted in the context of the church which stands in the apostolic tradition. The fathers unanimously concurred that the inspired Scriptures had a central message and that the Holy Spirit, the divine author, illuminated this unified message. Tertullian employed the analogy of the seed and its fruit, Clement spoke of the ecclesiastical symphony of the two choirs of the Old and New Testaments, Origen maintained that the unity of the Scriptures was the result of the Spirit's *skopos*, and Cyril and Chrysostom held that the agreement of the message of both Testaments attested to their divine origin—Christ being their main subject. The whole Bible, therefore, was viewed as an organic whole. Patristic interpretation of the Scriptures presupposed that Christian message of the New Testament did not just augment, but clarified and fulfilled the message of the Old Testament. As the Word of God, the Scriptures provided a theological framework for doctrines such as Christology, soteriology, and ecclesiology. The church furnished the platform where the interpretation of the Scriptures found their application. This functional relationship between scriptural interpretation and its application, which was common among the fathers, is most apparent in Chrysostom's exegesis.

The Old Testament enshrined the truth of the coming messiah in types and shadows. The New Testament contained the apostolic witness to Christ, who fulfilled all the prophecies of the Old Testament concerning him. The incarnation was viewed as the pinnacle of God's love for humanity, a theme that was prefigured in the Old Testament. Christological and typological interpretations of the Old Testament were common among the Alexandrian and Antiochene fathers. Although they did not agree on every detail, both schools shared a common christological understanding of the Scriptures. The Alexandrian fathers generally resorted to an allegorical approach in order to find the spiritual message of the Scriptures. The Antiochenes, on the other hand, opted to seek the spiritual sense behind the historical expressions and events. The fathers from both schools agreed fundamentally that the Scriptures had a spiritual message. While Alexandrian exegetes looked for hidden meanings concealed in the text, the Antiochenes considered the *theōria* to comprehend the higher spiritual meaning of the Scriptures. Origen admonished his hearers to look beyond the literal meaning of the text to understand its spiritual value, while Chrysostom admonished his hearers to mine the Scriptures carefully in order to gain insight and appreciation of their spiritual teaching. Exegesis and praxis were inseparable in the understanding of the fathers; this union was forged in their hearts because they maintained that the purpose of doctrine was not just to inform and educate, but also to govern the Christian life.

The differences in exegesis were due to the philosophical and rhetorical traditions prevalent in the academia of that day. Scholars often prefer to highlight the differences between Alexandrian and Antiochene fathers to the extent that the common motifs between them are overlooked. The two schools had more in common than is portrayed in current scholarship. The exposition of the Scriptures by the fathers, at the end of the day, was done for the spiritual edification of the recipients. Clement interpreted the Scriptures with the preconception that the church's faith was the basis for all scriptural knowledge. The scope of all Scripture, according to Origen, is to restore the soul. Cyril remarked that the knowledge of the Scriptures is the path to the knowledge of God and Christ inaugurated a new covenant through his incarnation. Diodore maintained that the Scriptures teach what is useful, expose what is sinful and correct what is deficient. According to Theodore, the Scriptures provide a coherent teaching for life and must be studied in their proper context. For Chrysostom, the Scriptures are a treasury of medicine containing healing for all; they nourish the soul and prepare the individual to commune with God. Furthermore, concurring with Origen that Christ (the Word according to the flesh) appears in the Bible according to the letter, Chrysostom understood the existence of the Scriptures as God's *sunkatabasis*. As in the incarnation of the Word, so in the Bible the glory of God is veiled in the flesh of the text—human language and thought. It is by the careful reading and study of the Scriptures that one encounters its true subject: Jesus Christ. The historical incarnation therefore is viewed as a paradigm for the nature of the Scriptures: God's message is inextricably fused in the human language of the text. God accommodates himself to the reader in the interpretive encounter, thus providing a divine pedagogy for the reader's edification and spiritual life.

In Chrysostom's view exegesis, doctrine, and application form a complex whole with strong interconnections between them. Doctrine was complemented by application, and they both found their provenance in Scripture. A study of Chrysostom's reading and interpretation of the Scriptures, therefore, is an essential starting point in understanding the relation between Christology and the practice of the Christian life in his exegesis. Patristic reading, interpretation, and application of the Scriptures should be viewed as a three-stranded cord, closely intertwined. Emphasizing one aspect alone is akin to separating and dividing the strands, thus weakening the whole cord. The beauty and strength of the cord is fully appreciated only when one treats this functional relationship as a whole: unified and undivided.

3

The Doctrine of Christ in Chrysostom's Homilies on the Gospel of John

Introduction

THE READING AND INTERPRETATION OF SCRIPTURE WAS NOT ONLY AN integral part of the life of the early church, it also shaped the church's faith and tradition. The previous chapter underscored the centrality of Scripture, examining how the fathers read, interpreted, and applied its teaching in their unique ecclesiastical contexts. In so far as doctrine and application form a cohesive unit in the teaching of the fathers, the main objective of this chapter is to illustrate how Chrysostom's Christology relates with his view of the Christian life. In order to accomplish this I will survey Chrysostom's preaching on the person and work of Christ, underscoring the skillful use of images in his exegetical homilies on the Fourth Gospel—a *locus classicus* for patristic Christology. As one of the church's celebrated preachers and pastors, Chrysostom's Christology is inextricably linked to his understanding of the Christian life. Thus his portrait of Christ makes most sense from within this perspective. Moreover, it will be pointed out that his understanding of the Christian life is the outworking of his christological thought.

Chrysostom's christological picture will be examined employing a threefold analytical framework that corresponds with the three christological perspectives of this chapter: ontological considerations, sacramental mediation, and the practical outworking. In the final analysis, Chrysostom's picture of Christ will be surveyed from three perspectives: a *Christology of Restoration*, where the redemptive ministry of Christ is portrayed in the context of incarnational theology; a *Christology of Participation*, where Christ is depicted as the source and giver of life in the sacramental context of the Eucharist; and a *Practical Christology*, where Christ is viewed as an exemplar for the faithful.

Contextual Overview

Survey of Scholarship on Chrysostom's Exegesis and Christology

A cursory survey of the divergent ways Chrysostom is viewed in patristic scholarship will set the background for my approach to his portraiture of Christ in John's Gospel. The majority of scholarly readings of Chrysostom accuse him of mutually inconsistent forms of one-sidedness. The first misreading accuses him of being purely a moralizer with no doctrinal sophistication; the second misreading interprets him as having too much of a doctrinal focus shaped by the Christology of the Antiochene school. Since Chrysostom is typically regarded as a moralist the scholarly focus thus tends to be directed to his ethical and moral teaching, rather than on how his theology and his understanding of the Christian life inform this moral preaching. For instance, Liebeschuetz has remarked that dogma does not occupy much space in Chrysostom's preaching and that "his immediate aim was to propagate Christian morality, and persuade his hearers to let Christianity play a larger part in their lives and thoughts. Presumably he assumed that if this objective was achieved allegiance to state orthodox religion would follow automatically."[1] Likewise, Simonetti's critique of Chrysostom's exegesis highlights a similar sentiment, "his predominantly ethical or exhortatory interest account for the fact that often the actual illustration of the text remains superficial . . . The illustration of the letters of Paul is similarly [to the Gospel of John] deficient."[2] However, Mitchell has convincingly argued that Simonetti's negative judgment of Chrysostom's exegesis is due to an illegitimate dichotomy he posits between moral exhortation and exegesis, viewing them as two different tasks.[3] She contends that "ancient biblical interpretation consisted of a much wider set of practices than Simonetti has confined it to here. Moreover, his own definition is predicated upon a non-existent ideal, for no ancient Christian interpreters illustrated the

---

1. Liebeschuetz, *Barbarians and Bishops*, 167. For a similar perspective on Chrysostom as a moralist, see Osborn, *Ethical Patterns in Early Christian Thought*, 116.

2. Simonetti, *Biblical Interpretation*, 74.

3. See, e.g., ibid.

text 'for its own sake' (a claim of modern historical-critical exegesis that has itself been buffeted severely in the last half century). Chrysostom's vivid exegetical moralizing may be more extensive or artful than many others, but that does not remove his homilies from the realm of biblical interpretation."[4] One might also add that his "vivid exegetical moralizing" is better understood when surveyed from the perspective of his understanding of the practical Christian life, as will be shown later in this chapter.

Mitchell's extensive and helpful documentation of the various depictions of Paul as the archetype of virtue from Chrysostom's oeuvre, and her thorough analysis of it as products of fourth-century Christian oratory, usefully build on Young's proposal of Antiochene "ikonic" mimetic scriptural reading and paraenetic exegesis. She further observes that "the firm foundation of Antiochene exegetical practice was the *paideia* of the rhetorical schools."[5] However, the present study's objective is not to underscore the techniques employed for reading patristic texts, but rather to outline Chrysostom's christological doctrine as it emerges from his preaching on the Fourth Gospel.[6]

Scholarly studies on the Christology of Chrysostom tend to examine his christological thought in relation to the Alexandrian and Antiochene traditions from dogmatic perspectives, which hardly bear any resemblance to the Christ that is portrayed by him from the pulpit. In doing so, the sole focus of such scholarship tends to be directed at Christ, whose person (and work) is studied in isolation from the life of faith in a sacramental and ecclesiastical context. The aim here is to frame Chrysostom's picture of Christ in the context in which he portrays it: the life of faith and the church's worship. To divorce the study of

---

4. Mitchell, *Heavenly Trumpet*, 385.

5. Ibid., 387.

6. Young argues that the Alexandrian school with its roots in the philosophical schools viewed the text's mimetic role as "symbol" of true realities and the Antiochene school influenced by the rhetorical schools regarded the text as "ikon" of moral and dogmatic teachings: "They saw the biblical text as 'ikonic,' as imparting dogma and ethics through 'images.'" Young, *Biblical Exegesis and the Formation of Christian Culture*, 211. Elsewhere, she observes, "Where philosophy found abstract doctrines or virtues through verbal allegory, rhetoric looked for concrete ethical examples in a narrative." See Young, "The Rhetorical Schools and Their Influence on Patristic Exegesis," in Williams, *Making of Orthodoxy*, 169–85, 188. See also Schäublin, *Untersuchungen zu Methode und Herkunft der antiochenischen Exegese*.

Chrysostom's Christology from its churchly context is to undermine the very foundation on which his doctrinal thought is erected.

A survey of the studies both past and present on the Christology of Chrysostom underscores this point. Juzek maintained that Chrysostom's Christology is Antiochene to the extent that he asserted two complete natures in Christ but, unlike Diodore and Theodore of Mopsuestia, did not employ terminology to speak of the natures separately after the union. He points out that Chrysostom, in common with the Antiochenes, emphasized the integrity of the two natures of Christ in opposition to the Apollinarian heresy, which denied a rational soul in Christ. With particular reference to Chrysostom's interpretation of Christ's prayer in the garden (where he allegedly speaks of two wills in opposition to each other), Juzek sees a twofold will and, by implication, dual centers of activity in Christ. He shows that Chrysostom's Christology is to some extent a reflection of the Chalcedonian understanding of the unity of Christ and the relationship between the two natures.[7]

Hay argued against Juzek's position that Chrysostom's emphasis on the integrity of the human nature of Christ places him in the same category as his fellow Antiochenes.[8] He explains that the term "flesh" is the normal expression employed by Chrysostom to refer to the humanity of Christ and underscores his assertion of the reality of the human nature of Christ. Chrysostom uses the term *sarx* instead of *anthrōpos* to refer to Christ's human nature concretely considered, avoiding the danger of positing two persons in Christ. For Chrysostom "flesh" signified a perfect human nature, a union of body and soul, whereas "man" implied a perfect human person. Hay argues that Chrysostom's apparent description of the two wills opposed to each other in Christ's prayer in Gethsemane is to be understood as an instinct of self-preservation and not a deliberate act of the will.[9] He notes that though Chrysostom affirmed that Christ possessed a human soul in common with his fellow Antiochenes, it had no theological significance in Chrysostom's Christology. He asserts that Chrysostom was not preoccupied to any degree with the Apollinarian heresy.[10] Hay concludes that while Chrysostom affirmed the reality and

---

7. Juzek, *Christologie des hl. Johannes Chrysostomus*.

8. Hay, "St. John Chrysostom and the Integrity of the Human Nature of Christ," 298–317.

9. Ibid., 315, 305–9.

10. Hay observes that in Chrysostom's voluminous writings, he refers to and refutes Apollinarius only once, and this is to be found in his commentary on *Philippians*, where

integrity of the human nature of Christ, it can hardly be said that this was an emphasis of his christological thought.

Grillmeier, subscribing to Hay's conclusions, notes that if one prejudges Chrysostom's Christology as Antiochene, one would expect him to be openly opposed to Apollinarius and thereby emphasize the soul and the complete human nature of Christ.[11] Contrary to what is expected, Chrysostom's Christology, Grillmeir notes, is quite similar to that of the younger Cyril of Alexandria and his model, Athanasius. He points out that Chrysostom's picture of Christ suggests that everything is understood in light of the person of the Logos and the predominance of the divine nature. Therefore, the "typically Antiochene difficulties in the interpretation of the unity of Christ do not exist for Chrysostom."[12] Grillmeier concludes that Chrysostom's doctrine of Christ is much more Alexandrian than Antiochene, and that Antiochene Christology really begins with Theodore of Mopsuestia.

Barnard places Chrysostom's Christology within the Antiochene tradition and calls it a "dyophysite christology."[13] He observes that the prevalent philosophical, theological, anthropological influences "caused Chrysostom to deny that the incarnation has an effect upon God, and to conceive that its movement was wholly toward man and that its effects remained on earth. God therefore had no experience in the incarnation. The advantage in Chrysostom's Christology is merely the obverse of his feeling that the incarnation was too thorough going a human experience for God himself to enter it."[14] In other words, Barnard maintains that Chrysostom undermines the personal continuity of the Logos-Son in Christ.

Lawrenz's balanced study shows that Chrysostom's Christology contains elements of both approaches and observes that he should not be considered as a classic example of either.[15] Further, Lawrenz

---

Chrysostom clearly affirms the existence of a soul in Christ and attacks those who refute it. (Homily 7, in *Philippians* [*PG* 62.231–32]). Ibid., 301–2.

11. Grillmeier, *Christ in Christian Tradition*, 1:418–21.

12. Ibid., 421.

13. Barnard, "Christology and Soteriology in the Preaching of John Chrysostom."

14. Ibid., 6. Moreover, Bernard observes that it is "likely that Chrysostom escaped obloquy and oblivion because he differed from Antiochene theology only in respect to the doctrine of *apokatastasis*, for there is little difference between his Christology and the condemned christologies of Theodore and Nestorius." Ibid., 67.

15. Lawrenz, "Christology of John Chrysostom."

observes, "While we find a methodology that is clearly similar to that of Theodore of Mopsuestia and other Antiochene exegetes and theologians, Chrysostom's theological foundations most often reflect those of Athanasius and of later Alexandrians."[16] Lawrenz concludes that Chrysostom is Antiochene to the extent that his theology is exegetical in nature—inasmuch as the biblical text provides the theological language that enables him to describe the person of Christ and (as far as possible) the nature of the incarnation; Chrysostom is Alexandrian to the extent that he speaks of Christ as one divine acting subject, the Logos, who determines every rational and volitional experience in the incarnation. In this respect, Chrysostom is similar to Athanasius, Cyril, and others who maintain a real unity in Christ, while distinguishing the characteristics of the flesh. Lawrenz's study focuses solely on Chrysostom's Christology apart from how it relates to the Christian life.

These divergent accounts of the Christology of Chrysostom, where his understanding of the person of Christ is bifurcated from the life of faith, and where no importance is attached to the context in which he frames his christological thought, sufficiently demonstrate that the picture of Christ, which emerges from this method of investigation is entirely monochromatic. Therefore, a new study is warranted—one that grounds Chrysostom's Christology in the life and context of the church's faith. With this objective in mind, I shall now turn to Chrysostom's christological picture as it emerges in his preaching on the Fourth Gospel.

Chrysostom's Homilies on the Gospel of John

John Chrysostom's *Commentary on Saint John the Apostle and Evangelist* is comprised of eighty-eight exegetical homilies preached during his priesthood in the city of Antioch, sometime circa 391.[17] These homilies

---

16. Ibid., 196.

17. Although not much is known about his personal life during his priesthood, significant portions of his work from this period are extant and give a glimpse of the issues that Chrysostom was dealing with in his capacity as a priest. Kelly notes that the ten years from 387 to 397 were not just busy ones for Chrysostom but they also had a formative impact on his career as he began to gain notoriety, adding to his growing stature in the community. Chrysostom's ninety homilies on Matthew, considered the earliest and the most extensive patristic commentary on the First Gospel, were delivered in 390, a year prior to the ones delivered on John's Gospel. For an exhaustive list of homilies, commentaries, and treatises that were published by Chrysostom during his priesthood at Antioch, see the chapter titled "Decade of Development," in Kelly, *Golden Mouth*, 90–103.

have been translated into two English volumes by Stupart in *A Library of the Fathers* (1848–1852), and later revised with a few additional notes by Marriott in *A Select Library of the Nicene and Post-Nicene Fathers* (volume 14, 1889; reprinted 1975).[18] The most recent translation of Chrysostom's homilies on the Gospel of John is by Goggin and appears in two volumes of *The Fathers of the Church* series (volume 33, 1957; volume 41, 1960).[19] The Greek text of Chrysostom's homilies on the Gospel of John was edited by the Benedictine Bernard de Montfaucon (1718–38) and reworked by Theobald Fix (1834–39), and can be found in Migne's *Patrologia Graeca* (volume 59, 1863).[20] Due to the absence of a proper critical edition for these homilies, all Greek citations used herein are taken from the *Patrologia Graeca*. The updated English translation by Goggin of Chrysostom's *Commentary on Saint John the Apostle and Evangelist* (volumes 33 and 41) will be used for all English citations unless otherwise specified.

Chrysostom's eloquence in these homilies is striking. He musters all his rhetorical skills in communicating the truth of the Scriptures persuasively, betraying his earlier training in the principles of Atticism under the renowned fourth century orator Libanius. Hubbell pointed out that after the official recognition of Christianity by Constantine, large numbers of people started attending churches, "who were but little affected by the finer moral and spiritual ideas of religion, and who demanded that the Christian priest should furnish them the same entertainment which they could receive from a Libanius or a Themistius. And the Christian priests, many of them trained under the best rhetoricians of the day,

---

18. Chrysostom, *Homilies on the Gospel of St. John and The Epistle to the Hebrews*, NPNF, vol. 14.

19. Chrysostom, *Commentary on Saint John the Apostle and Evangelist*, FOC, vols. 33 and 41.

20. For a more detailed chronological list of complete and partial editions of the Greek text of the *corpus Chrysostomicum* containing the *Commentary of John*, see Harkins, "Text Tradition of Chrysostom's Commentary on John," 404–12. Cf. Fee, "Text of John and Mark in the Writings of Chrysostom," 525–47. Fee offers an analysis of Chrysostom's text of the Fourth Gospel and concludes that it was distinctly Byzantine and had a considerable influence on the emerging text in the Greek church. Riddle notes that Chrysostom ignores the pericope of the woman accused of adultery (John 7:53—8:11), as do all the Greek fathers before the eighth century. One may surmise that Chrysostom's text of the Gospel of John may not have contained that passage. See also the "Introductory Essay" in NPNF 10:21.

were not loath to accept the challenge."[21] Chrysostom certainly was one such priest; his oratorical skills were extraordinary. As a gifted speaker he drew large crowds to the Great Church in Antioch. Sometimes the enthralled congregation had to be warned not to get too engrossed or even captivated with his preaching, lest they get pickpocketed by thieves who took advantage of such large gatherings.[22]

As an exegete and teacher, Chrysostom preached through the Gospel text carefully, repeating the same texts several times in the homily to familiarize his listeners with Scripture. He sometimes insisted that they read the passage carefully in advance and come prepared for the lesson. Some of his homilies were quite lengthy and would have taken more than an hour to preach. As the internal evidence suggests, it is quite possible that these homilies were delivered in a church setting in the morning.[23]

Chrysostom's homilies follow a particular pattern: each homily begins with a brief exordium (or introduction), often in the form of an exhortation, and a call to pay close attention to what is to follow. The introduction is followed by the body of the homily, which forms the explanation of the text or passage that is being dealt with. Then follows the paraenetic section with its practical and moral admonition usually highlighting a virtue to emulate or a vice to avoid. It is customary with

---

21. Hubbell, "Chrysostom and Rhetoric," 262–63. Kennedy notes that "the preaching of the Cappadocian Fathers and John Chrysostom developed the philosophical basis of Christian doctrine to a high level of sophistication." Furthermore, Kennedy adds, "For the next 1000 years these (Athanasius, the Cappadocians, John Chrysostom, Theodore of Mopsuestia) remain the major models of Christian eloquence, Nazianzus and Chrysostom the most, the others in varying degrees depending on the values and objectives of their successors. A great deal of subsequent Greek preaching not only imitates Gregory and John, but quarries phrases, sentences and whole passages from their works. Their achievements were never surpassed and rarely equaled." Kennedy, *Greek Rhetoric under Christian Emperors*, 50, 255–56. See also Pelikan, *Divine Rhetoric*, specifically chapter 5, "Chrysostom: 'Golden-Tongued' Preacher," 67–80.

22. See Chrysostom, Homily 4, *Incomprehensible Nature of God*, FOC 72:134 (PG 48:735).

23. Chrysostom, Homily 23, in *John*, FOC 33:222 (PG 59.137); cf. Homily 31, in *John*, FOC 33:310 (PG 59.182), where Chrysostom contrasts the hot midday meeting of Christ with the Samaritan woman at the well with the comfort and shade provided by the roof that the congregation is sitting under in the early morn. Some scholars suggest that Chrysostom's normal pulpit was in the Old Church, where he carried out his priestly duties. The Great Church, which was built by Constantine, was the episcopal church where Chrysostom might have been summoned on several occasions to assist the bishop. See Mayer and Allen, *John Chrysostom*, 17–18.

Chrysostom that he bring his homilies to a close by spurring his listeners to action, exhorting them to put into practices what they have heard. Every sermon was capped by the following doxology, albeit slightly varied at times: "the grace and loving-kindness of our Lord Jesus Christ, through whom and with whom, to the Father and the Holy Spirit, be glory forever, Amen."

Chrysostom on the Gospel Accounts

Of over six hundred extant homilies of Chrysostom, 178 are on the Gospels of Matthew and John. Chrysostom preached ninety homilies on the Gospel of Matthew, a work for which, it is said, Aquinas would have exchanged the city of Paris.[24] In his opening homily, Chrysostom's description of the Gospel of Matthew as ἱστορία (*historia*) suggests that he views the Gospel narratives as inspired accounts of salvation-history.[25] Furthermore, he maintained that this history is also called good news, for it announced, "the removal of punishment, and remission of sins, and 'righteousness, and sanctification, and redemption,' and adoption, and an inheritance of Heaven, and a relationship with the Son of God, which he came declaring to all; to enemies, to the perverse, to them that are sitting in darkness."[26]

Treating the Scriptures as an organic whole, like a body connected by nerves, veins, arteries, blood, and bones, Chrysostom sees no contradictions in the Gospel narratives. Unlike pagan philosophers who contradict themselves and speak in opposition to one another even on matters of the same discipline, the evangelists, in Chrysostom's view, concur with each other on significant points in their Gospel accounts with minor variations in wording that do not undermine their credibility.[27] He asks, "What then? Was not one evangelist sufficient to tell all? One indeed was sufficient; but if there be four that write, not at the same times, not in the same places, neither after having met together, and conversed one with another, and then they speak all things as it were out of one mouth, this becomes a very great demonstration of the truth."[28] Furthermore, Chrysostom contends that the fact that there are

24. Quinn, "Saint John Chrysostom on History in the Synoptics," 140.
25. Chrysostom, Homily 1, in *Matthew*, section 3, NPNF 10:2 (PG 57.17).
26. Ibid.
27. Ibid., section 8–9, NPNF 10:4 (PG 57.17–18).
28. Ibid., section 5–6, NPNF 10:3 (PG 57.16).

variations concerning minor issues is evidence itself that they did not collude with each other to contrive and devise falsehood, or mislead in the matters concerning truth. He affirms that the slight variations in the Gospel accounts, however trivial, actually authenticate the evangelists' character in communicating the good news. "But now even that discordance (διαφωνία) which seems to exist in little matters delivers them from all suspicion, and speaks clearly in behalf of the character of the writers."[29] He maintains that if there was complete harmony (συμφωνία) in all details then the Gospel accounts must be treated with suspicion and should not be considered as products of honest integrity. The minor discrepancies among the Gospels are insignificant because they are only a difference of wording; the truth is that the evangelists recorded everything as if it were "from one mouth."

In Chrysostom's view, the Gospels are a historical account of the incarnation from four evangelists who complemented and supplemented each other's teaching. He maintains that the Gospel of Matthew was written for the Jews and seeks to illustrate that Christ was from the lineage of Abraham and David. The Gospel of Mark was written after Matthew's Gospel, hence its brevity. Luke's Gospel was written for all in general and therefore traces the genealogy of Christ all the way back to Adam. Since Matthew's Gospel predates his writing, Luke sought to supplement it with more teaching.[30] Discussing John's purpose for writing the Fourth Gospel, Chrysostom observes:

> forasmuch it had been the care of the three to dwell upon the account of the dispensation, and the doctrines of the Godhead were near being left in silence, he, moved by Christ, then and not till then set himself to compose his Gospel. And this is manifest both from the history itself, and from the opening of his Gospel. For he does not begin like the rest from beneath, but from above, from the same point, at which he was aiming, and it was with a view to this that he composed the whole book. And not in the beginning only, but throughout all the Gospel, he is more lofty than the rest.[31]

Chrysostom asserts that the real harmony of the Gospels is seen in their common teaching on the historical incarnation of Christ—that the eter-

---

29. Ibid.
30. Chrysostom, Homily 1, in *Matthew*, sections 5–6, *NPNF* 10:3–4 (*PG* 57.17).
31. Ibid., section 7, *NPNF* 10:3 (*PG* 57.16–17).

nal Son, consubstantial with the Father, became human. He maintains that they all agreed on the following points of importance:

> But what are these points? Such as follow: That God became man, that He wrought miracles, that He was crucified, that He was buried, that He rose again, that He ascended, that He will judge, that He hath given commandments tending to salvation, that He hath brought in a law not contrary to the Old Testament, that He is a Son, that He is only-begotten, that He is a true Son, that He is of the same substance with the Father, and as many things as are like these; for touching these we shall find that there is in them a full agreement.[32]

For Chrysostom, Christ is the central theme of the Gospels, and the incarnation is the starting point for the restoration and redemption of humanity. The following section will examine the ontological and soteriological aspects of Chrysostom's christological picture as they emerge in his exposition.

A Christology of Restoration

Introduction

The focus of this section is on the relation between Chrysostom's incarnational theology and his soteriological thought, with particular reference to his understanding of how baptism structures Christian life. The first subsection investigates the ontological aspects of Chrysostom's incarnational thought. Here I will examine Chrysostom's understanding of the incarnation as it emerges in his polemical preaching against the Neo-Arians. These polemics demonstrate that he views the Logos as the single subject in Christ, underscoring his personal continuity in and after the incarnation. Chrysostom's christological thought is undergirded by the idea of God's personal involvement in the economy of salvation: only if Christ is the natural Son of God can he make us by grace what he is by nature. The following subsection will examine the soteriological implications of Chrysostom's christological thought. Here I highlight two interrelated soteriological motifs that are characteristic of his incarnational theology: restoration of human nature and adoption as sons. It will be shown that Chrysostom's understanding of the Christian life is

---

32. Ibid., section 6, *NPNF* 10:3 (*PG* 57.16–17).

underpinned by a soteriology that is relational in nature. Furthermore, I will examine Chrysostom's understanding of how baptism—of Christ and the believer—provides a vital means for the application of the incarnation. In Chrysostom's view, the soteriological ideas of the gift of adoption and the conforming of the Christian to the likeness of Christ are one and the same. It is the baptismal context where they are actualized. So it will be argued that Chrysostom's understanding of the Christian life is the outworking of his unitive Christology.

The Ontology of the Incarnation

The polemic tone of Chrysostom's statements on the person of the Logos is unmistakable in his homilies on the Johannine prologue. Although his refutation of the Neo-Arian doctrine of the essential dissimilarity (*anomoios*) of the Logos and the Father is scattered and unsystematic, he consistently emphasizes the divinity and consubstantiality of the Logos by pointing out his co-eternality and equality with the Father.[33] In a critical passage he clearly distinguishes the person of the Logos from the Father, mentioning his eternal nature, his consubstantiality, and his procession. Chrysostom maintains that the Logos is "a Being, a distinct Person, proceeding from the Father Himself without alteration. He [John] has indicated this, as I have said, by his appellation 'the Word.' Therefore, just as the expression 'In the beginning was the Word' reveals His eternity, so 'He was in the beginning with God' has revealed to us His co-eternity."[34] The Logos is co-eternal with the Father; he has always existed—there never was a time when he was not. Consistent with the creedal pronouncements Chrysostom affirms that the Father is unbegotten and the Son is the begotten of the Father.[35] Furthermore, he asserts that the Logos was not created and then chosen by God to have a transitory sovereignty, "but one that is His by nature and essence.[36] Chrysostom often argued against the Neo-Arian doctrine of the dissimilarity between

---

33. For a comprehensive and in-depth treatment of Neo-Arianism from primary source material, see Kopecek, *History of Neo-Arianism*.

34. Chrysostom, Homily 4, in *John*, FOC 33:45–46 (PG 59.47). Further, Chrysostom adds that the Logos was as "eternal as the Father himself, for the Father was never without the Logos but always God was with God, though each in His own Person." Ibid. (PG 59.47).

35. Chrysostom, Homily 2, FOC 33:22 (PG 59.33).

36. Chrysostom, Homily 3, FOC 33:35 (PG 59.41).

the essences of the Son and the Father, which they associated with the subsequent existence of the former. He contended that there was no essential difference between the Father and the Son, and asserted that the Logos was not subsequent to but co-eternal with the Father. Illustrating this point employing the well-known Cappadocian example he says that just like light has its origin in the sun, the Son likewise is neither created, subsequent, nor inferior to the Father, but rather is co-eternal with Him, possessing all the qualities of divinity.[37] Moreover, Chrysostom reasoned that because the Son is co-eternal with the Father he is not a creature, and since he is begotten processionally he shares the same divine essence: "For if the son were not of the same Essence (οὐσία), there must be another God and if He were not co-eternal, He would exist later than the Father; and if He did not proceed from the Father's Essence, it is evident the He must have been made."[38] Chrysostom further substantiates his argument by asserting that the Father would not have anyone dissimilar or distinct in essence from him in his bosom. The fact that the only begotten Son came from the Father's side (John 1:18) is the ultimate proof that he is of the same substance and shares in the natural communion of the Godhead. Affirming this perichoretic union of the Father and the Son, he observes:

> That is also the reason, as I have said, why the Evangelist mentioned the Father's bosom: to clear up the whole matter for us by this one word. [It implies] that They have full conformity and agreement of substance, that Their knowledge is identical, that Their power is equal. For, the Father would not have anyone distinct [ἑτερούσιον] from His own essence in His bosom, nor would any other have dared—since he was a slave and an ordinary person, to be himself in the bosom of the Lord, for this is a prerogative only of His own Son who is on terms of complete equality with Him who begot Him and is in no way inferior to Him.[39]

If the Evangelist wanted to show the inferiority of the Son's divinity, argues Chrysostom, he would not have used terms like "life and light" (vv. 3–5), which refer to the Son as a personal agent in creation (because through him all things were made) and revelation (because he illumines all things), attesting to his equality and identity with the Father. "What is

---

37. Chrysostom, Homily 4, *FOC* 33:46–47 (*PG* 59.48). Cf. Homily 7, *FOC* 33:78 (*PG* 59.61); Homily 8, *FOC* 33:81 (*PG* 59.65).

38. Chrysostom, Homily 4, *FOC* 33:49 (*PG* 59.49).

39. Chrysostom, Homily 15, *FOC* 33:146 (*PG* 59.99).

said of the Father as creator is meant also of the Son; he would not have said it if he had not the same opinion of Him as of the Creator and as not inferior to anyone."[40] Elsewhere, commenting on the words, "Let us make man in our image" (Gen 1:26), Chrysostom discusses the Son's role in creation underscoring his equality with the Father. He argues:

> So who is this to whom he says, "Let us make a human being? Who else is it than the Angel of Great Counsel, Wonderful Counsellor, Figure of Authority, Prince of Peace, Father of the age to come, Only-begotten Son of God, like the Father in being, through whom all things were created? To him is said, "Let us make a human being in our image and likeness." This text also deals a mortal blow to those entertaining the position of Arius. I mean, he did not say by way of command, Make such a creature, as though to a subordinate to one inferior in being, but "Let us make" with great deference to an equal. And what follows shows us further the equality in being.[41]

Besides being active in creation and its sustenance, the life and light of Logos have brought about a change; death has lost its foothold and the darkness of sin has been vanquished. "When Life came to us, the power of death has been destroyed, and when the Light has shone for us, darkness is no more, but Life always remains in us and death cannot overcome it."[42] For Chrysostom, the divine nature of the Logos is evident in his participation in creation, revelation, and redemption.[43]

In the incarnation the Logos suffered no alteration, for in the assumption of flesh he remained unchanged in his divine nature: "His substance [οὐσία] was not transformed into flesh, but remaining what He is, He thus took the form of a slave."[44] Furthermore, the Logos always remains in the same state of perfection;[45] "not that His substance changed into flesh, but that, after assuming flesh, His substance remained intact."[46] Moreover, Chrysostom asserts, "He can do all things as long as

---

40. Ibid., *FOC* 33:52 (*PG* 59.50); Chrysostom likens the creative activity of the only-begotten to an incessant spring that produces fathomless depths. Homily 5, *FOC* 33:63 (*PG* 59.56).

41. Chrysostom, Homily 8, in *Genesis*, *FOC* 74:109 (*PG* 53.72).

42. Chrysostom, Homily 5, in *John*, *FOC* 33:65 (*PG* 59.57).

43. Ibid.

44. Chrysostom, Homily 11, *FOC* 33:107 (*PG* 59.79).

45. Chrysostom, Homily 14, *FOC* 33:130–31 (*PG* 59.91).

46. Chrysostom, Homily 11, *FOC* 33:107–8 (*PG* 59.79).

He remains God; but if He receives a transformation, and one for the worse, how would He be God? Change is out of keeping with that pure nature."⁴⁷ The reason Chrysostom consistently defends the notion of the unchanging nature of the Logos, even after the incarnation, is because he views the Logos as the personal subject in Christ. In asserting that the person of Christ is the eternal Logos who added humanity to himself without a transformation, Chrysostom maintains the personal continuity and unity in Christ. This perspective will be substantiated further in the final section, where I shall underscore its implications in conjunction with how it relates to the restorative sacramental benefits in the context of Chrysostom's incarnational theology.

In keeping with his down-to-earth attitude with respect to metaphysical speculation, Chrysostom asserts that in the incarnation the divine Logos and flesh have been united in a way that is beyond explanation. In a crucial passage he emphasizes the point that, in the incarnation of Christ, God the Logos and the flesh have become one in a union that defies human epistemology but is well within the bounds of divine comprehension. "By Their union and conjoining, God, the Word, and the flesh are one, not as a result of commingling or disappearance of substances but by some ineffable and inexplicable union. But do not seek the how; it "was made" in a way which He Himself knows."⁴⁸

It is worth noting that Chrysostom uses both ἕνωσις and συναφεία to describe this union in Christ. At this pre-Chalcedonian stage in the history of the controversies between the Alexandrians and the Antiochenes, where the issue of the union—be it the "hypostatic union" (ἕνωσις καθ' ὑπόστασιν) favored by the former (e.g., Cyril) or the "union by grace" (ἕνωσις κατ' εὐδοκιάν) favored by the latter (e.g., Theodore of Mopsuestia and Theodoret)—had not yet come up for explicit debate. Chrysostom does not attempt to explain this union; he is content simply stating that the union is "an inexplicable union" where the Logos and the flesh are one, yet maintaining that this does not imply confusion or commingling of substances. The emphasis here is on the unity of the incarnate Logos and not on how this union takes place. For Chrysostom the union of the two realities in Christ is a mystery to the human mind and beyond all speculation. His focus in these homilies is mainly on the relation of

---

47. Ibid., *FOC* 33:108 (*PG* 59.79).
48. Ibid., *FOC* 33:109 (*PG* 59.80).

Christ to God the Father, rather than on the relation of the divine and human natures in the person of Christ.

The Soteriological Ramifications of the Incarnation

Consonant with the teaching of the Fathers, the doctrinal threads of incarnation, restoration, and salvation are interwoven in the intricate tapestry of Chrysostom's soteriology. Underscoring this *consensus patrum*, Florovsky has rightly stated that "in this lifting up of human nature into an everlasting communion with Divine Life, the Fathers of the early church unanimously saw the very essence of salvation, the basis of the whole redeeming work of Christ."[49] The historical incarnation of which Chrysostom speaks as the *oikonomia* is underscored as being the cause of the restoration of sinful and fallen humanity and is correspondingly inseparably united to Chrysostom's understanding of redemption.[50] In so far as the *philanthrōpia* of God and the *oikonomia* of Christ are related, the incarnation is understood as integral, a cornerstone of the divine plan of redemption and not just a cosmic event. For Chrysostom the incarnation, life, and death of Christ—viewed as a composite picture—is a reflection of God's love, manifested in the divine condescension of the second person of the Trinity. Discussing this issue in his commentary on *Genesis*, Chrysostom writes:

> Do you see the Lord's inventive love [*philanthrōpia*]? . . . Why are you surprised if to this end he has devised all those stratagems and countless others? He who by nature was in the bosom of the Father deigned to take the form of a servant, to submit himself to all other bodily conditions, to have a woman for mother, to be born of a virgin, to be carried in the womb for nine months, to be wrapped in swaddling clothes, to be thought the son of Joseph, Mary's husband, to grow up gradually, to be circumcised, to offer sacrifice, to suffer hunger and thirst and weariness, finally to meet his death, and not simply death but that death thought most

---

49. Florovsky, "Lamb of God," 17.

50. Prestige observes that term οἰκονομία is a constant favorite with Chrysostom. He concludes that "it need only be added that the supreme instance of divine economy, whether in the sense of dispensation, condescension, or special providence, was exhibited in the Incarnation, for which the word 'oekonomia' without any verbal qualification is the regular patristic term from the third century onwards." For the patristic use of the term οἰκονομία and the variety of meanings attached to it, see Prestige, *God in Patristic Thought*, 57–67.

shameful—I mean crucifixion. All of this was accepted for us and for our salvation by the Creator of everything, the one who never changes, who brings everything from non-being to being, who looks down upon the earth and makes it tremble, the splendor of whose glory not even the Cherubim, those incorporeal powers, cannot see but cover their eyes with their wings as they reveal the marvel to us; he whose praise angels, archangels and countless hosts forever sing—he it is who for us and for our salvation deigned to become man, plotted for us the way of exemplary living and bequeathed to us adequate instruction by the example he personally gave in assuming the same nature as ours.[51]

Fallen human nature, marred by sin and consequently corrupted by death, had to be restored to its original fullness. This reversal found its provenance in the incarnation and its ultimate termination in the death of Christ. In the historical incarnation the union of the human and the divine natures provided the context for the restoration and redemption of humanity. Through his death Christ vanquished the curse of sin and overturned the consequences of the fall. Between these two crucial events of the incarnation and crucifixion in the history of salvation, his exemplary life is viewed as a mimetic paradigm for the practice of the Christian life.[52]

The doctrine of the incarnation is the cardinal doctrine of the church for Chrysostom. "This doctrine forms no small teachings of the church, and is its chief doctrine with regard to our salvation and one through which all things have come to exist and are directed. Through it death has been destroyed, and sin has been removed, and the curse has vanished, and countless blessings have come into our lives."[53] In the assumption of the flesh "the Lord and Ruler of all" condescended to bring about this restoration and redemption.[54] The sacramental ramifications of this doctrine have very practical implications: the Christian life is viewed as a response to the redemptive work, and a reflection of the incarnational presence, of Christ in the church. Christ is the source of life and grace and he mediates these benefits to us through the sacraments. The reality of restoration of humanity therefore is firmly rooted in union

51. Chrysostom, Homily 23, in *Genesis*, FOC 82:102 (PG 53.205).
52. Chrysostom, Homily 16, in *Genesis*, FOC 74:221 (PG 53.134). Cf. Homily 12, in *John*, FOC 33:117 (PG 59.84).
53. Chrysostom, Homily 31, in *John*, FOC 33:299 (PG 59.177).
54. Chrysostom, Homily 12, FOC 33:113 (PG 59.82).

with him, manifesting itself in the life of the Christian.⁵⁵ Commenting on the words, "In him was life and his life was the light of men" (John 1:4), Chrysostom observes, "When Life has come to us, the power of death has been destroyed, and when the Light has shone for us, darkness is no more, but Life always remains in us and death cannot overcome it."⁵⁶ Moreover he observes that Christ himself is both the, "the fountain and root of all virtues. He Himself is life, and light, and truth, not keeping within Himself the wealth of these blessings, but pouring it forth upon all others, and even after the outpouring still remaining full. He suffers loss in no way by giving His wealth to others, but, while always pouring out and sharing these virtues with all men, He remains in the same state of perfection."⁵⁷

There are two interrelated soteriological motifs that are characteristic of Chrysostom's incarnational theology, both of which emphasize the divine nature of Christ and his equality with the Father. The first motif can be characterized as restorative, where the incarnation of Christ is perceived as the basis for the restoration of fallen human nature. The second motif can be described as relational and views salvation as humanity enjoying fellowship with God, through Christ. By virtue of becoming incarnate, Christ the eternal Son gave us the privilege of relating to God as sons. These relational privileges are appropriated by the Christian through sacramental participation in Christ, identifying oneself with the Savior in his life, death, and resurrection.

The Restoration of Human Nature

The fellowship that humanity enjoyed with God at creation was subsequently severed by sin leading to corruption and death.⁵⁸ The Savior himself remedied this distance by assuming flesh and providing the context for redemption in the incarnation. This redemption involved restoring human nature from the corruption of death to life eternal. Chrysostom points out that the fall had a detrimental effect on human nature. Taking his cue from Amos 9:11 ("I will raise up the tabernacle of David that has fallen"), Chrysostom associates the condition of fallen humanity with

---

55. Chrysostom, Homily 14, FOC 33:137–38 (PG 59.95–96).
56. Chrysostom, Homily 5, FOC 33:65 (PG 59.57).
57. Chrysostom, Homily 14, in *John*, FOC 33:130–131 (PG 59.94).
58. See Homily 27, FOC 33:264 (PG 59.159).

the "tabernacle" of David, observing that the "tabernacle" of human nature had an "irreparable fall" and only God as its creator could restore it. By assuming human nature, Christ restored it, raised it up, and thereby "deemed it worthy of His royal throne." The only way this could have been accomplished was through the incarnation of the Savior himself because he "who fashioned it in the beginning" was able to reform it. This restoration is realized in the believer through the "regeneration of the water and the Spirit."[59]

Chrysostom employs two metaphors to illustrate how human nature was restored by the incarnation of the Logos. One from the sphere of building construction depicts Christ as a skilled architect. The other, a matrimonial metaphor, portrays Christ as a royal bridegroom, the son of a king. Chrysostom likens the fallen human condition to a dilapidated building lying in a state of complete disrepair and in need of the immediate attention of a skilled builder. Discussing how Christ affected its renovation, Chrysostom observes, "Even as some skilled architect who restores a house fallen to decay with age, so He restored our common human nature. Like the architect, He supplied parts that had been broken off, fastened together the separated and disjointed portions, and raised up again that which had completely fallen down."[60] The human condition, continuing in its state of corruption and death, needed the creator of humankind, the one who "fashioned Adam from the earth," to step into the situation and restore humanity to its original fullness. This transformation required the very creator himself to become incarnate and bring about the restoration of human nature and to refashion the soul.[61]

Secondly, he pictures Christ as a royal bridegroom marrying a maiden of low estate, observing that in spite of being the son of a king, the Logos condescends to the point of taking the initiative in her betrothal and afterwards escorts the bride to his Father's house. Correspondingly, in the incarnation Christ assumed and united human nature to himself and led it upwards: "Human nature did not go up to heaven, but He Himself came to it, rightly despised and worthless as it was, and when

---

59. Chrysostom, Homily 11, FOC 33:109 (PG 59.80). Commenting on the same thought elsewhere, Chrysostom affirms, "The forming of our nature is from above, of the Holy Spirit and water." Chrysostom, Homily 26, FOC 33:251(PG 59.153).

60. Chrysostom, Homily 12, FOC 33:114 (PG 59.83).

61. Ibid.

the espousals had taken place He did not permit it to remain longer here, but took it away and brought it to His Father's house."[62] By uniting human nature to himself Christ reestablished it, thereby returning it to divine fellowship. Chrysostom firmly holds to the notion that the incarnational union forms the basis for a redeeming union, in the sense that salvation is made possible because of the union of human and divine natures in Christ. "In truth, to mingle the high with the low works no harm to the honor of the high, but raises the lowly up from its very humble estate. Accordingly, this is also true in the case of Christ. He in no wise lowered his own nature by His descent, but elevated us, who had always been in a state of ignominy and darkness, to ineffable glory."[63] The incarnation of Christ is therefore viewed as the zenith of God's redemptive act of restoration in that human nature and divine nature have been brought together in an intimate fellowship and communion in the person of Christ: "even so has he done, joining the old covenant with the new, God's nature with man's, the things that are His with ours."[64] The onus was on the Savior to bring this about. The Redeemer himself condescended and assumed human nature in order to realize the central purpose of the divine economy: "God himself, remember, despite his divinity, took to himself our human flesh, and for no other reason than the salvation of the human race became man."[65]

Adoption as Sons

The other soteriological motif associated with Chrysostom's incarnational theology is the conferral of the gift of adoption through Christ, a concept that is relational in nature. When the Son of God assumed flesh and became man, he entered into brotherhood with us in order to make us by grace what he is by nature. Through grace we are made the sons of God by the Son of God in order that we might share in the natural fellowship of the Father and the Son. Therefore, the one who can make us the sons of God has to be divine himself. Consistent with the words of Irenaeus, Chrysostom affirmed the soteriological import of the incarnation in relational terms of the bestowal of sonship. "It is that the

62. Chrysostom, Homily 18, *FOC* 33:176 (*PG* 59.115).
63. Chrysostom, Homily 11, *FOC* 33:106 (*PG* 59.79).
64. Chrysostom, Homily 2, in *Matthew*, section 2, *NPNF* 10:10 (*PG* 57.26).
65. Chrysostom, Homily 3, in *Genesis*, *FOC* 74:46 (*PG* 53.37).

'Word became flesh' and the Master took on the form of the slave. He became the Son of Man, though He was the true Son of God, in order that He might make the sons of men children of God."[66] Similarly, in commenting on the first verse of the Gospel of Matthew Chrysostom observes, "When therefore you are told that the Son of God is Son of David and of Abraham, do not doubt that you too, the son of Adam, shall be son of God. For not at random, nor in vain did He abase Himself so greatly, only He was minded to exalt us. Thus He was born after the flesh [κατὰ σάρκα], that you might be born after the Spirit [κατὰ πνεῦμα]. He was born of a woman, that you might cease to be the son of a woman."[67] By making us his sons, and therefore brothers of the only-begotten, God by his grace has enabled us to share in the blessings of heaven.[68]

Once the curse of sin held sway, divesting humanity of fellowship with God and distancing both parties from each other; now through Christ we are deemed worthy to be called his friends and even his body.[69] Chrysostom highlights the change that is brought about through grace in relational terms underscoring the unique standing that we have with God through Christ. Commenting on John 1:16–17 Chrysostom contrasts the superiority of the gifts of grace we receive through Christ to the ones that were merely shadows of the reality to come in the Old Testament. "Not only was pardon for our sins granted to us, since we shared in this with them—since all have sinned—but also justice, and holiness, and adoption of sons, and grace of the Spirit, much more splendid gifts and richer by far. Through this grace we have become dear to God, no longer merely as servants, but as sons and friends. That is why he said: 'grace for grace.'"[70]

Chrysostom posits a sharp distinction between the sonship by grace (κατὰ χάριν) and Christ's natural sonship (κατὰ φύσιν). The Son of God and the sons of God may share in the divine life, but there is a difference in their ontological state: Christ is divine by virtue of his being and nature, whereas we are not divine either by being or nature, but have been reformed and grafted into the divine life by grace. Arguing against

---

66. Chrysostom, Homily 11, in *John*, FOC 33:106 (PG 59.79). Cf. Homily 6, FOC 33:72 (PG 59.61).
67. Chrysostom, Homily 2, in *Matthew*, section 2, NPNF 10:10 (PG 57.26).
68. Chrysostom, Homily 79, in *John*, FOC 41:363 (PG 59.431).
69. Chrysostom, Homily 19, FOC 33:190–91 (PG 59.122).
70. Chrysostom, Homily 14, FOC 33:135 (PG 59.93–94).

the confusion of titles when applied to God and us, Chrysostom contends (presumably against the Neo-Arians), "Thus, when we are called gods and sons of God, the expression, though used both in regard to us and in reference to God, does not have the same potency for both. Moreover, the Son is called the image and glory of God. And so are we, but there is a great difference. And again: You are Christ's and Christ is God's, but Christ is not God's in the same way as we are Christ's."[71] He presses the point that though we are called the sons of God, this is to be understood as an adoptive relationship. It subsists purely by grace and not by nature; natural sonship belongs to the only-begotten Son alone. The logical implication of his argument is that only a son by nature, one consubstantial with the Father, can enable us to participate in the natural relationship he shares with him:

> Well, in that case, since Christ is called the Son of God, and also God, man, too, who is called the son of God, must be God. For Scripture says; "I have said, ye are all gods and sons of the Most High." will you strive with the only begotten about sonship and will you say that He has nothing more than you in this regard.? "by no means" is the answer. Yet, you do this even though you do not say it in word. How? Because you say He, like you, has shared in the adoption of sons by grace; for by maintaining that He is not Son of God by nature, you declare that he is one not otherwise than by grace.[72]

The incarnation reversed the consequences of the fall. Through Christ we have been redeemed from a state of mortality, corruption, and imperfection to a state of immortality, incorruption, and perfection. The restoration and renewal of humanity in and through Christ culminates in an intimate relationship: the privilege of being adopted into the family of God, and by grace to share in the natural relationship of the Godhead. Citing Psalm 82:6, Chrysostom asserts that the fact that Christ has vouchsafed this privilege to us is sufficient proof of his deity, for only God could make us sons. "He [the Evangelist] did not say that Christ did not have power unless he had received it, but that He even gave to others 'the power of becoming sons of God.' Moreover, Paul likewise declared that He is equal to God."[73] Chrysostom affirms that the gift of adoption

---

71. Chrysostom, Homily 75, *FOC* 41:305 (*PG* 59.406).

72. Chrysostom, Homily 3, *FOC* 33:30–31 (*PG* 59.39).

73. "What, then? Will the Son not be God? But, if the Son is God, and if He is Son of the Father who is called 'the only God,' it is very evident both that He is true God . . .

through Christ is granted in the sacramental context of baptism where we receive the restorative grace of the Spirit and are placed into the same relation to the Father that the Son has naturally "Having been born from above and, so to speak, reformed [ἀναστοιχειωθέντες], it is in this way that we have been called sons."[74] The believer is conformed to the likeness of Christ and made the son of God, having been renewed by grace through the sacramental relationship with the Son of God.

Chrysostom's Sacramental Understanding of Baptism

This subsection highlights the point that the two soteriological motifs of restoration and adoption are held together in Chrysostom's view, and it is in the baptismal context that these are sacramentally actualized. The majority of Chrysostom's statements on baptism in his homilies on John occur in his treatment of John 3:1–21. He stresses its sacramental character, mindful of the catechetical need of his audience. His statements on baptism are varied and largely paraenetic in nature, mainly exhortatory rather than speculative. Chrysostom's statements on baptism accent the inner change brought about through the Holy Spirit and the ensuing moral implications of the Christian's identification with Christ. The catechumens are urged to remember their commitment to Christ as they aspire to live a radically changed life after baptism. The new believers, who have received the grace of God, are exhorted to live a life worthy of that honor. Further, the baptized are warned of the dire consequences of transgressing their commitment and promise made to Christ. The unbaptized are entreated to follow suit and not put off their baptism until the hour of death in order to avoid the obligations of the Christian life.[75]

Chrysostom's view of the sacramental benefits of baptism closely parallels his understanding of the soteriological implications of the baptism of Christ. In what way did the baptism of Christ benefit us sacramentally? What is the relationship between the baptism of Christ and the baptism of the Christian? In order to see how Chrysostom views the sacramental nature of baptism and its concomitant benefits for the

---

Thus, if the Son is not true God, how is he God? Moreover, how does He make us gods and sons, if He is not true God?" Chrysostom, Homily 80, *FOC* 41:371 (*PG* 59.435).

74. Chrysostom, Homily 14, *FOC* 33:134 (*PG* 59.93). Cf. Homily 11, *FOC* 33:109 (*PG* 59.80).

75. See Homilies 24–28, *FOC* 33:232–77 (*PG* 59.143–66).

Christian, a brief survey of his treatment of the baptism of Christ is in order.[76]

THE SOTERIOLOGICAL AND SACRAMENTAL IMPLICATIONS OF THE BAPTISM OF CHRIST

Chrysostom does not primarily focus on baptism of Jesus at in his teaching on John 1:29–34, where the latter is proclaimed as the one who takes away the sins of the world. Rather, he discusses this event as an occasion for John the Baptist to dispel the notion that Jesus needs his sins to be forgiven like the others coming forth for baptism. By referring to Jesus as the "Lamb of God who takes away the sins of the world," Chrysostom contends that John removed this notion entirely. Thus this passage is mainly interpreted as the announcement of Christ and his mission by John the Baptist, who was fulfilling his call by preparing the way for Christ, as was prophesied in Isaiah 40:3.[77] Chrysostom maintains that Christ came to John the Baptist twice and states that the evangelists (Matthew and John) focused on different periods and different events in the life of Christ. Matthew recorded the first meeting when Jesus went to John the Baptist to be baptized (Matt 3:13–17). The Fourth Evangelist, on the other hand, recorded the second time when Christ went to John the Baptist. He did so in order that others might hear the latter's proclamation that he is the "Lamb of God who takes away the sins of the world," reminding them of the words of the prophet Isaiah, and also fulfilling the type prefigured in the time of Moses. Chrysostom remarked that Christ came to purify everyone and to dispense the power of the Holy Spirit to those who will be baptized after him.

Moreover, Chrysostom notes that the descent of the Spirit at the baptism of Christ (Matt 3:13–17) happened for the sake of pointing out Christ and not because he needed the Spirit, as he was the one who would baptize others in the Holy Spirit.[78] "Christ, then did not need baptism—

---

76. For an overview of the preparation for initiation rites and the liturgy of baptism in the fourth century, see Harkins, "Pre-Baptismal Rites in Chrysostom's Baptismal Catecheses," 219–38; Yarnold, *Awe-Inspiring Rites of Initiation*; Finn, *Liturgy of Baptism in the Baptismal Instructions of St. John Chrysostom*; Riley, *Christian Initiation*.

77. Chrysostom, Homily 16, in *John*, FOC 33:157 (PG 59.105).

78. Chrysostom, Homily 17, FOC 33:165 (PG 59.109). Contra Michaud, who exaggerates the image of the dove's descent on Christ as him receiving the Spirit and by implication underscoring the idea of an adoptionist Christology. See Michaud, "La christologie de St. Jean Chrysostome," 275–91.

not John's nor any other's; rather, baptism was needful of the power of Christ."⁷⁹ What was lacking in the baptized "was the chief of all blessing," namely, the baptized being considered worthy of the Spirit and only Christ was able to convey this gift.⁸⁰ The purpose of the descent of the Spirit at Christ's baptism, maintains Chrysostom, was to make him manifest and known. This event mentioned in the Fourth Gospel (1:29–34) was John's proclamation of Christ's power to remit the sins of humanity. It was also an announcement that Christ would be the one who would baptize the faithful with the Spirit. Chrysostom seems to steer clear of an adoptionist Christology and the interpretation that Christ received the Holy Spirit at his baptism, as the latter could possibly be misconstrued to mean that he was not essentially divine and was in need of an infilling of the Holy Spirit, as Paul of Samosata had maintained.⁸¹

But the question of the need for Christ to be baptized still remains unanswered. Before I examine Chrysostom's actual treatment of the baptism of Jesus in the Gospel of Matthew with its soteriological and sacramental implications, a brief survey of Cyril's thoughts on this topic will serve as a good contrasting background.⁸²

Wilken has drawn attention to the fact that the narrative account of the baptism of Jesus posed a challenge to the early church. The conundrum of how is it that Jesus the Lord can receive the Spirit was a difficult one to get around, and needed to be answered satisfactorily. If Christ received the Spirit, does it mean that the he was inferior to the Father and therefore needed to be sanctified?⁸³ Reviewing Cyril's interpretation

---

79. Chrysostom, Homily 16, in *John*, FOC 33:166 (PG 59.110).

80. Ibid.

81. "Let those who have accepted the insane teachings of Paul of Samosata be ashamed, since they are opposing such manifest truth." Ibid., FOC 33:164 (PG 59.109).

82. Ferguson's study of the Epiphany sermons of Chrysostom and Gregory of Nyssa discusses the centrality of baptism in the pastoral theology of the fourth-century church. The feast of Epiphany, celebrated on the sixth of January in the Eastern Church, commemorates the day of the baptism of Christ. It is called the feast of Epiphany because Christ was revealed and proclaimed to many through the Holy Spirit's descent at his baptism. The feast day provided both Gregory and Chrysostom with a ready occasion to address issues relating to baptism and was part of the preparation for the catechumens who were going to be baptized on Easter Sunday. Ferguson mainly treats Gregory's and Chrysostom's views on the baptism of Christ with the focus on their respective pastoral interests and homiletical practices, without drawing any sacramental implications for the Christian life. See Ferguson, "Preaching at Epiphany," 1–17.

83. Wilken, "Exegesis and History," 146f. See also Wilken, *Judaism and the Early Christian Mind*, 93–142.

of John 1:32–33, Wilken observes that Cyril broached this theologically delicate issue by employing the Adam-Christ typology. Cyril maintained that Christ was both one with the Father and yet true man. It was as man, Cyril argued, that Christ was able to receive the Spirit at his baptism. The main point of Cyril's argument is that the first Adam did not preserve the grace that was given to him by God. Therefore God the Father sent the second Adam, his own Son, in the likeness of man in every way—except without sin. Just as through the disobedience of the first Adam humanity was subject to divine wrath, the obedience of the second Adam reversed the curse. After the incarnation Christ, as the one who knew no sin, received the Spirit from the Father, thus restoring to human nature the grace that had been lost in the Fall. The reception of the Spirit by the second Adam therefore transforms and renews humanity, providing a new beginning. Cyril continues:

> But when the Word of God became Man, He received the Spirit from the Father as one of us, (not receiving ought for Himself individually, for He was the Giver of the Spirit); but that He Who knew no sin, might, by receiving It as Man, preserve It to our nature, and might again root in us the grace which had left us. For this reason, I deem, it was that the holy Baptist profitably added, I saw the Spirit descending from Heaven, and It abode upon Him. For It had fled from us by reason of sin, but He Who knew no sin, became as one of us, that the Spirit might be accustomed to abide in us, having no occasion of departure or withdrawal in Him.[84]

Contra Wilken, Welch has noted that Cyril's usage of the Adamic typology had a christological rationale: Cyril employed the seemingly paradoxical Adamic typology mainly to insist on the historical unity of the one Christ. The reception of the Spirit by Christ, Welch adds, is closely related to Cyril's emphasis on the kenosis, a theme that he invokes four times in interpretation of this passage (John 1:32–33). He maintains that Cyril was keen on showing that the Son who emptied himself is the selfsame second Adam who receives the Spirit not because he was sinful, but because he was in the "condition" of sinful flesh. He concludes that Cyril's kenotic language and use of Adamic typology influence one another in the sense that kenosis is used to explain the historical events in the life of Christ, the second Adam. Conversely, the second Adam, who

---

84. Cyril, *Commentary on John*, 1:41–42 (Pusey, 1.184).

in the condition of fallen humanity needs the Spirit, is always spoken of as one and the same Christ.[85]

Chrysostom deals with the topic of the baptism of Christ (as mentioned in Matt 3:13–17), specifically in his twelfth homily on the Gospel of Matthew.[86] Chrysostom's interpretation of the baptism of Jesus has soteriological overtones akin to Cyril's view. Both stress the incarnational aspects of Christ the eternal Son in regard to his baptism: Cyril employs Adamic typology and kenotic language to explain the reception of the Spirit, while Chrysostom highlights the condescension of Christ in the incarnation and his willingness to be baptized in fulfillment of the law for the redemption of humanity. Without specifically deploying a typology, Chrysostom also makes reference to the transgression of Adam and Christ's reversal thereof. The first Adam incurred through his disobedience the wrath of God; the second Adam delivered humanity from its curse through his obedience. Adam had paradise for his share and lost it through sin, but Christ has now made the baptized joint heirs with him, restoring the possibility of that privilege once again.[87]

Whereas Cyril highlights the reception of the Spirit by Christ, Chrysostom focuses on the act of baptism by underscoring Christ's claim that he did so to fulfill the law of God at all points. For Cyril, Christ as man received the Spirit to refashion humanity; for Chrysostom, Christ as man had to fulfill the law and be baptized. The main difference between Cyril and Chrysostom's interpretation is that Cyril acknowledges and explains why Christ "received" the Spirit at his baptism, whereas Chrysostom views the descent of the Spirit as an announcement and a witness to his identity and not as a "reception." Chrysostom's initial focus is directed to the paradox of the eternal Son who humbles himself and submits to baptism:

> With the servants the Lord, with the criminals, the Judge, comes to be baptized. But do not be troubled; for in these humiliations His exaltation does most shine forth. For He who vouchsafed to be borne so long in a Virgin's womb, and from there to take our

85. Welch, *Christology and Eucharist in the Early Thought of Cyril of Alexandria*, 66–67.

86. See Chrysostom, Homily 12, in *Matthew*, NPNF 10:75–79 (PG 57.201–8).

87. "For if he who had paradise for his portion, for one disobedience underwent such dreadful things after his honor; we, who have received Heaven, and are become joint heirs with the Only Begotten, what excuse shall we have, for running to the serpent after the dove?" Ibid., *NPNF* 10:78 (PG 57.207).

> nature, and to suffer all the rest which He suffered; why do you marvel if He vouchsafed to be baptized, and to come with the rest to His servant. For the amazement lay in that one thing, that being God, He would be made Man; but the rest after this all follows in course of reason.[88]

Chrysostom views the obedience of Christ as being central to his mission of fulfilling the law at all points and dismissing the condemnation that held sway over humanity. The judge of all sinners himself condescended to be baptized and thereby secured a pardon for all. Christ was baptized not because he needed to receive the Spirit as man, but to reverse the curse of sin by being obedient to the law. Chrysostom uses the title "Judge" twice in this homily to emphasize the divinity of Christ and to dispel the idea that he was baptized for the remission of sins, since he himself will judge all sinners. Christ satisfied the law of God at all points by fulfilling the commandments; thus he has done away with the curse of the transgression. The obedient Son overruled the curse written against humanity; this was the main purpose of the incarnation.[89] Moreover, Chrysostom observes that the reason the heavens opened and the Spirit descended in the likeness of a dove along with the voice, was to "proclaim the dignity of the Only Begotten" and to show us that the Spirit likewise comes to those who are baptized. Chrysostom does not employ language suggesting any "reception" of the Spirit by Christ. For him, the descent of the Spirit in the form of a dove served only to point out the one whom the voice called "my beloved Son."[90]

Chrysostom affirms that the Holy Spirit comes to the believer at baptism just like He did at Christ's baptism. The difference being that at the baptism of Christ the Spirit descended to point out the Savior; at the baptism of the Christian the Spirit descends to convey adoption into the family of God—"the greatest mark of dignity." The Spirit's action here *causes* us to become the "sons of God."[91] So Chrysostom's understanding of the baptism of Christ has both soteriological and sacramental implications for the Christian. The Son of God condescended to be baptized as part of his redeeming mission, and made us worthy to receive the grace

---

88. Chrysostom, Homily 12, *NPNF* 10:76 (*PG* 57.202).

89. Ibid., *NPNF* 10:76–77 (*PG* 57.203–5).

90. Ibid.

91. Ibid., *NPNF* 10:77–78 (*PG* 57.205–6). Cf. Chrysostom, *Homily on the Baptism and the Epiphany of Christ* (*PG* 49.363–72).

of the Spirit, which renews and refashions us to become like Christ. Here soteriological and sacramental dimensions of the baptism of Christ are inseparably connected. The work of the Holy Spirit is highlighted in the process of adoption, whereby the Christian is conformed to the likeness of Christ at baptism.[92] Commenting on John 1:12—"To as many as received Him he gave them power of becoming sons of God"—Chrysostom asserts:

> Such is the power of faith in Him; such the greatness of His grace. And even as the element of fire, having come in contact with ore from mines, forthwith makes the ore true gold; so also, and even more, does baptism make those who have been washed in it golden instead of earthy, since the Spirit at that time falls like fire on our souls, both burning away "the likeness of the earthy," [εἰκόνα τοῦ χοϊκοῦ] and restoring "the likeness of the heavenly," [εἰκόνα τοῦ ἐπουρανίου] freshly formed and shining, gleaming as if from the smelting furnace.[93]

Through the mediation of the Holy Spirit, Christ makes us the "sons of God" by replacing the "likeness of the earthy" with the "likeness of the heavenly."[94] Unlike the baptism of John, which does not possess the power either to remit sin or renew the believer, the grace of Christ has inaugurated a new way of life by making us the children of God: "Because henceforth He leads us away from the old to the new way of life, both opening to us the gates on high, and sending down His Spirit from thence to call us to our country there; and not merely to call us, but also with the greatest mark of dignity. For He hath not made us angels and archangels, but He has caused us to become 'sons of God,' [υἱοὺς Θεοῦ] and 'beloved' [ἀγαπητοὺς], and so He draws us on towards that portion of ours."[95]

As Cyril later would, Chrysostom views the baptism of Christ as a reversal and a restoration from the curse of sin and understands it to be

---

92. Chrysostom, Homily 12, *NPNF* 10:77–78 (*PG* 57.205–6).

93. Chrysostom, Homily 10, in *John*, *FOC* 33:100 (*PG* 59.76). Elsewhere Chrysostom associates the remission and the sacramental cleansing of sins with the conferral of filial adoption: "For where remission of sins is there is sonship. Even so at least we are able to call God Father until we have washed away our sins in the pool of the sacred water." Chrysostom, *Homily on the Paralytic Let Down through the Roof*, *NPNF* 9:217 (*PG* 51.58).

94. Cf. Homily 78, in *John*, *FOC* 41:346–47 (*PG* 59.424f).

95. Chrysostom, Homily 12, in *Matthew*, *NPNF* 10:76 (*PG* 57.206).

integrally related to the incarnation and atonement. Through baptism the subjects of divine wrath become the sons of God. The dominant thrust of both Cyril's and Chrysostom's views on the sacramental benefits obtained by Christ through his baptism are, in the final analysis, parallel with one another and both are deeply linked to their incarnational theology. Cyril observes: "For he sends in our likeness his own Son who is by nature without alteration or change and not knowing sin in any way, that is by the disobedience of the first we became subject to divine wrath, so through the obedience of the second, we might both escape the curse and the evils from it might come to nought."[96]

And Chrysostom has Christ say: "Because I have come to do away the curse that is appointed for the transgression of the law. I must therefore fulfill it all, and having delivered you from its condemnation, in this way to bring it to an end. It is proper for me therefore to fulfill the whole law, by the same rule that it becomes me to do away the curse that is written against you in the law: this being the very purpose of my assuming flesh, and coming here."[97]

Cyril's view tends to stress the ontological transformation rooted in Christ's baptism, while Chrysostom underscores the functional and moral requirements to which the incarnate Son subjected himself for the redemption of humanity. Broadly speaking, both developed similar soteriological and sacramental conclusions from their understanding of the baptism of Christ. Through sinful disobedience fallen humanity lost fellowship with God, marring his image and likeness, and leading to corruption and death. Through the incarnation and the life of obedience (even that of baptism and the cross) Christ humbled himself and, as human, fulfilled all the requirements of the law. He reversed the disastrous effects of the corruption of sin and condemnation against humanity, thus conferring the grace of the Holy Spirit, who renews and refashions the believer into a new creation at baptism. Although Chrysostom speaks of other sacramental benefits of baptism, this concept is integral to his understanding of the Christian life.

---

96. Cyril, *Commentary on John*, 1:42 (Pusey, 1.182–83).
97. Chrysostom, Homily 12, in *Matthew*, NPNF 10:76 (PG 57.203).

Baptism, Adoption, and Restoration of the Divine Image in the Christian

In Chrysostom's view the conferral of the gift of adoption and the conforming of the Christian to the likeness of Christ are one and the same, and the sacrament of baptism is the means through which this is actualized. To be made a son of God is to be conformed to Christ's likeness and thus be renewed in the image of God. Consequently, to be sacramentally renewed in the divine image is to become by grace what Christ is by nature.[98] The Christian's identification and union with Christ at baptism initiates a new life with its unique privilege: the heavenly kinship of adoption. This spiritual regeneration has implications for the Christian life because a genuine change has occurred.[99] Chrysostom illustrates this regeneration through the use of different metaphors.

Employing the spiritual birth imagery, Chrysostom distinguishes sharply between the earthly birth according to the flesh and the heavenly birth according to the Spirit, and warns of the eternal consequences for those who have not experienced the latter. The individual who has not been born of water and the Spirit has not yet received the renewal of the divine image, which Chrysostom sometimes refers to as the "the image of sonship,"[100] or the "Master's stamp,"[101] or the "the royal stamp."[102] He understands baptism as bringing a radical change in the life of the believer, comparing it with the first creation and contrasting it with the eschatological implications of this spiritual birth. In the beginning man was created after the earth was formed, but the re-creation of humanity happens before this world will be transformed. In the former creation man was made in the "image of God," but now (at baptism) man is made "one with God Himself."[103] Here Chrysostom emphatically relates the restoration of the divine image in the new creation with divine fellowship, a condition from which sinful humanity had departed and can now be restored through the work of the Spirit at baptism.[104] Adhering to the

---

98. Chrysostom, Homily 15, in *Romans*, NPNF 11:453 (PG 60.541).
99. Chrysostom, Homily 10, *FOC* 33:101 (PG 59.76).
100. Ibid., (PG 59.76).
101. Chrysostom, Homily 25, *FOC* 33:243 (PG 59.148).
102. Chrysostom, Homily 10, *FOC* 33:100 (PG 59.75).
103. Chrysostom, Homily 25, *FOC* 33:245 (PG 59.150).
104. Chrysostom, Homily 8, in *Genesis*, FOC 74.110f. (PG 53.72–73). Cf. Homily 10, in *Genesis*, FOC 74.133 (PG 53.85); Homily 9, in *Genesis*, FOC 74.120 (PG 53.78).

common practice of catechetical instructions drawn from the creation account of Genesis, he alludes to the events from the primeval prologue in reference to the life sustaining features of water and the work of the Holy Spirit in bringing about this change in the baptized, "as the womb is to the embryo, so the water is to the believer, since he is formed and shaped in the water."[105] The sacramental context of baptism is the means of this spiritual birth, for the believer is born of the Spirit and has experienced a new birth in conformity to Christ because the "image of sonship" has been impressed in this process.[106]

Whereas the catechumen is a stranger and a foreigner, the one who is baptized has a heavenly kinship and has received adoption. The one who is initiated is renewed, changed, and mystically united to the body of Christ. Individual merit cannot earn this gift, as it is solely the work of God through the Holy Spirit.[107] In keeping with the renewal motif, Chrysostom alludes to Pauline terminology from Romans 6, underscoring the distinction between "the old man" and "the new man" and noting how the individual identifies with and participates in the mystery of Christ's death, burial, and resurrection:

> In it the divine covenant is fulfilled: burial and death, and resurrection and life and all these take place at once. When we immerse our heads in water, just as if in a grave, the old man is buried, and having sunk down, is entirely hidden once for all; then, when we emerge, the new man rises again. Just as it is easy for us to be immersed and to emerge [from the water], so it is easy for God to bury the old man and raise up the new. This is done thrice that you may learn that the power of the Father and of the Son and of the Holy Spirit performs all this.[108]

Through baptism the believer also appropriates the sacramental benefits of the crucifixion, in that not only pardon for sins but also a new quality of life are granted.[109] Furthermore, Chrysostom associates the renewal

---

105. Chrysostom, Homily 26, in *John*, FOC 33:251 (PG 59.153).

106. Chrysostom, Homily 10, FOC 33:100 (PG 59.76).

107. Chrysostom, Homily 25, FOC 33:248 (PG 59.151).

108. Ibid., FOC 33:247 (PG 59.151). See also Homily 11, in *Romans*, NPNF 11:408 (PG 60.483).

109. Chrysostom, Homily 27, in *John*, FOC 33:261–62 (PG 59.158). The believer has now been given a new lease of life by Christ, who not only erased the certificate of the ancestral sin debt but also shred it to pieces: "the nails of the cross tore up the decree and destroyed it utterly, so that it would not hold good for the future." Chrysostom, *Baptismal Instructions*, 3.21–22, ACW 31.63 (SC 50.163–64).

and restoration of the divine image in the baptized with being conformed to the likeness of Christ. Employing Pauline language on matters relating to this discussion, Chrysostom notes that in baptism the old person marred by sin has been buried, and has been raised to new life. In this process we have "put off" the old and "put on" the new—Christ himself: "Baptism is a burial and a resurrection. For the old man is buried with his sin and the new man is resurrected being renewed according to the image of his Creator. We put off the old garment, which has been made filthy with the abundance of our sins; we put on the new one, which is free from every stain. What am I saying? We put on Christ Himself. For all you, says St. Paul, who have been baptized into Christ, have put on Christ."[110] Moreover, for Chrysostom, "to put on Christ" or to be "clothed with Christ" at baptism is to have Christ indwell the Christian, resulting in the individual's nature being conformed to the nature of Christ, the eternal Son. Elaborating on what this means in his *Commentary on Galatians* 3:26–27, Chrysostom remarks: "Why did Paul not say: 'All you who have been baptized in Christ have been born of God?' For this was the conclusion of the proof that they were sons. But he puts it in a much more awe-inspiring way. For if Christ is the Son of God and you have put on Christ, since you have the Son in yourself, you have become like to Him and you have been brought into one relationship and into one nature with Him."[111] Therefore, to receive the gift of adoption at baptism or to be impressed with "image of sonship" is the same as saying that the Christian has been conformed to the likeness of Christ, and to be conformed to Christ is to be renewed in the image of God.

This is central to Chrysostom's sacramental understanding of baptism. The inner change and renewal of the image of God in the Christian at baptism, to a large extent, underpins Chrysostom's preaching on the Christian life. This thought is echoed in his *Baptismal Instructions*. In his catechetical homilies, Chrysostom often quotes 2 Corinthians 5:17

---

110. Chrysostom, *Baptismal Instructions* 2.11, ACW 31.47.

111. Chrysostom, *Commentary on Galatians* 3:26–27, NPNF 13.30 (PG 61.656). Cf. Chrysostom, *Commentary on Romans* 13:14, NPNF 11.518 (PG 61.623–624). Likewise, discussing the same thought in his catechetical instructions, he maintains: "St. Paul says: *For all you who have been baptized into Christ have put on Christ.* So I exhort you to do your every deed and action just as if you had Christ, the Creator of all things and the Master of our nature, dwelling within you. And when I say Christ, I mean also the Father and the Holy Spirit. For this is what Christ Himself promised us when He said: *If anyone love me and will keep my commandments, the Father and I will come and make our abode with him.*" Chrysostom, *Baptismal Instructions* 4.3, ACW 31.67.

("Therefore, if anyone is in Christ, he is a new creation; the old has gone, the new has come") as a reminder of the gift of transformation that the catechumen has received at baptism.[112] The soul is purified like a stained statue of gold that has been smelted and refined again; the rust and soot of sin has been removed and the individual has received new life.[113] Chrysostom describes various sacramental benefits of baptism, the common theme is that of restoration and renewal wrought through Christ the redeemer, who is the source of grace.[114] To be renewed in the image of God, in Chrysostom's view, is to enjoy by grace the privilege of divine fellowship that belongs to the Son by nature. To be conformed to the likeness of Christ is to be restored in the divine image. The conferral of adoption at baptism inaugurates a new way of life, because the Christian by definition is Christ-like.[115]

In keeping with his emphasis on the practical implications of this renewal for the Christian life, Chrysostom observes, "Do you see how a new creation has truly taken place? The grace of God has entered these souls and molded them anew, reformed them, and made them different from what they were."[116] In Chrysostom's thought doctrinal teaching and praxis are intertwined: the evidence of the restoration and renewal of hu-

---

112. Chrysostom's *Fourth Instruction* addressed to the neophytes is based on 2 Cor 5:17. See *Baptismal Instructions* 4.1–33, ACW 31.66–78. As a mystagogue, Chrysostom makes reference to 2 Cor 5:17 about nine times, more than any other passage in his catechetical instructions.

113. "So, too, God takes this nature of ours when it is rusted with the rust of sin, when our faults have covered it with abundant soot, and when it has destroyed the beauty He put into it in the beginning, and he smelts it anew. He plunges it into the waters as into the smelting furnace, renewed like newly-molded vessels, to rival the rays of the sun with our brightness. He has broken the old man to pieces but has produced a new man who shines brighter than the old." Chrysostom, *Baptismal Instructions* 9.22, ACW 31.139.

114. Chrysostom describes about ten benefits (or "the graces") of baptism in his address to the neophytes. Contrasting their former condition with the blessings received at baptism, he declares, "Before yesterday you were captives, but now you are free and citizens of the Church; lately you lived in the shame of your sins, but now you live in freedom and justice. You are not only free, but also holy; not only holy, but also just; not only just, but also sons; not only sons, but also heirs; not only heirs, but also brothers of Christ; not only brothers of Christ, but also joint heirs; not only joint heirs, but also members; not only members, but also the temple; not only the temple, but also instruments of the Spirit." See *Baptismal Instructions* 3.5, ACW 31.57 (SC 50.153).

115. See Torrance, "God the Physician," 163–76.

116. Chrysostom, *Baptismal Instructions* 4.14, ACW 31.72.

man nature is reflected in the moral and virtuous life of the Christian.¹¹⁷ The starting point for the Christian life is firmly grounded in the restorative ministry of Christ. The consequences of the fall have been overturned, mortality and corruption have been reversed, and through sacramental participation in Christ, humanity can enjoy fellowship with God again. None other than the divine Savior himself actualizes such a restoration in the believer. The Christian life therefore is a reflection of a sacramental relationship with Christ, which is sustained through grace as it is mediated through the sacraments of the church.

The Christological Implications of Chrysostom's Incarnational Theology

This portrayal of the restoration (and renewal) of human nature through the incarnation as mediated to the believer through the sacraments suggests that the infrastructure of Chrysostom's understanding of the Christian life is underpinned by a firm correspondence between his christological and sacramental thought. His emphasis on the person of Christ as the Word who assumed flesh without a transformation implies that he maintains a personal continuity in Christ. The divine nature of the pre-incarnate Word and post-incarnate Word is the same. In keeping with this emphasis, Chrysostom consistently highlights the point that Christ is the changeless eternal Son, who is consubstantial and equal with the Father. It is he who makes it possible for us to relate with God as sons in a personal way, enabling us to share in the natural fellowship of the Godhead by renewing and restoring us in the image of God, in the sacramental context of baptism. This is consistent with saying that God gives us himself in and through Christ.¹¹⁸ Such a Christology requires

---

117. Chrysostom, Homily 28, in *John*, FOC 33:273 (PG 59.164). For an overview of Chrysostom's understanding of the church and salvation, see Korbacher, *Ausserhalb der Kirche kein Heil?*, 122ff.

118. Fairbairn's recent study of grace in the early church underscores this very point from Cyril's perspective: "Christ does not simply give us grace, he *constitutes* the grace that he gives us. God the logos incarnate is both the giver and the gift." Fairbairn convincingly argues that there was a theological consensus at the turn of the fifth century with regard to the person of Christ and the mediation of grace. He notes that Chrysostom's christological terminology is similar to both Athanasius and Cyril. His contention is that Athanasian and Cyrillian thought mirrored this consensus of the fathers from both the Alexandrian and the Antiochene schools. See Fairbairn, *Grace and Christology in the Early Church*, 69.

that the personal subject of Christ to be the Logos himself and therefore views the incarnation as a condescension of grace.

The different epithets Chrysostom ascribes to Christ in his ministry of restoration emphasize the same point. Chrysostom's portrayal of Christ as a skilled architect who restores fallen human nature to its original condition suggests that only the creator who fashioned human nature in the beginning could repair and restore it as it was intended to be. Christ as the royal bridegroom, who reaches out to fallen humanity to unite us with himself, points to the divine initiative in this redemption and restoration. Christ as the fountain and root of all blessings, who mediates these gifts to us and yet remains in the same state of perfection, signifies that he is the sacramental source through whom these gifts are conveyed. All three aspects of Christ's restorative ministry have a personal dimension: we receive these benefits through the person of Christ; only if Christ is Son by nature can he bring about this restoration, and only if the Logos is the personal subject in Christ can he convey these benefits to us.

Furthermore, Chrysostom's understanding of regeneration as being conformed to the likeness of Christ also reflects a Christology that points to the unity of Christ with the Father and his consubstantiality. To be made a son of God is to be conformed to the likeness of the Son of God. To be clothed with Christ at baptism is to have the eternal Son dwell in us, and to be conformed to his likeness is to experience a renewal in God's image. In this sacramental vouchsafing we have been made "one with God" through Christ. Chrysostom's association of the conferral of adoption with being conformed to the likeness of Christ and thus with our renewal in the divine image is consistent with saying that only if Christ is divine and one with God can we receive these benefits by being made like him. Chrysostom's portrayal of Christ as the Creator, Lord, and Ruler who condescended to restore the heavenly kinship that humanity enjoyed before the fall can therefore be appropriately described as a *Christology of Restoration*. This perspective, viewed through the lens of the life of faith, has on going implications for life in the church. It is on this canvas of the sacramentally mediated relationship between Christ and the Christian that Chrysostom's complete picture of Christ continues to develop. The following section, the second christological perspective, will discuss the participatory nature of Chrysostom's eucharistic theology as a function of the relation between Christ's joint consubstantiality with the Father and us.

A Christology of Participation

In this section, I examine Chrysostom's view of our union with Christ in the sacramental context of the Eucharist, and investigate its implications for his understanding of our participation in the divine life. The following question will serve as a *vade mecum* as this terrain of his thought is explored: what do we receive from God in this sacrament and who must Christ be in order for us to receive this gift? In his study of the interpretation of the Fourth Gospel in the early church, Wiles made a brief statement regarding Chrysostom's conception of our ultimate union with God. He maintained that in Chrysostom's view, our ultimate union with the Father was different from the union that exists eternally between the Father and the Son; he noted that Chrysostom, in his commentary on the closing verses of the seventeenth chapter, was quite explicit that "in view of the radical difference between divine and human nature, the word καθώς ('even as,' 17:14–26) cannot be understood to imply an exact parallelism or equality."[119] In other words, Wiles suggested that Chrysostom did not hold to the idea that humanity can enjoy full participation in the life of God because he maintained that there was a drastic ontological difference between the divine and human natures. I intend to show from other contexts that Chrysostom did maintain the idea that our union with the Father is the same as that, which is shared between him and the Son. The reason for his insistence on the radical difference between the natures of the Father and the Son on the one hand, and us on the other, in his commentary on John 17 is polemic. The Son and the Father share the same nature and glory; therefore (and in response to Arian and Sabellian thought), Chrysostom contends that the Son is consubstantial and equal with the Father and highlights the distinctions among the persons in the Godhead.[120] His discussion here is not about our ultimate union with

---

119. Wiles, *Spiritual Gospel*, 152.

120. Commenting on John 17:14, Chrysostom remarks, "Furthermore, do not be troubled because He said: 'Even as I am not of the world.' For the expression 'even as' does not here imply complete identity. Just as when He used the expression 'even as' with reference to Himself and the Father, Their complete equality was intimated because Their nature is the same, so, when He used it with regard to Him and us, the abysmal difference between us is implied, because there is a great, even infinite, difference between the two natures." Chrysostom's discussion here is about natural sonship: the Son is divine and possesses this characteristic by virtue of his nature. The point being made relates to the Son's relationship and his consubstantiality with the Father; therefore Chrysostom mentions "the suspicious reasoning" of Arius and Sabellius further along

God, but rather on the ontological status that the Father and Son possess by nature. Chrysostom consistently maintains the ontological distinction between the Son of God and the sons of God, as has been pointed out in the previous section. This distinction in Chrysostom's understanding between the divine and human natures, I argue, does not preclude the idea of our ultimate participation in the natural fellowship between the Father and the Son in his soteriological thought. My contention is that Chrysostom affirms the view that we acquire the status of sons by grace, and can therefore share in the divine life that the Son enjoys by nature. Before I examine Chrysostom's understanding of our union with Christ and its implications with reference to our participation in the divine life, I will substantiate my view by surveying his portrayal of Christ as it is presented within the framework of his preaching on the hope of eternal life. I shall commence my survey by considering Chrysostom's view of Christ as the source of life, and as the one who has power and authority over death, before I explore the soteriological and sacramental implications of Christ's ultimate victory over death from his homilies on various pericopes in John's Gospel.

The Narrative Framework for Christ's Victory over Death

Christ as the Source of Life

Aulén's classic study of the main ideas of atonement maintained at different stages in the history of the church underscored the close relationship between sin and death in the thought of the fathers. He noted that for the fathers the idea of sin was inseparable from the idea of death. The reversal of the Pauline motif of death as the wages of sin was central to their understanding of what the incarnation and atonement of Christ accomplished. Christ's power over sin and death was the dominant

---

his comments on this passage. He asserts that the Son shares in the same glory as the Father and that there is a distinction between the persons in the Godhead. Furthermore, the discussion centers on the divinity and equality of the Son and the Father and not our ultimate union with God. Although Chrysostom underscored the distinction between the divine and human natures, this does not lead to the conclusion that he did not maintain the idea that we cannot share in the natural fellowship of the Father and the Son. I argue that by virtue of affirming the idea of sonship by grace, Chrysostom views salvation as our sharing by adoption in the natural relationship between the Son and the Father. See Chrysostom, Homily 82, in *John*, FOC 41:388–92 (PG 59.442). Cf. Homily 15, in *Romans*, NPNF 11:453 (PG 60.541).

thrust of their soteriological thought: "death, which is sometimes almost personified, as 'the last enemy that shall be destroyed' (1 Cor. 15:26), is most closely connected with sin. Where sin reigns, there death reigns also. To be set free from sin through Christ is to be delivered also from death's dominion; the salvation won by Christ has come 'unto all men to justification of life' (Rom. 5:18); 'even so reckon ye also yourselves to be dead unto sin, but alive unto God in Christ Jesus' (Rom. 6:11)."[121] For the fathers, to be set free from sin is to be set free from death. A victory over death is therefore victory over sin. This correlation was also discussed by Pelikan in his survey of the soteriological thought of the early fathers. He asserted that one of the proof-texts employed by the Greek fathers to highlight the relation between salvation from death and salvation from sin was the healing of the paralytic in Matt 9:2-9. Citing this relation in Irenaeus's thought, Pelikan obeserves: "According to Irenaeus, this passage meant that the only Son of God had come from God for the salvation of man. Through his Son, he against whom man had sinned came to grant the forgiveness of sins. Because disease was one of the consequences of sin, it was appropriate that the bringer of 'salvation [σωτηρία]' be the bringer of 'health [σωτηρία],' and against the Gnostics Irenaeus insisted that the bringer of salvation from sin and the bringer of salvation from disease had to be the same."[122] Discussing this particular motif in one of his homilies on this passage, Chrysostom develops the picture of healing and restoration by portraying Christ as an able physician who not only treats the symptoms of sickness, but also deals with the root and origin of the infirmity. By healing the paralytic from his disease and forgiving his sins, Christ demonstrated that he is the source of grace, has authority and power over disease (which eventually led to death and was the result of sin), and restores us to communion with God.[123] Akin to the early fathers, Chrysostom refers to this incident and the words of Christ ("Take heart, son: your sins are forgiven," Matt 9:2) to stress a similar

---

121. Aulén, *Christus Victor*, 67.

122. Pelikan, *Emergence of the Catholic Tradition*, 1:154-55.

123. Chrysostom employs this image interchangeably with reference to both God and Christ. He discusses the idea that God uses various ways to restore us back to spiritual health. He pictures God as a versatile physician who uses different means in order to bring healing, sometimes through tender care, sometimes though cautery and surgery: "He seeks by means of each to lead us back to health, and to communion with Himself, and He knows our several needs, and what is expedient for each one, and how and in what manner we ought to be saved, and along that path He leads us," *Homily on the Paralytic Let Down through the Roof*, NPNF 9:212 (PG 51.51).

point in his homilies on the Fourth Gospel. He usually resorts to this incident as theological shorthand to point out the divinity of Christ and his equality with the Father. The one who can remit sins and heal diseases is the very one who also offers us the hope of salvation.[124] Chrysostom discusses this topic in his treatment of the fifth chapter of John's Gospel, capitalizing on the motif of Christ as the source of life who offers hope in the context of healing.

Chrysostom views this event of healing as a picture of baptism, which offers cleansing from sin and life through Christ. He highlights the perseverance of the paralytic man who, having been afflicted by his infirmity for thirty-eight years, did not lose hope. To this end, Chyrsostom cites Romans 5:5, "Hope does not disappoint."[125] Analogous to a good physician who can bring about internal healing by external treatment, Christ brought healing to the paralytic's soul by healing his body. His words "sin no more" were evidence that, besides being healed, the man was forgiven of his sins, and that this was due to Christ's grace alone.[126] Restoring the body from sin and restoring the soul can only be accomplished by God, and so Christ furnished the paralytic a clear proof of His own divinity.[127] In keeping with this emphasis on the divinity of Christ, Chrysostom points out that Christ healed the man on the Sabbath to demonstrate through his deeds that he was equal to God. Only if he is God could he have healed the paralytic, and he did so on the Sabbath in order to prove that as the author of the Law, he is not subject to it. Illustrating Christ's dignity and authority to carry out such an operation from the sphere of royal politics, Chrysostom remarks, "If He were not truly the Son of God and of the same substance as He, the defense was out of proportion to the accusation. For, if a subordinate official who had changed a royal law, upon being charged with this, should then make this sort of defense and say that he made the change because the king could even nullify the law, he would not be able to escape punishment, but would incur a still more serious charge."[128] The main thrust of Chrysostom's thought on this passage is Christ's equality with the Father.

---

124. See Chrysostom, Homily 14, in *John*, *FOC* 33:137–38 (*PG* 59.95); Homily 24, *FOC* 33:235 (*PG* 59.144–45); Homily 64, *FOC* 41:196 (*PG* 59.356).

125. Chrysostom, Homily 36, *FOC* 33:355 (*PG* 59.205).

126. Chrysostom, Homily 38, *FOC* 33:371(*PG* 59.213).

127. Ibid., *FOC* 33:372 (*PG* 59.213).

128. Ibid., *FOC* 33:373 (*PG* 59.214).

He emphazises the identity of their purpose, power, and strength by noting that whether it is resurrection from the dead, creation, or forgiveness of sins, Christ acts in the same manner as the Father. In his homilies on John's Gospel, Chrysostom often cites verse 5:21 ("For Just as the Father raises the dead and gives them life, even so the Son gives life to whom he is pleased to give it") to stress the point that Christ is the means of life, even eternal life and because he has power to raise the dead, he is not inferior to the Father.[129] It is with this in mind that he admonishes his audience to flee the "diseases that corrupt the soul" and to look forward to the glory that accompanies us in the life to come. He maintains that our hope of salvation is fostered by dwelling on things of God, and though we dwell on earth it is imperative that we do not become strangers to the things of heaven.[130]

Continuing with the thought of a future hope, he discusses the point from a juridical perspective. Following the theme of judgment in the fifth chapter (vv. 22–27), Chrysostom notes that there will be a future tribunal where all will have to render an accounting to Christ, who will sit in judgment. He who now forgives sin and died for our sake will appear to judge the universe. The one who was begotten of the Father is both the source of life and judge, and therefore has power to heal and authority to forgive sins.[131] As judge who is the source of life, only he can deliver us from the judgment of death by giving us eternal life.[132] Chrysostom affirms that Christ as judge is on par with God the Father, and does nothing contrary to the latter's will. Emphasizing this harmony between the Son and the Father, he has Christ say, "I judge as if it were

---

129. Chrysostom often cites this verse as a proof-text in different contexts to highlight Christ as the source of life, his power and authority over death, his equality with the Father, and as one who gives eternal life. This chapter is the most quoted chapter in his homilies on the Fourth Gospel. He cites various verses from this chapter about twenty-five times in his eighty-eight homilies. He quotes 5:21 some eight times. E.g., see Homily 3, *FOC* 33:38 (*PG* 59.43); Homily 5, *FOC* 33:63 (*PG* 59.56); Homily 45, *FOC* 33:456 (*PG* 59.255); Homily 49, *FOC* 41:18 (*PG* 59.276); Homily 64, *FOC* 41:193–94 (*PG* 59.355); Homily 68, *FOC* 41:238 (*PG* 59.375); Homily 69, *FOC* 41:246 (*PG* 59.379); Homily 80, *FOC* 41:369–70 (*PG* 59.434).

130. Chrysostom, Homily 38, *FOC* 33:384 (*PG* 59.220).

131. Cf. Homily 40, *FOC* 33:405 (*PG* 59.229).

132. Chrysostom, Homily 39, *FOC* 33:391 (*PG* 59.222f). For Chrysostom's statements on Christ as the means of eternal life, see Homily 27, *FOC* 33:264 (*PG* 59.159f). Cf. Homily 68, *FOC* 41:235, 238 (*PG* 59.373f; 375).

the Father Himself who is judging."[133] As judge, Christ both forgives and wipes out the record, without keeping an account of sins.[134] Moreover, contrasting this life with the life to come, he asserts, "There death is not to be feared, nor need we anticipate any end of those blessings. Blessed and thrice blessed, and that many times over, are they who are enjoying that blessed lot."[135] Chrysostom firmly maintains that our hope of salvation lies in the veracity of the statements and promises of Christ. For the one who can forgive sins and deliver us from future judgment also has power over death.[136] Because Christ is the source of life, he is portrayed as the one who can heal, forgive sins, and as the one who has power and authority over death.

Christ's Power and Authority over Death

The raising of Lazarus from the dead is viewed as a vignette of the reversal of the corruption of death and a preview of Christ's ultimate victory over it. The words of Christ—"I am the resurrection and the Life"—not only attest to his intrinsic power and authority, but also point out that he himself is the giver of life. Therefore, death is subject to him. It is this thought that captures Chrysostom's attention in his exegesis of the Lazarus passage (11:1–44). The theme of Christ's power and authority over death is the dominant motif in Chrysostom treatment of this pericope. Apart from Christ's ultimate victory over death at his crucifixion and resurrection, nowhere is his complete power over death more lucidly demonstrated in his earthly ministry than the raising of Lazarus. Chrysostom notes that Christ, who shares in the same glory as the Father, deliberately allowed the consequences of death, the "corruption of the body," to take place in order to confirm the fact that the one whom Christ raised to life was dead, thereby underscoring the authenticity of the miracle.[137]

---

133. Chrysostom, Homily 39, *FOC* 33:397 (*PG* 59.225).

134. Ibid., *FOC* 33:400 (*PG* 59.227).

135. Ibid., *FOC* 33:401 (*PG* 59.227). Chrysostom often speaks of the everlasting blessings of heaven that may be enjoyed after one's departure from this life, and pictures the blessed life as enjoying communion with the King and the angelic host. See Homily 31, *FOC* 33:311(*PG* 59.182). Cf. Homily 87, *FOC* 41:465 (*PG* 59.476f); Homily 62, *FOC* 41:177 (*PG* 59.348).

136. Chrysostom, Homily 40, *FOC* 33:404 (*PG* 59.229).

137. Chrysostom, Homily 62, *FOC* 41:167 (*PG* 59.343).

Christ's true identity and power were beyond the comprehension of Lazarus's sisters Mary and Martha, "For they did not yet understand clearly either that He was God or that He performed these miracles by His own power and authority, though he had instructed them regarding both these facts."[138] By claiming that he himself was the "resurrection and the life," and by promising that anyone who believes in him "even if he die, shall live," Christ intended to show that he needed no external help in reviving Lazarus. Chrysostom continues to press the point that, because Christ is the source of life, his power is not restricted to time and space, citing the account of the healing of centurion's servant (Matt 8:8) as an example.[139] The assuring words of Christ to the sisters offered hope and consolation that he had power over both the death of the body as well the death of the soul. Having been troubled in his spirit and overcome with emotion, he sympathized with their grief, confirming his human nature.[140] Besides pointing out Christ's human emotions and actions in this passage in terms of condescension of the incarnation, Chrysostom notes that Christ affirmed his consubstantiality with the Father in different ways and proved it by his works: "By saying: 'I am in the Father and the Father in me,' He was also indirectly telling us of Their equality [ἰσότης] . . . when the subject of His discourse was His power [δύναμις], He said: 'I and the Father are one.' And when the subject concerned His authority [ἐξουσία], once again He said: 'For as the Father raises the dead and gives life, even so the Son also gives life to whom he will.' But He could not say this if His substance [οὐσία] was different from that of the Father."[141] The raising of Lazarus was incontestable proof his power over death and fulfillment of his words, "The hour is coming in which the dead shall hear the voice of the Son of God, and those who hear shall live" (5:25). Chrysostom stresses the point that Christ did everything of his own power and authority and did not derive it from someone else. The ocular and tactile proof of this authoritative power was demonstrated by Christ in bringing the dead man to life. He possessed this power intrinsically because he was able to conquer death in others.[142] If Christ

138. Ibid., *FOC* 41:171 (*PG* 59.345).
139. Ibid., *FOC* 41:173 (*PG* 59.346).
140. Chrysostom, Homily 63, *FOC* 41:181–83 (*PG* 59.450–51).
141. Chrysostom, Homily 64, *FOC* 41:193–94 (*PG* 59.355).
142. Ibid., *FOC* 41:198–99; 200–201 (*PG* 59.357–58). Elsewhere Chrysostom speaks of the marks of Christ's divinity: sins forgiven, secret thoughts revealed, death taking flight, and miracles performed with authority. See Homily 74, *FOC* 41:294 (*PG* 59.401).

is the source of life and has power and authority over death, what are the soteriological implications of his death and resurrection? This will be my focus in the following sections.

Christ's Ultimate Victory over Death on the Cross

Commenting on the events of the crucifixion, death, and resurrection of Christ, Chrysostom paints a dreadful picture of death and its consequences. He notes the difference between how it is perceived by different people: fear and despair for the nonbeliever (because death is viewed as the end of life) and bright hope for the believer (because death is viewed as a transition to the life to come). This hope is firmly rooted in the grace of God, through whom we can enjoy the blessed life:

> Death is an awesome thing, and one that inspires great fear—not, however, to those who have knowledge of the true wisdom from above. The man who has no clear understanding of the life to come, but considers death as a kind of annihilation and end of life, with good reason shudders and is afraid, under the illusion that it means passing on to a state of non-existence. We on the contrary, who by the grace of God have learned the mysteries and secrets of His wisdom, and who consider death merely as a transition, have no reason to tremble at it. We ought to rejoice and be of good heart, because, leaving behind this ephemeral life, we are going to another, much better and brighter, and one that is without end.[143]

The underlying theme of Chrysostom's portrayal of Christ's final hours is that he was in complete control of events, even his death on the cross. Depending on the context, Christ's actions are viewed either as acts of divine condescension or viewed as humanly exemplary. His prayer in the garden was for the sake of his disciples. His ability to blind the soldiers to his identity when they came for him and their falling to the ground are viewed as acts of his "insuperable power."[144] Chrysostom is keen to point out that the events in the garden that led to Christ's arrest were not due to the power of his antagonists, but were brought about by his own will. This was done in obedience to his Father even to the point of death, which was for the salvation of the world.[145] Continuing this

---

143. Chrysostom, Homily 83, *FOC* 41:399 (*PG* 59.447).
144. Ibid., *FOC* 41:401 (*PG* 59.448).
145. Ibid., *FOC* 41:404 (*PG* 59.449).

thought at Christ's trial before Pilate, he highlights the point that Christ's sovereignty was far beyond any human power; his kingdom is not of this world and neither is it transient. Christ's reply in the affirmative to Pilate's question of whether he was a king suggested that "all His other attributes are also innate and He has nothing which He has received." And the words of the evangelist, "As the Father has life in himself, even so he has given to the Son also to have life in himself," refer to his eternal generation.[146]

Besides noting (in line with patristic concerns) the fact that the crucifixion of Christ was fulfillment of type and prophecy, Chrysostom particularly highlights the figure of Christ carrying the cross on his shoulders. He associates the picture of Christ bearing the wood of the cross on his shoulder with the figure of Isaac who carried wood on his shoulder for the sacrifice on mount Moriah, and affirms that the former was the typological fulfillment latter. Building on this figurative interpretation, Chrysostom views the crucifixion of Christ as a decisive triumph over death, portraying him as a conqueror and the cross as his trophy. He writes, "Some say that there Adam had died and lay buried, and that Jesus set up His trophy over death in the place where death had begun its rule. For He went forth bearing His cross as a trophy in opposition to the tyranny of death, and, as is customary with conquerors, He also carried on His shoulders the symbol of His victory."[147]

Discussing the events at the crucifixion, Chrysostom once again notes that Christ's power was in control of everything. This power was displayed in foiling the devil's strategy, as evidenced by the fact that one of the two men who crucified with Christ was conducted to heaven.[148] The theme of Christ's power and his divine nature is thus central to Chrysostom's account of the crucifixion of Christ. Whereas his agony in the garden was a demonstration of the frailty of his human nature, his composure at the crucifixion is evidence of the infinite extent of his power.[149] The evangelist's description of Christ's tunic is said to highlight the same point: the "garment was woven from the top," suggesting an allegory, and means that the "crucified One was not man merely, but also possessed His Godhead from above."[150] Moreover, Chrysostom points

146. Ibid., *FOC* 41:413 (*PG* 59.453).
147. Ibid., Homily 85, *FOC* 41:428 (*PG* 59.459).
148. Ibid., *FOC* 41:429 (*PG* 59.460).
149. Ibid., *FOC* 41:432 (*PG* 59.461).
150. Ibid., *FOC* 41:431 (*PG* 59.461).

out that the evangelist emphasized the uniqueness of the crucifixion and death in order to make it clear that "Christ Himself is Lord of all." "Every detail was controlled by the One who was dying, and death did not enter His body until He Himself willed it, and He willed it only after all had been fulfilled. That is why he said: "I have power to lay down my life and I have power to take it up again."[151] Remarking on the words, "There came out blood and water" from the Christ's pierced side, Chrysostom asserts that the crucified body of Christ is the source through which the church and its sacraments of baptism and Eucharist have been instituted. "It was not accidentally or by chance that these streams came forth, but because the church has been established from both of these. Her members know this, since they have come to birth by water and are nourished by Flesh and Blood. The Mysteries have their source from there, so that when you approach the awesome chalice you may come as if you were to drink from His very side."[152] Christ is the source through whom we receive the benefits mediated sacramentally through baptism and the Eucharist. Thus the objective events of the crucifixion and the death of Christ are firmly associated with the sacraments of the church, where the believer subjectively appropriates the benefits through individual participation.

Commenting on the words of the resurrected Christ regarding his ascension to God ("I ascend to my Father and your Father, to my God and your God" [20:17]), Chrysostom says that although we became his brothers in the incarnation, he alone is worthy to sit on the royal throne in heaven, while his disciples only stand near him. There is a great difference in dignity between him and us: he alone is the Son and is therefore worthy to be enthroned. Nevertheless, through the incarnation and death of Christ we have the privilege of enjoying by grace what Christ possesses in his natural dignity as the Son. By virtue of the Son assuming flesh and eventually being glorified in heaven, human nature is also considered worthy of sharing in this privilege. Echoing this thought elsewhere, Chrysostom notes that through the incarnation and the assumption of human nature, and his subsequent resurrection and glorification (John 17:4–5), Christ raised our nature with him and considered it worthy of heaven, even that of the heavenly throne: "He dwells always in this tabernacle, for he put on our flesh, not to put it off again, but to have it always with him. If this were not so, he would not have deemed it

---

151. Ibid., *FOC* 41:434 (*PG* 59.462).
152. Ibid., *FOC* 41:435 (*PG* 59.463).

worthy of his royal throne, and bearing it, would not have had it adored by all the host above."[153]

We shall be able to share in his glory in our bodies as we fellowship with him in the blessed life to come. The Christian therefore has the privilege of looking forward to the promises of the beatific vision and eternal fellowship with Christ.[154] For such there is "great peace of conscience and great hope for the future; also bright glory and abundant esteem, and, more valuable than all these, the approval of God and promise of security from Him."[155] Citing 2 Timothy 2:12 ("if we endure we will also reign with him") and 2 Corinthians 4:17–18 ("For, our present light affliction, which is for the moment, prepares for us an eternal weight of glory that is beyond all measure; while we look not at the things that are seen, but at the things that are not seen"), Chrysostom asserts that this hope of our glorious reign with Christ is actualized through a relationship with him by faith and patient endurance in the here and now.[156] For Chrysostom, to be given the privilege of reigning with Christ and being glorified with him is the result of him making us sons and fellow-heirs by grace. Elaborating on this thought further while commenting on the words from Ephesians 1:3 ("Praise be to God, . . . who has blessed us with every spiritual blessing in the heavenly places in Christ"), he observes that the spiritual blessings through Christ include: being given immortality; being made a son, a brother and fellow-heir with Christ; and thereby being given the privilege of reigning and being glorified with him.[157] Since our nature has been exalted and is seated with him on the throne, it therefore shares in the intimate fellowship of heaven.[158] This was the reason, Chrysostom insists, for the incarnation and death of Christ: "His descent has become our ascent."[159]

Chrysostom maintains that the prize achieved by the cross was peace (through reconciliation), and this was the reason Paul often said, "Grace to you and peace." Further, he notes that gifts and power of the

---

153. Chrysostom, Homily 11, *FOC* 33:109 (*PG* 59.80).

154. Chrysostom, Homily 85, *FOC* 41:450 (*PG* 59.469); Homily 87, *FOC* 464–65 (*PG* 59.476).

155. Chrysostom, Homily 87, *FOC* 41:469 (*PG* 59.478).

156. Ibid., *FOC* 41:465f. (*PG* 59.476).

157. Chrysostom, *Commentary on Ephesians* 1:3–6, *NPNF* 13:50 (*PG* 62.11).

158. Chrysostom, Homily 5, in *Hebrews*, *NPNF* 14:388 (*PG* 63.46–47).

159. Chrysostom, Homily 65, in *Matthew*, *NPNF* 10:401 (*PG* 58.623).

Father, the Son, and the Holy Spirit are one. What belongs to the Father also belongs to the Son and to the Holy Spirit. It is through the sacramental ministry of the church, Chrysostom affirms, that one is able to possess the Holy Spirit within oneself.[160] By inference, then, to possess the Holy Spirit within oneself is to possess the fullness of God, enjoy the eternal fellowship of the Trinity, and thus share in the blessings of heaven.

Chrysostom points out that Christ's post-resurrection appearances were acts of condescension as well. In particular, attention is drawn to Christ's incorruptible body, which bore the marks or wounds of the crucifixion, was touched by the mortal hand of Thomas and also partook of food after the resurrection. All this was done in order that the doctrine of resurrection might be believed and to indicate that Christ was the Son of God. This was the reason why he came, for it is through him that we have eternal life, "for He Himself is the Life."[161]

Images of Christ's Victory and Their Implications

The motifs of Christ's absolute victory over death's tyranny, the reversal of the curse of death, and the hope of eternal fellowship with God through reconciliation form the background of Chrysostom's soteriological picture. He personifies death in various ways. One of his favorite images of death is that of a defeated tyrant, under whose dominion humanity was held captive. Christ on the other hand is portrayed as a conqueror, a victorious athlete, and a savior who routed death once and for all and released captive humanity to effect reconciliation with God. Speaking on the Holy Pascha (the feast in celebration of the resurrection), Chrysostom discusses the soteriological implications of Christ's death and resurrection:

> Indeed now present for us is the desired and saving feast, the day of resurrection of our Lord Jesus Christ, the event of peace, the occasion of reconciliation, the elimination of the wars, the abolishment of death, the defeat of the devil. Today humans have mingled with the angels and those who possess a body offer their doxology with the bodiless powers. Today the tyranny of death

---

160. Chrysostom underscores the ministry of the priesthood here with particular reference to the forgiveness of sins. Chrysostom, Homily 86, in *John*, FOC 41:454 (PG 59.471).

161. Ibid., FOC 41:460–62, 464 (PG 59.474–75).

is abolished. Today the bonds of death were loosened, and the victory of Hades was eliminated. Today is the appropriate time to say this prophetic cry, "Where, O death, is your victory? Where, O death, is your sting?" (I Cor. 15:55). Today Christ our Master broke the copper gates and the countenance [πρόσωπον] of death itself is eliminated.[162]

Through his resurrection Christ conquered and abolished death, defeated the devil, and thereby broke the fetters that bound us in such a decisive way that the very *prosōpon* of death was terminated. Through Christ we have peace with God having been reconciled with him. The image here is that of a powerful conqueror who has successfully defeated the forces led by death, and his victory is primarily understood in terms of securing freedom from the dominion of death and granting humanity the possibility of immortality.

This redemptive theme of Christ's victory over the powers of darkness recurs in Chrysostom's homilies on the Fourth Gospel. Commenting on the words, "Just as Moses lifted up the serpent in the desert, even so the Son of Man be lifted up . . . that those who believe in him might have eternal life (3:14–15)," he asserts that salvation came through Christ's triumph over the principalities and powers that held humanity captive under the grip of death. He affirms that the powers opposed to Christ were vanquished at his crucifixion and death. Portraying Christ as a victorious athlete who wrestles with his antagonist, overpowering him by humiliating him in the contest, Chrysostom writes:[163] "And this it is also which Paul said: 'Disarming the principalities and Powers, he displayed them openly, leading them away in his triumph by force of it (Col. 2:15).' As a great athlete, when he makes his victory more splendid because of having lifted up his opponent on high and hurled him down again, so Christ, with the whole world looking on, cast down the powers opposing Him, and having healed those smitten in the desert, He freed them from all wild beasts by hanging suspended on the cross."[164] Furthermore, he

---

162. Chrysostom, *On the Holy Pascha*, section 1 (PG 52.767). For ET, see Fotopoulos, "John Chrysostom," 123–34.

163. Wrestling was one of the most popular sports among the Greeks and the Romans, and was commonly held in high regard in the Byzantine world. Chrysostom liberally borrowed terms and illustrations from athletic contests to illustrate his points and did so with great eloquence. For Chrysostom's use of athletic phrases and metaphors in his homilies and commentaries, see Sawhill, "Use of Athletic Metaphors in the Biblical Homilies of St. John Chrysostom."

164. Chrysostom, Homily 27, *FOC* 33:263 (PG 59.159).

says that because Christ was the Son of God, death could not keep him for long: "His death would simply be a transition."[165] Consequently, he was able to bring a speedy end to its power over humanity: "He was no ordinary man; namely that He was able to set up a trophy over death and so quickly terminate its long tyranny and relentless warfare."[166] As a victorious conqueror that cannot be held back, he eliminated the slavery of death that humanity was under, and is therefore able to raise up those who are subdued by it.[167]

Christ's decisive victory over the tyranny of death weakened the latter's dominion; hence its effects over humanity are temporary and transient. Chrysostom portrays the transitory nature of death in different ways. Death is viewed as nothing more than sleep. "Because Christ our God was offered as a sacrifice and resurrected, the loving Master removed from our midst those names and brought a new and foreign behavior to our life, instead of death, then, the separation from the present life is called repose and sleep."[168] Comparing type with reality, Chrysostom points out that, before Christ came, the uplifted serpent mentioned in the Numbers account was able to stave off death temporarily. The cross, on the other hand, is efficacious to overcome eternal death. The crucified Christ reverses temporal death caused by the wounds inflicted by the spiritual dragon, and thus the faithful will be able to escape its momentary affliction.[169]

By prevailing over death through his victory, Christ loosened its permanent grip on us; we can thus be assured of our absolute victory over death through him. For the faithful, death is passing, not permanent, and will not affect our ultimate destiny. Because of Christ's victory over death we can now wrestle with our enemy with the knowledge that he has been weakened and his power diminished. The fact that we still experience death and corruption in our bodies must not be understood as our defeat, since we will rise again to prove that the consequences of death are impermanent and our victory through Christ eternal.

---

165. Chrysostom, Homily 79, *FOC* 41:352 (*PG* 59.427).

166. Chrysostom, Homily 23, *FOC* 33:229 (*PG* 59.142).

167. Chrysostom, Homily 78, *FOC* 41:342 (*PG* 59.422); Homily 5, *FOC* 33:67 (*PG* 59.58).

168. Chrysostom, *On the Holy Pascha*, section 1 (*PG* 52.767). Cf. Chrysostom, Homily 79, *FOC* 41:359 (*PG* 59.429).

169. Chrysostom, Homily 27, *FOC* 33:262–63 (*PG* 59.159).

Chrysostom portrays death in terms of an ephemeral blush whose effects are fleeting:

> Surely the wrestler will be famous, not when he does not grapple with his opponent, but when, after grappling with him, he is not worsted. Well, then, because we come to grips with death we are not therefore merely mortal, but we are immortal because of our victory over it. For we should be mortal if we remained forever in its power . . . so also when a man is going to rise again after death he is not mortal, even though laid low by death. Indeed, if a man should blush for a little while, tell me, please: shall we say then say he is always red? . . . If someone should become pale, shall we call him jaundiced? "By no means, because the affliction is only temporary." Well, then, you will not call him mortal who comes for a short time under the dominion of death. If we did so, we should also call those who are asleep "dead," for they have died, so to speak, and are inactive. "But death corrupts the bodies of the dead?" And what of that? For it does not do so that they may remain in a state of corruption, but that they may become better.[170]

Chrysostom goes on to mention that as a community of the redeemed, we are like strangers on earth, and "our sojourn here is brief and passing" as we make our way to the city whose builder and architect is God. We can look forward to enjoying the eternal benefits of Christ's redemptive death, for by being made the sons of God we are brothers of the only-begotten Son. We are therefore promised all the blessings of heaven.[171]

Christ's death is also viewed as a means of purification and as a prerequisite for the descent of the Holy Spirit, whose indwelling is promised to the faithful. Through his death, and our identification with him in baptism, we are cleansed from sin and have the privilege of receiving the Spirit. This would not have been possible unless Christ had died first. We would not be able to enjoy the benefits of the Holy Spirit's ministry had it not been for Christ's death and his sending of the Holy Spirit. Again employing imagery from athletic contests, Chrysostom alludes to the Holy Spirit as the "Anointer" with reference to the individual who prepares the athletes by anointing them before they engage with their opponents in the wrestling arena. He points out that the prerequisite of Christ's death had to be in place before we could receive the assistance of the Holy

---

170. Chrysostom, Homily 79, FOC 41:358–59 (PG 59.429).
171. Ibid., FOC 41:363 (PG 59.431).

Spirit: "The sacrifice had to be offered and sin had to be destroyed" and, as athletes preparing for the contests, they had to await the "Anointer."[172] The only way the Holy Spirit could come was after the departure of Christ. Chrysostom is very specific about the benefits of the death of Christ with regard to the removal of the curse of sin. Elsewhere, in reply to an imaginary interlocutor inquiring as to why the Holy Spirit had not come before Christ's departure, he contends, "He could not come, since the curse had not yet been lifted, the original sin had not yet been forgiven, but all men were still subject to the penalty for it. 'Therefore,' He said, 'that enmity must be destroyed and you must be reconciled to God, and then you will receive that gift.'"[173] It is through the death of Christ that we are enabled to receive the indwelling of the Holy Spirit, who is equal in power and dignity with the Father and the Son. He asserts that the gift of sonship is bestowed through the Holy Spirit, whereby we are cleansed and forgiven of our sins and given new life. Moreover, it is he who gives life to our mortal bodies, and enables us to relate with the Father as sons, having made us righteous by the cleansing and sanctification that he accomplishes in us.[174] Associating the mystical implications of Christ's death and resurrection with our renewal, Chrysostom point out that "He Himself paid the penalty for sin by the birth pangs of His death and caused the new man to be regenerated by that means."[175] It is because of Christ's redemptive death that this regeneration is accomplished in us through the ministry of the Holy Spirit.

Whereas the incarnation is considered as the root of God's plan of redemption, the benefits of Christ's death and resurrection are viewed as its fruit. Though the starting point of redemption is the incarnation, ultimately it is only through Christ's death and resurrection that the dominion and tyranny of death are finally overcome.[176] The underlying theme of Chrysostom's portrayal of the cross of Christ is reconciliation with God. The redemptive and propitiatory implications of Christ's victory over death and the devil are depicted in various ways. Chrysostom

---

172. Chrysostom, Homily 75, *FOC* 41:302 (*PG* 59.404). Presumably Chrysostom has the act of chrismation in mind, where the initiated are anointed with oil after baptism, symbolic of the descent of the Holy Spirit.

173. Chrysostom, Homily 78, *FOC* 41:345 (*PG* 59.423).

174. Ibid., *FOC* 41:346–47 (*PG* 59.423–24).

175. Chrysostom, Homily 79, *FOC* 41:354 (*PG* 59.427).

176. Chrysostom, Homily 80, *FOC* 41:372 (*PG* 59.435). Cf. Homily 39, section 2, in *First Corinthians*, *NPNF* 12:235 (*PG* 61.334).

resorts to his favorite depiction of Satan as an evil tyrant who perpetrates crimes against the innocent, and as a creditor who ill-treats his debtors by imprisoning them. If a tyrant unjustly kills the king's son he will have to pay the penalty for it; and if a creditor imprisons someone who owes him nothing he will pay a high price for his mistake. In both cases the guilty party will be punished and will have to make retribution. Likewise, Satan exercises his power over humanity justly (for they are guilty of sin and therefore worthy of such punishment), but he unjustly wielded his power over Christ, the guiltless one, when he subjected him to death and will therefore be penalized for overstepping his authority and power. It was through the redemptive sacrifice of Christ on the cross that Satan received his just deserts:

> Suppose that there is a certain tyrant, given to violence, who inflicts evils without number on all who come into his hands. If, on coming to grips with a king, or the son of a king, he should destroy the latter unjustly, his death will cause retribution to be made for the others, also. Suppose that some creditor is exacting with his debtors, and beats them, and casts them into prison. Then suppose that out of the same high-mindedness he puts someone who owes nothing into the same prison. The creditor will pay the penalty for what he has done to the others, for that innocent man will destroy him. Thus has it also happened in the case of the Son. For the Devil will have punishment demanded of him for what he has done to us, because of what he dared to do to Christ.[177]

Because Satan had no right to kill Christ, in doing so he lost his authority over him and all those who were subject to the power of death. Through Christ's death we have been redeemed from the dominion of death and its consequences. This understanding is drawn from words of Christ in Matthew 20:28, where he says that he would give his life as a ransom for many. This is said to mean that the retribution demanded on behalf of humanity will be its freedom from the bondage of death. Commenting on this motif but employing different imagery, Chrysostom discusses the redeeming aspects of Christ's ministry, noting how humanity was delivered from death's captivity. He explains how Christ's death liberated us from our bondage and imprisonment:

---

177. Chrysostom, Homily 67, in *John*, FOC 41:232–33 (PG 59.372).

> Adam sinned and died, but Christ did not sin and died. Why did this happen and for what purpose did this occur? So that he who sinned and died could be freed from the bonds of death with the help of him who did not sin and died. Someone owes money to someone else and they are not able to repay it, and for this reason they are imprisoned. But another person, who is not in debt but is able to pay, liberates the one responsible by paying the sum. This is what happened to Adam and to Christ. Adam owed death and was imprisoned. But Christ came and eliminated death for the one held captive, so that he could liberate him from the bonds of death. Do you see the achievements of the resurrection? Do you see the loving-kindness of the Master? Do you see the greatness of his protection?[178]

In this transaction, even though Christ did not owe anything to anyone, he paid the penalty for our sin by his sacrificial death and liberated us.

In another context Chrysostom discusses the redemption won by Christ from a juridical perspective. Citing Romans 5:12, he observes that because Adam was guilty of sin, he was liable to death. Sin was the reason death came upon humanity, and ever since then humanity has been in subjection to it. Christ was sinless, yet he died in order to redeem humanity from the curse of death. Consequently, Satan, "the prince of this world" (John 12:30), will ultimately be vanquished and there will be "judgment and retribution."[179] Having trapped Satan in the dock of God's court of justice, the question that will be asked of him is this: "Granted that you destroyed all men because you found them guilty of sin; but why did you destroy Christ? Is it not very evident that you did so unjustly? Well then, through Him the whole world will be vindicated."[180] This vindication is possible because Christ voluntarily laid down his life as a sacrifice in order to redeem us from our bondage and reconcile us with God. Chrysostom stresses the idea that Christ substituted himself in order to liberate us and reconcile us with God: "He Himself becomes the offering, presenting Himself to the Father as sacrifice and oblation."[181] He gave himself on behalf of those who were condemned and suffers the humiliation of death in their place.

---

178. Chrysostom, *On the Holy Pascha*, section 4, (PG 52.770).
179. Chrysostom, Homily 67, in *John*, FOC 41:231 (PG 59.372).
180. Ibid., FOC 41:232 (PG 59.373).
181. Chrysostom, Homily 78, FOC 41:345 (PG 59.423); Homily 14, FOC 33:138 (PG 59.95).

Our alienation from God resulted in death and corruption; the cross was the only means of reconciliation and eternal life. Chrysostom often stresses the view that our redemption was accomplished through the cross. Some of his most forceful statements on the cross of Christ highlight this motif:

> For the cross destroyed the enmity of God towards man, brought about the reconciliation, made the earth heaven, associated men with angels, pulled down the citadel of death, unstrung the force of the devil, extinguished the power of sin, delivered the world from error, brought back the truth, expelled Demons, destroyed temples, overturned altars, suppressed sacrificial offering, implanted virtue, rounded Churches . . . the cross has broken our bond, it has made the prison of death ineffectual, it is the demonstration of the love of God. "For God so loved the world that He gave His only-begotten Son, that every one who believes in Him should not perish." And again Paul says, "If being enemies we were reconciled to God by the death of His Son."[182]

Prior to the event of the cross, we were enemies of God and imprisoned by death, but now through Christ we have been reconciled, freed, and granted life, peace, and eternal fellowship with him. Salvation is also described in terms of the "dissolution of death and the destruction of the devil."[183] This was the very reason for the incarnation; Christ became like us in order to make retribution for our sin through the cross and enable us to enjoy eternal communion with God. Commenting on Christ's ministry of reconciliation through his incarnation and death, Chrysostom writes:

> He was earnestly willing to become our brother in all things, and for this cause did He leave the angels and the other powers, and come down to us, and took hold of us, and wrought innumerable good things. He destroyed Death, He cast out the devil from his tyranny, He freed us from bondage . . . For this cause He took on Him our flesh, only for love of man, that He might have mercy upon us. For neither is there any other reason for the incarnation, but this alone. For He saw us, cast on the ground, perishing, tyrannized over by Death, and He had compassion on us. "To make reconciliation" he says, "for the sins of the people. That He might be a merciful and faithful High Priest."[184]

---

182. Chrysostom, *Against Marcionites and Manichaens*, NPNF 9:203 (PG 51.35).
183. Chrysostom, Homily 3, in *Hebrews*, NPNF 14:379 (PG 63.33).
184. Chrysostom, Homily 5, in *Hebrews*, NPNF 14:389 (PG 63.47).

The soteriological thought of Chrysostom is framed by the twin themes of the incarnation and death of Christ, and their redemptive benefits are viewed together. Christ entered brotherhood with us in order that through his death he might reconcile us with God. The ultimate reversal of the consequences of sin (*viz.*, death and corruption) due to Christ's death is viewed in terms of receiving immortality and incorruption through our reconciliation with God. Christ descended to the point of death in order that we might be raised up with him and share in the eternal fellowship of God. This reconciliation offers us the hope of divine communion whereby, through our union with Christ, we can share in the blessings of heaven. The sacramental benefits of the death of Christ are conveyed to us in the context of our participation in the Eucharist. It is through our union with Christ, the "bread of life," that we continue to enjoy the blessings of this reconciliation. Ultimately, Christ entered brotherhood with us in order that we might have everlasting life through our union with him. Chrysostom has Christ say, "I wished to become your brother when for your sake I had assumed flesh and blood, I gave back again to you the very Flesh and Blood through which I became your kinsman."[185] The soteriological consequences of the incarnation and death of Christ are inseparable in Chrysostom's thought. Christ assumed flesh and shed his blood on the cross in order that we might be spiritually nourished by his "flesh and blood" through our participation in the Eucharist. Consequently, we enjoy the blessings of our kinship with him through this sacramentally mediated union. In overcoming death once and for all he rescued humanity from its dominion and gives us the privilege of enjoying immortality and incorruption.

The Eucharistic Appropriation of Christ's Victory

Before I discuss Chrysostom's view of the eucharistic appropriation of Christ's redemptive work, I will briefly survey Cyril's view as a contrasting background in order to see if their perspectives converge or diverge on this issue. In an insightful article, Chadwick highlights the close relationship between the Eucharist and Christology in Cyril's thought by examining how the sacramental benefits of the Eucharist are directly related to his understanding of the person of Christ.[186] Cyril, he maintains,

---

185. Chrysostom, Homily 46, in *John*, FOC 33:469 (*PG* 59.261).

186. See Chadwick, "Eucharist and Christology in the Nestorian Controversy," 145–64.

perceived the threat from Nestorius's insistence on the dual personality of Christ as undermining the soteriological implications of the incarnation from a eucharistic point of view. Chadwick notes that Cyril's fundamental objections to Nestorius' doctrine were the repercussions that such a view had on the doctrines of the Eucharist and the atonement. Conversely, by insisting on the existence of the two *hypostases* in Christ, Nestorius was trying to do justice to Christ's soul playing a real part in the work of redemption but ended up instead making him into a dual personality. Both Cyril's and Nestorius' soteriological concerns governed their understanding of the person of Christ.

The Eucharist, Chadwick points out, was central to Cyril's Christology. Cyril maintains that in the Eucharist, Christ comes among the faithful visibly and invisibly: invisibly as God and visibly as being in the body that can be touched in the ὁμολογία καὶ ἀνάμνησις (confession and remembrance) of his death and resurrection.[187] A dual personality in Christ could not communicate salvation to humanity, Cyril argues, for the flesh of Christ that is received at the Eucharist must be the very flesh of the Logos by which the communicant is united to him. Therefore, those who refrain from participating in the sacrament exclude themselves from the blessed life, because they are not intimately united to the life-giving flesh of the Logos. To Nestorius, Cyril's doctrine implied that the humanity was transformed into divinity, the body losing its uniqueness so that Christ's humanity no longer has any solidarity with ours. This in turn is closely connected to Nestorius's soteriology, which views the duality of the natures imperative to safeguard the integrity of the human nature and the soul of Christ. For Cyril, to divide the natures is to separate Christ's flesh from the life-giving source, thus making his flesh the flesh of the ordinary man and not the ἰδία σάρξ (very flesh) of the Logos and reducing the Eucharist to an act of cannibalism.

In a similar vein, Welch has proposed that Cyril's soteriological and eucharistic concerns shape and govern his early christological thought.[188] Arguing from Cyril's commentary on the Gospel of John, and reassessing Cyril's early Christology, Welch maintains that in Cyril's view, salvation is the unity of the baptized in the Spirit with Christ, and that this is communicated through the Eucharist. The baptized partake of the

---

187. Cyril, *Commentary on John* 12:26 (PG 74.725); Chadwick, "Eucharist and Christology in the Nestorian Controversy," 155.

188. Welch, *Christology and Eucharist in the Early thought of Cyril of Alexandria*.

life-giving flesh of Christ and are joined to him. Once the baptized are united to Christ, they are also united to the Father through Christ, who as the eternal Son is consubstantial with the Father. The christological implications of such a view demand an understanding of the incarnation in which the eternal Son of God becomes flesh in order to restore divine communion. Thus Cyril's soteriological and eucharistic views require the unity of Christ and the communication of properties. He concludes that Cyril "no more worked out a Christology apart from his understanding of the eucharistic liturgy anymore than he constructed a Christology apart from his soteriological concerns."[189] Scholars have highlighted this relationship in Cyril's thought, but have not given similar attention to the christological implications of Chrysostom's eucharistic thought. How is Chrysostom's understanding of the Eucharist similar to or distinct from what has been proposed in Cyril's case? What are the christological implications of Chrysostom's eucharistic thought?

Chrysostom's View of Christ as "The Bread of Life"

Chrysostom briefly discusses the implications of our participation in the Eucharist in his homilies on John 6:25–59, employing the "bread of life" imagery to make his point. Underscoring the distinction between the figure of manna and the reality of the true bread, he notes that, unlike the figure (which was only sufficient for bodily nourishment), the bread that came from heaven is able to impart eternal life. By declaring "I am the bread of life," Christ introduced his hearers to the "revelation of the mysteries." The expression "bread of life" refers to Christ's divinity, and this is central to Chrysostom's understanding of the implications of our participation in the Eucharist. The reference to Christ's body will be made later in the chapter with the words, "the bread that I will give you is my flesh." Chrysostom affirms that the "bread of life" is God the Word, just as after the epiclesis the bread becomes the body of Christ because of the Spirit coming upon it.[190] Moreover, Christ called himself the "living bread" because he "welds together for us this life and the life to come" and revealed himself as God.[191]

---

189. Ibid., 130.
190. Chrysostom, Homily 45, in *John*, FOC 33:452 (PG 59.253).
191. Chrysostom, Homily 46, FOC 33:465 (PG 59.258–59).

Whereas those who partook of the manna died in the wilderness, those who partake of the "bread of life" will live forever. Indicating how the faithful can enjoy the privilege of sharing in the divine life through Christ, Chrysostom invokes the Pauline head-body image of Christ and his church (Eph 5:30) and points out that "we are one body, and members made from his flesh and his bones."[192] We become one with Christ through our union with him in the eucharistic participation. He continues: "Therefore, in order that we may become of His Body, not in desire only, but also in very fact, let us become commingled with that Body. This, in truth, takes place by means of the food which He has given us as a gift, because He desired to prove the love which He has for us. It is for this reason that He has shared Himself with us and brought His Body down to our level, namely, that we might be one with Him as the body is joined with the head."[193] Christ has given the faithful the privilege not just to look upon him and touch him, but also to consume him and be intimately united with him in this sacramental participation. The reason he assumed flesh was to give us back the flesh and blood through which he became our kinsman. His blood has opened the way to heaven, and it is through it that we have salvation. He is the head and we are his body, and we are spiritually nourished through the partaking of the flesh and blood. "This Blood makes the seal of our King bright in us; it produces an inconceivable beauty; it does not permit the nobility of the soul to become corrupt, since it refreshes and nourishes it without ceasing."[194] Chrysostom regards the mysteries of the church as "awe-inspiring" and compares them to a fountain of paradise; the spiritual streams arising from it are able to cleanse our souls.[195] Christ purchased and adorned the church by his blood, and those who participate in the Eucharist are united with him. This is described as wearing the royal robe of Christ, and therefore "wearing the King Himself," as well as enjoying the heavenly communion of the angels, the archangels, and the powers above.[196] Because this union has metaphysical implications, the initiated are warned of the consequences of partaking in the Eucharist unworthily,

---

192. Ibid., *FOC* 33:468 (*PG* 59.260).
193. Ibid.
194. Chrysostom, Homily 46, *FOC* 33:469 (*PG* 59.261).
195. Ibid., *FOC* 33:470 (*PG* 59.261).
196. Ibid., *FOC* 33:471 (*PG* 59.262).

and are reminded of the repercussions of treating the blood of the covenant in an unholy way.[197]

Commenting on the words of John 6:53 ("unless you eat the flesh of the Son of Man, and drink his blood, you shall not have life in you. He who eats my flesh and drinks my blood has life in himself"), Chrysostom observes that by referring to his flesh as food and his blood as drink, Christ was underscoring the central nature of the mysteries and the reality of the initiated being united with him through the sacrament. Eternal life is promised to those who abide in Christ by partaking of the elements. This is but a logical conclusion of the fact that by being united to Christ, one is united to the source of life and therefore has everlasting life.[198] The life that Christ gives us through our participation in his flesh and blood is the "glorious and ineffable" blessed life, which stands in stark contrast to figure of manna, which could only provide bodily nourishment. Through Christ we can look forward to the hope of our future resurrection and this is the due to "revoking the punishment resulting from sin, destroying that well-known sentence of death and substituting for former blessings, not merely life, but everlasting life."[199] Chrysostom contends that Christ commented on the manna repeatedly in this context to highlight the difference between it and the bread from heaven, the latter reversing the punishment of death by giving us immortality. Thus by partaking of the "bread of life" through our participation in the Eucharist we can participate in the divine life. Chrysostom maintains that since such imagery has both spiritual and mystical elements in it, it can only be comprehended and appreciated through our spiritual senses. Just as the words of Christ were offensive to his audience because of their fleshly thinking, the spiritual nature of mysteries might incite a similar response in us if not comprehended by the inner eyes and spiritual faculties.[200]

197. Chrysostom, Homily 17, in *Hebrews*, NPNF 14:449 (PG 63.133). For an overview of the duties of a priest at the liturgical service of the Eucharist, see chapter 9, "Chrysostom as Liturgist," in Baur, *John Chrysostom*, 1:190–200. For commentaries on eucharistic practices in the East, see Schulz, *Byzantine Liturgy*; Taft, *Liturgy in Byzantium and Beyond*.

198. He has Christ say, "For if a man abides in me, and I am alive, it is evident that he also will be alive," and cites John 5:26, "For as the Father has life in himself, even so he has given to the Son also to have life in himself." Chrysostom, Homily 47, in *John*, FOC 33:473–74 (PG 59.263).

199. Ibid., FOC 33:475 (PG 59.264).

200. Chrysostom, Homily 47, FOC 33:477 (PG 59.265) When speaking of the mys-

The Implications of One's Sacramentally Mediated Union with Christ

The sacraments are regarded as an expression of the church's faith in the sense of embodying and conveying the reality of God's grace through symbols. It has been suggested that, generally speaking, the fathers' understanding of the symbols was far more positive and realistic than ours. When the fathers spoke in realistic terms of the bread and wine as the very body of Christ, their main purpose was to press the point that the life-giving, propitiatory benefits of the once-for-all sacrifice of Christ were fully available to the initiated in the here and now.[201] This realism dominates Chrysostom's view of the bread and wine in the Eucharist: that which is in the cup is that which flowed from the side of Christ, and the bread of which the initiated partake is the very body of Christ.[202] According to Chrysostom, the sacraments of baptism and Eucharist find their provenance in Christ's death on the cross; the crucified body of Christ was the source of the water and blood that flowed from his pierced side.[203] Because eternal life is communicated through Christ, Chrysostom often stressed our union with him through participation in the Eucharist. Christ took on flesh like ours and shares this life-giving flesh with us in the mysteries, uniting us to himself.[204] Commenting on this intimate union with Christ and reminding his hearers of the words of Christ ("eat Me, drink Me"), Chrysostom has him say, "I am not only

---

teries, Chrysostom frequently urged his hearers to see with the "eyes of the soul" or "spiritual eyes" or the "eyes of faith." See *Baptismal Instructions* 2.9–10 (SC 50.138); 2.17, 28 (SC 50.143); 4.20 (SC 50.193).

201. See chapter 5, "The Sacraments," in Wiles, *Christian Fathers*, 110–34.

202. Chrysostom, Homily 24, in 1 *Corinthians*, NPNF 12:139 (PG 60.200).

203. Chrysostom, Homily 85, in *John*, FOC 41:435 (PG 59.463). "It is from both of these that the Church is sprung through the bath of regeneration and renewal by the Holy Spirit, through baptism and the mysteries. But the symbols of baptism and the mysteries come from the side of Christ. It is from His side, therefore, that Christ formed His Church, just as He formed Eve from the side of Adam." Chrysostom, *Baptismal Instructions* 3.17, ACW 31.62 (SC 50.161).

204. Chrysostom, Homily 82, in *Matthew*, NPNF 10:495 (PG 58.743). Discussing this theme elsewhere, Chrysostom notes that Paul underscores this point by saying our participation is communal and that we are the body of Christ, "Because he intended to express something more and to point out how close was the union: in that we communicate not only by participating and partaking, but also by being united. For as that body is united to Christ, so also are we united to him by this bread." Chrysostom, Homily 24, in 1 *Corinthians*, NPNF 12:139–40 (PG 61.200).

mingled with you, I am entwined in you. I am masticated, broken into minute particles, that the interspersion, and commixture, and union may be more complete. Things united remain yet in their own limits, but I am interwoven with you. I would have no more division between us. I will that we both be one."[205]

Chrysostom asserts that Christ ordained the institution of the Eucharist at the time of the Passover to point out that, as the Lawgiver in the Old Testament, only he had the authority to fill the type with the truth by replacing the Jewish feast with the Eucharist. He made this chief of feasts obsolete in order to lead us to the awe-inspiring table, saying, "take, eat, this is my body, which is broken for many."[206] Therefore this celebration is called εὐχαριστία (*eucharistia*) as commemoration of the benefits that we receive and is done in grateful response to the salvific work of Christ.[207] Furthermore, the Eucharist is representative of the sacrifice of Christ and is reenacted to appropriate the benefits of Christ's death: "it is not a another sacrifice, as the High Priest, but we offer always the same, or rather we perform a remembrance [*anamnēsis*] of a Sacrifice."[208] The church as the body of Christ is one body, not many bodies, and this communal unity is reflected by the bread, which consists of many grains and yet is one.[209] To partake of the "bread of life," the life-giving flesh, is to be united to Christ and share in the eternal life of God. Underscoring the soteriological and sacramental implications of our participation in the Eucharist, Chrysostom observes: "For he gave not simply even His own body; but because the former nature of the flesh which was framed out of earth, had first become deadened by sin and destitute of life; He brought in, as one may say, another sort of dough and leaven, His own flesh by nature indeed the same, but free from sin and full of life; and gave to all to partake thereof, that being nourished by this and laying aside the old dead material, we might be blended together unto that which is living and eternal, by means of this table."[210] Baptism, as we have noted earlier, is where the individual has

205. Chrysostom, Homily 15, in 1 *Timothy*, NPNF 13:464 (PG 62.586).
206. Chrysostom, Homily 82, in *Matthew*, NPNF 10:491 (PG 58.738).
207. Chrysostom, Homily 25, in *Matthew*, NPNF 10:174 (PG 57.331).
208. Chrysostom, Homily 17, in *Hebrews*, NPNF 14:449 (PG 63.131). For the early church's use of images in reenacting biblical events in catechetical and eucharistic contexts, see Frank, "Taste and See."
209. Chrysostom, Homily 24, in 1 *Corinthians*, NPNF 12:140 (PG 61.200).
210. Ibid.

received pardon from sin and has been granted sonship, such that the divine image has been renewed and fellowship with God restored. This communion is granted as the result of Christ's redemptive death and is actualized through our participation in the Eucharist. Christ gives us the privilege of being united with him as we partake of "his own flesh" in the Eucharist; as the "bread of life," he enables us to share in the life of God because he is God the Word. By virtue of our union with the eternal Son, we can share in the eternal fellowship of the Father and the Son: "By being in them and having the Father with Him [so that] He joined them together."[211] Through our eucharistic participation and union with Christ, we share by grace in the divine life that he as the eternal Son possesses by nature. Since the Son participates in the life of the Trinity, our union with him grants us this privilege. Therefore our union with Christ, sacramentally mediated through the Eucharist, is understood as sharing by grace in the natural fellowship of the Godhead.

The Christological Implications of Chrysostom's Soteriological and Sacramental Thought

The imagery that Chrysostom employs in his soteriological and sacramental thought, concomitant with his incarnational theology, also points to Christ's unity and his consubstantiality with the Father. Chrysostom's portrayal of Christ as physician and judge suggests that only if he were one with God could he have healed diseases and remitted sins in the manner in which he did. Restoring the body from disease and death indicates that, as the savior who is the source of life, he has authority and power to deliver humanity from the effects of sin. The one who pronounced forgiveness of sins after healing the body from its infirmity, and the one who will sit in judgment in the future are the same person. Chrysostom often cites John 5:21 to describe Christ's consubstantiality with the Father and does so in order to emphasize Christ's power and authority over death and corruption. The one who has the power to raise the dead and give life like the Father is equal to him in all respects. Chrysostom stressed this point in his account of Christ's victory over death on the cross. His description of Christ as being in control of events at his passion and crucifixion is made in terms of his authority

---

211. Chrysostom, Homily 82, in *John*, FOC 41:392 (PG 59.444).

and power: his sovereign power extended to all details, to the point that even death did not enter his body until he willed it.

Chrysostom views the incarnation and death of Christ as two sides of one doctrinal coin. This is seen in his statements on the soteriological aspects of cross. The idea that the Son descended not merely to human life but also to death in order reconcile us with the Father suggests a unitive Christology. The whole life and work of Christ is viewed in terms of what was accomplished through the cross. By underscoring the point that his descent was our ascent, Chrysostom was complementing his earlier thought as to the reason the Word became flesh: he became the Son of Man in order to make us the children of God. Christ's victory over death is viewed as the pivotal point in our redemption from sin and possibility of fellowship with God.

Chrysostom holds to both classical (in Aulén's sense) and juridical perspectives in his depiction of Christ's atoning work. The incarnation, life, death, and resurrection of Christ are viewed as a victory over sin and death. In assuming flesh, God the Son entered brotherhood with us. He entered the dominion of Satan and subjected himself to death in order to redeem us from its tyranny; he allowed the devil to take his sinless life, even though Satan by rights had no power over him. Through Christ's death Satan incurred the penalty for overstepping his authority and forfeited his power over death. The resurrection of Christ was the proclamation of this victory, which he secured through the cross.

The imagery employed to depict Christ's decisive victory over death and Satan is rich with redemptive themes that require the Son's personal presence in the transaction. The depiction of Christ as a heavenly conqueror and a victorious athlete who defeated and routed the principalities and powers suggests that only if Christ is Son of God could he have been able to prevail over his enemy. The view that Christ substituted himself as a perfect sacrifice in order turn away the Father's anger towards sin and guilt and to reconcile us with him, demands an understanding of the savior as the Son of God himself.

The one who reconciles us with God also enables to share in the divine fellowship. By virtue of his resurrection, ascension, and glorification the eternal Son raised human nature to the royal throne to share in the intimate communion of heaven. The prospect of sharing in the divine life is given to the baptized through union with Christ in the sacramental context of the Eucharist. In partaking of the "flesh and blood" of Christ, we also partake of the "bread of life," and thereby share in the divine life. Because the elements of Eucharist are viewed as the very life-giving flesh and blood of Christ the eternal Son, Chrysostom often stressed the idea of an our intimate union with him in this sacrament. In receiving the elements we receive Christ himself; grace is viewed in personal and not impersonal terms. By inference then, grace is understood as God giving himself to the baptized through Christ.

Our union with Christ allows us to share in the divine life, because as the Son, he is equal and consubstantial with the Father; to be united to the Son is to be united to the Father and receive the privilege of sharing in the eternal fellowship of God. The view that we can share in the divine communion through our union with Christ reflects a unitive Christology in that it requires his person to be the Logos himself: for only the Son who possesses this privilege by nature can enable us to share in the divine life. The idea of reconciliation with God is central to Chrysostom's soteriological and sacramental thought. Sin and death alienated us, but through Christ we have been reconciled with God, having been delivered from death, corruption, and mortality. Our reconciliation is viewed as sharing by grace in the divine communion of the Father and the Son.

My study of the relationship between Chrysostom's eucharistic and Christological thought corroborates the correlation between Christology and the Eucharist proposed in the work of scholars like Chadwick and Welch with respect to Cyril's thought. It also shows that Cyril's early christological thought is essentially similar to that of Chrysostom insofar as the understanding of the unity of the person of Christ is concerned. Their view of the nature of the sacraments is very similar also, except that Chrysostom emphasizes the practical implications that ensue from our sacramental participation, stressing that the intimate union with Christ demands moral purity in the life of the Christian. For Chrysostom, then, the life of virtue is but a reflection of our sacramental participation in Christ. The church is viewed as a sacramental community and its liturgical praxis in communicating the awe-inspiring mysteries to the individual reinforces the reality of this relationship. Chrysostom's portrayal of the Christ as the source of life, the one who demonstrates his authoritative power over death and offers divine fellowship and eternal life sacramentally mediated through our union with him, can therefore be called a *Christology of Participation*.

A Practical Christology

Introduction

The objective of this final section is to examine Chrysostom's view of the practical outworking of the Christian life as it relates to his Christology and to study its implications with respect to these questions: what does a life that is conformed to Christ's image look like? What are the moral implications of our sacramentally mediated union with Christ? How does this translate into practice in an ecclesiastical context? For Chrysostom, our sacramentally mediated union with Christ has existential and practical consequences. He affirms that the Christian life is a transformed life in which an ontological change has occurred through God's grace. Commenting on Romans 6:4, he says: "When you hear about the newness of life, look for a great change, for a great transformation." In this transformation the old age of sin is replaced by the vitality of grace because "the souls of the righteous are youthful and vibrant, and are permanently in the very prime of life, ever ready for any fight and struggle."[212]

This change is the result of being made sons and being conformed to Christ, for what Christ is by nature we have become by grace.[213] As noted in the previous section, according to Chrysostom, to be conformed to the image of Christ is to be clothed with him. To be clothed with Christ is to have him indwell us, and therefore, our life is in effect a reflection of Christ's life in us. To put on Christ, in Chrysostom's view, is to have absolute virtue indwell us. Stringing together multiple metaphors from various pericopes, Chrysostom elaborates on this thought, declaring:

> But in saying, "Put ye on," he [Paul] bids us be girt about with Him upon every side. As in another place he says, "But if Christ be in you." (Rom. 8:10.) And again, "That Christ may dwell in the inner man." (Eph. 3:16, 17.) For He would have our soul to be a dwelling for Himself, and Himself to be laid round about us as a garment, that He may be unto us all things both from within and from without. For He is our fullness; for He is "the fullness of Him that fills all in all" (Eph. 1:23): and the Way, and the Husband, and the Bridegroom; for "I have espoused you as a chaste virgin to one husband," (2 Cor. 11:2): and a root, and drink, and meat, and life; for he says, "I live, yet not I, but Christ lives in me;" (Gal.

---

212. Chrysostom, Homily 10, in *Romans*, NPNF 11:406 (*PG* 60.480).
213. Chrysostom, Homily 15, in *Romans*, NPNF 11:453 (*PG* 60.541).

2:20) and Apostle, and High-Priest, and Teacher, and Father, and Brother, and Joint-heir, and sharer of the tomb and Cross; for it says, "We were buried together with Him," and "planted together in the likeness of His Death" (Rom. 6:4, 5): and a Suppliant; "For we are ambassadors in Christ's stead" (2 Cor. 5:20): and an "Advocate to the Father; for "He also makes," it says, "intercession for us:" (Rom. 8:34) and house and inhabitant;—for He says, "He that abides in Me and I in Him" (John 15:5): and a Friend; for, "Ye are My friends" (John 5: 14): and a Foundation, and Cornerstone. And we are His members and His heritage, and building, and branches, and fellow-workers. For what is there that He is not minded to be to us, when He makes us cleave and fit on to Him in every way? And this is a sign of one loving exceedingly. Be persuaded then, and rousing thee from sleep, put Him on, and when thou hast done so, give your flesh up to His bridle.[214]

This genuine existential change wrought through our sacramental participation in Christ has practical and moral implications. The life of virtue is viewed as a reflection of the transformation that has taken place in one's life. It is against this contextual background that Chrysostom's constant exhortations to his listeners to imitate Christ and live a virtuous life should be viewed. Furthermore, Chrysostom views piety and morality as an art, implying that it has to be learned from a skilled teacher.[215] Therefore the life of Christ is portrayed as a paradigm for the Christian life; he "took flesh from our clay in order that by this means He might teach us virtue."[216] The idea of Christ as an exemplar and teacher whom the Christian is expected to imitate and follow is central to Chrysostom's view of the practice of the Christian life. This relationship between Christ and the Christian is often emphasized in his paraenetic exegesis of John's Gospel.

Christ as Exemplar

Young notes that the idea of *mimesis* was a key concept in ancient literary criticism and an important interpretive feature of scriptural exegesis in the early church. Specifically, the wording and content of the Scriptures were viewed as "mimetic" of divine truths and doctrinal teaching: "In the

---

214. Chrysostom, Homily 24, in *Romans*, NPNF 11:518–19 (*PG* 60.623–24).
215. Chrysostom, Homily 58, in *John*, FOC 41:118–19 (*PG* 59.322).
216. Chrysostom, Homily 70, FOC 41:250 (*PG* 59.381).

ancient Church *mimēsis* or 'representation' was important. It underlay the enactment of the saving events in the sacraments as well as the 'exemplary' use of scripture: great heroes were listed to illustrate a particular virtue, so a character like Job came to embody patience, and Christ's life and death were set forth as ways to be imitated. Such 'mimetic' use of literary heroes reinforced the paraenetic use of scripture . . . and provided 'types.' 'Mimetic exegesis' assumes the replay of a *drama*—an act or plot—and so had a place in forming ethics, lifestyle and liturgy."[217]

Similarly, Cameron observes that early Christian discourse presented its audience with images that were mimetic in intent: "Through lives, Christian writers could present an image not only of the perfect Christian life but also of the life in imitation of Christ, the life that becomes an icon."[218] Mitchell underscores the point that imitation of exemplary figures was central in ancient ethical and pedagogical theory, citing Aristotle's claim that "human beings learn their first lessons by imitation (*Politica* 3.4.2)."[219] That these literary influences shaped Chrysostom's exegesis and preaching is indisputable.[220] The life of Christ is viewed as an icon, a picture, or a model for Christian ethics and practice. However, it must be noted that Chrysostom's preaching on the imitation of Christ and practical morality is grounded in the context of faith and sacramental life. The virtuous and moral life is viewed as a life that is consistent with the existential change that has been wrought in the Christian and is essentially an imitation of the life of Christ. Therefore the life of Christ is viewed as an example for the faithful. Chrysostom's emphasis on Christian praxis suggests that he does not consider our mimetic response to the example set by Christ to be an academic exercise, or a hermeneutical device consistent with the literary theories of his day, but a recognition of a sacramentally mediated transformation that has taken place in the Christian. Further, the reality of Christ's human na-

---

217. Young, *Biblical Exegesis and the Formation of Christian Culture*, 209.

218. Cameron, *Christianity and the Rhetoric of the Empire*, 57.

219. Mitchell, *Heavenly Trumpet*, 50.

220. Commenting along similar lines, Benin helpfully explains that as individuals who profited richly from pagan and Christian learning, both Augustine and Chrysostom appreciated the power and influence of teachers and of pedagogical techniques: "Both viewed God as the teacher, and both were captivated by the divine method of instruction. They saw this method as one of divine accommodation; that is the Lord adapted his lessons and plan to human capacities." See Benin, "Sacrifice as Education in Augustine and Chrysostom," 7.

ture, coupled with the defense of his human experience and the call to imitate him, are integral features of Chrysostom's view of spirituality.[221] Christ was not only consubstantial with the Father but he also entered brotherhood with us and therefore truly identifies with us in every way. The condescension of the incarnation is thus viewed in explicitly pedagogical terms in that Christ's sinless life provides a demonstration of the exemplary Christian life:

> Therefore, since we have been deemed worthy of a greater and more perfect teaching, no longer through Prophets, but through the Son of God preaching to us in these latter days, let us give evidence of a much better life and one more worthy of the honor. It would be strange if, while He condescends to such an extent that He no longer wills to speak to us through servants, but through Himself, we show no greater effects of this than our predecessors. To be sure, they had Moses as instructor, but we have the Lord of Moses. Well, then, let us give evidence of a philosophy [of life] worthy of this honor and let us not have anything in common with the earth. It is for this reason that He has furnished us with teaching from above, from heaven, in order that he may remove our thoughts thither, that we may become imitators of our Teacher according as we are able.[222]

Chrysostom often emphasizes the actions of Christ as exemplary and admonishes his hearers to follow suit. Christ's life is portrayed as a pattern for Christians to imitate. To be a disciple of Christ is to be like him in his meekness and gentleness;[223] Christ's endurance of insults and mockery is viewed as worthy of our imitation;[224] his magnanimity and unselfishness are likewise viewed as commendable examples for us;[225] his simplicity, his experience of hardship, and his disregard for basic needs

---

221. See Chrysostom, Homily 27, in *Genesis*, FOC 87:160 (PG 54.509–10).

222. Chrysostom, Homily 15, in *John*, FOC 33:148 (PG 59.100–101).

223. Chrysostom, Homily 60, FOC 41:142 (PG 59.332). "All virtue is good, but especially that of meekness or gentleness. It proves that we are men; it distinguishes us from wild beasts; it makes us fit to dwell in the company of the angels. That is why Christ repeatedly spoke at some length about this virtue and bade us to be meek and gentle. Moreover, not only did He speak of it, but He also instructed us by His example. At one time He was struck and bore it patiently. At another, He was insulted and plotted against. Yet again, He went forth into the midst of those who were plotting against Him . . . but replied them with great meekness." Homily 61, FOC 41:151 (PG 59.335–36).

224. Chrysostom, Homily 83, FOC 41:414 (PG 59.453).

225. Chrysostom, Homily 15, FOC 33:148 (PG 59.100–101).

are regarded as exemplary virtues;[226] his committing the care of Mary to his disciple from the cross is viewed as a praiseworthy act of making provision for one's parents;[227] his controlled and minimal expression of grief at Lazarus' tomb, his patience and gentleness in dealing with Nicodemus' questions, his willingness to lay down his life and his readiness for death are all viewed as virtues worth emulating in the practice of the Christian life.[228] Illustrating the exemplary character of Christ's earthly life, Chrysostom borrows practical examples from various trades and professions to underscore how Christ concretely demonstrated the virtuous life through his deeds:

> Christ having come to earth wished to instruct men in all virtue: now the instructor teaches not only by word, but also by deed: for this is the teacher's best method of teaching. A pilot for instance when he makes the apprentice sit by his side shows him how he handles the rudder, but he also joins speech to action, and does not depend upon words alone or example alone: in like manner also an architect when he has placed by his side the man who is intended to learn from him how a wall is constructed, shows him the way by means of action as well as by means of oral teaching; so also with the weaver, and embroiderer, and gold refiner, and coppersmith;—and every kind of art has teachers who instruct both orally and practically. Inasmuch Christ Himself came to instruct us in all virtue, He both tells us what ought to be done, and does it. "For," he says, "he who does and teaches the same shall be called great in the kingdom of heaven." Now observe; He commanded men to be lowly-minded, and meek, and He taught this by His words: but see how He also teaches it by His deeds. For having said, "Blessed are the poor in spirit, blessed are the meek," He shows how these virtues ought to be practiced. How then did He teach them? He took a towel and girded Himself and washed his disciples feet. What can match this lowliness of mind? For He teaches this virtue no longer by His words only but also by His deeds.[229]

Like a master pedagogue, Christ has left Christians concrete examples both from his teaching and life in order that we might learn from him.

---

226. Chrysostom, Homily 31, *FOC* 33:304 (*PG* 59.179).

227. Chrysostom, Homily 85, *FOC* 41:431 (*PG* 59.461).

228. Chrysostom, Homily 62, *FOC* 41:176 (*PG* 59.347); Homily 26, *FOC* 33:257 (*PG* 59.156); Homily 83, *FOC* 41:399 (*PG* 59.447).

229. Chrysostom, *Against Marcionites and Manichaens*, *NPNF* 9:206 (*PG* 51.38).

Besides underscoring the reality of the incarnation, Christ's human experience is viewed as all-encompassing, such that his followers could be assured that his life was no different from theirs. His perfect life is an example of virtuous living. Discussing the pedagogical and didactic principle behind the actions of Christ, Chrysostom writes: "The actions performed by Christ in a human way were so performed not merely for the purpose of confirming the incarnation, but also that he might instruct us to virtuous living. For, if he did everything as God, whence would we be able to learn what we ought to do when faced with trials outside the realm of our experience?"[230] Christ in his human nature exemplified the Christian life in the sense that he modeled it for all believers. He demonstrated that virtuous living is possible on the human level. The virtuous life is a reflection of the life of Christ, who became incarnate in order not only to restore human beings from the corruption of death and renew their fellowship with God, but also to empower them through grace and to show them the way to live.

Since the practical Christian life is viewed as an emulation of the life of Christ, his actions are consistently highlighted in Chrysostom's paraenetic exposition. Chrysostom views the occasion of Christ washing his disciples' feet as a particularly apt picture of utter humility: "He who had come from God and was going to Him, He who is the Ruler of all things, performed this action, and thus did not disdain to stoop to such an office."[231] The hands that opened blind eyes, cleansed lepers, and raised people from the dead were also willing to wash feet. Moreover, Chrysostom asserts that if he who is seated on the royal throne washed the traitor's feet, how much more should we humble ourselves and follow his lead.[232] For Chrysostom, the life of virtue is also viewed as our obedient response to, and a demonstration of our relationship with Christ.[233] Commenting on the words of Christ to his disciples in John 13:14 ("If, therefore, I the Lord and Master have washed your feet, you also ought to wash the feet of one another. For I have given you an example, that as I have done to you, so you also should do"), he says: "This precept

---

230. Chrysostom, Homily 49, in *John*, FOC 41:12 (PG 59.273).

231. Chrysostom, Homily 70, FOC 41:253 (PG 59.382).

232. "He who is seated upon the Cherubim washed the traitor's feet, and do you, O man, who are but earth and ashes, and cinders, and dust, magnify yourself and act arrogantly?" Chrysostom, Homily 71, FOC 41:262 (PG 59.386).

233. Chrysostom, Homily 21, FOC 33:210 (PG 59.132).

He recorded not merely with reference to the washing of feet, but also with regard to all the other things in which He gave us His example."[234] Following the example of Christ is perceived as being faithful to his teaching, and this is evidence of our obedience and submission to his Lordship. Christ's condescension in the incarnation is the ultimate picture of humility and the Christian response must be similar. Commenting on Philippians 2:5–8, on the humility of Christ, Chrysostom elaborates:

> What then is humility? To be lowly minded. And he is lowly minded who humbles himself, not he who is lowly by necessity. To explain what I say; and do ye attend; he who is lowly minded, when he has it in his power to be high minded, is humble, but he who is so because he is not able to be high minded, is no longer humble. For instance, If a King subjects himself to his own officer, he is humble, for he descends from his high estate; but if an officer does so, he will not be lowly minded; for how? he has not humbled himself from any high estate. It is not possible to show humble-mindedness except it be in our power to do otherwise. For if it is necessary for us to be humble even against our will, that excellency comes not from the spirit or the will, but from necessity. This virtue is called humble-mindedness, because it is the humbling of the mind.[235]

Moreover, he observes that although Christ left his disciples an example to follow, he recognized that our imitation of his life would not be perfect: "That is why He selected His examples from matters of greater importance: namely, that we might at least accomplish the lesser ones. I say this, for teachers write the letters for children very beautifully, so that they may attain to at least an imperfect imitation."[236] The life of Christ is viewed as a pattern for our imitation, and the virtuous Christian life is our response to the archetype provided by his life. By portraying Christ as an instructor and a teacher whose exemplary human life set a standard for us, Chrysostom seems to suggest that our endeavor to imitate him is a reflection of an abiding relationship between two living subjects: Christ the teacher and the Christian disciple. A follower of Christ, therefore, is expected to be Christ-like. The life of virtue is the external reflection of the inner transformation, and evidence that the Christian is conformed to Christ both internally and externally. In this respect the Christian life

---

234. Chrysostom, Homily 60, *FOC* 41:149 (*PG* 59.335).
235. Chrysostom, Homily 6, in *Philippians*, *NPNF* 13:208 (*PG* 62.221).
236. Chrysostom, Homily 71, in *John*, *FOC* 41:260 (*PG* 59.385).

The Christian Life as a Life of Faith and Virtue

Chrysostom underscores faith in God as a *sine qua non* in the process of salvation and transformation, noting that it is the means by which God's promises are appropriated.[237] He depicts faith as the mother of all virtues, the medicine of salvation, and a sacred anchor.[238] Divine assistance precedes one's faith in Christ; the soul has to be drawn to Christ by God.[239] Our union with Christ begins with faith, and nothing can be done without the power of Christ; therefore one must be "united to Him by faith as the branch is to the vine."[240] Chrysostom maintained that Christ is the light who becomes present through faith.[241] He came not only to pardon, but also to remit sins and provide salvation by faith,[242] for he is "the author and finisher of [our] faith" (Heb 12:2).[243] Moreover, Chrysostom affirms that "faith is a great blessing, then, when it proceeds from a fervent mind, from great love, and a zealous soul. It shows that we are practical Christians."[244] He insists that Christianity requires both "correctness of doctrine and an upright life."[245]

237. Chrysostom, Homily 87, FOC 41:460 (PG 59.473–74). Commenting on Romans 3:27–31, he asserts that the law of faith is to be saved through grace. See Homily 7, in *Romans*, NPNF 11:379 (PG 60.446).

238. Chrysostom, Homily 33, in *John*, FOC 33:322 (PG 59.187). "It is impossible to be saved otherwise than by faith." Chrysostom, Homily 8, in *Romans*, NPNF 11:385 (PG 60.453).

239. Chrysostom, Homily 45, in *John*, FOC 33:455–56 (PG 59.254).

240. Chrysostom, Homily 76, FOC 41:317 (PG 59.411).

241. Chrysostom, Homily 5, FOC 33:67 (PG 59.58).

242. Chrysostom, Homily 28, FOC 33:272 (PG 59.164).

243. Chrysostom, Homily 77, FOC 41:333 (PG 59.418).

244. Chrysostom, Homily 63, FOC 41:185–186 (PG 59.352). Chrysostom occasionally speaks of the Christian life as philosophy. He refers to faith in God as true philosophy as opposed to pagan philosophy: "Philosophy is a very good thing—I mean, of course, our philosophy. Pagan philosophy, to be sure, is merely talk and fables and not even the fables themselves possess any trace of true wisdom. In fact, all their teachings are uttered with a view to worldly pride." Ibid., FOC 41:179; 185–187 (PG 59.349; 352f.). For a brief overview of Chrysostom's understanding of Christian philosophy, see Packard, "Chrysostom's True Christian Philosophy."

245. Chrysostom, Homily 28, in *John*, FOC 33:272 (PG 59.164).

For Chrysostom faith in God is not a mere verbal confession, but a way of life. He holds that the practical Christian life is a reflection of one's faith in operation: "Therefore, since the profession [of our love for God] by words alone, and the denial of it by deeds, is not merely senseless but even harmful to us, I beseech you, let us make our confession by deeds, in order that we likewise may obtain acknowledgment from Him in that day when He will confess before His Father those who deserve it."[246] When speaking on the external proof of one's faith, Chrysostom often repeated Christ's words from the Sermon on the Mount, which stress the point that true disciples are recognized by the fruit they bear and that not everyone who merely confesses and calls him Lord will enter the kingdom of God (Matt 7:21f.):

> "Is it not, therefore, enough to believe in the Son." you will say, "to have eternal life?" By no means. Listen to Christ making this point clear by saying: "Not everyone who says to me, 'Lord, Lord,' shall enter into the kingdom of heaven." Furthermore, blasphemy against the Spirit is sufficient, even of itself, to cast into hell. But why do I mention only part of the doctrine? Even if one believes in an orthodox manner in the Father and the Son and the Holy Spirit, but does not live a moral life, he does not gain profit from his faith for his salvation.[247]

The comprehension and belief of proper doctrine needs to be coupled with application; orthodoxy should lead to orthopraxy. One of the hallmarks of Chrysostom's ethical teaching is the insistence that the "orthodoxy of faith is of no profit if one's life is corrupt."[248] Chrysostom's view of saving faith was that it had to be exemplified by virtue and good deeds in the life of the individual.[249] An unethical life is viewed as being inconsistent with the teachings of Christ and does not accurately reflect true faith in God: "See to it that we, also, while we glory in the true Faith, do not dishonor God by failing to give the example of a life in accordance with our faith, and so cause Him to be blasphemed. And I say this for He wishes the Christian to be a teacher of the world, its 'leaven,' and 'light,' and 'salt.'"[250] The doxological emphases of Chrysostom's preaching on

---

246. Chrysostom, Homily 20, *FOC* 33:201 (*PG* 59.128).
247. Chrysostom, Homily 31, *FOC* 33:297 (*PG* 59.176).
248. Chrysostom, Homily 63, *FOC* 41:187 (*PG* 59.352).
249. Chrysostom, Homily 84, *FOC* 41:425 (*PG* 59.458).
250. Chrysostom, Homily 52, *FOC* 41:53 (*PG* 59.292).

the Christian life can be summarized by his pleas to his congregation to glorify God not just by their faith, but also by their life and their works.[251]

Depictions of the Virtuous Life

Chrysostom portrays the Christian life as a journey or a voyage to heaven. He depicts the true Christian as an ambitious merchant who is not satisfied with merely thinking about his business plans, but actually does something about them. He prepares a ship, gathers a crew, hires a pilot, and sets off across the sea, enduring many dangers. He is even willing to suffer other risks in order to realize his ambition.[252] There is no room for either epistemic complacency or spiritual indifference in the practice of the Christian life. Moreover, the ship of the Christian life needs the help of the seasoned pilot (Christ) or else it will be shipwrecked on the shoals of hypocrisy and the rocks of dead faith. He elaborates:

> We also are sailing on a voyage, not from one land to another but from earth to heaven. Therefore, let us prepare our reasoning power as a pilot fit to conduct us on high, and let us gather a crew obedient to it. Let us fit out a strong ship, of the kind that will not be submerged by the buffeting and discouragements of this life, nor raised up by the wind of false pretense, but will be sleek and swift. If we thus prepare the ship, thus the pilot and the crew, we shall sail with a favoring wind, and shall draw to ourselves the Son of God, the true Pilot. He will not permit our bark to be overwhelmed; even if countless winds blow, He will rebuke the winds and the sea and will bring about a great calm in place of the tempest.[253]

The voyage of the Christian life can be successful only if Christ the pilot accompanies and guides us towards our eschatological union with God. Therefore the grace of God plays a crucial role in the progress and completion of this journey. Moreover, Chrysostom affirmed that virtuous living was the result of godly wisdom applied in one's life, rendering the Christian merciful, kind, gentle, and refined: "Nothing makes men so wise as virtue." Furthermore, "Virtuous living is really the root

---

251. Chrysostom, Homily 67, *FOC* 41:233 (*PG* 59.374); Homily 46, *FOC* 33:472 (*PG* 59.262).

252. Chrysostom, Homily 86, *FOC* 41:454 (*PG* 59.471). Cf. Homily 87, *FOC* 41:465 (*PG* 59.476).

253. Chrysostom, Homily 1, *FOC* 33:9–10 (*PG* 59.28).

and source of all wisdom, just as wickedness had its source in folly."[254] Moreover, those who practice it enjoy its blessings not just in this life, but also in heaven. Chrysostom consistently exhorts his hearers to apply themselves to good works in order that they may obtain their future crown.[255] He also urged his hearers to "clothe themselves with it," implying that the practical Christian life is a virtuous life.[256]

Chrysostom considered charity (*agapē*) the basis of all virtue and referred to it as the distinctive mark of saintly men.[257] "Love is the chief blessing of them all. In it all blessings have their root and source and mother. If there is no love, other blessings profit nothing. Love is the mark of the Lord's disciples; it stamps the servants of God. By it we recognize his apostles. Christ said: 'This is how all will know you for my disciples.'"[258] Further, he asserted that loving concern for one's neighbor was particularly pleasing to God, an office which Christ asked of Peter: "There are many virtues which can make us pleasing to God and cause us to appear illustrious and worthy of esteem, but the one that more especially wins favor from on high is loving concern for the welfare of our neighbor."[259] The Christ-like virtues of humility and gentleness are described by Chrysostom as the very foundation of the Christian life:

> The example of Moses demonstrates how great a virtue this is, for it made him the kind of man he was and as great as he was. Truly, there is nothing equal to humility. For this reason Christ began the Beatitudes with this virtue. In the manner of one who intends to set in place the foundation stone and firm basis for a very large building, so He has set humility in first place. Indeed, without it, it is not possible—it is not possible, I repeat—to be saved; but even if one fasts, prays and gives alms, if he does so with a proud spirit, all these are trifling and foolishly done, since this virtue is not present.[260]

---

254. Chrysostom, Homily 41, *FOC* 33:422 (*PG* 59.238).

255. Chrysostom, Homily 40, *FOC* 33:414 (*PG* 59.234).

256. Chrysostom, Homily 85, *FOC* 41:445 (*PG* 59.468).

257. Chrysostom, Homily 72, *FOC* 41:278–79 (*PG* 59.394).

258. Chrysostom, Homily 1, section 5, *On the Incomprehensible Nature of God*, *FOC* 72:52 (*PG* 48.701–2).

259. Chrysostom, Homily 88, in *John*, *FOC* 41:470 (*PG* 59.477).

260. Chrysostom, Homily 33, *FOC* 33:329–30 (*PG* 59.192).

These virtues were not just verbally expressed and preached by Christ, but were exemplified and demonstrated by him as well.²⁶¹ So with us, the message of the Word has to be enfleshed in the life of obedience and practice.²⁶²

The virtue that is most often underscored in Chrysostom's preaching, in general, and in his homilies on the Gospel of John, in particular, is that of ἐλεημοσύνην (*eleēmosynēn*), translated variously as almsgiving, mercy, or charity.²⁶³ In contrast to vainglory (*kenodoxia*), he admonishes his flock to be benevolent to the needy, saying, "Do you wish to enjoy real glory? Practice charity; then the angels will praise you; then God will give you approval."²⁶⁴ Chrysostom views *eleēmosynē* as a practical way of demonstrating repentance and a beneficial remedy for the sinful soul. Almsgiving and charity to the poor are viewed as ways to demonstrate the love of God and as a reflection of the work of grace in the life of the Christian. Divine forgiveness follows human repentance and true generosity of the heart reflects that gift. God's *eleēmosynē* towards the Christian in turn demands the same attitude towards the needy: "If indeed you wish to reconcile the Lord to you, show Him the evidence of your deeds: become acquainted with the debris of misfortunes; take note of the naked, the hungry, those suffering injustice. He has created for you countless ways of loving your neighbor."²⁶⁵ In Chrysostom's view, all *eleēmosynē* extended to the poor is done unto Christ and therefore is done in response to and in acknowledgment of his goodness: "Let us not seek for more, but expend all our possessions on the needy. Indeed, what excuse shall we have when He Himself promises heaven to us, and we give Him not even a loaf? What excuse, when He makes his sun rise on you and furnishes you with the service of all creation, while you do not even give Him a garment, or share your dwelling with Him? . . . He has given His body to you, and His precious Blood, and do you not even provide Him with a drink of water?"²⁶⁶

261. Chrysostom, Homily 61, *FOC* 41:151 (*PG* 59.335).

262. Chrysostom, Homily 82, *FOC* 41:396 (*PG* 59.446).

263. In his ninety sermons on Matthew, Chrysostom mentions ἐλεημοσύνην about forty times. See Baur, *John Chrysostom and His Time*, 1:217. In his eighty-eight homilies on John, Chrysostom mentions ἐλεημοσύνην some twenty-five times.

264. Chrysostom, Homily 69, in *John, FOC* 41:248 (*PG* 59.380).

265. Chrysostom, Homily, 73, *FOC* 41:288 (*PG* 59.398).

266. Chrysostom, Homily 77, *FOC* 41:336 (*PG* 59.419). Cf. Homily 27, *FOC* 33:265 (*PG* 59.160).

Of all the sins that Chrysostom preached against, vainglory (*kenodoxia*) tends to be singled out for his vitriolic invective. One of his favorite adjectives to deplore sins was the word *terrible* (δεινὸν), and he employed it to describe all evils. He denounced vainglory as a "terrible thing" (δεινὸν ἡ κενοδοξία, δεινὸν), with the following caveat to his listeners: "Let us then flee from this beast above all. For it has many colors and shapes, and spreads its peculiar poison everywhere: in riches, and in luxury, and in beauty of body."[267] Chrysostom stressed that vainglory was a passion that was more despotic than other evils[268] and remarked that greed, desire for wealth, hatred, enmity, and quarrels are different manifestations of it. He called it the cause of all evils[269] and a plague that is capable of destroying any virtue that one might possess.[270] He often urged his hearers to flee from the love of glory and empty praise with much zeal and earnestness.[271] He pleaded with his hearers to not fall prey to this vice and illustrated its destructive qualities thus:

> The love of glory is a terrible thing, terrible and prolific of many evils. It is a kind of thorn, hard to remove; or a wild beast, impossible to tame; a many-headed monster, taking up arms against the very ones who feed it. Just as the worm gnaws through the wood by which it is generated, and the rust feeds on the iron whence it proceeds, and moths feed on wool, so also does vainglory destroy the soul that feeds it. Wherefore we must be very much in earnest if we are to get rid of this disease.[272]

Besides vainglory, Chrysostom preached against the love of wealth and the deceit of riches, both of which he believed to be inconsistent with the ethos of the Christian lifestyle.[273] He explicitly denounced extravagant funerals held by rich families in Antioch. He reproved them by asking them to cease from the "senseless and exaggerated care of the dead" and urged them to bury the departed in a way that glorified God.[274] Similarly, covetousness, anger, envy, and pride were common

---

267. Chrysostom, Homily 69, *FOC* 41:248 (*PG* 59.380).
268. Chrysostom, Homily 28, *FOC* 33:276 (*PG* 59.166).
269. Chrysostom, Homily 29, *FOC* 33:286 (*PG* 59.170).
270. Chrysostom, Homily 38, *FOC* 33:382 (*PG* 59.218).
271. Ibid.
272. Chrysostom, Homily 30, *FOC* 33:288 (*PG* 59.171).
273. Chrysostom, Homily 24, *FOC* 33:241 (*PG* 59.148); Homily 74, *FOC* 33:298 (*PG* 59.403).
274. Chrysostom, Homily 85, *FOC* 41:444 (*PG* 59.467).

unchristian attitudes that bore the brunt of Chrysostom's moral preaching. He described covetousness as a terrible vice.[275] He called anger a terrible beast and a strong fire consuming all things, corrupting the soul.[276] He taught that envy was a terrible thing, which reeked with pretense and had filled the world with innumerable evils.[277] Pride, in his view, was the mother of all evils; it estranges those who possess it from the mercy of God and gives them over to the fire of hell.[278]

Chrysostom did not shy away from preaching about social evils that enticed the members of his church. He urged his hearers not to frequent the theaters and dances, and implored them to stay away from prostitutes.[279] He chided his listeners for their apathetic attitude in church and scriptural teaching, in contrast to the excitement they gained from public entertainments: "If a musician, or a dancer, or anyone else connected with the theater should summon them to the city, they all hurry eagerly, and thank the one who invited them, and spend an entire half a day with their attention fixed on the performer exclusively. Yet when God addresses us through prophets and Apostles, we yawn, get bored and become drowsy."[280] At a time when chariot races were a popular entertainment for the masses—including the people in his congregation who patronized them by flocking to the hippodrome, even in inhospitable and inclement conditions—Chrysostom rebukes his hearers for not displaying similar devotion in regard to assembling in church where there was a "roof over their head and the temperature is admirable."[281] Furthermore, he asserts that with regard to unhelpful knowledge of horses and chariots, some of his hearers "can compose a discourse more cleverly than sophists or rhetors," yet when it comes to aspects of scriptural and spiritual knowledge like the names of prophets, the essentials of salvation, and what it means to be a Christian, they are ignorant.[282]

---

275. Chrysostom, Homily 65, *FOC* 41:211 (*PG* 59.365).

276. Chrysostom, Homily 4, *FOC* 33:56 (*PG* 59.52).

277. Chrysostom, Homily 64, *FOC* 41:202 (*PG* 59.359).

278. Chrysostom, Homily 9, *FOC* 33:194 (*PG* 59.72).

279. Chrysostom, Homily 87, *FOC* 41:469 (*PG* 59.478). Cf. Homily 74, *FOC* 41:298 (*PG* 59.402).

280. Chrysostom, Homily 58, *FOC* 41:116 (*PG* 59.320).

281. Ibid.

282. Chrysostom, Homily 58, *FOC* 41:116–17 (*PG* 59.320).

There are two favorite pericopes that recur in Chrysostom's preaching on the Christian life in general: the parable of the Ten Virgins (Matt 25:1–13) and the Final Judgment (Matt 25:31–46).[283] These are often cited in the moral application section at the end of the homily. Chrysostom commonly resorts to these passages in his homilies on John's Gospel, especially when he wants to stress the continual need of seeking God's grace in order to live the Christian life. Capitalizing on the theme of the forethought of the five wise virgins, Chrysostom often emphasizes the need for the Christian's willing participation in showing goodwill to the poor in order to receive God's sustaining grace. He says, "If we will it, we shall make even brighter that light which we received as soon as we received the grace of the Spirit, but, if we are not willing to do so, we shall quickly lose it. When it has gone out, there will be nothing else but darkness in our soul."[284] He interprets the oil in the lamp as *eleēmosynē* and admonishes his hearers to keep bright their lamps (which he associates with purity and holiness)[285] by practicing charity and being generous to the needy:

> It is by this means that the brightness of this fire is preserved. Let us, then, put oil in our vessels as long as we are here. It is not possible to buy it when we have taken our departure hence, or to receive it from any source other than the hands of the poor. Let us, therefore, collect it from there in great abundance, that is, if we wish to enter in with the bridegroom; if we do not do this, we must remain outside the bridal chamber. It is impossible, I repeat, even if we perform countless good works, to enter the portals of the kingdom without charity [ἐλεημοσύνης].[286]

He warns his congregation that the unwise virgins had oil in their lamps, but not enough, and therefore they were not able enjoy the company of the bridegroom.[287] In acts of mercy and charity to the needy, the Christian's true piety shines forth brightly. Employing similar imagery, Chrysostom discusses the practical implications of being made sons through Christ. He observes that as sons we glorify the Father by let-

---

283. He refers to Matthew 25:31–36 as the "most delightful portion of Scripture," which he often mentions in his preaching. Chrysostom, Homily 79, in *Matthew*, NPNF 10:470 (PG 58.717).

284. Chrysostom, Homily 50, in *John*, FOC 41:32–33 (PG 59.282).

285. Chrysostom, Homily 78, in *Matthew*, NPNF 10:470 (PG 58.711).

286. Chrysostom, Homily 23, in *John*, FOC 33:231 (PG 59.144).

287. Chrysostom, Homily 77, FOC 41:336 (PG 59.420).

ting the light of the virtuous life shine brightly through acts of charity. Furthermore, the virtuous life is portrayed as a lamp with a glowing flame, reflecting an ample supply of oil. It has been rightly suggested that Chrysostom might be using a play on the words for mercy (ἔλεον) and oil (ἔλαιον) in this particular instance:

> To give the proper glory to God, and it is the proper kind [if given] not in words only but much rather in deed. "Let your light shine before men," Scripture says, "in order that they may see your good works and give glory to your Father in heaven (Matt. 5:18)." Indeed, nothing is more productive of light, beloved, than a virtuous life. One of the wise men also affirms this as follows: "The ways of the just shine as the light (Prov. 4:18)." And they shine not only for those men themselves who kindle the light by their deeds and act as beacons on the straight path, but also for their neighbors. Well, then, let us pour out oil [ἔλαιον] for these lamps so that the flame may become higher, so that the light may appear richer. This oil not only has great strength now, but, even at the time when the offering of sacrifices was highly approved, its efficacy was commended more highly than theirs by far, for God said: "I desire mercy [ἔλεον] and not sacrifice (Hos. 6:6)," and with good reason. That altar was lifeless, and this is living. Moreover, there, all that was lying thereon was consumed by the fire and ended in cinders and was dispersed in ashes and the smoke perished in the substance of the air; here, on the contrary, not so, but it bears other fruits.[288]

The virtuous Christian life is the external proof of the inward spiritual work; the gift of grace must be complemented by virtue in order to ensure that the supply of God's grace for the ongoing Christian life does not cease. The reception of grace is continual, and the practice of virtue plays an important role in this active process. For Chrysostom, the progressive transformation of human nature by grace through Christ is correspondingly reflected in the continual moral life of the Christian.

Closely connected to the parable of the virgins are the words of Christ in Matthew 25:31–46, where he refers to his coming at the end of the age where he is portrayed as a shepherd who separates the sheep from the goats, the righteous from the unrighteous. The difference be-

288. Chrysostom, Homily 13, FOC 33:128 (PG 59.90). Goggin notes that the Greek words ἔλεον (mercy) and ἔλαιον (oil) were pronounced the same way in Chrysostom's day. It is likely that Chrysostom intended his audience to make the association between "mercy" and the "oil of virtue"—that God desires the oil of virtue and not sacrifice. See FOC 33:128.

tween the righteous and the unrighteous is that the righteous reached out and showed kindness to the needy by caring for them, whereas the unrighteous failed to do so. Commending the benevolence and generosity of the righteous, Christ will say: "I tell you the truth, whatever you did for one of the least of these brothers of mine, you did for me." Condemning the unrighteous, he will state: "I tell you the truth, whatever you did not do for one of the least of these, you did not do for me." Behind Chrysostom's persistent philanthropic appeal to his flock to care for the needy, be generous to the poor, feed the hungry, give the homeless shelter, and be charitable to the underprivileged is the conviction that in so doing one is actually serving Christ, the ultimate judge, who will reward the righteous and punish the unrighteous. Moreover, by recognizing Christ in the poor and responding to his appeal through them, the Christian in turn secures God's benevolence and forgiveness. "Therefore, in order that we may hear these words (Matt 25:35–36), let us clothe the naked, let us take in the stranger, let us feed the hungry, let us give drink to the thirsty, let us visit the sick, let us go to see the prisoner, in order that we may receive the fulfillment of His pledge and pardon our sins, and may share in those blessings which are too great for speech or thought."[289] According to Chrysostom, it is not the measure of the contribution that matters the most in God's opinion; it is the measure of one's goodwill that God notices.[290] Bridging the themes from his two favorite passages on the virtuous Christian life, he underlines their common message of the need of God's grace, and, in turn, of the Christian's willingness in seeking it by living a charitable life that will glorify God. He observes: "When we do not recognize the hungry Christ, He will not recognize us when we are without oil, and rightly so. Indeed, if a man ignores a person in distress and does not give him what he has, how will he expect to receive in his turn what is not his? Therefore, I beseech you, let us conduct all our affairs and expend every effort so that the oil may not fail us, but we may fill our lamps and go to the marriage with the Bridegroom."[291]

In Chrysostom's view, faith in God and the life of virtue are inseparable; there cannot be one without the other. His emphases on deeds and good works arise from his conviction that the Christian life is a reflection of the exemplary life of Christ. The virtuous Christian life is a Christ-

289. Chrysostom, Homily 59, *FOC* 41:132–33 (*PG* 59.328).
290. Chrysostom, Homily 74, *FOC* 41:299 (*PG* 59.404).
291. Chrysostom, Homily 50, *FOC* 41:32–33 (*PG* 59.282).

indwelt life. To be clothed with Christ is to be conformed to his image and likeness, with existential implications for the here and now. Thus the idea of the Christian's participation in Christ and transformation by grace is the undergirding theme in Chrysostom's preaching on the practical Christian life.

The Christological Implications of Chrysostom's View of Christ as Exemplar

Chrysostom's portraiture of Christ as our exemplar suggests that he views the reality of Christ's human experience as integral to his Christology. In particular, he emphasizes the Son's double consubstantiality with the Father and us. The Word became flesh and experienced life as a human being not only to restore, redeem, and transform humanity, but also to show us the way to live in the here and now. Furthermore, in Chrysostom's view, humanity experienced a drastic change after the incarnation. Before it our flesh was easy prey to the assaults of sin, but after Christ the struggle for virtue became easy, since we now have his assistance and example.[292] The virtuous Christian life is possible because Christ's life in the flesh freed humanity from its bondage of sin and released it to experience life to the full.

Christ's life and ministry did make a difference for believers; the empowerment that we receive through grace enables us to live a transformed life. The Christian life is not just about our participation in the mysteries and looking forward to the eschatological hope of communion with God, but also about embodying the teaching and example left by Christ. Christ is consubstantial with the Father and us. Therefore he can identify with us in his humanity. His perfect life is viewed as an exemplary paradigm for us and thus he is variously portrayed as our teacher and example. The condescension of the incarnation itself is viewed as a picture of humility in that God became man and experienced life as a human being. The one who is described as the Judge, Ruler, and the Lord of Moses, humbled himself to the point of suffering the indignity of being mocked, insulted, mistreated, and crucified. His meekness, humility, simplicity, patience, graciousness, generosity, and benevolence are not viewed as mere mannerisms to be mimicked, but are regarded as commendable virtues worthy of our imitation. As our instructor in virtuous

---

292. Chrysostom, Homily 11, *NPNF* 11:411 (*PG* 60.487–88).

living, Christ leads the way; as the pilot of the ship of the Christian life, he charts the course and guides it to its destination.

The existential transformation wrought through Christ precedes our imitation of him in our lives. Our conformity and identity with Christ both have practical ramifications. As sons who have been conformed to Christ's likeness, in whom the divine image has been renewed, we have now been clothed with virtue because Christ is in us. The virtuous Christian life is the external evidence of the inward spiritual renewal because Christ is formed in us. Our identity with Christ is manifested in the practice and is a response to our sacramental union with him. Chrysostom's pastoral, practical, moral, and ethical exhortations to his congregation are framed around the canvas of the Christian life, which is a reflection of the example left by Christ. As the Word became flesh, so must doctrine be enfleshed in application. In Chrysostom's view, theology and application, doctrine and practice, faith and virtuous living are inseparable. In the final analysis, the picture of Christ that emerges in Chrysostom's preaching on John's Gospel is a reflection of his understanding of the practical Christian life.

Conclusion

The christological picture that develops from the three perspectives of *restoration, participation,* and *practice* is thus framed around the life of faith in a sacramental and ecclesiastical context. Chrysostom's pastoral theology colors his picture of Christ and highlights the relationship between divine philanthropy and divine economy. This is apparent in the depictions of his christological thought which emphasize God's initiative in restoring humankind from the corruption of sin, giving them the privilege of enjoying divine communion, and enabling them to live a life consistent with the existential transformation that has taken place in the Christian. The paraenetic nature of Chrysostom's exegesis invariably produces a doctrine that is praxeological in nature. His preaching on the Christian life is superimposed on his christological thought and therefore these two aspects must be viewed together. The imagery employed in conveying the soteriological, sacramental, and practical aspects of Chrysostom's christological thought in the Fourth Gospel highlights the Son's consubstantiality and equality with the Father. Furthermore, Chrysostom's view of the personal continuity of the Logos in Christ points to the fact that he maintains the Logos as the personal subject in Christ. This unitive christological thought leads Chrysostom to view Christ as the source of life, grace, and virtue. In restoring and reestablishing human nature through the incarnation, the Son rescues humankind from corruption and mortality, and makes it possible for us to enjoy eternal life. By entering into brotherhood with us and enabling us to participate in the divine life, he gives us by grace what he enjoys by nature. Through his sacramental presence in the mysteries we have been renewed, reformed, and conformed to his likeness by being made the sons of God. Through our sacramentally mediated union with Christ, we enjoy the propitiatory benefits of his victory over death and are given the privilege of divine fellowship.

Our union with Christ, the head of the church, has practical implications for life in an ecclesiastical context. The virtuous Christian life is viewed as an icon of a Christ-indwelt life. For Chrysostom the sacramental participation in the mysteries and the practical Christian life are interrelated and viewed as complementary. The invisible is reflected in the visible, and the mysterious in the practical; in both cases, the former precedes the latter. The restoration and renewal has existential consequences for the individual, for the ethical life is but a proof of the Christian's active faith. The sacramental life is represented as life in Christ, and the practical Christian life is understood as reflection of the life of Christ. He is viewed as our teacher who leads the way for us and as a pilot who steps alongside as our navigator. Christ's sacramental presence in the church, along with the Holy Spirit's influence and work in the Christian, are reflected in Chrysostom's portraiture of the church as a spiritual clinic where the wounds of sin are healed and its stains cleansed. The church is also pictured as a perfumery where a visitor is scented with fragrant smell regardless of whether the person is wiling or aware of it; the sacramental and ecclesiastical participation makes an objective difference in the life of the believer.[293] The sacramental life and the virtuous Christian life both have Christ as their center; he is viewed as the very personification of grace and virtue. As the eternal Son, he enables us to enjoy fellowship with God as sons. As an exemplar he models the Christian life for us. And as the fountain and root of virtue he gives us the grace to live a virtuous life. Chrysostom's picture of Christ, therefore, is better appreciated when viewed from the perspective of the life of faith in a sacramental and ecclesiastical context.

293. Chrysostom, Homily 2, in *John*, FOC 33:25 (PG 59.36); Homily 53, FOC 41:61–62 (PG 59.295).

4

The Doctrine of Christ in Chrysostom's Homilies on Hebrews

Introduction

Continuing with the theme of the picture of Christ in Chrysostom's preaching, the objective of the present chapter is to examine its development in his exegetical homilies on Hebrews. The previous chapter underscored the importance of studying Chrysostom's Christology in the context of the life and faith of the church, and argued that Chrysostom's expositional portrait of Christ is colored by his understanding of the Christian life. Likewise, the assertion of this chapter is that Chrysostom's christological picture in his preaching on Hebrews is best viewed in the context in which it originates. The perspectives that emerge in his commentary on Hebrews are pastoral in nature and cannot be bifurcated from his understanding of the church's worship and the Christian life. The picture of Christ that develops in his exposition is unitive and incorporates the rich christological imagery of the epistle. In keeping with the threefold analytical structure (ontological considerations, sacramental mediation, and practical outworking), I shall survey Chrysostom's christological portrait in Hebrews from three perspectives: a *Christology of Identification*, where Christ's Sonship and brotherhood with us is depicted in the context of his human nature, suffering, and death; a *Christology of Mediation*, where the Christ's sacerdotal role as our high priest is illustrated in the context of his heavenly ministry; and a *Christology of Grace*, where Christ is viewed as the author and finisher of our faith and the Christ-likeness of the believer is portrayed in the context of the practical Christian life.

Contextual Overview

A Brief Survey of Scholarship on John Chrysostom's Exegesis of Hebrews

The dominant thrust of the scholarly readings of Chrysostom's christological exegesis of Hebrews labels it as being typically Antiochene. Hardly any focus is put on the doctrinal framework that undergirds this preaching on the Christian life. Greer's study of Antiochene exegesis of Hebrews presupposes that Chrysostom's commentary is essentially similar to his fellow pupil Theodore. He even argues that Chrysostom's Christology is Antiochene in nature because of the emphasis on the moral aspects of the Christian life. This is said to betray an assumed Man Christology. Such a Christology underscores the cooperation of the free will of the assumed Man with the divine will of Word: "The incarnation is totally the work of God, but that work could never have been effective had not the free will of the assumed Man allied him with the divine purpose."[1] Greer deduces the aforementioned conclusion from Chrysostom's use of double predication when speaking of Christ and artificially imposes an "assumed Man" concept wherever Chrysostom speaks of Christ's humanity in his exegesis of Hebrews.[2] Moreover, Greer contends that Chrysostom's understanding of salvation in moral terms, with its emphasis on the life of virtue, excludes the idea of divinization in his theology. "Chrysostom prefers to conceive salvation in moral than metaphysical terms. That is, the perfection of man as a moral creature more than it is the transformation of his nature. Certainly, despite Chrysostom's use of philosophical categories attendant upon the notion of mutability, he never regards salvation as the divinization of man's nature."[3] My contention that reading Chrysostom's exegesis without reference to its context can be misleading, and therefore unappreciated, is reflected in Greer's conclusion. He writes that Chrysostom nowhere develops a "satisfactory Christology" in his exegesis of Hebrews, and that much of what he says has no "explicit basis in the text of the epistle. But one must give him credit for attempting to

---

1. Greer, "Antiochene Exegesis of Hebrews," 22.

2. For instance, commenting on Chrysostom's exegesis of Heb 1:2ff., Greer asserts, "What Chrysostom seems to mean is that the Word is Son by nature, and the assumed Man Son by grace, and that through the incarnation there is but one Son." Ibid., 49.

3. Ibid., 37–38.

preserve in more careful language the religious insights of the text. Thus the strong double judgment of Hebrews regarding Christ's person finds expression in Chrysostom's double predication."[4]

In a later revised publication of his work, Greer seems to have altered his views slightly, admitting that there are instances in Chrysostom's exegesis of Hebrews where the "absence of the assumed Man is most severely felt." However, this absence "introduces a considerable degree of confusion and obscurity into his thought." Yet, Greer maintains that Chrysostom's exegesis and Christology must be viewed in reference to the classical Antiochene exegesis presented by Theodore, and wherever he departs from the Antiochene line he does so deliberately in order "to avoid controversy."[5]

Discussing christological ideas in Greek commentaries on Hebrews both from Alexandrian and Antiochene perspectives, Young categorizes Chrysostom's homilies on Hebrews as typical of the Antiochene commentaries which focus on the theme of Christ's human achievement of obedience through temptation and suffering. In other words, the exemplary nature of Christ's human struggle and triumph is highlighted in the work of salvation. This is in contrast to Cyril, who speaks of the pre-incarnate Logos and the post-incarnate Logos (and not of the distinction between the Logos and Man) in order to safeguard the unity of Christ's person. Although the presupposition of the commentators is the Nicene Faith, where the idea of any change or improvement in the person of Christ through the incarnation is inconceivable, Young remarks that Cyril concentrates on the "invincible activity of divine power, the injection of divinity into humanity, while Chrysostom underscores the exemplary power of human suffering and the achievement of human victory over sin."[6] Furthermore, Young points out that whereas Cyril's anxiety to safeguard the unity of Christ "tended to underplay the suffering apart from the physical aspects which he could attribute to the flesh alone, Chrysostom emphasizes his experience of the human condition to such an extent that he is obliged to separate the Logos from it; this is the only way he knows of safeguarding both the reality of Christ's involvement, and the divine nature of the Logos."[7]

4. Ibid., 59–60; 74.

5. Greer, *Captain of Our Salvation*, 289, 291.

6. Young, "Christological Ideas in the Greek Commentaries on the Epistle to the Hebrews," 150–63.

7. Ibid., 157.

Young also finds Chrysostom's understanding of Christ's sacrifice for sin, and his attribution of our salvation to the love of God, as reflecting a Christology that is typically Antiochene in character. It is said to be such in the sense that the human nature (which functions as mediator) and the divine nature (as one sitting on the throne) are divided, consequently implying a division of will and purpose, and thus a division in Christ's person. She concludes: "Chrysostom wants to attribute salvation to the love of God dealing with sin, and yet he assumes that the sacrifice offered by the Man, Christ, propitiates the wrath of God, the Father. Father and Son are apparently divided, but since he consistently speaks of the High Priesthood of Christ being a function of his Manhood, while his sitting on the throne of judgment is a function of his Divinity, the implication is an uncomfortable division between God and Man within the Person of Christ himself."[8] Essentially, Young makes the point that Chrysostom's Christology is divisive in nature and is therefore consistent with Antiochene Christology.

In his study of the human experience of Christ and the salvation of man among Antiochene theologians, Wallace-Hadrill notes that "it was the Letter to the Hebrews that the Antiochenes turned especially for assurance of God's presence with them in the tribulations of this present age, and for assurance of salvation in the age to come."[9] He also makes an important observation in regard to the Antiochene emphasis on the reality of Christ's humanity as a means of opposing Gnostic docetism. He rightly observes that "Gnostic docetism had been the enemy in the early second century as it was in the fourth, and the defence of the human experience of Christ was the perennial preoccupation of Antiochene theologians."[10] Moreover, Wallace-Hadrill surmises that the emphasis on the reality of Christ's humanity and his brotherhood with mankind were well suited to the humanist tendency of Antiochene Christianity and "to its passionate rejection of Gnostic docetism."[11]

The aforementioned studies on Chrysostom's exegesis of Hebrews presuppose Chrysostom's Christology to be Antiochene in nature and study it in light of the Antiochene christological thought of his contemporaries, without much qualification. Scholars like Greer and Young

8. Ibid., 159.
9. Wallace-Hadrill, *Christian Antioch*, 151.
10. Ibid., 118.
11. Ibid., 156.

seem to take Chrysostom's use of double predication when speaking of Christ's human and divine nature as implying a division in the person of Christ, and therefore assume that his Christology is not a unitive one in the sense of viewing the Logos-Son as single subject in Christ. Wherever Chrysostom's Christology appears to be strongly unitive in character it is dismissed as being obscure or confusing (Greer), or whenever he speaks of the different operations of Christ's humanity and divinity it is taken as lending support to a duality in Christ's person (Young). I will demonstrate that Chrysostom's picture of Christ, as it emerges in his homilies on Hebrews, is a unitive one, consisting of a varied mosaic that is rich in practical theology when viewed from the perspective of the Christian life, and in the context of the life and faith of the church.

Chrysostom's Homilies on Hebrews

The Greek text of Chrysostom's thirty-four homilies on the Epistle to the Hebrews compiled by the Benedictine Montfaucon can be found in Migne's *Patrologia Graeca*, volume 63 (1862). This work was initially edited by Field and published in *Bibliotheca Patrum Ecclesiae Catholicae Qui ante Orientis et Occidentis schisma floruerunt* (1862). The English translation was originally made from Montfaucon's text and later revised from Field's edited text by Keble and his brother, the vicar of Hursley. This translation appeared in the last volume of the Oxford *Library of the Fathers* (1877). It was further revised by Gardiner and published in the *Nicene and Post-Nicene Fathers*, First Series, volume 14 (1889).[12]

The geographical and chronological provenance of Chrysostom's homilies on Hebrews is disputed among scholars. Quasten maintains that the homilies were composed in the last year of his episcopal office at Constantinople (ca. 403/404) because the title suggests that they were published after his death from stenographic notes by Constantine, a priest of Antioch.[13] Baur, on the other hand, seems a bit cautious, and asks, If Chrysostom's manuscript actually originated in Constantinople, how did it get into the hands of the priest who surely lived in Antioch?[14] Baur suggests that the individual named Constantine could possibly be

---

12. Chrysostom, *Homilies on the Gospel of St. John and The Epistle to the Hebrews*, NPNF 14.

13. Quasten, *Patrolology*, 3:450.

14. Baur, *John Chrysostom and His Time*, 2:94.

the priest that Chrysostom communicated with during his banishment, and the one who visited him in his exile.[15] Baur concludes that a reliable answer to this question is difficult to ascertain from the available material. Kelly surmises that this series of homilies belong to the "closing stages" of Chrysostom's ministry in Constantinople and, since they do not betray any sign of strained relations between him and the imperial couple, they might have originated during the period of friendship after his return from his first exile in the autumn of 403. It might seem more probable, Kelly asserts, that they were preached in the preceding winter, as Chrysostom mentions the extreme cold in his eleventh homily and chides his audience for neglecting the poor in such adverse conditions.[16]

More recently, Allen and Mayer have challenged the arguments of scholars who have adduced a Constantinopolitan provenance for the homilies on Hebrews. They argue that a priori assumptions regarding provenance, supported by selective use of internal or external material evidence, need to be identified at the outset for what they are.[17] Allen and Mayer argue that there is evidence of material from both locations, *viz.*, Antioch and Constantinople, in the thirty-four homilies on Hebrews and, consequently, that they must not be exclusively ascribed to Chrysostom's time in Constantinople. Therefore, a careful reading of each individual homily of Chrysostom's entire series is suggested as a positive strategy and methodology in determining their date and place.[18] My objective in this chapter, however, is not to determine or establish where or when Chrysostom might have preached this series of homilies, but rather to examine his christological exegesis of Hebrews and thereby formulate his picture of Christ in light of his practical and pastoral theology.

---

15. See Chrysostom, *Letters* 221 & 225 (*PG* 52.732, 735); 13 & 114 (*PG* 52.611, 670).
16. Kelly, *Golden Mouth*, 133–34.
17. Allen and Mayer, "Thirty-Four Homilies on Hebrews," 309–48.
18. Ibid., 327–35. Cf. Allen, "Homilist and the Congregation," 397–421. For an account of Chrysostom's life as a preacher and his audience make-up both in Antioch and Constantinople, see the chapter by W. Mayer, "John Chrysostom: Extraordinary Preacher, Ordinary Audience," in Cunningham and Allen, *Preacher and Audience*, 105–36.

The Pastoral and Polemic Framework of Chrysostom's Homilies

Chrysostom's homilies on Hebrews are less paraenetic in their tone when compared to his homilies on the Gospel of John. It is possible that the differing degrees of moral and doctrinal emphases in his homilies are contingent on his pastoral and polemic concerns. Throughout his thirty-four homilies, Chrysostom assumes Paul to be the author of the Epistle to the Hebrews without offering an explanation of such an assumption. In the introductory homily, he remarks that although Paul viewed himself as an apostle to the Gentiles (Rom 11:13–14)—in contrast to Peter, who was viewed as the apostle to the Jews (Gal 2:8)—he had a burden for the suffering Christians in Jerusalem and Palestine and therefore sent this epistle to them. Chrysostom observes:

> Why, then, not being a teacher of the Jews, does he send an Epistle to them? And where were those to whom he sent it? It seems to me in Jerusalem and Palestine. How then does he send them an Epistle? Just as he baptized, though he was not commanded to baptize. For, he says, "I was not sent to baptize" (1 Cor. 1:18): not, however, that he was forbidden, but he does it as a subordinate matter. And how could he fail to write to those, for whom he was willing even to become accursed? (Rom. 9:3) . . . He who prays to become accursed for those who were not yet believers, and who so ministers to the faithful, as to journey himself, if need be, and who everywhere took great care of them;—let us not wonder if he encourage and comfort them by letters also, and if he set them upright when tottering and fallen.[19]

In Chrysostom's view, Paul wrote the epistle to Hebrew Christians who were experiencing hardship and suffering on account of their faith. The general tenor of these homilies is both pastoral and practical. The fact that Chrysostom views the letter as a "message of encouragement" (*Logos Paraklēseōs*) to Christians can be seen from his view of affliction as "instruction" (*paideusis*), for he maintains that discipline in the form of affliction originates in the love of God and proves that we are true sons and not illegitimate children. Developing this thought further, he states, "For if the chastisement [παιδεία] be of love [κηδεμονίας], if it begin from loving care, if it end with a good result . . . why are you discouraged?

---

19. Chrysostom, Introduction, in *Hebrews*, sections 2–3, NPNF 14:364–65 (PG 63.11–12).

For such are they who despair, who are not strengthened by the hope of the future."[20] Chrysostom often adduces the words of Christ from John 16:33 ("Take courage, I have overcome the world") in his homilies on Hebrews to assure his audience that suffering is part of the Christian life—for Christ himself suffered and endured affliction, thereby leaving us a fitting example.[21] We can take courage because he identified with us in his suffering, and sympathizes with us as he intercedes in heaven on our behalf. "He knows what tribulation is; He knows what temptation is, not less that we who have suffered, for He Himself also suffered."[22] If Christ entered brotherhood with us and endured suffering, then chastisement and discipline in the Christian life should be viewed as a benefit of sonship and partaking of God's holiness.[23] Chrysostom capitalizes on the epistle's focus on the humanity of Christ and exhorts his listeners that Christ led the way for others to follow. The dual emphasis on the reality of the incarnation and the reality of Christ's identification with us in every aspect forms the bedrock of Chrysostom's exegesis of Hebrews. Christ was "born, brought up, grew, suffered all things necessary and died"; by entering into brotherhood with us, he sympathizes with us, for he knows our plight not only as God but also as man, and as our high priest, he is able to purify and deliver us from our sins.[24] The images that Chrysostom employs underscore various aspects of Christ's relationship with God, his identification with humanity, and his mediation through his continuing ministry to those who are united with him in faith and practice.

Although Chrysostom does not deal with polemic issues in depth in these homilies, he does make his position clear when dealing with passages that were the focus of the polemical controversies of his day. He counters the Sabellian teachings of people like Paul of Samosata, Marcellus, and Photinus. Often insisting on the distinction of the Persons in the Godhead,[25] he argues against the Docetists and asserts the

---

20. Chrysostom, Homily 30, section 1, *NPNF* 14:503 (*PG* 63.209).

21. See Homily 7, section 6, *NPNF* 14:400 (*PG* 63.63); Homily 21, section 5, *NPNF* 14:463 (*PG* 63.151); Homily 25, section 1, *NPNF* 14:477 (*PG* 63.172); Homily 28, section 5, *NPNF* 14:494 (*PG* 63.195); Homily 29, section 4, *NPNF* 14:501 (*PG* 63.206).

22. Chrysostom, Homily 5, section 2, *NPNF* 14:389 (*PG* 63.48).

23. Chrysostom, Homily 29, section 3, *NPNF* 14:500 (*PG* 63.205).

24. Chrysostom, Homily 5, section 1-2, *NPNF* 14:388–89 (*PG* 63.47–48).

25. Chrysostom, Homily 2, section 1, *NPNF* 14:370 (*PG* 63.20).

reality of the incarnation.²⁶ He also affirms the divinity of the Son against the Arians.²⁷ Blending the pastoral with the polemic, he admonishes his hearers to adopt a humble attitude and reverential mind when speaking of the *mysterium tremendum* of the divine nature, underscoring the need for faith in matters pertaining to our conception of God and his attributes:

> Everywhere indeed a reverential mind is requisite, but especially when we say or hear anything of God: Since neither can tongue speak not thought hear anything suitable to our God. And why speak I of tongue or thought? For not even the understanding which far excels these, will be able to comprehend anything accurately, when we desire to utter aught concerning God. For if "the peace of God surpasses all understanding" (Phil. 4:7), and "the things which are prepared for them that love Him have not entered into the heart of man" (I Cor. 2:9); much more He Himself, the God of peace, the Creator of all things, does by a wide measure exceed our reasoning.²⁸

Chrysostom warns that unbelief causes one's soul to be hardened, just like atrophied parts of the body that become callous, hard, and unyielding make it difficult for the physician to administer proper treatment.²⁹ Faith for Chrysostom is the very "principle of our subsistence" and the means of our salvation. "Faith is indeed great and brings salvation, and without it, it is not possible ever to be saved. It suffices not however of itself to accomplish this, but there is need of a right life also. So that on this account Paul [*sic*] also exhorts those who had already been counted worthy of the mysteries; saying, 'Let us labor to enter into that rest.' 'Let us labor' (he says), Faith not sufficing, the life also ought to be added thereto, and our earnestness to be great; for truly there is need of much earnestness too, in order to go up into Heaven." ³⁰

The practical Christian life is a reflection of true faith in God; there cannot be one without the other. "Faith involves purity of life. And without this it is not possible to be a Christian, as without foundations there can be no building; nor skill in literature without the letters. Still if one

---

26. Chrysostom, Homily 4, section 5, *NPNF* 14:385 (*PG* 63.41). Cf. Homily 8, section 3, *NPNF* 14:404 (*PG* 63.69).

27. Chrysostom, Homily 3, sections 2–3, *NPNF* 14:376 (*PG* 63.29).

28. Chrysostom, Homily 2, section 1, *NPNF* 14:370 (*PG* 63.19).

29. Chrysostom, Homily 6, section 3, *NPNF* 14:394 (*PG* 63.55).

30. Chrysostom, Homily 7, section 1, *NPNF* 14:398 (*PG* 63.59–60).

should be always going round about the letters, or if about the foundation, not about the building, he will never gain anything."³¹ Commenting on the words, "without faith, it is impossible to please God" (Heb 11:5), Chrysostom posits that faith takes precedence over reason not just in the practical Christian life but also in reference to our limited perception of the being and essence of God:

> It is necessary to "believe that He is," not "what He is." If "that He is" needs Faith, and not reasonings; it is impossible to comprehend by reasoning "what He is." If that "He is a rewarder" needs Faith and not reasonings, how is it possible by Reasoning to compass His essence? For what Reasoning can reach this? For some persons say that the things that exist are self-caused. Do you see that unless we have Faith in regard to all things, not only in regard to retribution, but also in regard to the very being of God, all is lost to us?³²

Capitalizing on the words of the letter to hold fast to one's faith (4:14), Chrysostom notes that our profession (*homologia*) is true because Christ, our high priest, is in heaven and this fact confirms what we believe. Since our high priest has experienced temptation, and knows well our afflictions, he can therefore sympathize with us in our weaknesses. Consequently, it is imperative that we hold on to our profession of faith without wavering:

> What sort of profession does he mean? That there is a Resurrection, that there is a retribution: that there are good things innumerable; that Christ is GOD, that the Faith is right. These things let us profess, these things let us hold fast. For that they are true, is manifest from the fact that the High Priest is within. We have not failed of [our hopes], let us confess; although the realities are not present, yet let us confess: if already they were present they were but a lie. So that this also is true, that [our good things] are deferred. For our High Priest also is Great.³³

Furthermore, Chrysostom goes on to note that because of our high priest's presence in heaven, we can approach God's throne boldly "because now it is a throne of Grace, not a throne of Judgment." He admonishes his listeners to "bring Faith" as they do so, for it is God who gives

---

31. Chrysostom, Homily 9, section 3, *NPNF* 14:409 (*PG* 63.77). Cf. Homily 22, section 1, *NPNF* 14:465 (*PG* 63.153).

32. Chrysostom, Homily 22, section 5, *NPNF* 14:467 (*PG* 63.157).

33. Chrysostom, Homily 7, section 5, *NPNF* 14:400 (*PG* 63.63).

all things graciously. Chrysostom illustrates the thought thus: "now is the time of the gift; let no man despair of himself. Then [will be] the time of despairing, when the bride-chamber is shut, when the King is come in to see the guests, when they who shall be accounted worthy thereof, shall have received as their portion the Patriarch's bosom: but now it is not as yet so. For still are the spectators assembled, still is the contest, still the prize in suspense."[34] Ultimately, Chrysostom affirms that it is Christ who is the author and the finisher of our faith, and as his followers we are meant to look to him as our example and leader, who not only mediates on our behalf in heaven but also instills in us the grace to practice what we confess. For if he endured all things nobly, how much more should we? He elaborates:

> For as in all arts and games, we impress the art upon our mind by looking to our masters, receiving certain rules through our sight, so here also, if we wish to run, and to learn to run well, let us look to Christ, even to Jesus "the author and finisher of our faith." What is this? He has put the Faith within us. For He said to His disciples, "Ye have not chosen Me, but I have chosen you" (John 15:16); and Paul too says, "But then shall I know, even as also I have been known." (1 Corinthians 13:12) He put the Beginning into us, He will also put on the End.[35]

For Chrysostom, the Christian life begins and ends with the grace of God manifested in and through Christ.

For Chrysostom, the incarnation and the death of Christ provide the soteriological and sacramental basis for his preaching on Hebrews. In keeping with the broad contours of the epistle he begins with the idea that in the incarnation the Son entered brotherhood with us, identifying with us in his human nature, suffering, and death. He says that, in his sacerdotal role as our high priest, Christ offered himself as a willing sacrifice in order to obtain our salvation, thereby uniting us with God in his heavenly ministry of mediation. We are conformed into his image through the sacramental ministry in the ecclesiastical context of faith and practice.

I shall begin my survey of Chrysostom's picture of Christ in Hebrews with the study of the perspective titled, a *Christology of Identification*. Herein Christ's Sonship and brotherhood with us is depicted in the context of his human nature, suffering, and death.

34. Ibid.
35. Chrysostom, Homily 28, section 4, *NPNF* 14:493 (*PG* 63.193).

A Christology of Identification

Introduction

In light of scholarly readings that portray Chrysostom as less than surefooted with respect to Christology, with some even suggesting a duality in his understanding of Christ's person and consequently viewing his soteriology as inconsistent, my purpose here is to offer an account that shows the profound potency of Chrysostom's christological thought. Also, it will be remembered from the introduction to the previous chapter that a distinctive Antiochene Christology denies the direct personal presence and experience of God in the incarnation. Barnard argued that the philosophical, theological, and anthropological influences of the Antiochene christological school "caused Chrysostom to deny that the incarnation has an effect upon God, and to conceive that its movement was wholly toward man and that its effects remained on earth. God therefore had no experience in the incarnation."[36] In contrast to Barnard, who characterized Chrysostom's Christology as divisively positing a duality in his person and thus undermining the personal continuity of the Logos-Son in Christ, I intend to demonstrate that in Chrysostom's view, God the Son entered the human experience in the incarnation, identified with us in every way, and raised human nature to heaven in his ascension. I will proceed by examining his christological thought from the perspective of the ontology of the incarnation (especially Christ's consubstantiality with humanity) in Hebrews. I posit that Chrysostom's christological thought is unitive: he views the Logos-Son as the single subject in Christ who entered brotherhood with humanity, identifying with us in his human nature, suffering, and death in order to make us members of one family and restore our fellowship with God. I will also emphasize that there is a consistency between his incarnational thought across his homilies on John's Gospel and Hebrews. Chrysostom's polemic arguments reflect his Nicene presuppositions and highlight the unitive element in his christological thought. As in his homilies on the Fourth Gospel, the canvas of his preaching on the Christian life in Hebrews is framed by his Christology and soteriology.

---

36. See Barnard, "Christology and Soteriology in the Preaching of John Chrysostom," 6, 67.

The Ontology and Personal Continuity of the Son in His Incarnate and Post-Resurrection Existence

Chrysostom's christological picture of the ontology of the Son in Hebrews is structured by two intertwined foci: incarnation and humiliation (*kenosis*). The exegetical use of the prologue of John's Gospel and the *kenosis* theme of Philippians 2 in his exposition of the first two chapters of Hebrews, suggests that he views the christological concepts of these passages as being consonant with each other. For Chrysostom, the motif of the Word becoming flesh from the Johannine prologue is parallel to the motif of the humiliation of Christ in Philippians 2:6–7, and he often blends these two themes together in his exegesis. This is apparent from his commentary on these two key christological passages. Conflating the two ideas of the incarnation and humiliation in his commentary on John 1:14, he writes: "The Word became flesh and the Master took on the form of the slave. He became the Son of Man although he was the true Son of God, in order that he might make the sons of men children of God . . . He did not lower his own nature by his descent, but elevated us, who had always been in dishonor and darkness, to ineffable glory."[37] The Logos, the true Son of God, descended and assumed human nature (took on the form of the slave) in order to make us God's children and bring us to glory. Likewise, in his exposition of Philippians 2:6–7, Chrysostom observes:

> Speaking here of his divinity, Paul no longer says, he became, he took, but he says he emptied Himself, taking the form of a servant, being made in the likeness of men. Speaking here of his humanity he says, he took, he became. He became [ἐγένετο] the latter [i.e., human], he took [ἔλαβεν] the latter; he was [ὑπῆρχε] the former [i.e., God]. Let us not then confuse or divide. There is one God, there is one Christ, the Son of God, when I say, 'one' I mean a union [ἕνοσιν], not a confusion [σύγχυσιν]; the one nature [φύσεως] did not degenerate into the other, but was united [ἡμωμένης] with it.[38]

Three points in particular are noteworthy in these two passages, and they shed light on Chrysostom's discussion of the sonship of Christ in Hebrews. First, in the incarnation the Logos descended to assume hu-

---

37. Chrysostom, Homily 11, in *John*, FOC 33:106 (PG 59.79).
38. Chrysostom, Homily 7, in *Philippians*, section 3, NPNF 13:214–15 (PG 62.232).

man nature without undergoing any change in his own nature. Second, it is apparent that Chrysostom views the Logos as the Christ's personal subject because he equates God, Christ, and the Son of God ("there is one God, there is one Christ, the Son of God"). Third, the Logos is viewed as the person to whom being and becoming is applied, in that Chrysostom distinguishes being (who the Logos is in his divinity) from becoming (what the Logos does in his humanity). Christ, the Logos-Son, did not become God or assume deity, because he always was. Rather, the Son of God became man and took the form of a servant upon himself. These presuppositions animate Chrysostom's christological exegesis of the first two chapters of Hebrews, where he speaks of the one subject, Christ the Son of God, and refers to his person as the Word—the express image of the Father, the brightness of the Father's glory, and the one who took the form of a servant (or slave). A distinction is often made between who the Word is and what the Word does.[39]

Chrysostom begins his homilies on Hebrews by quoting Romans 5:20, which intimates the sufficiency of God's grace to the afflicted recipients of the letter. As one wishing to lead a child to lofty heights is gentle and patient in the journey upwards in order not to let the child be seized with vertigo and stagger with dizziness, the writer likewise gently leads the readers of the epistle to the lofty heights of the summit: the "unapproachable light and the very brightness" of the glory of the Son.[40] The recipients were partakers of exceeding grace because it is through the agency of his preexistent Son, the "heir of all things," that God has spoken and acted. Commenting on the Son's appellation as the "heir" of all things (1:2), Chrysostom asserts that it declares two things: "His proper sonship and His indefeasible sovereignty."[41] This prerogative, he adds, belonged to the Son from eternity and was not merely given after his incarnation and exaltation.[42]

According to Chrysostom the Logos-Son always enjoyed the status of deity by virtue of his nature; his assuming flesh in the divine economy and atoning for our sins did not compromise his natural (and filial) relationship with the Father. Moreover, he observes that when speaking of the ascended Christ, the writer of Hebrews sometimes refers to his

---

39. See Homily 1, in *Hebrews*, sections 2–4, *NPNF* 14:367–68 (*PG* 63.21–24).
40. Ibid.
41. Chrysostom, Homily 1, section 2, *NPNF* 14:367 (*PG* 63.15).
42. Ibid., section 3, *NPNF* 14:368 (*PG* 63.16–17).

human nature and sometimes to his divine nature depending on the context. Although the predications may differ with respect to their application to who he is and what he does, the writer refers to the same person. He illustrates the use of double predication with a body and soul analogy. Chrysostom reasons:

> So truly it is our way also when we talk of man, to speak of things both high and low. Thus when we say, "man is nothing," "man is earth," "man is ashes," we call the whole by its inferior aspect. But when we say, "man is an immortal animal," and "man is rational, and akin to things above," we call the whole by the better aspect. So also in the case of Christ, sometimes Paul discusses from the less and sometimes from the better; wishing both to establish [the union of] the incarnation and to teach concerning the incorruptible nature.[43]

Just as one speaks of the physical and spiritual aspects of a human being, while referring to the same (whole) person, so does the writer in regard to the person of Christ. Therefore, when speculating on metaphysical matters of such significance, Chrysostom warns, a reverential mind and a life of faith are requisite because our conception of God is limited and finite, for even the writer of Hebrews struggled to "put out his illustrations with exactness."[44]

Chrysostom moves on to discuss the Son's consubstantiality, his personal distinction, and his equal honor with the Father. In his commentary on Hebrews 1:3 ("Who being the brightness of his glory"), he asserts that the expression means, "He (Son) is of Him (Father) without passion."[45] He cites the Sabellian stance of Marcellus and Photinus, and warns his hearers not to be "sick of their disease" because they insist that the "brightness is not substantial, but has its being in another." Further, he contends, "Just as He [the Father] is personally subsisting, being in need of nothing, so also the Son. For he says this here, showing the undeviating similitude and peculiar image of the prototype, that He [the Son] is in subsistence by Himself."[46] Moreover, because the Son is "the express image" of the prototype (i.e., the Father), there is a distinction of person but a similarity of essence. The express image differs from the proto-

---

43. Ibid., *NPNF* 14:368 (*PG* 63.17).
44. Chrysostom, Homily 2, section 1, *NPNF* 14:370 (*PG* 63.19).
45. Ibid., *NPNF* 14:370 (*PG* 63.19–20).
46. Chrysostom, Homily 2, section 2, *NPNF* 14:370 (*PG* 63.20).

type in that it exists hypostatically.⁴⁷ Chrysostom is keen to underscore the unique hypostatic existence of the Son, while maintaining that he is similar in essence (or nature), and therefore no different from the Father.

Besides being similar in nature and distinct in person, the Son has absolute authority, for he enjoys equal honor with the Father. The phrases "He appointed Him heir of all things" and "by Him He made the worlds" (1:2) are spoken of the one Son. The former refers to his human nature assumed after the incarnation, and the latter to his preexistent divine nature. Chrysostom states that because the Son's complete equality with the Father is suggested by the writer, this idea led some (like Sabellius and others) to conclude wrongly that there was no distinction between the persons in the Godhead.⁴⁸ In a polemical diatribe against Marcellus, Sabellius, Paul of Samosata, Arius, and Marcion, he argues that predications concerning the Son, whether humble or sublime, need to be interpreted with reference to his natural and filial relation with the Father, with whom he is equal in power and honor.⁴⁹ As in his homilies on John's Gospel, Chrysostom resorts to two of his favorite images whenever he speaks of Christ's equality with the Father: Christ as judge and agent of creation. Just as it is said of the Father that he judges no man, but has entrusted all judgment to the Son (in that the Son was begotten a Judge [John 5:22]), so also he created the universe through the Son (in that the Son was begotten by him a Creator). The Son is therefore equal in all respects for he is the brightness of the Father's glory.

Further, Chrysostom equates the phrase "the Son is the brightness of God's glory" (Heb 1:3) with the words of Christ from John 8:11, "I am the light of the world." He views these phrases as two sides of the same ontological coin with reference to Christ's nature and person (in that he is consubstantial in nature with the Father and yet distinct in person), and understands them as being said in the sense of "Light of Light," associating these words with the phrase in the Nicene Creed that Christ is God of God, Light of Light, very God of very God. Besides Christ's being of the same essence and equal to the Father in all things, Chrysostom presses the point that all that pertains to the Son pertains to Christ.⁵⁰ He adduces passages from the Johannine prologue in his interpretation

---

47. Ibid., *NPNF* 14:372 (*PG* 63.22).
48. Ibid., section 1, *NPNF* 14:371 (*PG* 63.21).
49. Ibid.
50. Ibid.

of Hebrews 1:2–3 in order to sustain his view of the personal continuity of the Son in the incarnation, reiterating that the Son is God (John 1:1), that all things were made by him (John 1:3), that he was life (John 1:4), and that as God he is before all ages as Creator and maker of all things.[51]

In keeping with the personal continuity motif, Chrysostom invokes the *kenosis* theme to expound Hebrews 1:5 ("For to which of the angels did God say, 'You are my Son, this day I have begotten you'? And again, 'I will be his Father, and he will be my son.'"), asserting the following:

> For these things indeed are spoken with reference also to the flesh: "I will be to Him a Father, and He shall be to Me a Son"—while this, "You art My Son, this day have I begotten You," expresses nothing else than "from [the time] that God is." For as He is said to be, from the time present (for this befits Him more than any other), so also the [word] "Today" seems to me to be spoken here with reference to the flesh. For when He hath taken hold of it, thenceforth he speaks out all boldly. For indeed the flesh partakes of the high things, just as the Godhead of the lowly. For He who disdained not to become man, and did not decline the reality, how should He have declined the expressions? . . . For [if] He Himself being God and Lord and Son of God, did not decline to take the form of a slave, much more ought we to do all things, though they be lowly.[52]

Chrysostom equates God, Lord, and Son of God with Christ, noting once more that, without giving up his identity as God, he partook of flesh in the incarnation—he took on the form of a slave. In this union the divine partakes of the lowly and the flesh partakes of the divine. Earlier in his commentary, Chrysostom refers to this same thought, making use of the kenotic motif again to explain who the Son is in his deity (the brightness of his Father's glory) and what is accomplished through the incarnation. The one who now sits at the right hand of the Father is the same who partook of the flesh in his humiliation: "Therefore just as 'the form of a slave' (Phil. 2:6–7) expresses no other thing than a man without variation [from human nature], so also the 'form of God' expresses no other thing than God . . . Having said, 'Who being the brightness of His glory,' he added again, 'He sat down on the right hand of the Majesty.'"[53] The one who descended in the incarnation is the one who now sits on the throne.

---

51. Ibid., section 2, *NPNF* 14:372 (*PG* 63.23).
52. Ibid., *NPNF* 14:373 (*PG* 63.24).
53. Ibid., *NPNF* 14:372 (*PG* 63.22).

Furthermore, the ontological consistency of the Son is highlighted from the perspective of his ministry of reconciliation and subsequent exaltation; the Son himself purged our sins and then sat down. "'By Himself,' he says, 'having purged our sins, He sat down on the right hand of the Majesty on high.' He here sets down two very great proofs of His care: first the 'purifying us from our sins,' then the doing it 'by Himself.' And in many places, you see him making very much of this,—not only of our reconciliation with God, but also of this being accomplished through the Son. For the gift being truly great, was made even greater by the fact that it was through the Son."[54] He illustrates the soteriological exigency of the Son's personal continuity in the incarnation using two images. He calls the first image a "going out" (*exodos*), where the Son himself "went out" in order to effect reconciliation between God and humanity. The image is that of a king who wishes to be reconciled with those who have offended him and are in chains outside, and therefore he himself goes out of his palace to bring about this reconciliation. Commenting on Hebrews 1:6, he observes: "For as in royal palaces, prisoners and those who have offended the king, stand without, and he who desires to reconcile them, does not bring them in, but himself going out discourses with them, until having made them meet for the king's presence, he may bring them in, so also Christ has done. Having gone out to us, that is, having taken flesh, and having discoursed to us of the King's matters, so He brought us in, having purged the sins, and made reconciliation."[55] The other image is that of obtaining an inheritance or receiving something as a possession, and this is viewed as a "coming in" (*eisodos*), where the Son is depicted as returning with human nature and thus exalting it to the throne of God: "For the saying, 'and when again He brings in the First-Begotten into the world,' means this, 'when he puts the world into His hand.' For when He was made known, then also He obtained possession of the whole thereof, He did not say these things concerning God the Word, but concerning that which is according to the flesh. For if according to John, 'He was in the world, and the world was made by Him' (John 1:10): how is He 'brought in,' otherwise than in the flesh?"[56] In both of these images Christ the Son is viewed as the one who "goes out" and "comes in"; he proceeds from the Father in order to enter the

---

54. Ibid., *NPNF* 14:373 (*PG* 63.24).
55. Chrysostom, Homily 3, section 1, *NPNF* 14:375 (*PG* 63.27).
56. Ibid. Cf. Homily 5, section 1, *NPNF* 14:388 (*PG* 63.45–46).

ranks with his adopted brothers, and he proceeds to the Father, taking us with him to glory.

Furthermore, Chrysostom capitalizes on the theme of the heavenly session of Christ, and the reverence and worship that is extended to him, to underscore the continuity of the Son in his pre-incarnate and post-resurrection existence. In his commentary on 1:6, "Let all the angels worship Him," he glosses the meaning of the worship given to the Son by the angels. Adoration is extended to the ascended Son, who, after assuming human nature in the incarnation, is now seated on the throne. Like a master who introduces someone into the house and commands all those entrusted to his care to respect and reverence him, the ascended Christ likewise receives the reverence and worship that is extended to him by all the angelic beings in heaven.[57] The one who is the object of angelic worship cannot but be divine intrinsically. This becomes the focus of Chrysostom's exposition in the rest of the chapter. Continuing his discussion of the enthroned Son, Chrysostom notes that the phrase "Your throne O God is for ever and ever"(1:8), reflects the kingly office of the Son and is a symbol of royalty, adding that the definite article (ὁ Θεὸς) clearly points to the his divinity.[58] On the other hand, the reference to the exaltation of the Son above his companions (1:9) refers to his human nature, stressing the idea that when the writer speaks of the "doctrine concerning the uncreated nature he always joins also that of the 'Economy.'"[59] The Son possessed this honor by virtue of his nature; it was not something that was granted, for "He Himself remains ever existing, and lives without end" (1:12).[60] Similarly, in his discussion of 1:13, Chrysostom asserts that the Son being enthroned at the right hand of the Father is a reflection the Father's love and honor extended to him by virtue of his filial dignity. "This again belongs to the sovereignty, to equal dignity, to honor and not weakness... This belongs to His great love and honor towards the Son."[61] The ascended Christ who is now worshiped in heaven is the preexistent Son. This was not an external honor bestowed on him, but something that belonged to him before the incarnation.

---

57. Chrysostom, Homily 3, section 1, *NPNF* 14:375 (PG 63.27–28).
58. Ibid.
59. Ibid., section 2, *NPNF* 14:376 (PG 63.29).
60. Ibid., section 3, *NPNF* 14:376 (PG 63.29).
61. Ibid., section 4, *NPNF* 14:376-377 (PG 63.29–30).

Although the Son is now enthroned and exalted, he has entered brotherhood with us, having assumed our nature in the incarnation, identifying with us in his suffering and death in order reconcile us to God. He who sits at the right hand of God is the humiliated Son who became our brother in order to make us the children of God. In a crucial passage, Chrysostom emphasizes these issues and lays out the reason for the very incarnation of the Son:

> He that is so great, He that is "the brightness of His glory," He that is "the express image of His person," He that "made the worlds," He that "sits on the right hand of the Father," He was willing and earnest to become our brother in all things, and for this cause did He leave the angels and the other powers, and come down to us, and took hold of us, and wrought innumerable good things. He destroyed death, He cast out the devil from his tyranny, He freed us from bondage: not by brotherhood alone did He honor us, but also in other ways beyond number. For He was willing also to become our High Priest with the Father: for he adds, "That He might become a merciful and faithful High Priest in things pertaining to God." For this cause (he means) He took on Him our flesh, only for love to man, that He might have mercy upon us. For neither is there any other cause of the economy, but this alone. For He saw us, cast on the ground, perishing, tyrannized over by death, and He had compassion on us.[62]

As the pre-incarnate Logos, the Son was willing to enter brotherhood with us in all things. He condescended in the incarnation in order to free us from the bondage of death and to reconcile us with God. As a result, we share in the fellowship of heaven as sons through his personal mediation.

The Necessity of Christ's Solidarity with Us in His Humanity, Suffering, and Death

Chrysostom's exposition of the motif of Christ's entrance into brotherhood with us in his homilies on Hebrews reflects a soteriological thrust consistent with the incarnational thought in his commentary on the Johannine prologue. In partaking of flesh and identifying with us in his human nature, suffering, and death Christ made it possible for us to become his brothers and share in his glory. Consequently, in identify-

---

62. Chrysostom, Homily 5, sections 1–2, *NPNF* 14:389 (*PG* 63.47).

ing with him in faith and in the participation of the sacraments we are made joint-heirs and express that reality in the practice of the Christian life. Before studying Chrysostom's view of Christ's experience of suffering and death, I shall briefly examine his understanding of the need for Christ's solidarity with us in his humanity.

Christ's oneness with us in his humanity is viewed from both incarnational and sacerdotal perspectives, themes that are closely connected in Chrysostom's soteriology. By entering brotherhood with us, the divine Son united human nature to himself, and by virtue of his ascension and exaltation raised it to glory.[63] Chrysostom consistently emphasizes the idea that the incarnation was not an appearance but a reality; the Son of God partook of flesh and blood just like humans are made of flesh and blood.[64] Out of divine love he pursued human nature and took hold of it in the incarnation in order to elevate it to be adored in heaven:

> For when human nature was fleeing from Him, and fleeing far away (for we "were far off"—Ephesians 2:13), He pursued after and overtook us. He showed that He has done this only out of kindness [φιλανθρωπία], and love [ἀγάπη], and tender care [κηδεμονία]. As then when he saith, "Are they not all ministering spirits, sent forth to minister for them who shall be heirs of salvation" (c. 1:14)—he shows His extreme interest in behalf of human nature, and that God makes great account of it, so also in this place he sets it forth much more by a comparison, for he says, "He taketh not hold of angels." For in very deed it is a great and a wonderful thing, and full of amazement that our flesh should sit on high, and be adored by Angels and Archangels, by the Cherubim and the Seraphim.[65]

Although we have been given the privilege of being made the brothers of Christ and therefore sons of God, Chrysostom safeguards (as always) the distinction between the Son and us as sons by noting who Christ *is* in relation to the Father and what he *does* in his function as the one who entered brotherhood with us. The difference between him and us is made clear by the fact that he possessed that dignity by nature. In order to bring many sons to glory and make us members of the same family (2:10–11), the Son of God became our brother. The divine Son united us as members of one family. Chrysostom writes, "For when He clothed

---

63. Chrysostom, Homily 4, section 5, *NPNF* 14:384 (*PG* 63.59–60).
64. Ibid.
65. Chrysostom, Homily 5, section 1, *NPNF* 14:388 (*PG* 63.46).

Himself with flesh, He clothed Himself also with the brotherhood, and at the same time came in the brotherhood."⁶⁶

In distinguishing who Christ is by nature and what he does in his function as our brother, Chrysostom safeguards the unity of Christ's person by pointing out the ontological distinction between him and us. Being of the same substance as the Father, he clothed himself with flesh in order to enable us to enjoy God's gracious fellowship.

Moreover, in Chrysostom's view, Christ entering brotherhood with us and his function as our high priest are two aspects of one soteriological picture. The corresponding motifs of adoption and reconciliation are viewed as complementary. As the Son he gives us the privilege of relating with him as members of the same family, and in his function as our high priest, he reconciles us with God having purified us from our sins:

> For the Son is a faithful High Priest, able to deliver from their sins those whose High Priest He is. In order then that He might offer a sacrifice able to purify us, for this cause He has become man. Accordingly he added, "in things pertaining to God,"—that is, for the sake of things in relation to God. We were become altogether enemies to God, (he would say) condemned, degraded, there was none who should offer sacrifice for us. He saw us in this condition, and had compassion on us, not appointing a High Priest for us, but Himself becoming a High Priest. In what sense He was "faithful," he added [viz.], "to make reconciliation for the sins of the people."⁶⁷

The Son himself became our high priest in the incarnation out of divine compassion; he did so in order to restore us to fellowship with the Father, from whom we had become alienated. He was not only willing to become man and identify with us in his humanity, but also to act as our high priest, representing us before God. "Even the mere willing to become man was a proof of great care and love; but now it is not this alone, but there are also the undying benefits which are bestowed on us through Him, for, he says, 'to make reconciliation.'"⁶⁸ Christ's solidarity with humanity is viewed in tandem with his ministry of reconciliation as our high priest. He is God's Son and our personal representative. Furthermore, Chrysostom employs the head-body image to explain Christ's identifica-

---

66. Chrysostom, Homily 4, section 4, *NPNF* 14:384 (*PG* 63.41).
67. Chrysostom, Homily 5, section 2, *NPNF* 14:389 (*PG* 63.47).
68. Ibid., section 3, *NPNF* 14:389 (*PG* 63.48).

tion with us and its implications for the faithful. His oneness with us in his humanity ultimately leads to our exaltation. He partook of our nature in order that we might be able to partake of his; this union is actualized through our sacramental participation. Discussing the phrase "For we have been made partakers of Christ" (3:14), Chrysostom comments, "We partake of Him (he means); we were made One, we and He—since He is the Head and we the body, 'fellow-heirs and of the same body; we are one body, of His flesh and of His bones.' (Eph. 3:6; Rom. 12:5; Eph. 5:30) 'If we hold fast the beginning of our confidence [or, the principle of our subsistence, our faith] steadfast unto the end.'"[69] The reason we can enjoy the privilege of being called fellow heirs of Christ is that we have been united to him in the incarnation. As the ascended Son and our high priest he has accomplished the task of restoring our fellowship with God.

Moreover, Chrysostom notes that in entering brotherhood with us in the incarnation, Christ also identified with us in suffering and death. His suffering was part of his human nature: "he was willing and earnest to become our brother in all things," for "He was born, was brought up, grew, suffered all things necessary and at last He died."[70] In partaking of the flesh, he also entered the realm of human suffering, making our suffering his own. His suffering was no different from our experience. Chrysostom presses the point that the divine Son identified with us in every way in his human nature, except sin.

Discussing his understanding of Christ's suffering as his glory, Chrysostom adduces the words of Christ from John 12:23 (where he refers to his sufferings and subsequent death as "glory") in his interpretation of Hebrews 2:7 ("you crowned him with glory and honor") to affirm that the cross of Christ was his glory and honor. He endured suffering for our salvation and called it his glory in order to persuade us to bear our affliction and to look forward to our sharing in the "fruit of the Cross" and future glory.[71] Furthermore, Christ became the "Captain of our salvation" through his suffering (2:10). In enduring the suffering that he was subjected to, he was made perfect (*teleiōsai*), like a champion wrestler who serves as an example to others. Commenting on how Christ has "become" the "Captain of our salvation," Chrysostom says:

---

69. Chrysostom, Homily 6, section 4, *NPNF* 14:394 (*PG* 63.56).
70. Chrysostom, Homily 5, section 1, *NPNF* 14:388 (*PG* 63.47).
71. Chrysostom, Homily 4, section 3, *NPNF* 14:383 (*PG* 63.39).

> He [God] has done what is worthy of His love towards mankind, in showing His First-born to be more glorious than all, and in setting Him forth as an example to the others, like some noble wrestler that surpasses the rest. "The Captain of their salvation," that is, the Cause of their salvation . . . "To make perfect through sufferings." Then sufferings are a perfecting, and a cause of salvation. Do you see that to suffer affliction is not the portion of those who are utterly forsaken; if indeed it was by this that God first honored His Son, by leading Him through sufferings? And truly His taking flesh to suffer what He did suffer, is a far greater thing than making the world, and bringing it out of things that are not. This indeed also is [a token] of His loving-kindness, but the other far more. And [the Apostle] himself also pointing out this very thing, says, "That in the ages to come He might show forth the exceeding riches of His goodness, He both raised us up together, and made us sit together in the heavenly places in Christ Jesus." (Eph. 2:7, 6.) "For it became Him for whom are all things and by whom are all things in bringing many sons to glory, to make the Captain of their salvation perfect through sufferings." For (he means) it became Him who takes tender care, and brought all things into being, to give up the Son for the salvation of the rest, the One for the many. However he did not express himself thus, but, "to make perfect through sufferings," showing the suffering for any one, not merely profits "him," but he himself also becomes more glorious and more perfect. And this too he says in reference to the faithful, comforting them by the way: for Christ was glorified then when He suffered. But when I say, He was glorified, do not suppose that there was an accession of glory to Him: for that which is of nature He always had, and received nothing in addition.[72]

Several points are noteworthy in this passage. First, Christ's experience of suffering is exemplary; he was allowed to suffer in order to set an example for the faithful, and not because he was sinful or imperfect and needed to be perfected morally. Second, his suffering was a means of perfection in the sense that he qualified (humanly speaking) as an exemplary champion. The Son was honored through this process, whereby he was willing to suffer in his flesh for our salvation. Third, he did not need to be perfected in order to be glorified, for glory is his by nature; his perfection belonged to his incarnate experience. Finally, Christ's suffering is viewed as a prerequisite for our glorification. As an accom-

---

72. Ibid., section 4, *NPNF* 14:384 (*PG* 63.40–41).

plished wrestler who has been perfected through enduring affliction sets an example to others, Christ through his exemplary suffering has done the same for the faithful. In this sense he has become the "cause of our salvation" through his experience of suffering and ascension to glory. This thought is complemented in Chrysostom's exposition of Hebrews 5:13 where he speaks of perfection through suffering. He points out that this perfection (*teleiotēs*) is not of nature but of virtue (*aretē*).[73] Christ therefore is viewed as the archetype of perfection for the faithful. His suffering is a paradigm for the virtuous Christian life, for perfection of virtue comes through suffering. The language of perfection, therefore, is ascribed to the process by which we are saved and perfected, and not to the Son's being.

Two points in particular can be inferred from Chrysostom's interpretation of the passages that deal with Christ's suffering in his homilies on Hebrews. First, he draws attention to the reality of Christ's experience of suffering, underscoring the idea of knowledge through experience. Second, in keeping with the epistle's focus, he maintains that because the ascended Christ knows what it means to suffer, he truly sympathizes with us. In his commentary on 2:18 ("For he himself suffered, when he was tempted, he is able to help them who are tempted"), Chrysostom observes that in entering brotherhood with us and enduring affliction, Christ knows not only as God but also as man:

> He went through the very experience of the things which we have suffered; "now". He is not ignorant of our sufferings; not only does He know them as God [ὡς Θεὸς], but as man [ὡς ἄνθρωπος] also He has known them, by the trial wherewith He was tried; He suffered much, He knows how to sympathize. And yet God is incapable of suffering: but he describes here what belongs to the Incarnation, as if he had said, Even the very flesh of Christ suffered many terrible things. He knows what tribulation is; He knows what temptation is, not less than we who have suffered, for He Himself also has suffered.[74]

Just as the experience of suffering in the flesh was real, so is the knowledge that was gained thereby. Further on in his commentary on the passage, Chrysostom underscores the latter point again, saying: "since many men consider experience the most reliable means of knowledge,

---

73. Chrysostom, Homily 8, section 6, *NPNF* 14:406 (PG 63.73).
74. Chrysostom, Homily 5, section 2, *NPNF* 14:389 (PG 63.47).

he wishes to show that He who has suffered knows what human nature suffers."[75] In Chrysostom's view, Christ's experience of suffering was necessary to make him a sympathetic representative on behalf of humanity. By underscoring Christ's experiential knowledge gained through suffering, Chrysostom can confidently speak of Christ's knowledge as being complete. He can sympathize with us because he himself entered our suffering and knows it firsthand.

Moreover, Chrysostom maintains that Christ's road of suffering was "more rugged" than ours and that, as our representative, he is not ignorant of our hardship because he endured much affliction before he ascended. In his discussion of Hebrews 4:14–15 ("For we do not have an high priest who cannot be touched with the feeling of our infirmities"), Chrysostom says, "He is not ignorant of what concerns us, as many of the High Priests, who know not those in tribulations, nor that there is tribulation at any time. For in the case of men it is impossible that one should know the affliction of the afflicted who has not had experience, and gone through the actual sensations. Our High Priest endured all things. Therefore He endured first and then ascended, that He might be able to sympathize with us."[76] As the one whose ascension came only after much suffering, he readily sympathizes with us in our travails.

Further, Chrysostom emphasizes another characteristic of Christ's qualification as our sympathetic high priest. Besides gaining experiential knowledge of human suffering and temptation, Christ also learned obedience through his suffering. Commenting on 5:7–9 ("though He were a Son, yet he learned obedience by the things which He suffered"), Chrysostom observes that Christ's "learning" obedience in this fashion was part of the humiliation of the incarnation. The Author of salvation had to be made perfect in his human experience, and this included learning of obedience. He continues, "But if He, being the Son, gained obedience from His sufferings, much more shall we. Do you see how many things he discourses about obedience, that they might be persuaded to it? ... 'From the things,' he says, 'which He suffered He' continually 'learned' to obey God. And being 'made perfect' through sufferings. This then is perfection, and by this means must we arrive at perfection. For not only was He Himself saved, but became to others also an abundant supply of salvation. For 'being made perfect He became the Author of salvation to

---

75. Ibid., section 5, *NPNF* 14:390 (*PG* 63.50).
76. Chrysostom, Homily 7, section 5, *NPNF* 14:400 (*PG* 63.63).

them that obey Him."⁷⁷ Being the Son and redeemer, he also became our example. In entering brotherhood with us, the Son endured suffering obediently. As the divine Son who united human nature to himself in the incarnation, and suffered in the flesh, his knowledge of both God and man is now complete.

If Christ willingly suffered, setting an example for us, then through our perseverance in suffering we identify with him. "Let us consider of what we have been thought worthy: we and Christ are One: let us not then distrust Him. And again, he hints at that which had been said in another place, that 'if we suffer, we shall reign with Him' (2 Tim. 2:12). For this is [implied in] 'We are made partakers,' we partake of the same things whereof Christ also partakes."⁷⁸ In partaking of flesh, he entered every human experience; he shared our suffering and knows our human condition. Chrysostom exhorts the faithful that in their affliction they have "communion with Him [Christ] in His sufferings" because he too suffered.⁷⁹ Furthermore, he maintains that if Christ himself was reproached and willingly suffered, calling his affliction glory, so should the faithful: "If then He calls the [sufferings] for His servants' sake 'glory,' much more should you the [sufferings] for the Lord."⁸⁰ Just as the ascended Christ has identified with us not only in his human nature but also in his suffering, our fellowship with him in our suffering is a preparation for our sharing in his glory.

Chrysostom illustrates the relationship between Christ's suffering and ours in his paraenetic comments using athletic imagery. He compares the Christian to a wrestler who, having perfected his skill in contests, is ready to face any contingency with confidence. A Christian likewise must be prepared to suffer and willing to experience hardship:

> Let us not then seek relaxation: for Christ promised tribulation to His disciples and Paul says, "All Who will live a godly life in Christ Jesus, shall suffer persecution." (2 Tim. 3:12.) No noble-spirited wrestler, when in the lists, seeks for baths, and a table full of food and wine. This is not for a wrestler, but for a sluggard. For the wrestler contends with dust, with oil, with the heat of the sun's ray, with much sweat, with pressure and constraint. This is the time for contest and for fighting, therefore also for be-

---

77. Chrysostom, Homily 8, section 3, *NPNF* 14:404 (*PG* 63.70).
78. Chrysostom, Homily 6, section 8, *NPNF* 14:396 (*PG* 63.58).
79. Chrysostom, Homily 33, sections 4–9, *NPNF* 14:515, 517 (*PG* 63.227; 63.229).
80. Chrysostom, Homily 4, section 3, *NPNF* 14:383 (*PG* 63.39).

ing wounded, and for being bloody and in pain. Hear what the blessed Paul says, "So fight I, not as one that beats the air." (1 Cor. 9:26.) Let us consider that our whole life is in combats, and then we shall never seek rest, we shall never feel it strange when we are afflicted: no more than a boxer feels it strange, when he combats. There is another season for repose. By tribulation we must be made perfect . . . These things I say, because I wish you to observe the laws of Christ who commands us to "pray that we enter not into temptation" (Matt. 26:41), and commands us to "take up the cross and follow" Him. (Matt. 16:24.) For these things are not contradictory, no they are rather exceedingly in harmony.[81]

To reiterate, in Chrysostom's view the Christian life is a reflection of the exemplary life of Christ. As a noble champion who has withstood the rigors of testing and affliction in his human experience, Christ has become our example. Christians must be willing to take up the cross and follow him. Christ not only identified with us in his human nature by entering brotherhood with us, he also experienced the pain of suffering. As the ascended Son and high priest he sympathizes with us, for he became an example by blazing a trail for the faithful to follow and can therefore rightly be called the Captain or Author of our salvation.

In addition to underscoring Christ's solidarity with us in his humanity and suffering, Chrysostom also considers the death of Christ. In keeping with the epistle's teaching, Chrysostom emphasizes the complete human experience of Christ: a Savior who has identified with us in his human nature, suffering, *and* death. The reality of our salvation depends on this complete identification with us. Chrysostom resorts to his oft-employed metaphor of a physician to expound the idea of Christ "tasting death" in his discussion of Hebrews 2:9 ("so that by the grace of God he might taste death for everyone"). Christ "tasted" death like a physician who partakes of what is prepared for his patient in order to persuade and encourage him to follow suit without fear: "For as a physician though not needing to taste the food prepared for the sick man, yet in his care for him tastes first himself, that he may persuade the sick man with confidence to venture on the food, so since all men were afraid of death, in persuading them to take courage against death, He tasted it also Himself though He needed not."[82] Christ's experience of death is viewed in connection with the grace of God: God's grace is available to all, Christ like-

---

81. Chrysostom, Homily 5, section 7, *NPNF* 14:392 (PG 63.51–52).
82. Chrysostom, Homily 4, section 3, *NPNF* 14:384 (PG 63.39–40).

wise died for all. Though all might not believe, he fulfilled his part by dying for all. Chrysostom notes that the expression Christ "tasted" death signifies that he genuinely partook of that experience, albeit only for a short period of time because he arose immediately thereafter. Christ's death is also viewed as a means of purification and a completion of what was foreshadowed in the old covenant. Capitalizing on the imagery presented in Hebrews 9, Chrysostom speaks of a real spiritual cleansing made possible through the death of Christ. In the Old Testament the sacrifices could only cleanse outwardly; because their efficacy was restricted to the physical, the purifying was bodily, and its effects were temporary. This contrasts with the sacrifice and death of Christ, where the purifying is spiritual and the effects are everlasting. Chrysostom draws a direct parallel between the inefficacy of the ritual sacrifices of the Old Testament and the death of Christ, underscoring the spiritual superiority of the latter in the sacramental context of eucharistic participation. Speaking to the faithful, he continues, "But in the case of the soul it is not so, but the blood is mixed with its very substance, making it vigorous and pure, and leading it to the very unapproachable beauty. Henceforward then he [the writer] shows that His death is the cause not only of confirmation, but also purification. For inasmuch as death was thought to be an odious thing, and especially that of the cross, he says that it purified, even a precious purification, and in regard to greater things."[83] Our complete purification is contingent on the sacramental appropriation of the death of Christ. The superiority of the spiritual benefits of Christ's death is but a reflection of God's grace realized through the sacrifice of Christ and made effective in our participation in the reality of his experience. The reconciliation between holy God and sinful humanity was brought about through God's loving initiative: "For us he spared not His only-begotten, for us when we were enemies He gave up His own Son to death; of what will He not count us worthy, having become His friends? What will He not impart to us, having reconciled us to Himself?"[84] The death of Christ is a *sine qua non* of the divine drama of reconciliation; it is firmly rooted in the divine love, which bridged the infinite distance between God and man. Chrysostom emphatically speaks of the death of Christ in regard to its role in the reversal of our alienation with God. Christ's death is understood as a once-for-all event,

---

83. Chrysostom, Homily 16, sections 5–6, *NPNF* 14:444 (*PG* 63.125).
84. Chrysostom, Homily 23, section 6, *NPNF* 14:471 (*PG* 63.164).

a drinking to the dregs of the sins of humanity: "He became a ransom by one death... His death nullified the tyranny of death... He died that He might deliver us... For He died indeed for all, that is His part: for that death was a counterbalance against the destruction of all men... Lo! He bore the sins. He took them from men, and bore them to the Father; not that He might determine anything against them [mankind], but that He might forgive them."[85] In order to restore fellowship with God, it was necessary that the Savior himself experience death on behalf of the ones whom he will release from its bondage. His death was more than just identification with us in our mortality; it was a means through which he accomplished deliverance for us. In this context salvation is viewed in terms of "the dissolution of death, the destruction of the devil, the kingdom of heaven, [and] everlasting life."[86] Christ could only "destroy death" and "cast out the devil from his tyranny" by entering brotherhood with us in all things.[87] His experience of death is viewed as the ultimate salve that saved humanity from its fatal disease of sin. Chrysostom, remarking on the uniqueness of Christ's death, observes: "For as a medicine, when it is powerful and productive of health, and able to remove the disease entirely, effects all after one application; as therefore, if being once applied it accomplishes the whole, it proves its own strength in being no more applied, and this is its business; whereas if it is applied continually, this is a plain proof of its not having strength. For it is the excellence of a medicine to be applied once and not often."[88] The sacrificial death of Christ is akin to a potent medicine, a remedy that brings about the salvation of humanity. Christ's death was the fulfillment of the shadow of the Old Testament ritual sacrifices, and its effectiveness is reflected in the soteriological effect—securing redemption on behalf of sinful humanity once and for all. Ultimately, in Chrysostom's view, this is the main purpose of the incarnation, that Christ "might destroy him that had the power of death, that is the devil."[89] In entering brotherhood with us in his incarnation, Christ entered the experience of death as well in order to secure our salvation. Our union with him in the sacramental context of baptism therefore represents our death and spiritual renewal. Chrysostom

---

85. Chrysostom, Homily 17, section 4, *NPNF* 14:447 (*PG* 63.129).
86. Chrysostom, Homily 3, section 6, *NPNF* 14:379 (*PG* 63.33).
87. Chrysostom, Homily 5, section 1, *NPNF* 14:389 (*PG* 63.47).
88. Chrysostom, Homily 17, section 5, *NPNF* 14:448 (*PG* 63.130).
89. Chrysostom, Homily 4, section 6, *NPNF* 14:385 (*PG* 63.41).

commonly associates baptism with the cross: "Baptism is a cross, and 'our old man is crucified with [Him]' (Rom. 6:6), for we were 'made conformable to the likeness of His death' (Rom. 6:5, Phil. 3:10), and again, 'we were buried therefore with Him by baptism into death' (Rom. 4:6)."[90] It is in the sacramental context of baptism that our identification with the death of Christ is portrayed. The salvific effects of Christ's death are actualized when the believer identifies with him in baptism. "For as Christ died on the cross, so do we in baptism, not as to the flesh but as to sin. There are two deaths. He died as to the flesh; in our case the old man was buried, and the new man arose made conformable to the likeness of His death . . . For baptism is nothing else than the putting to death of the baptized, and his rising again."[91] The conforming of the believer to the likeness of Christ and the inner spiritual renewal demonstrated in the practice of the Christian life is integral to Chrysostom's spiritual thought. Thus Christ's complete identification with us in his humanity, suffering, and death is viewed as a prerequisite for our spiritual renewal. He partook of the flesh in order that we might partake of the blessings of heaven. Chrysostom's threefold emphasis of Christ's solidarity with us in his humanity, suffering, and death suggests that he views the reality of these experiences as essential for our salvation. For Chrysostom a docetic Christology is untenable, for a Savior devoid of a complete incarnate experience is deficient and imperfect. Christ's solidarity with us is the means to our purification and perfection as sons. As the Son he is our redeemer, as the high priest he is our mediator, and as the captain of our salvation he is our example.

The Christological Implications of the Personal Continuity of the Son and His Identification with Us

Chrysostom's view of the personal continuity of the Son in the incarnation and ascension in Hebrews is consistent with his incarnational reflections on John's Gospel. The ontology of the preexistent Logos-Son, similar in nature and equal in power and honor to the Father, was not altered in the partaking of the flesh. The single personal subject of Christ in the incarnation was the Logos-Son. The one who is the heir of all things, the very brightness of the Father's glory, the express image of the

90. Chrysostom, Homily 9, section 6, *NPNF* 14:410 (*PG* 63.79).
91. Ibid.

Father, who had a distinct hypostatic existence before all ages, partook of the flesh by entering brotherhood with us. His humiliation in the incarnation, his solidarity with humanity, and his subsequent exaltation provide the means for us to enjoy the privilege of sharing in his glory. On this basis, Chrysostom can speak of the continuity of Christ the Son in his incarnate existence with regard to his identification with us in all things. His identification with us in his human nature, suffering, and death did not distort his personal integrity. The Logos-Son is the one to whom being and becoming are referred; therefore whatever is said of Christ with regard to his incarnate state refers to the person of the Son. Being who he is, the divine Son willingly identified with humanity in entering brotherhood with us in order that we might partake of the grace he enjoys by virtue of his nature.

In speaking of the incarnation of the Logos-Son in terms of "the flesh partaking of the high things and the Godhead of the lowly," Chrysostom is essentially making use of the *communicatio idiomatum* principle to affirm the divinity and unity of Christ's person.[92] When Chrysostom speaks of Christ's perfection through suffering, his learning of obedience, and his death on the cross, it is clear that he intends to refer to a single subject behind all of these—the Logos-Son. The Son made these human experiences his own by entering brotherhood with us in the humanity that he assumed. Chrysostom is aware of the confusion this might cause and is quick to point out the misuse of the principle by the Neo-Arians, in particular, who reasoned that since God cannot be born or suffer, Christ could not be God.[93] Although Chrysostom is careful not to ascribe the human experiences to the divine nature of the Son, he nevertheless speaks of the Son as the single subject of the union. Perfection through suffering, knowledge through experience, learning of obedience, and death are ascribed to the Logos-Son in his humanity. That is, he went through these human experiences as man rather than in his divine nature. The predications with reference to Christ should be considered with regard to his person and actions: who he is and what he does. Moreover, in speaking of Christ's actions in terms what he does "as

---

92. He also makes use of this idea in his homilies on John's Gospel. Commenting on John 17:6, he asks how can the divine Son receive anything since he is one with the Father? Chrysostom explains: "this cannot be said of the Son merely as man, for it is clearly evident to all that what belongs to the lesser nature belongs also to the greater, but the opposite is not the case." Chrysostom, Homily 81, in *John*, FOC 41:380 (PG 59.339).

93. See Homily 3, in *John*, FOC 33:35 (PG 59.41).

God" and what he does "as man," he is employing terminology that is essentially similar to that of Athanasius.[94] Chrysostom takes the same view as Cyril would later; both ascribe the experiences of Christ to the Logos, while still maintaining that the Logos did not change in his own nature. Chrysostom's Christology can therefore be regarded as being unitive, in the sense that he views the Logos-Son as the single subject of Christ, whose complete solidarity with humanity was exigent in order that he might become an effective representative on our behalf and conform us to his likeness through his mediation.

In Chrysostom's view, it was soteriologically imperative that Christ identify with us in every way, for the reality of our salvation is contingent on the authenticity of his identification with us. In order to make us partakers of the divine fellowship, the Son had to partake of the flesh, and this can only happen if there is a personal continuity of the Son in the incarnation, his human experiences of suffering, his knowledge through experience, and his "tasting of death." He can therefore sympathize with us in his ministry as our high priest, for he made our experiences his own. His identification with us is the ground of our reconciliation with God and adoption into his family. To say that the preexistent Son entered brotherhood with us is consistent with saying that God himself has personally entered the experiences of human life and identified with us. In this sense, Chrysostom's view can be regarded as a *Christology of Identification*. The following perspective, a *Christology of Mediation*, considers the sacerdotal and sacramental aspects of Chrysostom's theology as they relate to the person of Christ.

A Christology of Mediation

Introduction

In an article that examines the christological implications of the human priesthood of Christ, Torrance makes a pertinent observation with reference to how the early controversies shaped the church's worship and liturgy. He contends that one of the consequences of the controversies (especially the Arian and the Apollinarian) in the early church was that

---

94. See Wilken, "Tradition, Exegesis, and the Christological Controversies," 123–42. Cf. Kannengiesser, "Athanasius of Alexandria and the Foundation of Traditional Christology," 103–13.

it eventually influenced the worship and liturgy of the church negatively, resulting in a lopsided emphasis on the divine nature of Christ with reference to his priesthood and mediatorial role.[95] This disproportionate emphasis magnified the chasm between the divine and human and led to the deep sense of awe and dread in the practice of worship, an attitude that is also expressed in the sacerdotal ministry and liturgy of the church. In light of his survey of the liturgy of the Eastern Church (drawing on Jungmann's historical analysis), Torrance notes that this trend began "with and after Chrysostom," in whose thought the role of the human priesthood of Christ was downplayed and the role as the divine mediator was emphasized. Torrance observes that this misplaced emphasis negated the role of Christ's vicarious human priesthood and thus our continual participation in his worshiping and praying as man towards God. "The human priesthood in the church is apparently regarded not so much as participating in the vicarious priesthood of Christ, but rather as the priesthood on earth over against the priesthood of Christ addressed as God, which had the effect of investing the earthly priesthood with terrible and terrifying awe, in having to 'handle Christ in his body and blood.'"[96] One of the implications of this separation in the priestly work of Christ as man from the incarnation of the divine Son is that the mediation of Christ became exclusively related to his divine activity and thus undermined humanity's sharing in the worship and prayer of Christ in the fullness of his human priesthood.

In light of this argument, the twofold objective of the present perspective is to examine the mediatorial aspects of Christ's priesthood in Chrysostom's exposition of Hebrews, and consider its christological implications in order to verify if this disjunction is indeed reflected in his thought. Although the sacerdotal and sacramental aspects are closely connected in Chrysostom's thought, our focus here is not so much on the sacramental participation of the faithful, but rather on the Christ's role as high priest and mediator.

This section will highlight the point that although Chrysostom does emphasize the divine nature of Christ in his sacerdotal role, he no less consistently stresses the idea that Christ's priesthood must be viewed

---

95. See Torrance, "The Mind of Christ in Worship: The Problem of Apollinarianism in the Liturgy," in *Theology in Reconciliation*, 139–214.

96. Torrance concludes that Cyril's christological position, which he inherited from Athanasius, does view humanity as sharing in the vicarious priesthood of Christ in his presentation of himself and us to the Father. Ibid., 192.

as a function of the incarnation; it is the incarnate Son who fulfills the priestly role. My survey will highlight three aspects of Christ's role as priest and mediator as they emerge in Chrysostom's exposition. The first subsection considers the superiority of Christ's priesthood over that of Moses and Melchizedek, where the dominant thrust of Chrysostom's argument is that it is the incarnate Son who fulfills the mediatorial task. The second subsection considers the decisive nature of this mediation with reference to Christ's self-offering and atoning work. Chrysostom's point here is that Christ the Son makes our fellowship with God possible by removing the obstacle of sin. And finally, the third subsection surveys Chrysostom's view of the continuity of Christ's priestly office in the church, where the faithful appropriate the benefits of his heavenly liturgy in their sacramentally mediated union with him.

Chrysostom's View of the Incarnate Son's Priestly Mediation

Chrysostom views the incarnational and sacerdotal motifs as corresponding features of Christ's life and work, and unites these two concepts in his exposition. The humiliated Son became our brother and high priest in order to mediate between God and us, for we "were become altogether enemies to God, condemned, degraded, there was none who should offer sacrifice for us. He saw us in this condition, and had compassion on us, not appointing a High Priest for us, but Himself becoming a High Priest."[97] In Chrysostom's view, the Son's becoming our high priest is not of nature but of "grace [χάριτος], condescension [συγκαταβάσεως], and humiliation [κενώσεως]."[98] The efficacy of his ministry as priest and mediator is underscored by the fact that he secured eternal redemption for the faithful and presently sits on a throne of grace. Consequently, we can boldly draw near to God's throne through him, since "it is now a throne of grace, not a throne of judgment . . . for the affair is [one of] munificence, a royal largess."[99] For the time will come when the royal "bride chamber will be shut" and the faithful will enjoy fellowship with the King, whereas the rest will stand at the throne of judgment.[100] The regal and sacerdotal roles are fulfilled by the same person; "for King in-

---

97. Chrysostom, Homily 5, in *Hebrews*, section 2, NPNF 14:389 (PG 63.47).
98. Chrysostom, Homily 7, section 6, NPNF 14:400 (PG 63.64).
99. Ibid.
100. Ibid.

deed He always was, but has become Priest from the time He assumed flesh."¹⁰¹ Although the execution of Christ's priestly ministry is viewed as a function of his incarnate nature, Chrysostom affirms that it must be understood with reference to his whole person, "the manhood having Godhead, not dividing the one from the other."¹⁰² In viewing the priesthood as a function of the incarnation, Chrysostom does not see a disjunction between the state of the Son's exalted glory (his sitting on God's right hand) and the state of his humiliation (his priestly ministry). The royal and sacerdotal roles of the Son are united in his thought; God as man fulfils the mediatorial task. These intertwined motifs are highlighted in his exposition of the superiority of Christ's mediatorial role in comparison to that of Moses and Melchizedek.

The Incarnate Son's Mediatorial Role

Moses and Christ

Chrysostom compares the mediatorial roles of Moses and Christ (Heb 3:1–19) in order to convey the point that Christ's ministry is superior because it is exercised by the incarnate Son. Moses was a faithful servant, while Christ is the eternal Son; the former was a steward in God's house, while the latter is the owner. Whereas Moses was made a guardian and a steward, Christ, by virtue of being the Son, has authority over the members who constitute God's household. He is our apostle and high priest because he was sent by God, ministers to the faithful, and mediates on our behalf. These comparisons, Chrysostom asserts, should be understood with reference to Christ's humanity: "Therefore he [Paul] begins from the flesh, and goes up to the Godhead, where there was no longer any comparison. He began from the flesh [from His Human nature], by assuming for a time the equality, and says, 'as also Moses in all His house' . . . 'Who was faithful,' he says, 'to Him that made Him'— made [Him] what? 'Apostle and High Priest.' He is not speaking at all in this place of His essence, nor of His Godhead; but so far concerning human dignities."¹⁰³ The analogous roles of apostle and high priest refer to Christ's incarnate state and not to his divine nature. Therefore

---

101. Chrysostom, Homily 13, section 2, *NPNF* 14:427 (*PG* 63.103).
102. Ibid., section 7, *NPNF* 14:430 (*PG* 63.106).
103. Chrysostom, Homily 5, section 4, *NPNF* 14:390 (*PG* 63.49).

he can be compared with Moses with reference to his human nature in this context, and not with reference to his Godhead. Moreover, Christ's mediation is the basis of our hope and confidence, for through him we are assured the privilege of eternal rest in the kingdom of heaven. We are made partakers of Christ through his priestly ministry. "He that so loved us, He that counted us worthy of so great things, as to make us His Body, will not suffer us to perish."[104] The old covenant with its rules and regulations with regard to the seventh day typified the true rest to come: "What other rest then is there, except the kingdom of Heaven, of which the Sabbath was an image and type?"[105] The superiority of Christ's mediatorial role is reflected in the benefits conveyed to the faithful who are entrusted to him: "His care is greater, He protects them as His own, and would not have them fall away."[106] The contrast of the two roles is augmented by the fact that Christ the mediator entered the eternal rest of heaven, which was promised to the faithful, while Moses, the mediator of God's law did not enter the promised land.

In his humiliated state the Son learned obedience through his suffering, and through his experience of being perfected he is qualified to mediate on behalf of the faithful. The Son's humiliation in the incarnation is viewed in consonance with his sacerdotal role. This idea is elaborated in his discussion of Hebrews 12:18–24, where Chrysostom contrasts the mediatorial roles of Moses and Christ in the context of how one approaches God under the old and new covenants. The former was distinguished by fear and awe as Moses was required to approach God on behalf of the people, whereas the latter is characterized by divine condescension, whereby the incarnate Son himself mediates between God and his people:

> From the first therefore they [the people whom Moses led] were themselves the cause of God's being manifested through the Flesh. Let Moses speak with us, and "Let not God speak with us." (Exod. 20:9.) They who make comparisons elevate the one side the more, that they may show the other to be far greater. In this respect also our [privileges] are more gentle and more admirable. For they are great in a twofold respect: because while they are glorious and greater, they are more accessible. This he [Paul] says also in the Epistle to the Corinthians: "with unveiled counte-

---

104. Chrysostom, Homily 6, section 9, *NPNF* 14:396 (*PG* 63.56).
105. Ibid., section 2, *NPNF* 14:394 (*PG* 63.55).
106. Chrysostom, Homily 7, section 4, *NPNF* 14:399 (*PG* 63.63).

> nance" (2 Cor. 3:18), and, "not as Moses put a veil over his face." (2 Cor. 3:13.) They, he means, were not counted worthy of what we [are]. For of what were they thought worthy? They saw "darkness, blackness"; they heard "a voice." But you also have heard a voice, not through darkness, but through flesh. You have not been disturbed, neither troubled, but you have stood and held discourse with the Mediator . . . He declares here not that He is another; far from it. He does not set forth One and Another, but He appears terrible, when uttering His Voice "from Heaven." It is He Himself then, both the one and the other: but the One is terrible. For he [Paul] expresses not a difference of Persons but of the gift.[107]

Whereas Moses approached God with fear and trembling, and access to God's presence was restricted, the Christian faithful enjoy the better privilege of the Son as the God's spokesman. While the former approach was impersonal and limited access to God, the latter is characterized by God himself communicating with us in and through the condescension of his incarnate Son. Chrysostom adduces 2 Corinthians 3:18 in this context, alluding to the "gift" of access to God through Christ, such that through his mediation we are in God's glorious presence like Moses. The stark differences between the mediatorial roles of Moses (the faithful servant) and Christ (the faithful and eternal Son) serve to underscore the superior nature of the latter's mediation and priesthood.[108]

Furthermore, since Christ endured all things before he ascended, he is able to identify with the faithful in all things, unlike other priests who are ignorant of our infirmities. While earthly priests can reasonably bear with those whom they represent, Christ truly sympathizes with us as he exercises his priestly office.[109] Since we have a high priest who was afflicted and who persevered, we can approach the heavenly throne boldly with the assurance that in him we have a mediator who is faithful to God and is merciful towards us. Unlike other priests who have to stand in order to perform their ministerial duties, this high priest is seated at the Father's right hand. Having accomplished his sacerdotal mission, he is the source of grace to those who come to him. Chrysostom reiterates that, as the ascended high priest, he now sits on a throne of

---

107. Chrysostom, Homily 32, sections 3–4, *NPNF* 14:511–12 (*PG* 63.221).

108. Chrysostom, Homily 8, section 2, *NPNF* 14:403 (*PG* 63.67).

109. Chrysostom, Homily 5, section 3, *NPNF* 14:389f. (*PG* 63.47–48). Cf. Homily 8, section 1, *NPNF* 14:403 (*PG* 63.67–68).

grace; when the end is come, he will arise to judge the world and then it shall become a throne of judgment (he cites Ps 82:8, "Arise, O God, judge the earth").[110] His high priestly mediation and his sitting on the throne of grace are viewed in harmony with each other. The enthroned Son is our mediator through whom we obtain grace and have access to God.

Melchizedek and Christ

Chrysostom also considers the superiority of Christ's high priesthood with reference to it being in the order of Melchizedek (Heb 7:1–28). He does this in three ways: Christ's ministry is superior with reference to its location (it is exercised in heaven), its duration (it is eternal), and the nature of his oblation (it is a perfect sacrifice). As our forerunner, Christ has entered heaven as our high priest and offers true hope for the faithful. In this light, Christ's priesthood is superior because his ministry is exercised in heaven, "for we have our victim on high, our priest on high and our sacrifice on high."[111] Melchizedek the priestly king typified Christ and his priesthood. The latter surpasses the former because "not having beginning or end of life," his priesthood is eternal.[112] The reality of Christ's ministry is confirmed by the type both in name and mission. Elaborating on this further, Chrysostom remarks, "But who is 'King of righteousness,' save our Lord Jesus Christ? And after that also King of Salem, from his city, 'that is, King of Peace,' which again is [characteristic] of Christ. For He has made us righteous, and has 'made peace' for 'things in Heaven and things on earth.' (Col. 1:20.) What man is 'King of Righteousness and of Peace'? None, save only our Lord Jesus Christ."[113] The mystical meaning of Melchizedek's priesthood is embodied in Christ's priesthood such that his name and mission are united in his heavenly ministry of justifying and reconciling us with God through his atoning sacrifice. Moreover, since the reality of Christ's priesthood is superior to that of Melchizedek (whose priesthood was, in turn, superior to the Levitical priesthood), then, by implication, it supersedes the Aaronic priesthood as well. Christ's priesthood incorporates the radical changes that have taken place with regard to the covenant (i.e., he is the guarantor

---

110. Chrysostom, Homily 7, sections 5–6, *NPNF* 14:400 (*PG* 63.62–63).
111. Chrysostom, Homily 11, section 5, *NPNF* 14:419–20 (*PG* 63.92).
112. Chrysostom, Homily 12, section 3, *NPNF* 14:424 (*PG* 63.97).
113. Ibid.

and mediator of a better covenant) and the tribe (since he was from the tribe of Judah).[114] Moreover, his priesthood is of the new order, which is at once regal and sacerdotal, endless and indestructible. He did not carry out his priestly office in an earthly tabernacle but in the heavenly sanctuary. As the eternal priest-king, his heavenly sacerdotal ministry is superior in nature because of where it is exercised. Through his mediation we have a better hope of entering heaven and drawing near to God's throne, in contrast to the inferior (because imperfect) ministrations of human priests in the former dispensation.[115]

Chrysostom senses a potential tension in his reading of the twin infinitives of Hebrews 7:25: "Therefore He is able also *to save* them to the uttermost, that come to God through him, because he ever lives *to intercede* for them." Specifically, he queries why the one who is the source of life, and who possesses all power and authority, needs to intercede continually. In contrast to what Torrance might lead one to suspect, Chrysostom resolves the dialectic by treating the Son's intercession as a function of his human nature and not his divine nature. Commenting on Christ's permanent priesthood, Chrysostom asserts:

> "Therefore He is able also to save them to the uttermost, that come unto God by Him, seeing He ever lives to make intercession for them." Do you see that he says this in respect of that which is according to the flesh. For when He [appears] as Priest, then He also intercedes. Therefore also when Paul says, "who also makes intercession for us" (Rom. 8:34), he hints the same thing; the High Priest makes intercession. For He "that raises the dead as He will, and quickens them," (John 5:21), and that "even as the Father" [does], how [is it that] when there is need to save, He "makes intercession"? (John 5:22.) He that has "all judgment," how [is it that] He "makes intercession"? He that "sends His angels" (Matt. 13:41, 42), that they may "cast" some into "the furnace," and save others, how [is it that] He "makes intercession"? Therefore (he says) "He is able also to save." For this cause then He saves, because He dies not. Inasmuch as "He ever lives," He has (he means) no successor: And if He have no successor, He is able to aid all men. For there [under the Law] indeed, the High Priest although he were worthy of admiration during the time in which he was [High Priest] (as Samuel for instance, and any other such), but, after this, no longer; for they were dead.

---

114. Chrysostom, Homily 14, section 4, *NPNF* 14:434 (*PG* 63.112).
115. Chrysostom, Homily 13, sections 1–5, *NPNF* 14:427–29 (*PG* 63.101–6).

But here it is not so, but "He" saves "to the uttermost." What is "to the uttermost"? He hints at some mystery. Not here only (he says) but there also He saves them that "come unto God by Him." How does He save? "In that He ever lives" (he says) "to make intercession for them." Do you see the humiliation? Do you see the manhood? For he says not, that He obtained this, by making intercession once for all, but continually, and when ever it may be needful to intercede for them. "To the uttermost." What is it? Not for a time only, but there also in the future life. 'Does He then always need to pray? Yet how can [this] be reasonable? Even righteous men have oftentimes accomplished all by one entreaty, and is He always praying? Why then is He throned with [the Father]?' Do you see that it is a condescension. The meaning is: Be not afraid, nor say, Yes, He loves us indeed, and He has confidence towards the Father, but He cannot live always. For He lives forever.[116]

In contrast to the Levitical priests, whose ministrations were temporary and whose ministries were disrupted by death, the man Christ exercises an eternal priesthood and is able to mediate eternal salvation. To save and to intercede represent the two dimensions of Christ's priestly office. The certainty of our salvation is suggested by the continual intercession of the humiliated incarnate Son on our behalf. There is no temporal limitation to his ministry because he continues forever. We participate in the salvation made possible through the mediation of the Son who has entered into a new dimension in his sacerdotal role by virtue of his incarnation. Chrysostom insists on the personal integrity of the Son with regard to the exercise of his priestly mediation by asserting that one should not separate his divinity from his humanity.[117]

The superiority of his mediation is also attested by his perfect sacrifice. While the other high priests offered sacrifices of bulls and goats, Christ offered himself on behalf of the faithful. Chrysostom stresses the "exceeding greatness of the spiritual sacrifice," and in a crucial passage highlights the implications of Christ's once-for-all self-offering:

Do not then, having heard that He is a priest, suppose that He is always executing the priest's office. For He executed it once, and then "sat down." (10:12.) Lest you suppose that He is standing on high, and is a minister, he shows that the matter is [part] of a dispensation [or economy]. For as He became a servant, so also [He

116. Ibid., section 6, *NPNF* 14:429 (*PG* 63.105–6).
117. Ibid., section 7, *NPNF* 14:430 (*PG* 63.106).

became] a Priest and a Minister. But as after becoming a servant, He did not continue a servant, so also, having become a Minister, He did not continue a Minister. For it belongs not to a minister to sit, but to stand. This then he hints at here, and also the greatness of the sacrifice, if being [but] one, and having been offered up once only, it affected that which all [the rest] were unable to do.[118]

Christ offered himself as the final sacrifice and has therefore exercised a ministry that is superior to that of his predecessors. The finality of such a ministry is indicated by the fact that he is now seated at God's right hand.[119] Because of the atoning sufficiency of his offering, the enthroned Son does not need to stand anymore in order to offer another sacrifice. Only a superior priest could offer such a superior sacrifice; the legal priesthood had to be superseded by a royal priest in the order of Melchizedek, one who could exercise a permanent ministry in order to mediate eternal salvation. As our high priest, Christ embodies the images, types, and representations typified in the Old Testament. His office as the mediator supersedes Moses, Aaron, and Melchizedek, for he is the eternal Son who condescended to become our high priest. For a new covenant to be enforced, a new mediator is required, and the spiritual privileges under the new covenant are superior to the old. By means of his entrance into the heavenly sanctuary, and the acceptance of his sacrifice, he guarantees the spiritual blessings for the faithful. He now sits on God's right hand and enables us to share in the eternal life of heaven through his mediation.[120] The two dimensions of his once-for-all self-offering and his continual sitting on high are viewed as a unity, for the enthroned high priest is the enthroned Son.

---

118. Ibid., section 8, *NPNF* 14:430 (*PG* 63.107). Cf. Homily 17, section 3, *NPNF* 14:447 (*PG* 63.128).

119. Chrysostom consistently reinforces the image of the Son sitting at God's right hand with reference to the efficacy and finality of his sacrificial offering as an act of "His great loving kindness and His tender care for us," and with reference to this royal right belonging to him by virtue of his divinity. Chrysostom, Homily 14, sections 1–2, *NPNF* 14:433 (*PG* 63.109f). See also Homily 2, section 2, *NPNF* 14:372–73 (*PG* 63.21–22); Homily 5, section 1, *NPNF* 14:389 (*PG* 63.47); Homily 7, section 6, *NPNF* 14:400 (*PG* 63.63–64); Homily 13, section 8, *NPNF* 14:430 (*PG* 63.106-7); Homily 18, section 3, *NPNF* 14:452 (*PG* 63.135).

120. Chrysostom, Homily 14, sections 3–5 *NPNF* 14:433 (*PG* 63.112–13).

The Decisive Nature of the Son's Mediation

Three assertions in particular emerge in Chrysostom's view of Christ's mediation: the efficacy of his self-offering, the embodiment of what he mediates, and the unrestricted access to fellowship with God he gives to the faithful. One of the features that is stressed by Chrysostom with regard to Christ's sacerdotal role is the idea of the efficacy of his self-offering based on 7:27 ("When he offered himself, he sacrificed for their sins once for all"). He highlights this motif several times in his homilies. Christ's offering is viewed as "giving himself up for our sins (Gal. 1:4), and in doing so he 'gave himself as a ransom for us all (1 Tim. 2:6).'"[121] Because "He is Himself then both victim and Priest and sacrifice," his personal offering had the power to propitiate the Father and put away sin that grace may abound.[122] In his sacerdotal role, "the Son is a faithful High Priest, able to deliver from [their] sins those whose High Priest He is."[123] Moreover, our purification from sin and reconciliation with God can be secured only through the personal mediation of the Son, "For the gift being truly great, was made even greater by the fact that it was through the Son."[124] While the former offerings were characterized by their inability to atone for the sins of humanity, Christ's once-for-all offering is distinguished by its efficacy, "For inasmuch as he called the cross a sacrifice, though it had neither fire, nor logs, nor was offered many times, but had been offered 'once for all' in blood."[125] Chrysostom's emphasis on the unity of the offerer and the offering emphasizes the point that he views this aspect of the high priestly function and mediation of the incarnate Son as being crucial to the removal of sin.

Chrysostom also considers the symbolic relationship between Christ's body and the tabernacle as he points out that his entrance into the heavenly sanctuary as the atoning sacrifice was decisive. He contrasts the restricted access of the high priest to the inner sanctuary under the first covenant with Christ's direct access into the heavenlies, and capitalizes on the spatial imagery of the tabernacle to highlight the significance the relationship between Christ's body and the tabernacle. The point be-

---

121. Chrysostom, Homily 8, section 3, *NPNF* 14:404 (*PG* 63.70).
122. Chrysostom, Homily 17, section 3, *NPNF* 14:447 (*PG* 63.129).
123. Chrysostom, Homily 5, section 2, *NPNF* 14:489 (*PG* 63.47).
124. Chrysostom, Homily 2, section 2, *NPNF* 14:373 (*PG* 63.24).
125. Chrysostom, Homily 15, section 2, *NPNF* 14:439 (*PG* 63.118).

ing made is that the high priestly mediation performed in the heavenly sanctuary is exercised by God veiled in flesh. In his commentary on Christ's entering the heavenly tabernacle to appear before God (9:11), Chrysostom writes:

> "But Christ being come an High Priest of good things that are come by a greater and more perfect tabernacle not made with hands." Here he means the flesh. And well did he say, "greater and more perfect," since God The Word and all the power of The Spirit dwells therein; "For God does not give the Spirit by measure [unto Him]." (John 3:34.) And "more perfect," as being both unblamable, and setting right greater things. "That is, not of this creation." See how [it was] "greater." For it would not have been "of the Spirit" (Matt. 1:20), if man had constructed it. Nor yet is it "of this creation"; that is, not of these created things, but spiritual, of the Holy Ghost. Do you see how he calls the body tabernacle and veil and heaven? "By a greater and more perfect tabernacle. Through the veil, that is, His flesh." (Heb. 10:20.) And again, "into that within the veil." (Heb. 6:19.) And again, "entering into the Holy of Holies, to appear before the face of God." (Heb. 9:24.) Why then does he do this? According as one thing or a different one is signified. I mean for instance, the Heaven is a veil, for as a veil it walls off the Holy of Holies; the flesh [is a veil] hiding the Godhead; and the tabernacle likewise holding the Godhead. Again, Heaven [is] a tabernacle: for the Priest is there within. "But Christ" (he says) "being come an High Priest": he did not say, "become," but "being come," that is, having come for this very purpose, not having been successor to another. He did not come first and then become [High Priest], but came and became at the same time . . . "Neither by the blood," he says, "of goats and calves" (All things are changed) "but by His own Blood" (he says) "He entered in once for all into the Holy Place." See thus he called Heaven. "Once for all" (he says) "He entered into the Holy Place, having obtained eternal redemption." And this [expression] "having obtained," was [expressive] of things very difficult, and that are beyond expectation, how by one entering in, He "obtained everlasting redemption."[126]

In this rather dense passage, both Christ's body and heaven are compared to the veil and tabernacle. In employing the tabernacle imagery from the Johannine prologue, Chrysostom is drawing a parallel between the tabernacle of Christ's body and the heavenly tabernacle. The image

---

126. Ibid., section 4, *NPNF* 14:440 (*PG* 63.119).

of the Word "tabernacled" in flesh is likened to God dwelling in the heavenly sanctuary, and is employed to symbolize the embodiment and presence of God. The focus is then shifted to the priestly office, where Chrysostom presses the point that as the incarnate Son, Christ did not become (γενόμενος) a high priest but, having come (παραγενόμενος), he is the high priest. His entrance into heaven and his priestly service are exercised in his flesh. Eternal redemption is secured by the atoning sacrifice made by the one who is God in flesh. Again, in uniting the two themes of incarnation and priesthood in this context, Chrysostom combines the person (ontology) and work (mediation) of Christ. The inference here is that in entering the heavenly sanctuary, the incarnate Son (who has united flesh to himself and symbolically embodied the tabernacle in his earthly existence) enters the very presence of God in order to mediate on behalf of the faithful. The restricted access and the inadequacy of the former sacrifices are reversed by the Son in his person and work.

Consequently, the faithful are assured of the benefits of his priestly office because they are mediated by the incarnate Son. Capitalizing on the inheritance imagery of 9:15–18 in his discussion of Christ as the mediator of the new covenant, Chrysostom observes:

> A Testament is made towards the last day [the day] of death. And a testament is of this character: It makes some heirs, and some disinherited. So in this case also: "I will that where I am," Christ says, "they also may be." (John 17:24.) And again of the disinherited, hear Him saying, "I pray not for" all, "but for them that believe on Me through their word." (John 17:20.) Again, a testament has relation both to the testator, and to the legatees; so that they have some things to receive, and some to do, so also in this case . . . "And for this cause" (he says) "He is the Mediator of the New Testament." What is a "Mediator"? A mediator is not Lord of the thing of which he is mediator, but the thing belongs to one person, and the mediator is another: as for instance, the mediator of a marriage is not the bridegroom, but one who aids him who is about to be married. So then also here: The Son became Mediator between the Father and us. The Father willed not to leave us this inheritance, but was wroth against us, and was displeased [with us] as being estranged [from Him]; He accordingly became Mediator between us and Him, and prevailed with Him. And what then? How did He become Mediator? He brought words from [Him] and brought [them to us], conveying over what came from the Father to us, and adding His own death

thereto. We had offended: we ought to have died: He died for us and made us worthy of the Testament.[127]

Three points may be made in light of the above passage. First, there was a need for a mediator between God and estranged humanity. Second, the Son himself (Chrysostom substitutes "Son" for "Christ" in these verses) became the mediator in order propitiate God and restore humanity's fellowship with him. Third, as the mediator, the Son propitiated the Father by his atoning death and sacrifice in order to make us beneficiaries of the new covenant. The efficacy of the Son's self-offering is suggested by the fact that, through his mediation, the faithful are given the privilege of becoming heirs. Chrysostom adduces words from the high priestly prayer of Christ in John's Gospel to point out that as heirs the faithful will inherit the promise of divine communion; where Christ is, we shall also be. Our reconciliation and union with God is effected through the mediation of the incarnate Son whose office as mediator is predicated upon the decisive nature of his ministry. Further on in his commentary Chrysostom summarizes the benefits of the heavenly liturgy of Christ who, having died once for all, appeared on our behalf in the heavenly sanctuary as both victim and sacrifice, propitiating the Father through his self-offering and securing eternal redemption for the faithful.[128]

The definitive nature of Christ's mediation is underscored by the fact that he is now seated at the right hand of God, having offered his unique sacrifice. His ascension and subsequent exaltation have soteriological and sacramental implications for the faithful. Through his ministry their sins are forgiven, they are made fellow-heirs, and they are given the privilege of enjoying the very fellowship of heaven.[129] The faithful now have access to the throne of grace on which he sits because he made for them a new and a living way into heaven. Commenting on our participation in the benefits of Christ's heavenly presence, Chrysostom confidently affirms: "And yet neither was that priest visible, but stood within, and they all without, the whole people. But here not only has this taken place, that the priest has entered into the holy of holies, but that we also enter in."[130] Christ's once-for-all offering and personal mediation removed every obstacle to our sharing in the spiritual privileges of heaven.

---

127. Chrysostom, Homily 16, sections 1–2, *NPNF* 14:443–44 (PG 63.123–24).
128. Chrysostom, Homily 17, section 4, *NPNF* 14:447 (PG 63.129).
129. Chrysostom, Homily 19, sections 1–2, *NPNF* 14:454 (PG 63.139–40).
130. Ibid., section 2, *NPNF* 14:455 (PG 63.140).

The faithful can now share in the benefits of the incarnate Son's priestly mediation and appropriate them in their union with him.[131]

Christ's Heavenly Liturgy and Its Continuity in the Church

Chrysostom affirms that Christ's priestly office continues in the church, which is his body.[132] Christ's heavenly ministry is reflected in the sacramental community, both corporately and individually. His service (*leitourgia*) as our priest and mediator in the heavenly sanctuary is represented both in the church and in us, for "our things are in heaven and heavenly things are ours."[133] This thought is echoed in Chrysostom's treatise on the priesthood, where he asserts that "the work of the priesthood is done on earth, but it is ranked among the heavenly ordinances. And this is only right, for no man, no angel, no archangel, no other created power, but the Paraclete himself ordained this succession, and persuaded men, while remaining in the flesh, to represent the ministry of angels."[134] Furthermore, he maintains that the institutions of the church are patterns of heavenly truths. Consequently, in partaking of the sacraments, the faithful participate in the realities of heaven.[135] Commenting on the spiritual continuum between the sacramental and the heavenly realities, Chrysostom affirms:

> For although they are done on earth, yet nevertheless they are worthy of the Heavens. For when our Lord Jesus Christ lies slain [as a sacrifice], when the Spirit is with us, when He who sits on the right hand of the Father is here, when sons are made by the washing, when they are fellow-citizens of those in heaven, when we have a country, and a city, and citizenship there, when we are strangers to things here, how can all these be other than "heavenly things"? . . . Is not the altar also heavenly? How? It has

---

131. Chrysostom, Homily 20, section 3, *NPNF* 14:458 (*PG* 63.143–44).

132. Chrysostom, Homily 6, section 4, *NPNF* 14:394 (*PG* 63.55–56). Cf. Homily 17, sections 6, 9, *NPNF* 14:449, 450 (*PG* 63.131, 134); Homily 20, section 3, *NPNF* 14:458 (*PG* 63.144).

133. Chrysostom, Homily 14, section 3, *NPNF* 14:434 (*PG* 63.111–12). Cf. Homily 17, section 8, *NPNF* 14:449 (*PG* 63.132); Homily 34, section 4, *NPNF* 14:520 (*PG* 63.233–34).

134. Chrysostom, *De Sacerdotio* 3.4 (*PG* 48.642). *Six Books on the Priesthood*, ET by Neville, 70.

135. Chrysostom, Homily 33, in *Hebrews*, section 7, *NPNF* 14:517 (*PG* 63.229).

> nothing carnal, all spiritual things become the offerings (or the sacred elements). The sacrifice does not disperse into ashes, or into smoke, or into steamy savor, it makes the things placed there bright and splendid. How again can the rites which we celebrate be other than heavenly? For when He says, "Whosoever sins you retain they are retained, whosoever sins you remit, they are remitted" (John 20:23) when they have the keys of heaven, how can all be other than heavenly? ... The Church is heavenly, and is nothing else than heaven.[136]

The church as a sacramental community is a microcosm of heaven. Christ's sacerdotal ministry has sacramental implications such that, as sons, the faithful are enabled to share by grace in the privileges of a heavenly citizenship through the instrumentality of the Holy Spirit. The church's ministry represents spiritually the heavenly liturgy and the vicarious priesthood of Christ, who through his self-offering procured it on our behalf.

Moreover, because the institutions of the church figuratively and spiritually represent Christ's heavenly liturgy, our participation in the sacraments places us in the life of Christ. Comparing the eucharistic service with Christ's oblation, Chrysostom says that the ritual repetition of the church's worship is done as an *anamnēsis* (remembrance) of Christ's once-for-all priestly self-offering:

> And yet by this reasoning, since the offering is made in many places, are there many Christs? But Christ is one everywhere, being complete here and complete there also, one body. As then while offered in many places, He is one body and not many bodies; so also [He is] one sacrifice. He is our High Priest, who offered the sacrifice that cleanses us. That we offer now also, which was then offered, which cannot be exhausted. This is done in remembrance of what was then done. For (He says) "do this in remembrance of Me." (Luke 22:19.) It is not another sacrifice, as the High Priest, but we offer always the same, or rather we perform a remembrance of a sacrifice.[137]

The regular eucharistic liturgy in the church is viewed as a mimetic representation of Christ's unrepeatable self-oblation. His efficacious offering on our behalf cannot be duplicated. The sacerdotal ministra-

---

136. Chrysostom, Homily 14, section 3, *NPNF* 14:434 (PG 63.111–12). Cf. Homily 17, sections 2–3, *NPNF* 14:447 (PG 63.128–29).

137. Chrysostom, Homily 17, section 6, *NPNF* 14:449 (PG 63.131).

tions are performed in obedience to Christ, the high priest of the new covenant. The elements represent the atoning sacrifice, which removed the obstacle of sin and signifies our communion with Christ. The privileges of the new covenant (inaugurated by the atoning sacrifice of Christ, who secured eternal redemption for the faithful) are appropriated in the church. Christ's priestly office, performed and perfected in his humanity, is reflected in his sacramental presence and continues in the church's human liturgy.[138] As partakers of Christ, the faithful share in the benefits of his priestly office. In suggesting that the Son's priesthood is of grace, condescension, and humiliation, Chrysostom identifies Christ's ministry with his human nature such that there is a continuity in his person as the incarnate Son who mediates between God and man by virtue of being himself both God and man. He gives us the privilege of sharing in the divine life through his sacerdotal ministry, which is reflected in the church's liturgy.

For Chrysostom, the continuity of Christ's priestly office has practical implications for the individual members of the community of grace. Personalizing the tabernacle imagery in his paraenetic comments, he asserts that the faithful are God's "tabernacle," whom he inhabits. He cites 2 Corinthians 6:16, "I will dwell in them and walk in them," to support his view.[139] Just as the earthly tabernacle is viewed as a pattern of the heavenly, the Christian similarly is viewed as God's dwelling place. Therefore the Christian life is a life of participation in the heavenly realities: "our conversation [πολίτευμα] is in heaven, yet we live here."[140] The one who mediates in heaven also indwells us. Underscoring the need to live a life that reflects this reality, Chrysostom exhorts his hearers:

> Let us no longer continue on the earth; for even now it is possible for him that wishes it, not to be on the earth. For to be and not to be on the earth is the effect of moral disposition and choice. For instance; God is said to be in heaven. Why? Not because He is confined by space, far from it, nor as having left the earth destitute of His presence, but by His relation to and intimacy with the Angels. If then we also are near to God, we are in heaven. For what care I about heaven when I see the Lord of heaven, when I myself am become a heaven? "For," He says, "We will come," I and

---

138. See Homily 18, section 3, *NPNF* 14:452 (*PG* 63.135); Homily 6, section 9, *NPNF* 14:396 (*PG* 63.58); Homily 19, sections 3–5, *NPNF* 14:456–57 (*PG* 63.140f.).

139. Chrysostom, Homily 16, section 7, *NPNF* 14:445 (*PG* 63.124–25).

140. Ibid.

the Father, "and will make our abode with him." (John 14:23.) Let us then make our soul a heaven.[141]

As the sanctuary or dwelling place of God, the Christian's life is expected to reflect this intimacy. As members of the sacramental community, the heavenly and earthly realities come together in the lives of the faithful. The same Christ who mediates in heaven indwells the purified soul of the Christian—the earthly embodiment of the heavenly sanctuary.[142]

As members of the community of grace, the faithful share in the benefits of Christ's priestly office because it continues in the church. The sacramental benefits are assured because our high priest remains the same forever. In his commentary on Hebrews 13:8, "Jesus Christ is the same yesterday, today and forever," Chrysostom says:

> These words, "Jesus Christ the same yesterday and today and for ever," "yesterday" means all the time that is past: "today," the present: "for ever," the endless which is to come. That is to say: you have heard of a High Priest, but not a High Priest who fails. He is always the same. As though there were some who said, "He is not, another will come," he says this, that He who was "yesterday and to-day," is "the same also for ever" ... By Him therefore let us offer the sacrifice of praise to God continually, that is, the fruit of our lips giving thanks to His name.[143]

Christ's office and work are united in his person; what he does is reflected by who he is. His priestly office continues because he is the same yesterday, today, and forever. In his presence and working in the church, he allows us to share in his priestly mediation. In speaking of the implications of Christ's priestly office in sacramental and practical terms, Chrysostom essentially views the Christian life as a response to, and appropriation of, the benefits of Christ's mediation. His ascension, self-offering, appearance in the presence of God, and priestly office are viewed retrospectively as a unity. The eternal scope of Christ's mediation provides certainty to the sacramental community that the spiritual privileges they enjoy through their union with him are not bound by time.

---

141. Ibid. Elsewhere, Chrysostom compares Christ's self-offering with the eucharistic offering to underscore the continuity of Christ's priestly office in the church. See Homily 17, section 4, *NPNF* 14:447 (*PG* 63.129).

142. See Homily 19, section 3, *NPNF* 14:455 (*PG* 63.140).

143. Chrysostom, Homily 33, section 4, *NPNF* 14:515 (*PG* 63.226).

The Christological Implications of the Son's Mediatorial Role

Chrysostom's exposition of the priesthood of Christ incorporates three interrelated ideas that form the link between redemption and our union with God: The incarnate Son's fulfillment of the mediatorial task, the removal of the barrier of sin, and fellowship with God are all tied to the priestly role. In saying that the Son's becoming the high priest is of grace, condescension, and humiliation, Chrysostom is making the point that his role as priest must be viewed in conjunction with his role as servant (Phil 2). In the condescension of the incarnation, he unites us to himself. In his sacerdotal role, he mediates between God and us. By equating the Son's assuming flesh with him becoming a priest, Chrysostom views the incarnational and the mediatorial aspects in concert with each other. There is continuity in the soteriological and the sacerdotal roles; the one who secured eternal redemption for the faithful is the one who sits on the throne of grace. Chrysostom's consistent emphasis on the enthroned Son who is also our high priest points to the finality and efficacy of his atoning sacrifice. Atonement is seen as the incarnate Son making propitiation through his death, in order that human death might be removed and the faithful might inherit the promise of eternal life. Both ideas of substitution and representation are found in Chrysostom's language with regard to the theme of atonement in Hebrews. The fact that he makes use of juridical and classical terminology to make the same point suggests that he views the ideas as complementary. Chrysostom's view of the unity of the offerer and offering with reference to the heavenly liturgy underscores the Son's role as priest and mediator. As our high priest he has secured eternal redemption, making atonement through his once-for-all self-oblation, and as the enthroned Son he enables us to share in the blessings of heaven through his mediation.

The twin aspects of the Son's once-for-all self-offering and his continual sitting on high are viewed retrospectively as a unity: the enthroned high priest is the enthroned Son, whose self-offering was the means of reconciliation. Anticipating the uncomfortable division that is implied in the motifs of who he is and what he does, Chrysostom makes much about the Son sitting on the throne to suggest that in this respect his role as servant and minister is complete. Yet he continues his work of mediation as the enthroned high priest whose ministry is eternal because he is eternal. Chrysostom in this way posits a distinction is the roles and not a division in the person. The Son's role as our high priest and mediator does not diminish the integrity of his person.

In interpreting the spatial imagery of the heavenly sanctuary in ontological terms, Chrysostom goes on to posit a continuum between the Son's personal mediation and the sacramental community. The priestly office of the humiliated Son continues in the church, and those who are incorporated into Christ's body share in the benefits of his heavenly liturgy. By implication, then, the sacramental community participates in his sacerdotal role, in addition to sharing in its benefits. The church's sacerdotal ministry is a reflection of Christ's heavenly liturgy, and the faithful appropriate the spiritual benefits through their union with him in the sacramental context. In suggesting a spiritual continuum between the Christ's heavenly mediation and his priestly office in the church, Chrysostom views the Christian life as its extension.

As members of the sacramental community, the faithful are united with Christ through his priestly office, which is represented and continues in the ministry of the church. Believers are given the privilege of sharing by grace in the adoption as sons through the work of God the Son incarnate. Whereas Chrysostom's emphasis in John's Gospel was on participation in the divine life through our sacramentally mediated union with Christ, the focus here is on the role of the humiliated Son as our high priest and mediator who enables us to share in the divine life through his personal mediation which continues in the church. The following perspective, a *Christology of Grace*, will examine the relationship between the christological and charitological aspects of Chrysostom's thought as they pertain to the Christian life.

A Christology of Grace

Introduction

This perspective investigates the category of grace in Chrysostom's exposition of Hebrews in order to point out that his view of grace, as it pertains to the Christian life, also reflects a unitive Christology. A divisive Christology, which maintains a duality of subjects in Christ with a sharp distinction between the human and divine natures, views grace more in external terms of cooperation and favor than in terms of personal transformation and relationship with God through Christ as sons. A typical example would be Theodore's Christology, which views the union between the Logos and the assumed Man as one of grace or favor. Consequently, the soteriology of such a view regards God's grace mainly as assisting humanity in order that they might obtain salvation in the future *katastasis* (an age of incorruption and perfection). A divisive Christology does not associate grace with the idea of personal transformation of the Christian, and views salvation in moral terms of making progress towards the age to come. Therefore, the moral life is viewed as a means of obtaining salvation in the future age, with no emphasis placed on the priority of God's grace and its transforming effect in the life of the Christian.[144] Through my survey of the theme of grace as it emerges in Chrysostom's exposition of Hebrews, I will demonstrate that his view of grace takes a different shape compared to a divisive christological view of grace.

I take as my point of departure Fairbairn's perspective on the distinction between christological and anthropological aspects of grace. At the outset of his study of the relationship between Christology and grace in Cyril, Fairbairn lays out these two ideas of grace.[145] He describes christological grace as that which God gives people through the incarnation and atoning work of Christ, and anthropological grace as that which God uses to lead us to receive and to retain christological grace. He points out that the anthropological aspect of grace is primarily concerned with freedom that God has given to humanity at creation, and the grace of faith and perseverance that he gives in salvation. In contrast, the christological aspect of grace relates to what salvation is and what Christ gives the Christian.

Towards the end of his study, Fairbairn devotes a brief section to Chrysostom's Christology, and surveys Chrysostom's treatment of key New Testament passages like John 1:14; Romans 6:23, 8:2; and Philippians 2:6–7. He rightly concludes that Chrysostom views salvation as God's act of rescuing us from our fallen condition and restoring us to the glory of our original creation, and he views grace as the gift of fellowship by which God makes us his adopted children.[146] Fairbairn's brief survey only examines the christological aspect of grace and does not

---

144. For a fuller account of Theodore's Christology and view of grace, see Greer, *Theodore of Mopsuestia*; Greer, *Captain of Our Salvation*, 178–264.

145. Fairbairn, *Grace and Christology in the Early Church*, 13.

146. Ibid., 208.

treat the anthropological aspect—the aspect that deals with the practical Christian life. Not much is said about the role of God's grace as it relates to the Christian life, which I underscore is integral to Chrysostom's paraenetic thought and cannot be bifurcated from his doctrinal thought.

This final perspective will consider the theme of grace in Chrysostom's exposition as it relates to the christological aspect, and to its corresponding anthropological implications in the context of the Christian life. In contrast to Fairbairn's view, I will make a distinction between the christological and anthropological aspects of grace. The former will be viewed as being an objective gift and the latter as a subjective appropriation. The christological and anthropological aspects of grace correspond with the once-for-all character of Christ's sacrifice, on the one hand, and his ongoing ministry, on the other. These two aspects of grace are linked to Christ's person and work (which I have previously shown are inseparable in Chrysostom's thought) with implications for members of his body, the church. I will examine how these two aspects of grace are related in Chrysostom's thought, focusing mainly on the anthropological aspects in order to examine their christological implications.

The first section studies the priority of God's grace in salvation. Here I will highlight the point that in Chrysostom's view, God's grace (as it pertains to salvation) is identified with Christ's atoning work, and operates prior to human effort and response. Grace is viewed as being an objective gift (christological). The second and third sections view grace in subjective terms of appropriation (anthropological). The objective aspect is associated with facticity of Christ's sacrifice, where grace is viewed as a gift. The subjective aspect is associated with Christ's continual ministry, where grace is understood as the way in which God enables humanity to appropriate and be transformed by it. The second section stresses the internal effects of grace and examines the role of God's grace in the transformation of human nature, a motif which is equated with the idea of the Christian's conformation to Christlikeness. It will be pointed out that in Chrysostom's view believers already partake of God's fellowship as sons through Christ; the moral life is not a means to attain salvation but a willing response to God's grace given to us in Christ. The third section highlights the external effects of grace and looks at the relation between grace and the practical Christian life. Here I will note that in Chrysostom's view the reception of grace is a continual and active process in which the life of virtue plays a major role. I assert that in order to understand the relation between Christology and the Christian life in Chrysostom, the objective and subjective aspects of grace must be taken cumulatively.

The Priority of God's Grace

The idea of the priority of God's salvific grace is depicted in three ways in Chrysostom's exposition. First, it is identified with the finished work of Christ. Second, human actions are viewed as being subordinate to God's actions. Third, God's grace is bestowed according to his pleasure. In the very first homily on Hebrews, Chrysostom associates the grace of God with the Son's once-for-all atoning work. The opening sentence of his first homily is a quote from Romans 5:20, "where sin abounded, grace did much more abound," and is associated with the idea that the Son is now seated at God's right hand, having himself purged our sins. Chrysostom, it will be remembered, underscores the point that the throne on which the Son is seated is a throne of grace, and his mediatorial role as high priest is viewed as being that of grace, condescension, and humiliation. The inference that can be drawn from this view is that God's grace exists prior to one's appropriating it because it is associated with Christ's heavenly liturgy, which consists of his self-offering and is rooted in the definitive nature of his atonement. Chrysostom notes that it was the grace of the Spirit at work in the apostle that enabled him to communicate the wonderful truth of the Son's purgation of our sin and his heavenly session, both of which lead us gently to the brightness of God's glory.[147] Because Christ became our victim and sacrifice, grace has been abundantly poured out on the faithful; all sin has been dealt with and put away.[148] Moreover, Chrysostom affirms that since God wanted to extend his grace towards us, he did not spare his Son but delivered him up for us all (Rom 8:32). "He did not owe us this but has done it of grace ... 'Much more the grace of God, and the gift of grace which is by one man Jesus Christ, has abounded unto many. (Rom. 5:15.)'" Chrysostom says that God's abundant grace is the fruit of the cross and is rooted in the finished work of Christ.[149]

---

147. Chrysostom, Homily 1, sections 1–3, *NPNF* 14:366 (*PG* 63.13–16).
148. Chrysostom, Homily 17, section 3, *NPNF* 14:447 (*PG* 63.129).
149. Chrysostom, Homily 4, section 3, *NPNF* 14:383 (*PG* 63.39).

Furthermore, Chrysostom depicts the priority of God's salvific grace by noting that human actions are subordinate to it. He discusses this idea by declaring that, although we have to respond to God's grace and appropriate it, ultimately our efforts are secondary:

> All indeed depends on God, but not so that our free-will is hindered. "If then it depend on God," (one says), "why does He blame us?" On this account I said, "so that our free-will is not hindered." It depends then on us, and on Him. For we must first choose the good; and then He leads us to His own. He does not anticipate our choice, lest our free-will should be outraged. But when we have chosen, then great is the assistance he brings to us. How is it then that Paul says, "not of him that wills," if it depend on ourselves also "nor of him that runs, but of God who shows mercy." (Rom. 9:16.) In the first place, he did not introduce it as his own opinion, but inferred it from what was before him and from what had been put forward [in the discussion]. For after saying, "It is written, I will have mercy on whom I will have mercy, and I will have compassion on whom I will have compassion" (Rom. 9:15), he says, "It follows then that it is not of him that wills, nor of him that runs but of God who shows mercy." "You will say then to me, why does He yet find fault?" (Rom. 9:16, 19.) And secondly the other explanation may be given, that he speaks of all as His, whose the greater part is. For it is ours to choose and to wish; but God's to complete and to bring to an end. Since therefore the greater part is of Him, he says all is of Him . . . For so we ourselves also do. I mean for instance: we see a house well built, and we say the whole is the Architect's [doing], and yet certainly it is not all his, but the workmen's also, and the owner's, who supplies the materials, and many others', but nevertheless since he contributed the greatest share, we call the whole his . . . For do not consider that the well doing is your own. For if you do not obtain the impulse that is from above, all is of no purpose.[150]

Given the paraenetic context, Chrysostom initially comments on our willful action. He then reverses the order noting the prior and greater role of God's grace. He alludes to two important points with regard to God's grace in this passage. First, God's grace precedes human actions ("not him that wills but God who shows mercy"); our good works are the result of God's prior work in us. Second, God's grace plays a prominent role in this partnership ("all indeed depends on God"; "his is the greater part"). As in the construction of a house, although the laborers build

---

150. Chrysostom, Homily 12, sections 5–6, *NPNF* 14:425–26 (*PG* 63.99–100).

and the owner supplies the material, the actions of both are subordinate to the architect's plan and work. In the same way, our actions are subordinate to God's grace. Human free will is not hindered in this process because God's grace is at work to bring his plans to completion in the lives of the faithful, and this is done out of his mercy and compassion. For Chrysostom the priority of God's grace in giving us his fellowship does not exclude human action and free will. People do have a choice to accept God's gift and exercise their free will in doing so.[151]

The priority of God's grace is also seen in the fact that it is freely bestowed on people who do not deserve it. Chrysostom employs imagery of a royal pardon to illustrate this point:

> Suppose there are two soldiers, and that one of them steals, injures, overreaches, and that the other does none of these things, but acts the part of a brave man, does important things well, sets up trophies in war, stains his right hand with blood; then when the time arrives, suppose that (from the same rank in which the thief also was) he is at once conducted to the imperial throne and the purple; but suppose that the other remains there where he was, and merely of the royal kindness does not pay the penalty of his deeds, let him however be in the last place, and let him be stationed under the King. Tell me, will he be able to endure his despair when he sees him who was [ranked] with himself ascended even to the very highest dignities, and made thus glorious, and master of the world, while he himself still remains below, and has not even been freed from punishment with honor, but through the grace and kindness of the King? For even should the King forgive him, and release him from the charges against

---

151. It must be noted that for Chrysostom, the priority of God's grace in salvation does not undermine the importance of "free will" (αὐτεξούσιος) or "deliberate choice" (προαίρεσις), which are viewed as indispensable agents in the appropriation of that gift and the continual transformation of the Christian. In speaking of the need to exercise our free will here, he is highlighting the human factor in receiving God's gift of sonship. This in turn leads to the (Western) debate about dialectical relation between God's grace and human free will and the question whether Chrysostom can be labeled as a Pelagian. It is well known that both Augustine and Pelagius found material in Chrysostom to dispute each other. Although a discussion on this subject is beyond the scope of this study, I would point out that for Chrysostom God's grace operates prior to the human initiative in vouchsafing us his fellowship and making us joint-heirs with Christ, a gift that must be appropriated by the faithful. The sanctified Christian life is viewed as being synergistic, where God's grace and the human initiative are interwoven in the process of our conformation to Christ. For an extended and an open-ended discussion on this issue, see Hill, "Pelagian Commentator on the Psalms?" 263–71, and Kenny, "Was St. Chrysostom a Semi-Pelagian?" 16–29.

him, still he will live in shame; for surely not even will others admire him: since in such forgiveness, we admire not those who receive the gifts, but those who bestow them. And as much as the gifts are greater, so much the more are they ashamed who receive them, when their transgressions are great. With what eyes then will such an one be able to took on those who are in the King's courts, when they exhibit their sweatings out of number and their wounds, whilst he has nothing to show, but has his salvation itself of the mere loving-kindness of God?[152]

Chrysostom likens God to a King who grants a pardon to an irresponsible soldier. The gift is bestowed out of sheer grace and benevolence, so that the focus is on the one who bestows the gift. Chrysostom employs this illustration in the context of warning those who were considering baptism as a last resort. He wants to press the point that God's grace extends to the unworthy and that his gifts are bestowed on those who do not merit them. Further, Chrysostom affirms that Christ is now seated on the throne of grace where the affair is "one of royal munificence [θρόνος χάριτος] and royal largesse [θρόνος χρίσεως]."[153] God's grace exists and works apart from human effort and is bestowed freely on those whom God chooses, based on his good pleasure. This idea is also reflected in Chrysostom's comments on God's providence in the life of Moses, where attention is drawn to the precedence of God's grace with reference to Moses' protection and rescue as an infant: "Great was the grace that was poured out on that righteous man, this being not the work of nature... For observe, the child immediately on its birth appears beautiful and not disagreeable to the sight. Whose [work] was this? Not that of nature, but of the grace of God, which also stirred up and strengthened that foreign woman, the Egyptian, and took and drew her on. And yet in truth faith had not sufficient foundation in their case."[154] Moses' preservation by his parents and the fact that he was rescued by the Egyptian woman are both attributed to the grace of God. The first act portrays the priority of God's grace, and the second its influence on people. The two aspects of grace are interwoven in the passage: that it precedes human actions and that it supersedes human freedom. In Chrysostom's view, therefore, God's grace precedes human action and works apart from the human initiative. It is out of his good pleasure and favor that God bestows his grace

152. Chrysostom, Homily 13, in *Hebrews*, section 10, NPNF 14:431–32 (PG 63.108).
153. Chrysostom, Homily 7, section 6, NPNF 14:400 (PG 63.64).
154. Chrysostom, Homily 26, section 3, NPNF 14:483 (PG 63.180).

upon us. Commenting on this topic elsewhere, Chrysostom emphasizes the point that God extends his grace to us not as a reward for our labor, nor because he owes it us, but as a gift. Elaborating on Romans 6:23, he writes, "After he [Paul] has spoken of the wages of sin and turned to the blessings, he has not kept to the same order. For he does not say, 'the wages of good deeds,' but, the gift of God, so as to show that they were not freed of themselves, not did they receive something owed to them, neither yet a return or a recompense of labors, but by grace all these things came about."[155]

Chrysostom asserts that grace works apart from and prior to our efforts with regard to salvation. Furthermore, Chrysostom characterizes the benefits of grace as heavenly citizenship, reconciliation and friendship with God, and being made heirs through Christ. In his discussion of Hebrews 6:4, he lists the gifts associated with God's grace in Christ:

> What is, "having tasted of the heavenly gift"? It is, "of the remission of sins": for this is of God alone to bestow, and the grace is a grace once for all. "What then? Shall we continue in sin that grace may abound? Far from it!" (Rom. 6:1, 2) . . . He here shows that the gifts are many: and to explain it, you were counted worthy (he says) of so great forgiveness; for he that was sitting in darkness, he that was at enmity, he that was at open war, that was alienated, that was hated of God, that was lost, he having been suddenly enlightened, counted worthy of the Spirit, of the heavenly gift, of adoption as a son, of the kingdom of heaven, of those other good things, the unspeakable mysteries; and who does not even thus become better, but while indeed worthy of perdition, obtained salvation and honor, as if he had successfully accomplished great things.[156]

Through Christ, the faithful have their sins remitted; they have been given the gift of sonship, are counted worthy of the Holy Spirit, and have obtained salvation. The dominant feature of Chrysostom's view of grace is that of God's giving us his fellowship by adopting us into his family and making us joint-heirs with Christ, a recurring soteriological motif in his exposition.[157] All three aspects of the priority of God's grace un-

---

155. Chrysostom, Homily 12, in *Romans*, NPNF 11:417 (PG 60.496).

156. Chrysostom, Homily 9, in *Hebrews*, section 7, NPNF 14:411 (PG 63.79–80).

157. See Homily 23, section 7, NPNF 14:471–72 (PG 63.163–64); Homily 25, section 7, NPNF 14:480 (PG 63.177); Homily 20, section 3, NPNF 14:458 (PG 63.144); Homily 29, sections 2–4, NPNF 14:499–500 (PG 63.204f.); Homily 22, section 5, NPNF 14:467 (PG 63.156–57).

derscore the idea that God extends his largess to the faithful through Christ. God's grace precedes human effort as it is rooted in the finished work of Christ, and operates apart from and prior to our response.[158] In giving us his grace through Christ, God gives us himself. Salvation is not viewed as some distant future reality, but is experienced in the present. Through Christ, Christians are already sons, heirs, and counted worthy of the Spirit. Only if Christ is the Son is this possible.

God's Grace and the Transformation of Human Nature

It will be remembered from the previous chapter on John's Gospel that Chrysostom places much emphasis on the cleansing and renewal of the soul through baptism. One of the recurring themes in his catechetical discussions with reference to God's grace and the Christian life is the conforming of the individual to the likeness of Christ. Those who have put on Christ in baptism are conformed to his likeness and renewed in his image: "What the only begotten was by nature, this they [Christians] also have become by grace."[159] Chrysostom highlights the idea of God's transforming grace (its internal effect on the Christian) in three related ways in Hebrews. In characteristic fashion, he discusses the spiritual renewal motif, equating it with the idea of Christ-likeness (that Christ is formed in us) in his preaching on the Christian life. Second, the theme of grace is discussed with reference to inner renewal such that the Christian's soul is characterized as the dwelling place of God. Third, the idea of our fellowship with God through grace is viewed as a transforming experience in the present, which continues until the end. These three aspects are interlinked and not to be understood as being distinct.

Warning the faithful against the danger of falling away in his commentary on Hebrews 6:4f., Chrysostom stresses the point that although there is only one baptism, repentance is continual. In this context, Chrysostom mentions the renewal that takes place in the Christian at baptism:

---

158. Although Chrysostom speaks of the need to exercise faith and contribute what lies within us, he views the grace of God as preceding the human initiative. See, for example, Homily 58, in *Genesis*, FOC 87:165 (*PG* 54.513). Cf. Homily 9, in *Romans*, NPNF 11:396 (*PG* 60.468); Homily 10, in *Romans*, NPNF 11:404–5 (*PG* 60.479).

159. Chrysostom, Homily 15, in *Romans*, NPNF 11:453 (*PG* 60.541). Cf. *Commentary on Galatians* 3:26–27, NPNF 13.30 (*PG* 61.656).

To "be renewed," that is, to be made new, for to make men new is [the work] of the laver only: for (it is said) "thy youth shall be renewed as the eagle's." (Psalm 103:5.) But it is [the work of] repentance, when those who have been made new, have afterwards become old through sins, to set them free from this old age, and to make them strong. To bring them to that former brightness however, is not possible; for there the whole was grace. "Crucifying to themselves," he says, "the Son of God afresh, and putting Him to an open shame." What he means is this. Baptism is a cross, and "our old man was crucified with [Him]" (Rom. 6:6), for we were "made conformable to the likeness of His death" (Rom. 6:5; Phil. 3:10), and again, "we were buried therefore with Him by baptism into death." (Rom. 6:4.) Therefore, as it is not possible that Christ should be crucified a second time, for that is to "put Him to an open shame." For "if death shall no more have dominion over Him" (Rom. 6:9), if He rose again, by His resurrection becoming superior to death; if by death He wrestled with and overcame death, and then is crucified again, all those things become a fable and a mockery. He who is baptized a second time, crucifies Him again. But what is "crucifying afresh"? [It is] crucifying over again. For as Christ died on the cross, so do we in baptism, not as to the flesh, but as to sin. Behold two deaths. He died as to the flesh; in our case the old man was buried, and the new man arose, made conformable to the likeness of His death. If therefore it is necessary to be baptized [again], it is necessary that this same [Christ] should die again. For baptism is nothing else than the putting to death of the baptized, and his rising again. And he well said, "crucifying afresh unto themselves." For he that does this, as having forgotten the former grace, and ordering his own life carelessly, acts in all respects as if there were another baptism. It behooves us therefore to take heed and to make ourselves safe.[160]

In this passage Chrysostom makes three noteworthy points with regard to the work of grace in the Christian. First, through baptism the faithful identify with Christ in his death, burial, and resurrection. Second, through grace the baptized are conformed to the likeness of Christ. Third, the old nature is put to death and rebirth to a new life takes place in this process. Chrysostom's emphasis in this passage is on God's transforming grace, which both conforms the baptized to Christ and renews them by giving them the potential to live a life that is consistent with the inner change that has taken place. He warns that this grace needs to be

---

160. Chrysostom, Homily 9, in *Hebrews*, sections 5–6, NPNF 14:410-411(PG 63.78–79).

treated with reverence, for baptismal renewal and regeneration places the baptized in the life of Christ. Because baptism is likened to the cross, to be baptized again, or to live a life the laxity of which suggests one needs to be, is akin to crucifying Christ again.

Moreover, Chrysostom likens the Christian's soul to heaven, where Christ and the Father reside. "For what care I about heaven when I see the Lord of heaven, when I myself am become a Heaven? 'For,' He says, 'We will come,' I and the Father, 'and will make our abode with him.' (John 14:23.) Let us then make our soul a heaven . . . heaven has the sun; we also have the sun of righteousness. I said it is possible to become a heaven; and I see that it is possible to become even better than heaven. How? When we have the Lord of the sun."[161] Being conformed to Christ is to experience his indwelling such that through grace the faithful are enabled to share in the fellowship of the Father as if already in heaven, while still on earth. Further, Chrysostom also portrays the transforming character of God's grace as nourishing the soul, whereby it is sustained by the continual participation at the spiritual table of the mysteries of the church. Such a soul has the presence of the Spirit and is likened to a guest at a royal table, "having adornment of gold, [our] robe pure, [our] shoes royal, the face of [our] soul well-formed, the golden ornament put around it, even the girdle of truth," and merits union with Christ and the blessed life, "that being made worthy of the head who is set over us we may depart there where He wishes, for he says, 'I will that where I am, they may also be with me, that they may behold my glory' (John 17:24)."[162] The faithful are given the privilege of divine fellowship through Christ because they have received the Spirit of grace through whom the renewal to the divine image is wrought.[163] Chrysostom often adduces the words "Christ be formed in you" from Galatians 4:19 to remind his baptized audience of the work of God's transforming grace.[164] He also emphasizes the implications of the renewal through grace in the context of his comments on the mysteries. Chrysostom refers to baptism

---

161. Chrysostom, Homily 16, section 7, *NPNF* 14:445 (*PG* 63.125–26).

162. Chrysostom, Homily 17, sections 7–9, *NPNF* 14:449–50 (*PG* 63.131–34).

163. Chrysostom, Homily 20, section 3, *NPNF* 14:458 (*PG* 63.144).

164. Chrysostom, Homily 9, section 8, *NPNF* 14:411 (*PG* 63.80); Homily 21, section 3, *NPNF* 14:462 (*PG* 63.150); Homily 23, section 9, *NPNF* 14:473 (*PG* 63.166); Homily 31, section 3, *NPNF* 14:506 (*PG* 63.215).

as the washing of regeneration that gives us the privilege to call God our Father and enter the brotherhood of his family.[165]

Although Christians live on earth, their glory is in heaven; in obtaining grace and mercy through Christ, they continue to experience spiritual renewal in their union with God.[166] To be the recipient of God's grace through Christ is to be transformed through his fellowship in the here and now. In his discussion of 11:10ff. on the heroes of faith who looked forward to the fruition of God's promises, Chrysostom comments on the ways in which God extends his fellowship to us through Christ:

> For what language, what intellect can represent that blessedness and virtue, that pleasure, that glory, that happiness, that splendor? "What eye has not seen, and ear has not heard, and what has not entered into the heart of man" (1 Cor. 2:9), (he did not say, that they simply surpass [what we imagine]; but none hath ever conceived) "the things which God has prepared for them that love Him." For of what kind are those good things likely to be, of which God is the preparer and establisher? For if immediately after He had made us, when we had not yet done anything, He freely bestowed so great [favors], paradise, familiar intercourse with Himself, promised us immortality, a life happy and freed from cares; what will He not bestow on those who have labored and struggled so greatly, and endured on His behalf? For us He spared not His only begotten, for us when we were enemies He gave up His own Son to death; of what will He not count us worthy, having become His friends? what will He not impart to us, having reconciled us to Himself? He both is abundantly and infinitely rich; and He desires and earnestly endeavors to obtain our friendship; we do not thus earnestly endeavor. What am I saying, 'do not earnestly endeavor'? We do not wish to obtain the good things as He wishes it. And what He has done shows that He wishes it more [than we]... He, for our sake, gave even the Son who was His own...We [are] counted worthy to be sons; we His brethren and fellow-heirs.[167]

In this passage, Chrysostom weaves together two important aspects of God's grace that we have discussed earlier, and also speaks of our fellowship with God as the consequence of the work of grace in us. First, God's magnanimity was made evident prior to our exercising faith, in

---

165. Chrysostom, Homily 25, section 7, *NPNF* 14:480 (*PG* 63.177).
166. Chrysostom, Homily 9, sections 7–10, *NPNF* 14:410–11 (*PG* 63.79–80).
167. Chrysostom, Homily 23, sections 6–7, *NPNF* 14:471–72 (*PG* 63.163f.).

that he gave up his own Son to death while we were still estranged from him. Second, the splendor of God's grace is beyond comprehension. For as the one who prepares and establishes us in it, he enables us to have communion with him whereby as joint-heirs we enjoy the privileges of our brotherhood with the Son. In making us his sons through Christ, God gives us his fellowship such that we receive immortality by sharing in the divine life. Moreover, Chrysostom stresses the point that if God was ready to extend his largess to people before they responded, he will bestow it much more after they do. God has freely bestowed his grace through Christ and has counted us worthy of his communion; consequently, in our fellowship with him now, we are restored to the original glory that humanity enjoyed at creation. He views grace as transforming us such that we already partake of God's fellowship as sons. This is consistent with saying that to partake of the grace of God is to experience a transformation to the likeness of Christ in the present. To participate in Christ is to be changed into his likeness and to be the recipient of divine love and fellowship.[168]

Furthermore, the renewal and transformation that we receive through Christ is ongoing, and is brought to completion at the end of the Christian life in our complete union with God. Commenting on the words in Hebrews 13:21 ("through the blood of the everlasting covenant, our Lord Jesus Christ, make you perfect in every good work, to do His will, working in you that which is well-pleasing in His sight"), Chrysostom affirms, "For that is made 'perfect' which has a beginning and is afterwards completed." The work of grace in the Christian is seen as being progressive ("working in you"), implying that it subsequently leads to completion or perfection. The life of virtue is incomplete in itself, for to be made perfect for every good work, we need God working in us and with us. The "word of exhortation" (*Logos Parakléseōs*) of this letter is that we enjoy this grace through Christ, which is at work in us perfecting us until the end.[169] God's transforming grace has both ontological and functional implications for the Christian. Chrysostom views the grace of God not just as favor bestowed on the faithful, but also as an inner dynamic at work. One can infer that in Chrysostom's

---

168. Chrysostom also quotes John 14:23 (Christ and the Father abiding in the Christian) as a way to indicate one's sharing in the divine fellowship through grace. See, for instance, Homily 27, section 7, *NPNF* 14:489 (*PG* 63.189); Homily 16, section 7, *NPNF* 14:445 (*PG* 63.126).

169. Chrysostom, Homily 34, section 6, *NPNF* 14:520–21(*PG* 63.234ff.).

view, the moral life is the reflection of the ongoing transformation of the Christian, and not a means of salvation, which is already given to us in Christ by grace. A view that underscores personal transformation by grace through Christ demands a unitive Christology.

Grace and the Practical Christian Life

There are at least four aspects to how Chrysostom sees grace shaping the practical Christian life and conforming us to the likeness of Christ. First, grace is associated with the work of the Holy Spirit in us. Second, faith in Christ is viewed as the reflection of the work of grace. Third, repentance is seen as the means of being reestablished in God's grace. Fourth, the role of God's grace is said to conform us to Christ through suffering. These four aspects consider the external effects of grace as they pertain to the practical Christian life.

In his commentary on the epistle's concluding words, "Grace be with you all" (Heb 13:25), Chrysostom discusses the pneumatological aspect of grace as it is lived out in faith and perseverance. Here Chrysostom speaks of two aspects of grace as they pertain to the Christian:

> And what is "the grace"? Remission of sins, cleansing: this is "with" us. For who (he means) can keep the grace despitefully, and not destroy it? For instance; He freely forgave your sins. How then shall the "Grace be with" you, whether it be the good favor [εὐδοκία] or the effectual working [ἐνέργεια] of the Spirit? If you draw it to yourself by good deeds. For the cause of all good things is this, the continual abiding with us of the "grace" of the Spirit. For this guides us to all [good things], just as when it flies away from us, it ruins us, and leaves us desolate. Let us not then drive it from us . . . Do you see that a worldly soul cannot have Him?[170]

Chrysostom highlights grace as favor (*eudokia*) whereby the faithful receive the remission of sins and forgiveness from God. He also stresses another aspect of God's grace. He associates grace with the effectual working (*energeia*) of the Holy Spirit in the Christian. Grace is viewed as the empowering of the Holy Spirit, devoid of which the faithful are left desolate and helpless. It is not only divine favor but also divine empowerment. The effectual working of the Holy Spirit continues with us as we persevere in living a life consistent with the good favor that we have

---

170. Ibid., (*PG* 63.235).

received. In other words, grace is viewed as the Holy Spirit's activity in people. Shortly after this, Chrysostom goes on to illustrate the work of the Holy Spirit (and the perseverance of the Christian) by employing nautical imagery:

> For as a ship sailing with favorable winds is neither to be hindered nor sunk, so long as it enjoys a prosperous and steady breeze, but also causes great admiration according to the march of its progress both to the mariners, and to the passengers, giving rest to the one, and not forcing them to toil on at their oars, and setting the others free from all fear, and giving them the most delightful view of her course; so too a soul strengthened by the Divine Spirit, is far above all the billows of this life, and more strongly than the ship, cuts the way bearing on to heaven, since it is not sent along by wind, but has all the pure sails filled by the Paraclete Himself: and He casts out of our minds all that is slackened and relaxed. For as the wind if it fall upon a slackened sail, would have no effect; so neither does the Spirit endure to continue in a slack soul; but there is need of much tension, of much vehemence, so that our mind may be on fire, and our conduct under all circumstances on the stretch, and braced up ... For if we put it on the stretch on all sides by the hope of the things to come, it receives well the energy of the Spirit; and none of those perishable and wretched things will fall upon it, yea, and if any of them should fall, it does it no harm, but is quickly thrown back by the tightness, and is shaken off and fails down. Therefore we have need of much intentness. For we too are sailing over a great and wide sea, full of many monsters, and of many rocks, and bringing forth for us many storms, and from the midst of serene weather raising up a most violent tempest. It is necessary then if we would sail with ease, and without danger, to stretch the sails, that is, our determination: for this is sufficient for us.[171]

Just as a slackened sail is useless and practically ineffective for navigating a ship across the sea, the slackened soul likewise cannot be filled and infused with the wind of the Spirit to thrust it forward. Chrysostom underscores the need to stretch the sail of our souls by being willingly committed to the Christian life in order to benefit from the energy of the Spirit and be propelled to the haven of our union with God. In Chrysostom's view, grace (understood as the work of the Holy Spirit) plays a major role in the progress of the Christian life, and in actualizing the reality of our sonship in union with God. Chrysostom uses

171. Ibid., (PG 63.235–36).

the example of Abraham in order to explain how this commitment and intensity of faith relates to the Christian life:

> For Abraham also, when he had stretched forth his affections towards God and set before Him his fixed resolution: what else had he need of? Nothing: but "he believed God, and it was counted unto him for righteousness." (Gen. 15:6.) But Faith [comes] of a sincere will. He offered up his son, and though he did not slay him, he received a recompense as if he had slain him, and though the work was not done the reward was given. Let our sails then be in good order, not grown old (for everything "that is decayed and waxen old is close to vanishing away") (c. 8:13), not worn into holes, that so they may bear the energy of the Spirit. "For the natural man," it is said, "receives not the things of the Spirit." (1 Cor. 2:14.) For as the webs of spiders could not receive a blast of wind, so neither will the soul devoted to this life, nor the natural man ever be able to receive the grace of the Spirit: for our reasonings differ nothing from them, preserving a connection in appearance only but destitute of all power. Our condition, however, is not such, if we are watchful: but whatever may fall upon [the Christian], he bears all, and is above all, stronger than any whirlpool.[172]

Chrysostom notes that Abraham exercised faith sincerely and was willing to act upon it, and therefore God justified him through grace. Here Chrysostom highlights the anthropological aspect of grace as it pertains to faith and perseverance. The Christian who has benefitted from the grace of the Spirit is expected to persevere in faith while keeping the soul in good order (renewed) so that it may continue to be energized and rewarded by the Spirit's effectual work. The idea of God's grace as pneumatological empowerment is integral to Chrysostom's understanding of the Christian life.[173]

Secondly, Chrysostom describes faith as the basis for the Christian life. Just as one cannot build without a foundation, nor acquire skill in literature without letters, faith likewise is the prerequisite for the Christian life, and the means of receiving grace.[174] It is described as giving substance to hope: "For since the objects of hope seem to be unsubstantial,

---

172. Ibid.

173. See Homily 22, section 7, *NPNF* 14:468 (*PG* 63.159). Cf. Homily 13, in *Romans*, *NPNF* 11:435 (*PG* 60.517f.). Cf. Homily 14, in *Romans*, *NPNF* 11:440–41 (*PG* 60.525).

174. Chrysostom, Homily 9, in *Hebrews*, section 3, *NPNF* 14:409 (*PG* 63.77); Homily 7, section 1, *NPNF* 14:398 (*PG* 63.59–60).

faith gives them substantiality, or rather, does not give it, but is itself their substance. For instance, the resurrection has not come, nor does it exist substantially, but hope makes it substantial in our soul."[175] Chrysostom associates grace with faith and maintains that there cannot be one without the other; both are viewed as the building blocks of the Christian life. In his comments on Hebrews 13:9 ("For it is a good thing that the heart be established with grace; not with meats"), he says that "faith is all. If that establishes [it], the heart stands in security. It follows that faith establishes."[176] Faith and grace are interlinked; to be established by grace is to be strengthened in faith. In Chrysostom's view of the Christian life, true faith is reflected in acts of the will, and the one who exercises such faith is in turn helped by God's strengthening grace, which continues its work until the end. This is confirmed in Chrysostom's comments on Hebrews 12:2, where he asserts: "He has put the faith within us. For He said to His disciples, 'You have not chosen me, but I have chosen you' (John 15:16); and Paul too says, 'But then shall I know, even as also I have been known' (1 Cor. 13:12.). He put the beginning [ἀρχή] into us, He will also put on the end [τέλος]."[177] The teleology of grace is such that it begins and ends with God. The Christian life is lived between these two bookends; it begins with faith in Christ (the author of our faith), it is energized by the grace of the Spirit, and it is transformed continually until its complete union with God is actualized.

Further, Chrysostom discusses the significance for repentance in the Christian life in the context of his teaching on grace. Repentance is the means of receiving God's continual forgiveness and renewal in order that we might enjoy communion with him. In his commentary on Hebrews 6:4ff., he asserts that God has given us the medicine of repentance, which re-establishes our communion with him after our failings. The repentant faithful receive divine forgiveness through grace. For Chrysostom the alchemy of repentance consists of verbal confession of one's sins, humility of the mind, contrition of the heart, and charity.[178] The unrepentant person is likened to an ill-broken horse. Confession and repentance demonstrate the humility of the soul and make it worthy

---

175. Chrysostom, Homily 21, section 4, *NPNF* 14:463 (*PG* 63.151).

176. Chrysostom, Homily 33, section 6, *NPNF* 14:516 (*PG* 63.229).

177. Chrysostom, Homily 28, section 4, *NPNF* 14:493 (*PG* 63.193).

178. Chrysostom, Homily 9, sections 8–9, *NPNF* 14:411–12 (*PG* 63.80). See also Homily 20, sections 1–2, *NPNF* 14:457 (*PG* 63.113f.).

to receive the grace of God in the mysteries. A humble soul is a grateful soul, and therefore to be grateful to God is to appreciate his grace and mercy. Christian worship, accordingly, is a testimony to God's grace at work in the faithful.[179] Chrysostom associates charity with the mercy of God and highlights the relationship between God's mercy (ἔλεος) and our charity (ἐλεημοσύνη):

> And as when a queen is entering, no one of the guards stationed at the doors dares to inquire who she is, and whence, but all straightway receive her; so also indeed with mercifulness. For she is truly a queen indeed, making men like God. For, he says, "ye shall be merciful, as your heavenly Father is merciful." (Lk. 6:36.) She is winged and buoyant, having golden pinions, with a flight which greatly delights the angels . . . As some dove golden and living, she flies, with gentle look, and mild eye. Nothing is better than that eye. The peacock is beautiful, but in comparison of her, is a jackdaw. So beautiful and worthy of admiration is this bird. She continually looks upwards; she is surrounded abundantly with God's glory: she is a virgin with golden wings, decked out, with a fair and mild countenance. She is winged, and buoyant, standing by the royal throne. When we are judged, she suddenly flies in, and shows herself, and rescues us from punishment, sheltering us with her own wings. God would have her rather than sacrifices. Much does He discourse concerning her: so He loves her. "He will relieve" (it is said) "the widow" and "the fatherless" (Ps. 146:9) and the poor. God wishes to be called from her. "The Lord is pitiful and merciful, long-suffering, and of great mercy" (Ps. 145:8), and true. The mercy [ἔλεος] of God is over all the earth. She has saved the race of mankind (see Ps. 145:9): For unless she had pitied us, all things would have perished. "When we were enemies" (Rom. 5:10), she "reconciled" us, she wrought innumerable blessings; she persuaded the Son of God to become a slave, and to empty Himself [of His glory]. (Phil. 2:7.) Let us earnestly emulate her by whom we have been saved; let us love her, let us prize her before wealth, and apart from wealth, let us have a merciful soul. Nothing is so characteristic of a Christian, as mercy [ἐλεημοσύνη]. There is nothing which both unbelievers and all men so admire, as when we are merciful. For oftentimes we are ourselves also in need of this mercy, and say to God "Have mercy upon us, after your great goodness." (Ps. 51:1.) Let us begin first ourselves: or rather it is not we that begin first. For He has Himself already shown His mercy towards us: yet at least let

---

179. Chrysostom, Homily 33, section 1, *NPNF* 14:514 (*PG* 63.225).

us follow second. For if men have mercy on a merciful man, even if he has done innumerable wrongs, much more does God.[180]

In this rather ornate passage Chrysostom characterizes God's mercy in different ways: as a queen, a beautiful virgin, a golden dove, and a heavenly winged creature that swiftly comes to the rescue of the faithful, offering them shelter under its wings from God's judgment. He adds that God's mercy persuaded the Son to enter brotherhood with us. The zenith of divine mercy is seen in the incarnation: the Son of God emptied himself of his glory in order to bring us to glory. This calls for a similar attitude and a practical response from us. God's giving us his Son is viewed as a paradigm for our charity. In Chrysostom's view, mercifulness enfleshed in the charitable life is one of the definitive visible evidences of the work of grace in the Christian. To partake of the grace of God is to partake of his loving-kindness and embody it in practice.[181] The theme of grace is tightly interwoven in the tapestry of Chrysostom's thought on the Christian life.

Fourthly, the topic of God's grace also features in Chrysostom's discourse on the role of suffering in the Christian life. Suffering is viewed as part of being Christian, and a means through which God proves or tests our faith.[182] Citing the example of Abraham, Chrysostom notes that God tested Abraham not because he did not foreknow the outcome, but that he might make Abraham an example of fortitude to others:

> What then? Did not God know that the man was noble and approved? Why then did He tempt him? Not that He might Himself learn, but that He might show to others, and make his fortitude manifest to all. And here also he shows the cause of trials, that they may not suppose they suffer these things as being forsaken [of God]. For in their case indeed, it was necessary that they should he tried, because there were many who persecuted or plotted against them: but in Abraham's case, what need was there to devise trials for him which did not exist? Now this trial, it is evident, was by His command. The others indeed happened by His allowance, but this even by His command. If then temptations make men approved in such wise that, even where there is

---

180. Chrysostom, Homily 32, section 7, *NPNF* 14:513 (*PG* 63.223–24).

181. Chrysostom, Homily 11, section 10, *NPNF* 14:422 (*PG* 63.95–96).

182. Chrysostom, Homily 20, section 6, *NPNF* 14:459 (*PG* 63.146).

no occasion, God exercises His own athletes; much more ought we to bear all things nobly.[183]

The testing of Abraham was to strengthen his faith so that he might become an example to the faithful community. Moreover, suffering is not a sign of being forsaken, but the very opposite. God is involved in the lives of his people, and he tests the faithful to approve and fortify their faith. Further, God's testing of Abraham was part of his plan, typified in the death of his own Son:

> But these things were types: for here it is the Son of God who is slain. And observe, I beseech you, how great is His loving-kindness. For inasmuch as a great favor was to be given to men, He, wishing to do this, not by favor, but as a debtor, arranges that a man should first give up his own son on account of God's command, in order that He Himself might seem to be doing nothing great in giving up His own Son, since a man had done this before Him; that He might be supposed to do it not of grace, but of debt. For we wish to do this kindness also to those whom we love, others, to appear first to have received some little thing from them, and so give them all: and we boast more of the receiving than of the giving; and we do not say, we gave him this, but, we received this from him.[184]

Chrysostom says that Abraham's willingness to give up his son was illustrative of the grace of God, whereby the testing of Abraham was used to prefigure the eventual giving up of his own Son. The sufficiency of God's grace covers every aspect of the life of the faithful, even their suffering. God allows suffering in order that his grace may be manifested in the lives of the faithful. Chrysostom often cites the words of Christ, "In this world you shall have tribulation" (John 16:33), and the words of Paul, "My grace is sufficient for you" (2 Cor 12:8), sometimes in the same context, in order to drive home the point that the grace of God is at work even as the Christian undergoes suffering.[185] In such cases, therefore, "we have God working with us and acting with us," so that we may enjoy the "everlasting good things, which we may [all] attain in Christ."[186] Like a

---

183. Chrysostom, Homily 25, sections 1–2, *NPNF* 14:477–78 (*PG* 63.173).

184. Ibid.

185. For example, see Homily 25, section 2, *NPNF* 14:477 (*PG* 63.172); Homily 28, section 5, *NPNF* 14:494 (*PG* 63.195); Homily 29, section 4, *NPNF* 14:501 (*PG* 63.206); Homily 33, section 9, *NPNF* 14:518 (*PG* 63.230).

186. Chrysostom, Homily 16, sections 6–10, *NPNF* 14:444–46 (*PG* 63.128).

trainer, God works with the faithful, assuring them not to give up their confidence but to persevere in the Christian life, like an athlete who endures hardship until the very end before being crowned.[187]

Partaking of God's fellowship as sons also involves partaking of his discipline, which is viewed as instruction (*paideusis*). Chrysostom associates affliction with God's chastening and points out that all righteous people suffer, since all whom God treats as sons are disciplined. In his commentary on 12:5f., he declares, "You cannot say that any righteous man is without affliction: even if he appear to be so, yet we do not know his other afflictions. So that of necessity every righteous man must pass through affliction. For it is a declaration of Christ, that the wide and broad way leads to destruction, but the strait and narrow one to life. (Matt. 7:13-14). If then it is possible to enter into life by that means, and is not by any other then all have entered in by the narrow [way], as many as have departed unto life."[188] God's chastening is viewed as an act of his grace through which he conforms us to the image of his Son. As a father disciplines his son, God chastens his children through affliction. In his discussion of 12:7, "He scourges every son whom he receives," Chrysostom distinguishes between the suffering of the righteous and the unrighteous: "He who is not scourged, perhaps is not a son. What then, you say, do not unrighteous men suffer distress? They suffer indeed; how then? He did not say, Everyone who is scourged is a son, but every son is scourged. For in all cases He scourges His son: what is wanted then is to show, whether any son is not scourged."[189] In keeping with the epistle's flow of thought, Chrysostom stresses the idea that being chastised by God is a mark of a legitimate relationship with him, for God is treating us as his true sons when he disciplines us. Chrysostom asserts that God chastens us in order to purify us so that we might partake of his holiness. Commenting on Hebrews 12:10, he writes:

> What is "of his holiness"? It is, of His purity, so as to become worthy of Him, according to our power. He earnestly desires that you may receive, and He does all that He may give you: do you not earnestly endeavor that you may receive? "I said unto the Lord" (one says) "You are my Lord, for of my good things you have no need." (Ps. 16:2.) "Furthermore," he says, "we have had fathers of

---

187. Chrysostom, Homily 21, section 3, *NPNF* 14:462 (*PG* 63.150).
188. Chrysostom, Homily 29, section 2, *NPNF* 14:499 (*PG* 63.204).
189. Ibid.

our flesh which corrected us and we gave them reverence: shall we not much rather be in subjection to the Father of spirits, and live?" ("To the Father of spirits," whether of spiritual gifts, or of prayers, or of the incorporeal powers.) If we die thus, then "we shall live. For they indeed for a few days chastened us after their own pleasure," for what seems [so] is not always profitable, but "He for our profit." Therefore chastisement is "profitable"; therefore chastisement is a "participation of holiness." Yes and this greatly: for when it casts out sloth, and evil desire, and love of the things of this life, when it helps the soul, when it causes a light esteem of all things here (for affliction [does] this), is it not holy? Does it not draw down the grace of the Spirit?[190]

Chrysostom affirms that the grace of God is at work even as we endure his chastening. To be subjected to God's discipline is to partake of his holiness and be counted worthy of his grace. Affliction is one of the ways God continues to conform us to the likeness of Christ in our lives. He associates holiness with moral purity, and views it as the consequence of the work of grace in us. This is the basis of Chrysostom's emphasis on the moral and virtuous life in his homilies. For Chrysostom, to partake of God's holiness is to be morally pure inwardly and exemplify that reality outwardly. Moral purity is God's holiness embodied in the Christian and a reflection of one's fellowship with him.

Finally, the theme of Christ's suffering also colors Chrysostom's picture of grace. As the author and finisher of our faith, Christ exemplifies the work of God's grace in the Christian life. In his discussion of 12:2, "Looking to Jesus, the author and finisher of our faith," Chrysostom notes that if Christ endured reproach on our behalf, then as his disciples we are not above the master (Matt 10:25). He illustrates the importance of looking at the example of Christ, declaring: "For as in all arts and games, we impress the art upon our mind by looking to our masters, receiving certain rules through our sight, so here also, if we wish to run, and to learn to run well, let us look to Christ, even to Jesus 'the author and finisher of our faith.'"[191] Chrysostom asserts that if Christ, who had the power to both lay down his life and take it up again, suffered for our sake, how much more should we endure all things nobly. He cites Philippians 2:10, "God highly exalted him . . . and at the name of Jesus Christ every knee shall bow," to press the point that Christ was glori-

---

190. Ibid., (*PG* 63.206).

191. Chrysostom, Homily 28, section 4, *NPNF* 14:492–94 (*PG* 63.193).

fied after he suffered; therefore we too have a "great and unspeakable" prize set before us if we persevere in our suffering. Chrysostom commonly cites the example of Paul's suffering and adduces passages from 2 Corinthians 11–12 to point out that in the midst of his difficulties, Paul endured, and looked to Christ for help, and received grace in his affliction.[192] On one particular occasion, in his discussion on bearing affliction with gratitude, Chrysostom adduces 2 Corinthians 12:8–9, "My grace is sufficient for you, for my strength is made perfect in weakness," and avers that by *weakness* Paul means *affliction*.[193] In substituting affliction for weakness, Chrysostom views suffering not as antithetical to divine love, but as a means of conforming us to Christ. Christ's suffering does not exempt us from our suffering, but rather offers us the assurance that we have God working with us. The upshot of Chrysostom's argument is that he views suffering in the Christian life as the anvil on which God's grace continues to shape and conform us to the likeness of Christ, both spiritually (internally) and morally (externally). In this process we are more and more transformed by grace. The Christian's fellowship with God begins on earth and is consummated in heaven. A soul that is renewed and purified is a soul that is conformed to Christ. Therefore, the Christian life is framed by God's grace, which from beginning to end conforms us to Christ in order that we might continue in faith and look forward to the blessed life to come.

With regard to the christological aspect (the gift associated with Christ's finished work), priority is given to God's grace, whereas with reference to the anthropological aspect (the appropriation associated with the continual sacramental ministry of Christ in the church), human effort and the exercise of the will are underscored. Chrysostom does not posit a dichotomy between grace and works; the reception of grace is a continual, active process in which the Christian's striving after virtue is imperative. God's saving action of extending his grace to us through Christ operates prior to our response. But it incorporates our response by renewing and conforming us to the likeness of Christ both spiritually and morally. The virtuous life is the reflection of God's grace at work in us through his Holy Spirit, culminating in the ultimate goal of our eschatalogical union with God. Only if Christ is the Son can we be transformed to enjoy this favor and share by grace in God's fellowship.

192. Ibid.
193. Chrysostom, Homily 33, section 9, *NPNF* 14:518 (*PG* 63.230).

The Christological Implications of Chrysostom's View of Grace

Chrysostom's view of grace in Hebrews also points to a unitive Christology. In viewing grace as God's giving us his fellowship through Christ, Chrysostom is positing that the single subject of Christ is the Son. Taken cumulatively, the aspects of grace identified above reflect the view that the Son entered brotherhood with us in order to make us joint-heirs with him, and enjoy what he possesses by nature. Only if Christ is the Son can he extend God's fellowship to us through himself. Chrysostom's emphases on the renewal of our souls and our conformation to Christ's image reflect a similar emphasis. To be conformed to Christ is to be conformed to the likeness of the Son and partake of the divine fellowship. In positing the priority of God's grace, and associating it with the decisive nature of the atoning work of the Son who is now seated at God's right hand, Chrysostom integrates the work of grace with the Son. The one whose priesthood is of grace is the one who sits on the throne of grace and therefore embodies what he extends to us. Through the work of Christ, the faithful have been given the gift of adoption such that they have been renewed into the divine image and made to partake of the Holy Spirit. Partaking of the divine fellowship through Christ is viewed as a transforming experience: what he is by nature we are made so by grace. Only if the person of Christ is the Son can God give us this transforming grace.

The theme of God's grace plays a major role in Chrysostom's understanding of the practical Christian life. The moral life is not a means of aspiring to salvation or fellowship with God, but a response to what God has already done in making us his children and joint-heirs with Christ. An individual who is conformed to Christ reflects that reality in practice. Christ's *kenosis* is viewed as a paradigm for the practice of charity, and the humiliation of God's Son is identified with God's grace and mercy. To practice charity, in Chrysostom's view, is to exemplify the love of God that was manifested in the Son's becoming man in order to bring us to glory. The Christian's philanthropy is viewed as a willing response to the divine philanthropy which was the cause of the Son's economy.

The Christian life, in Chrysostom's view, is inseparable from the life of virtue, and is depicted as a journey that ultimately ends in unhindered eternal fellowship with God. The present life with its challenges is lived by the grace of God that is already at work in the Christian. The sanctification the believer is an ongoing process and is synergistic, with

God's grace complemented by human effort. Chrysostom makes much of exercising one's will in the practice of the Christian life and associates moral purity with the holiness of God, suggesting that he views the moral or the virtuous life as a reflection of our partaking of God's holiness. The divine agency is at work in and with us as we persevere in faith and practice. Grace is viewed as God's saving action in Christ, an outflow of divine love that is rooted in the atoning work of the Son, and works prior to and apart from human effort. Grace is also viewed as empowering the Christian in the practice of discipleship, with the work of the Holy Spirit energizing and stirring the soul to action. The Christian life involves human effort and is viewed as a reasonable service in response to God's giving us himself through Christ in salvation. Chrysostom's view of grace is grounded in the person of Christ the incarnate Son, the author and finisher of faith, into whose likeness we are being conformed in the progress of the Christian life.

Conclusion

The study of Chrysostom's Christology in this chapter highlights the point that his christological picture is better viewed in light of his understanding of the Christian life. It must also be noted that the Antiochene moral emphasis of Chrysostom's thought is due to the paraenetic context, not to his substantive christological positions. The picture of Christ that emerges from the three perspectives of *identification*, *mediation*, and *grace* in Chrysostom's exposition of Hebrews is consistent with the christological picture that I examined earlier in his homilies on John's Gospel. The emphasis on the humanity of Christ, however, contrasts and sharpens the contours of Chrysostom's picture of Christ in Hebrews. As the preexistent Logos, the Son added humanity to himself. In entering brotherhood with us, the Son identified with us in his humanity, suffering, and death in order that we might share in his glory. Christ the incarnate Son's solidarity with humanity was the means of our adoption into God's family; he became the first-born in order to make us joint-heirs. In entering brotherhood with us, he also suffered; therefore, as man, he is able to sympathize with us in our suffering. Christ's learning of obedience, like his suffering, was part of the humiliation of the incarnation. In partaking of flesh he entered every human experience, including death. In Chrysostom's view, Christ identified with us completely in his human nature, suffering, and death. The death of Christ was the way to reconcile us with God and bridge the distance between both parties. The only way the tyranny of death could be destroyed was if the Son entered brotherhood with us. The reality of our salvation is contingent on the authenticity of his identification with us. Only if there is a full personal presence of the Son in the incarnation, suffering, and death, can the natural separation between man and God be bridged in order that we might be able to partake of the divine fellowship.

In keeping with the focus on Christ's humanity, Chrysostom views the incarnational and sacerdotal aspects of his work as corresponding motifs. The incarnate Son entered brotherhood with us in order to mediate between God and us. The Son's becoming our high priest is viewed not in terms of nature but of grace, condescension, and humiliation. As the eternal high priest who is seated on the throne of grace, his ministry is superior because it is exercised in heaven. His once-for-all self-offering was decisive in atoning for humanity's sins. His sacerdotal ministry in heaven has implications for the faithful because it continues in the church. The church's sacerdotal ministry represents the heavenly liturgy of Christ. In partaking of the sacraments the faithful participate in the realities of heaven. Chrysostom identifies Christ's sacerdotal ministry with his human nature such that there is continuity in his person as the incarnate Son who mediates between God and man by virtue of being in himself both God and man. Both aspects of the Son's once-for-all self-offering and his continual sitting on the throne are viewed as a unity; the enthroned high priest is the enthroned Son whose self-offering was the means to our reconciliation. Chrysostom makes a distinction in the roles but not a division in the person: the Son's role as high priest and mediator does not diminish or compromise the integrity of his person.

Chrysostom views grace as God's saving action embodied in the person of Christ the Son, who purged our sins and is seated on God's right hand. The priority of God's grace in salvation is made clear by the fact that it is associated with the finished work of Christ, the benefits of which are extended to those who appropriate it in faith. God's salvific grace is depicted as working prior to and apart from human effort. He extends the good pleasure of his fellowship to us through Christ by making us his children. God's grace is also viewed as transforming human nature. When Chrysostom speaks of being clothed with Christ in baptism, he means that Christ is formed in us. Those who have been baptized have been conformed to Christ's likeness, and have been renewed in the divine image. Chrysostom makes much of the inner renewal of the soul. The soul, transformed by the grace of the Spirit is likened to heaven, where the fullness of God dwells. Grace is also associated with the work of the Holy Spirit in people. The divine agency is at work in the Christian, and the virtuous life involves human effort. The moral life is not a means to attain salvation, but a gratuitous response to God's adopting us as his children. In extending God's fellowship to us through his mediation, the incarnate Son enables us to share in the divine fellowship in our union with him. In Chrysostom's thought, the practical Christian life is the continual reflection of the embodiment of the grace of God. There is no dichotomy between grace and works at play here.

In contrast to scholarly views that characterize Chrysostom's Christology as being typically Antiochene and divisive, such that it underscores the cooperation of the free will of the assumed Man with the divine will of the Logos, I have argued that Chrysostom's Christology is unitive in that he sees the Logos-Son as single personal subject of Christ. Unlike Theodore, who viewed salvation as a future possibility, and grace as something which helps us to aspire to the second age, Chrysostom views the work of grace in us as a present reality such that we already enjoy fellowship with God as sons. God's grace in giving us his fellowship works apart from and prior to our efforts. The virtuous life is a response to God's making us his children not a means to obtain salvation in a future age.

The tendency among some patristic scholars to posit a division in Chrysostom's view of the person of Christ is reflected in their comments, which suggest that in emphasizing the human experience of Christ, Chrysostom was obliged to separate the Logos from it. Moreover, scholars have observed that the distinction in the roles of Christ's high priestly ministry and his being seated at God's right hand imply a division between God and man in the person of Christ. In response, it has been shown that Chrysostom maintains that there is a personal continuity of the divine Son in the human experiences of Christ. In entering brotherhood with us he also entered every human experience, and therefore identifies and sympathizes with us completely in his person. His heavenly liturgy consisting of his once-for-all self-offering is complete, but his ministry as the enthroned high priest continues because he is eternal. Both the divine and human aspects of the Son's ministry are viewed retrospectively as a unity. Chrysostom thus posits a distinction in the roles of Christ, but not a division in his person. My survey of the picture of Christ in Chrysostom's exposition in Hebrews reinforces the point that the particular form of Chrysostom's christological statements is better understood when examined in the context of the ecclesiastical, sacramental, and praxeological (versus speculative or theoretical) interests that govern the homilies.

Conclusion

THIS BOOK BEGAN WITH A SURVEY OF PATRISTIC HERMENEUTICS AND exegesis, underscoring the need to investigate more closely the context in which reading and interpretation of Scripture took place. I have highlighted the fact that patristic thought is bound to ecclesiastical life and is better understood when examined in that framework. The Alexandrian and Antiochene traditions of interpretation shared a common platform and goal: the church and the spiritual edification of its audience. Doctrine and application, exegesis and praxis were inseparable in the thought of the fathers. Although the approaches to reading and interpretation differed based on the different influences, be it philosophical or rhetorical, the fathers read the Scriptures (the Old and New Testaments) as the Word of God. They assumed holy writ had a coherent message, because they held that it was one and the same Spirit that inspired its various human authors. Irenaeus' and Tertullian's contests against the Gnostics underscored the need to interpret Scripture in accordance with the church's faith, which for them represented the body of truth, the centrality of Christ being their hermeneutical yardstick. This central christological idea worked as a unifying theme and was interpreted in different ways. Generally speaking, the Alexandrians preferred an allegorical hermeneutic and tended to stress the mystical aspects of the text, albeit without totally discarding the literal sense. The Antiochenes preferred a historical-literal hermeneutic, which tended to stress the moral aspects of the text. Individuals from both traditions commonly employed typology in order to make sense of Old Testament imagery, which they viewed as prefiguring Christ. The Alexandrian and Antiochene "schools" are better viewed as two parallel traditions that operated within the auspices of early church and that approximated the central idea of Christ in their own unique ways, both spiritually and practically.

Clement of Alexandria viewed Christ as the first principle, the one who spoke through the prophets, and therefore he read the Old Testament allegorically. He understood that religious truth was contained or encased in symbols and interpreted them as such. Origen viewed the Logos as the one who speaks throughout the biblical narrative and therefore viewed the Scriptures as containing spiritual truths. Christ the Word according to the flesh appears in the Scripture according to the letter. He affirmed that the teachings of Scripture must be understood in the light of its overarching christological framework. The spiritual meaning of the text was given more prominence in his interpretation than the literal sense. The exposition of Scripture was governed by the idea that spiritual knowledge imparted to the individual was imperative for the progress towards one's fellowship and union with God, and the context of the church provided the milieu in which this was actualized. Athanasius, the Cappadocians, and Cyril inherited the tendency for a spiritual hermeneutic from the Alexandrian tradition. Cyril was primarily an exegete engaged in ecclesiastical activity as the bishop of Alexandria before he became known as a christological thinker. Following the Alexandrian tradition of applying a dualistic framework in interpreting Scripture, he held to both the literal and spiritual senses of the text. Consonant with Origen and Athanasius's understanding of the *skopos* of the Scripture, Cyril explained the harmony of both Testaments by asserting that their message was confirmed and fulfilled in Christ. The recurring second Adam motif in Cyril's exegetical works pointed to a new way of life in Christ. Fallen humanity, represented by the first Adam, was restored in Christ, the second Adam. The first Adam sinned and the second Adam redeemed; the former transmitted death to humanity, while the latter through his victory over death gives them life. Cyril's exegetical works, which were more developed than his predecessors, were also paraenetic in nature and were invariably intended for the benefit of an ecclesiastical audience.

The Antiochene tradition of scriptural interpretation was not entirely dissimilar to this Alexandrian tradition. Though they had an affinity for a literal hermeneutic, the Antiochenes did not discard the spiritual sense of the Scriptures. Diodore underscored the point that reading Scripture according to its plain and historical sense provided the foundation for *theōria* or the higher spiritual sense. The moral application, associated with Antiochene paraenetic thought, was often based on the *theōria* of the text or passage. Theodore and Chrysostom inherited the Antiochene reluctance for allegorical interpretation, and their rhetorical training reinforced a hermeneutic methodology that was more philological and textual compared to the Alexandrians. The praxeological and moral emphases evident in their exposition were part of their spiritual understanding of Scripture. Moreover, the spiritual and moral aspects of scriptural interpretation were inseparable in Antiochene thought. In Chrysostom's view, the ultimate *skopos* of Scripture is the spiritual reformation of humanity, evidenced in the virtuous Christian life. God's *sunkatabasis* (condescension) in the incarnation is correspondingly reflected in the fleshly garb of human thought and language of Scripture, and therefore the latter needed to be studied with much precision and care. For Chrysostom, the types, figures, and shadows in the Old Testament were realized in the person of Christ. Christ is the truth, substance, and central theme of the Scriptures. The spiritual and moral aspects in the Antiochene tradition are akin to interpretation and application—they are not mutually exclusive.

The Alexandrian and the Antiochene traditions thus had much in common with regard to their understanding of Scripture: they held to the unity of the Testaments, viewed Christ as its central theme, underscored its spiritual and inspired nature, and commended its edificatory value. Doctrine was not isolated from practice, but was meant to govern life in the ecclesiastical context. It is this relationship between doctrine and application, theory and praxis, which comes to the fore in Chrysostom's exegesis. Chrysostom's doctrine of Christ is not speculative but exegetical and praxeological and is contoured by his pastoral concerns. His Christology is inseparable from his understanding of the life of faith and practice in the ecclesiastical context—in other words, the Christian life.

My examination of the picture of Christ in Chrysostom's exegesis of John's Gospel and Hebrews discussed the intertwined relationship between Christology and the Christian life from six perspectives: three from John's Gospel (*restoration, participation,* and *practice*) and three from Hebrews (*identification, mediation,* and *grace*). I will now review how these perspectives relate to each other and form the basis for my conclusions.

Ontological Considerations

The perspectives of *Restoration* and *Identification* focused on two related aspects, which frame Chrysostom's christological picture: his incarnational and soteriological thought. The personal continuity of the

Logos-Son in the incarnation, suffering, death, and ascension colors Chrysostom's soteriological thought and hightlights the idea that he views God's personal involvement as the *sine qua non* of the salvation of humanity. The initial focus of these related perspectives is on the ontology of the incarnation, and then later shifts to the soteriological implications of the Son's entrance into brotherhood with us. The ontology of the Logos-Son is considered in two ways: his essential similarity with the Father and his personal distinction from the Father. The polemic darts of Chrysostom's christological statements in his exposition of the Johannine prologue were mainly aimed at the Neo-Arians, a group of theologians who denied the consubstantiality of the Logos. In opposition to the Nicene teaching, they contended that he was not *homoousios* (identical in nature) with the Father, but *anomoios* (dissimilar in nature). Although Neo-Arianism was on the decline when Chrysostom was preaching (ca. 391), these heretics might have posed a threat still, for he consistently reinforces the Nicene position from his pulpit in Antioch. His exposition of the prologue to John's Gospel incorporates a wide range of statements, which underscore both the Logos' essential similarity and equality with the Father.[1]

According to Chrysostom, the Logos is identical in nature with the Father because he proceeds from the Father without alteration to his being, and is a distinct person apart from him. Similarly, arguing against the Sabellian stance of Marcellus and Photinus in his exposition of Hebrews 1:3, Chrysostom insists on the Son's distinct hypostasis, while maintaining that he is similar in essence (or nature) with the Father.[2] The Son and the Father are differentiated by their distinct hypostases. The Logos-Son, who is a distinct person, enjoys natural communion with the Father, and is consubstantial with him.

Furthermore, Chrysostom accentuates the continuity of the Logos-Son in the incarnation, noting that the integrity of his person remained undiminished in the partaking of the flesh. He asserts that in the incarnation, the Logos-Son added humanity to himself without any change to his essence: "When you hear: 'The Word became flesh,' do not be struck with consternation or downcast. His essence was not transformed into

---

1. Further, Chrysostom adds that the Logos was as "eternal as the Father himself, for the Father was never without the Word but always God was with God, though each in His own Person." Chrysostom, Homily 4, in *John*, FOC 33:45–46 (*PG* 59.47).

2. Chrysostom, Homily 2, in *Hebrews*, section 2, *NPNF* 14:370 (*PG* 63.20).

flesh . . . but remaining what He is, He thus took the form of a slave."³ Being who he is (consubstantial and co-eternal with the Father, yet distinct), he partook of the flesh in the incarnation without alteration to his person. He is the same person before and after the incarnation. In his comments on John 1:14, Chrysostom affirms that the Logos, the true Son of God, descended and assumed human nature in order to make us God's children and bring us to glory. The Logos-Son is viewed as the person to whom being and becoming is applied. Likewise, commenting on Philippians 2:6f., Chrysostom equates God, Christ, and Son of God and posits that the single personal subject of Christ is the Logos-Son, who added humanity to himself without undergoing any change to his own nature.⁴ Christ, the Logos-Son, did not become God or assume deity, because he always was such. Rather, the Son of God became man and took the form of a servant. Further, Chrysostom does not speculate much about the union of the two natures in the incarnate Christ; he is content to affirm that it is an ineffable and inexplicable union, and maintains that there is no confusion or commingling of substances.⁵ At this stage in the history of the early church—post-Nicea and pre-Chalcedon—the debate about the union between the two natures in Christ (whether hypostatic or prosopic) had not been resolved, or even clearly defined as a problem. Perhaps in the light of the prevailing Neo-Arian controversy and their position that insisted that one can define and know God in his essence, Chrysostom was less inclined to speculate on how the human and divine relate in the one Christ. His focus generally was on the unity of the incarnate Logos and his relation with the Father.

Chrysostom views the Logos-Son as the single subject in Christ, whose actions were often described as acts of condescension. Depending on the context, they are correspondingly viewed as exemplary or didactic. Certain characteristics and experiences are attributed to the one Christ according to his divine nature and others according to his incarnation. The distinction corresponds to that between who he is immanently and what he does economically, not to the duality of subjects in Christ's person. "He dwells always in this tabernacle, for he put on our flesh, not to put it off again, but to have it always with him."⁶ His person is the same

---

3. Chrysostom, Homily 11, in *John*, FOC 33:107 (PG 59.79).
4. Chrysostom, Homily 7, in *Philippians*, section 3, NPNF 13:214–15 (PG 62.232).
5. Chrysostom, Homily 11, in *John*, FOC 33:109 (PG 59.80).
6. Ibid.

before and after the incarnation, except that after the incarnation the Son partook of flesh, adding humanity to what he already possessed as God.

In Chrysostom's view, fallen humanity, through sinful disobedience, lost fellowship with God, marring the image and likeness of God. This lead to corruption and death, and thus humanity was dispossessed of the grace of the Spirit. The disastrous effects of the corruption of sin could be reversed, and fallen human nature restored to its original fullness, only if God was personally involved in the redemption process, as this was the common message of the Gospels for Chrysostom.[7] Our restoration and spiritual renewal is contingent on the reality of God's personal presence in the incarnation, suffering, death, and ascension of Christ. In keeping with this emphasis, Chrysostom elsewhere asserts, "God himself, remember, despite his divinity, took to himself our human flesh, and for no other reason than the salvation of the human race became man."[8] This soteriological paradigm requires the ontological continuity of the Son in the humiliation of the incarnation. Therefore Chrysostom emphasizes the idea that only if the Son truly entered brotherhood with us can he give us by grace what he possesses by nature. This suggests that the incarnational union forms the basis for the restoration of human nature, and is thus viewed as a redeeming union.

Chrysostom employs different images to illustrate this idea. In his commentary on John 1:14, he compares fallen human nature to the fallen tabernacle of David, which required the very creator to be incarnate in order that it might be restored to its original creation. Just as an able architect restores an edifice that has fallen into disrepair, so the Logos-Son—the agent of creation—acted in the incarnation. This idea is complemented by two related images that also depict the personal continuity of the Logos in the incarnation. Christ the Son is viewed as a royal bridegroom, who condescended from on high in the humiliation of the incarnation in order to escort human nature—portrayed as a

---

7. "But what are these points? Such as follow: That God became man, that He wrought miracles, that He was crucified, that He was buried, that He rose again, that He ascended, that He will judge, that He hath given commandments tending to salvation, that He hath brought in a law not contrary to the Old Testament, that He is a Son, that He is only-begotten, that He is a true Son, that He is of the same substance with the Father, and as many things as are like these; for touching these we shall find that there is in them a full agreement." Chrysostom, Homily 1, in *Matthew*, section 6, NPNF 10:3 (PG 57.16–17).

8. Chrysostom, Homily 3, in *Genesis*, FOC 74:46 (PG 53.37).

lowly bride—back to his Father's house to share in the divine fellowship of heaven through his ascension and exaltation. Similarly, commenting on Hebrews 1:6, Chrysostom portrays the continuity of the Son in the incarnation employing another royal image. He depicts the Son as a king who, wishing to be reconciled with those who have offended him and are in chains outside the palace, himself goes out in order to bring about this reconciliation. In partaking of the flesh and entering brotherhood with us, and through his subsequent ascension and enthronement, he exalted human nature to the royal throne. In these images, Christ the Son is viewed as the single acting subject: the one who condescends, the one who goes out, and the one who returns to heaven with human nature, suggesting the personal continuity of the Logos-Son in the incarnation and the heavenly session. The incarnation (the "origin and root of all our blessings") is viewed as the soteriological foundation and the basis of the restoration of human nature.[9] In partaking of the flesh and entering brotherhood with us, he restored human nature to its original glory and now extends the privilege of divine fellowship to us through grace.

The personal continuity of the Logos-Son is maintained not only in the incarnation, but also in the suffering and death of Christ: "He was born, was brought up, grew, suffered all things necessary and at last He died."[10] In partaking of the flesh, he added human attributes and human experiences to what he already possessed as God. Christ's human experience was complete and real; it was no different from ours and was part of the humiliation of the incarnation. Chrysostom also notes that in entering brotherhood with us and enduring affliction, Christ knows not only as God but also as man. The idea of knowledge through experience is stressed.[11] Moreover, in entering brotherhood with us, the Son also experienced death. Chrysostom depicts Christ as a physician who, though not needing to taste the food prepared for his patient, yet tastes it first in order to persuade and encourage his patient to partake of it. In Chrysostom's view, it was necessary to restore fellowship with God for the Savior himself to experience death on behalf of the ones whom he will redeem. His death is more than a matter of identifying with us in our mortality but also a means through which he delivered us. Death is depicted as a defeated tyrant under whose dominion hu-

---

9. Chrysostom, Homily 2, in *Mathew*, section 3, NPNF 10:10 (PG 57.27).
10. Chrysostom, Homily 5, in *Hebrews*, section 1, NPNF 14:388 (PG 63.47).
11. Ibid., section 5, NPNF 14:390 (PG 63.50).

manity was held captive. Chrysostom portrays Christ as a victorious conqueror who defeated death. For Chrysostom the tyranny of death could be overthrown only if Christ is the Son. Our complete salvation is contingent on the reality of the Son's entering brotherhood with us; the redemption of humanity is possible if the Son is personally involved in this process. In identifying with us completely in his humanity and suffering, Christ the eternal Son entered human experience, and through his death and ascension he has made it possible for us to enjoy divine fellowship. Chrysostom's insistence on the reality of Christ's human experiences should not be viewed solely as a polemic against docetic interpretations of the incarnation, but must also be seen as being integral to his soteriology.

Sacramental Mediation

The church's sacramental context is where the benefits of the divine economy are conveyed to the faithful. In identifying with Christ in baptism, the faithful are bestowed with the privilege of sonship, reversing the corruption of sin and condemnation against humanity through the grace of the Spirit, who renews and refashions the believer into a new creation. "He was born after the flesh, that you might be born after the Spirit, He was born of a woman, that you might cease to be the son of a woman."[12] In Chrysostom's view, sacramental participation has ontological and practical implications for the faithful. To be baptized is to be clothed with Christ, indwelt by him, renewed in his image, and given the privilege of divine fellowship through our union with him. Only if Christ is God's natural Son can he impart divine fellowship and enable us to become the sons of God by grace.

The corresponding perspectives of *participation* and *mediation* develop the sacramental and sacerdotal aspects of Chrysostom's theology as they relate to the person of Christ. Chrysostom depicts Christ in various ways: as the source of life who has complete power over death; as a physician who saves us from death and restores our communion with God; as a judge who has authority to pardon our sins; and as a heavenly conqueror and victorious athlete who overcame the tyranny of death. All these images suggest his equality with the Father, and his complete power and authority over death. Chrysostom also highlights the idea

---

12. Chrysostom, Homily 2, in *Matthew*, section 3, *NPNF* 10:10 (*PG* 57.27).

that the ultimate reason for the Son's incarnation is that—through his death—he might put an end to death and unite us with God. The Son's double consubstantiality is the basis for our sharing in the divine life. He is the "bread of life" who imparts life to those who are joined to him. In keeping with the traditional patristic interpretation, he associates the origin of the church's mysteries with the death of Christ, the benefits of which are appropriated by the faithful in the Eucharist. Chrysostom notes that as the "living bread," Christ "welds together for us this life and the life to come." Invoking the head-body imagery, he avers that we become one with Christ through our union with him in the eucharistic participation.[13] To partake of the "bread of life" or the life-giving flesh is to be united to Christ and share in the eternal life of God. Divine fellowship is promised to those who abide in Christ through their sacramental participation. As members of the sacramental community, the faithful are placed in the life of Christ.

Furthermore, Chrysostom views the incarnational and sacerdotal aspects of Christ as two dimensions of the same soteriological picture, thus linking the person and work of Christ. The incarnate Son who entered heaven mediates on our behalf. As the one who constitutes what he mediates, Christ's once-for-all self-oblation is decisive in atoning for our sins and reconciling us with God. By virtue of his glorification and enthronement, the eternal Son raises human nature to the royal throne to share in the heavenly fellowship: "It is a great and wonderful thing, and full of amazement that our flesh should sit on high, and be adored by angels and archangels."[14] The enthroned Son is the mediator who reconciles us with God and enables us to share in the divine life. As the one who unites both the human and divine realties in him, he gives us the privilege of participating in the benefits of his decisive atonement in the sacramental context.

Chrysostom's view of the priesthood of Christ does not posit a dichotomy in the state of the Son's exalted glory and the state of his humiliation. The enthroned Son is the enthroned high priest: the same person fulfills the royal and sacerdotal roles. The incarnate Son became our high priest in order to mediate between God and us. The heavenly liturgy consisting of his self-offering is complete, but his intercession continues because he is eternal. His decisive atonement and his continual interces-

---

13. Chrysostom, Homily 46, in *John*, FOC 33:468 (PG 59.260).
14. Chrysostom, Homily 5, section 1, in *Hebrews*, NPNF 14:388 (PG 63.46–47).

sion are considered together as a unity; the role as a servant and minister is complete, but his role as the mediator continues. Both aspects of his role as high priest and mediator are united in his person. God as man fulfills the mediatorial task and embodies what he mediates to us. Christ's heavenly liturgy has implications for the faithful in the church, his body. By participating in the institutions of the church, the faithful participate in the heavenly realities. In Chrysostom's view, there is a continuum between the heavenly and the earthly realms; the two are not viewed as being antithetical to each other. Christ who mediates in heaven indwells the purified soul of the Christian, the earthly embodiment of the heavenly sanctuary. The heavenly and earthly realities are united in the life of the Christian, for the Christian life is a participation in the life of Christ. Because the incarnate Son is consubstantial both with the Father and with us, by uniting human nature to himself he has made it possible for us to commune with God. Chrysostom's sacramental and sacerdotal views underscore the participatory character of his theology and betray a unitive Christology.

Practical Outworking

The corresponding praxeological and charitological perspectives shed light on the relationship between the practical Christian life and the grace of God. God's grace is characterized in two dimensions: objectively as what God gives us in Christ, and subjectively as spiritual empowerment. The former is viewed in conjunction with the once-for-all atoning work of Christ and is associated with God's largess. The latter is characterized as God's work in people, continually empowering them to live a life that is consistent with their union with Christ. Divine assistance precedes and incorporates human response. The inner renewal and transformation granted to the Christian in baptism has existential and practical implications. The baptized already enjoy the privilege of sonship by grace: "Not only was pardon for our sins granted to us ... but also righteousness, and holiness, and adoption of sons, and grace of the Spirit, much more splendid gifts and richer by far. Through this grace we have become dear to God, no longer merely as servants, but as sons and friends."[15] The moral or virtuous life is not a means to obtain salvation, but a gratuitous response to God's grace given to us in Christ.

15. Chrysostom, Homily 14, in *John*, FOC 33:135 (PG 59.94).

The sacramental and the practical go hand in hand in Chrysostom's understanding of the Christian life. The practical Christian life is also viewed as the imitation of Christ, the Word who became flesh.[16] Imitation and participation are coincident; imitation is participation, because the Christian life is lived out as a participatory response to one's sacramentally mediated union with Christ. In Chrysostom's view, to partake of God's grace is to be the recipient of his fellowship and embody this fellowship in practice. The Christian life is framed by God's grace from its inception to its end and is viewed as a progressive conformation to the likeness of Christ. Chrysostom characterizes the Christian life as a voyage with Christ as our pilot (John's Gospel). His work in us through the Holy Spirit (Hebrews) is viewed as energizing and propelling us forward to our eschatological and ultimate union with God. There is no disjunction between grace and works in Chrysostom's understanding of the Christian life; the reception of grace is continual, and the striving after virtue is imperative in the process of our transformation and union with God. Both aspects of grace are integrated with the person of Christ. The one who sits on the throne of grace constitutes what he extends to us through his continual ministry as the incarnate Son. The Christian life is the embodiment of the grace of God as it is extended to us through Christ. To partake of the grace of God through Christ is to partake of God's fellowship as his children, and enjoy the privileges of our adoption. The Christian life for Chrysostom is the visible representation of the inward work of grace, the evidence of our conformation to the likeness of Christ, both spiritually and morally.

Chrysostom's christological picture is sketched with a paraenetic stylus and is colored by his understanding of the Christian life. As one of the church's celebrated preachers who addressed Christians as a priest in Antioch, and subsequently as a bishop in Constantinople, his doctrinal thought is contoured by his pastoral concerns. In emphasizing the necessity and reality of the incarnation as the prerequisite for humanity's restoration to its original fullness, Chrysostom views God's personal involvement as imperative in the economy of redemption. Both aspects of the divine and human realities in the one Christ are stressed

16. "The actions performed by Christ in a human way were so performed not merely for the purpose of confirming the incarnation, but also that he might instruct us to virtuous living. For, if he did everything as God, whence would we be able to learn what we ought to do when faced with trials outside the realm of our experience?" Chrysostom, Homily 49, in *John*, FOC 41:12 (PG 59.273).

in Chrysostom's thought. The personal continuity of the Son in his incarnational and sacerdotal functions forms the basis of Chrysostom's sacramental thought. The church as a sacramental community is where the heavenly and the earthly realities are united in the head-body, human-divine relationship. The sacramental life is a life in Christ. The Christian's sacramentally mediated union with Christ is a redeeming, renewing, and a restoring union that places him or her in the life of God. The moral or virtuous life is the evidence of our being restored in the image of God's Son and being made joint-heirs. The sacramental and the practical aspects are inseparable in Chrysostom's doctrinal thought, and these interconnections are an outworking of his unitive Christology.

My study of Chrysostom's picture of Christ as it emerges in his exposition has shown that it is bound to the church's faith, and this fact colors his reading and interpretation of Scripture. The majority of scholarly readings of patristic doctrine tend to examine it apart from its context, bifurcating the doctrinal from the practical, the spiritual from the moral, and the paraenetic from the mimetic, resulting in lopsided views in binary, "either-or" categories.

In Chrysostom one sees elements of both Alexandrian and Antiochene traditions. The unitive aspects of his Christology, which are foundational to his soteriological thought, are consistent with the thought of Athanasius and later Alexandrians like Cyril. Given that Cyril was present at Chrysostom's deposition at the Synod of the Oak (where the grounds for his deposition were disciplinary and not doctrinal), and the fact that he eventually restored Chrysostom's name to the liturgical diptychs, one can speculate that it was possible that he might have been acquainted with some of the works of the bishop of Constantinople. The infrastructure of their christological and soteriological thought is parallel at many points.

The focus of Chrysostom's christological picture is on one subject: the Logos-Son who partook of flesh and entered brotherhood with us in order to restore our fellowship with God as sons. The reversal of the corruption of sin required God's personal presence in this world for humanity to be redeemed. God had to become human in order that humanity might enjoy divine fellowship. This foundational idea associated mainly with the Alexandrian tradition shapes Chrysostom's picture of Christ. His sacramental thought, which is not far removed from his christological thought, also bears resemblance to the Alexandrian tradition.

The inner renewal and the conformation of the baptized to the divine image, and their enjoying the privilege of divine communion through their sacramentally mediated union with Christ, are integral elements of Chrysostom's thought and reflect the participatory nature of his theology.

Chrysostom's hermeneutic methodology is characteristically Antiochene and is similar to that of Theodore's. The literal, historical, and philological aspects of the text are taken account of in the exercise of scriptural interpretation. The biblical text provides both the theological basis for his christological picture and the thematic background for his exegesis. The ethical and moral emphases of Chrysostom's preaching are consistent with the Antiochene tradition and complement his Christology. Chrysostom's stress on the imitation of Christ, however, is not a reflection of the idea that he views him, like Theodore, as the assumed Man and as an exemplar in the progressive moral march to the future age. Rather, it is an affirmation of the present reality of God's grace already at work in the Christian. The life of Christ is not viewed as a paradigm for moral accomplishment in order to obtain salvation, but is viewed instead as a demonstration of virtue for those who have already been made God's children. One's imitation of Christ ensues from one's participation in Christ and is viewed as a praxeological expression of God's work. This emphasis in Chrysostom's exposition must be associated with the paraenetic goals of his preaching, rather than being explained simply as an Antiochene rhetorical trait.

The role Scripture in the church, and the Christian faith as it was enshrined in the Creeds, were common motifs shared by the Alexandrians and the Antiochenes. The hermeneutic methodology might have differed superficially, but the approximation of scriptural authority and the core tradition remained the same foundationally. These two branches of the early church shared much in common. Consequently, their status as two opposing or rival schools of thought must not be exaggerated; rather, they should be understood as two traditions within the church that were trying to approximate what they commonly and uniquely maintained was the central message of the Scriptures: Jesus Christ. Chrysostom's Christology can be cited as evidence that these two parallel traditions overlapped, lending support to the view that there was concordance in patristic thought in the later decades of the fourth and early fifth centuries.

Chrysostom's usage of the head-body image to depict the continuity of Christ's heavenly ministry in the church suggests that he views the sacramental community, as a whole, as participating in the life and liturgy of Christ. This encapsulates the fact that his christological thought is inseparably bound to life in the ecclesiastical context. I have shown that such an understanding requires the person of Christ to be the divine Son himself. A view that underscores the incarnation of Christ as the basis of our enjoying adoption into God's family demands a unitive Christology; for only if he is Son by nature can he extend God's fellowship to us by grace. I have also demonstrated that Chrysostom's picture of Christ, as it emerges in his exposition of John's Gospel and Hebrews, is one in which the personal continuity of the Son is underscored. In the incarnation he entered brotherhood and identified with us in all things; in his exaltation and heavenly session, he is enthroned and continues his eternal ministry; and in the church, he extends God's fellowship and transforms us through grace. The enthroned Son is the incarnate Savior and high priest, whose ministry continues in the church—the sacramental community. In Chrysostom's view, only if Christ is the natural Son, in whom the divine and human are inseparably united, can he redeem and restore us to glory by enabling us to participate in his eternal relationship with God.

Bibliography

Reference Works

Altaner, Berthold. *Patrology*. Translated by Hilda C. Graef. Freiburg: Herder Druck, 1960.
Bauer, W. *A Greek-English Lexicon of the New Testament and Other Early Christian Literature*. 2nd ed. Translated by W. F. Arndt, F. W. Gingrich, and F. W. Danker. Chicago: University of Chicago Press, 1979.
Bindley, T. H., and F. W. Green. *The Oecumenical Documents of Faith*. 4th ed. London: Methuen, 1950.
Cross, F. L., and Elizabeth Livingstone. *The Oxford Dictionary of the Christian Church*. 3rd ed. Oxford: Oxford University Press, 1997.
Ferguson, Everett. *Encyclopedia of Early Christianity*. Garland Reference Library of the Humanities. New York: Garland, 1990.
Geerard, M. *Clavis Patrum Graecorum*. 5 vols. Corpus Christianorum. Turnhout: Brepols, 1974–1987.
Lampe, G. W. H. *A Patristic Greek Lexicon*. Oxford: Clarendon, 1961.
Lidell, H. G., and R. Scott. *A Greek-English Lexicon*. 9th ed. Oxford: Clarendon, 1940.
Pelikan, Jaroslav. *The Christian Tradition: A History of the Development of Doctrine*. 5 vols. Chicago: University of Chicago Press, 1971.
Quasten, Johannes. *Patrology: The Golden Age of Greek Patristic Literature*. 3 vols. Utrecht: Newman, 1963.
Richardson, Alan, and John Bowden. *A New Dictionary of Christian Theology*. London: SCM, 1983.
Schaff, Philip. *History of the Christian Church: From the Birth of Christ to the Reign of Constantine*. New York: Scribner, 1859.

Primary Sources, Texts, and Translations

Chrysostom, John. *Baptismal Instructions*. Edited by Johannes Quasten and Walter Burghardt. Translated by Paul W. Harkins. Ancient Christian Writers 31. Westminster: Newman, 1963.
———. *Commentary on Saint John the Apostle and Evangelist*. Vol. 1, Homilies 1–47. Translated by Sr. Thomas Aquinas Goggin. The Fathers of the Church 33. Washington, DC: The Catholic University of America Press, 1957.
———. *Commentary on Saint John the Apostle and Evangelist*. Vol. 2, Homilies 48–88. Translated by Sr. Thomas Aquinas Goggin. The Fathers of the Church 41. Washington, DC: The Catholic University of America Press, 1960.

———. *Commentary on the Psalms*. 2 vols. Translated by Robert C. Hill. Brookline: Holy Cross Orthodox Press, 1998.

———. *Huit catéchèses baptismales inédites*. Edited and translated by A. Wenger. Sources Chrétiennes 50. Paris: Cerf, 1957.

———. *On the Incomprehensible Nature of God*. Translated by Paul W. Harkins. The Fathers of the Church 72. Washington, DC: Catholic University of America Press, 1984.

———. *On Virginity, Against Remarriage*. Translated by Sally Rieger Shore. Studies in Women and Religion 9. New York: Mellen, 1983.

———. *S. Iohannis Chrysostomi opera omnia*. Patrologiae Cursus Completus, Series Graeca. Vols. 47–64. Edited by J. P. Migne. Paris, 1863–1864.

———. *Six Books on the Priesthood*. Translated by Graham Neville. London: SPCK, 1964.

———. *Sur l'incomprehesibilité de Dieu*. Edited by A. M. Malingrey. Translated by R. Flacelière. Sources Chrétiennes 13. Paris: Cerf, 1947.

———. *Works*. In *A Select Library of the Nicene and Post-Nicene Fathers*, First Series. Vols. 9–14. Grand Rapids: Eerdmans, 1975.

Clement of Alexandria. *Exhortation to the Heathen*. In *Ante-Nicene Fathers*. Vol. 2. Edited by A. Roberts and J. Donaldson. Grand Rapids: Eerdmans, 1989.

———. *Paedagogus*. Patrologiae Cursus Completus, Series Graeca 8. Paris, 1863.

———. *Protrepticum ad Graecos*. Die Grieschischen Christlichen Schriftsteller 1. Berlin: Berlin Academy, 1906.

———. *Stromata*. Edited by O. Stählin. Die Grieschischen Christlichen Schriftsteller 2. Berlin: Berlin Academy, 1906.

———. *Stromata*. In *The Ante-Nicene Fathers: Translations of the Writings of the Fathers Down to AD 325*. Vol. 2. Edited by A. Roberts and J. Donaldson. Grand Rapids: Eerdmans, 1989.

Cyril of Alexandria. *Commentarii in Johannem*. 3 vols. *Sancti Patris nostri Cyrilli Archiepiscopi Alexandrini in D. Joannis Evangelium: Accedunt fragementa varia necnon tractatus ad Tiberium diaconum duo*. Edited by P. E. Pusey. Oxford: Clarendon, 1872.

———. *Commentary on the Gospel according to St. John*. Vol. 1, *S. John 1–8*. Translated by P. E. Pusey. Library of the Fathers of the Holy Catholic Church. Oxford, 1884.

———. *Commentary on the Gospel according to St. John*. Vol. 2, *S. John 9–21*. Translated by Thomas Randell. Library of the Fathers of the Holy Catholic Church. Oxford, 1885.

———. *De adoration in spiritu et veritate*. Patrologiae Cursus Completus, Series Graeca 68. Paris, 1863

———. *Glaphyra in Pentatechum*. Patrologiae Cursus Completus, Series Graeca 69. Paris, 1863

Diodore of Tarsus. *Commentarii in Psalmos I–L*. Edited by J. M. Olivier. Corpus Christianorum, Series Graeca 6. Turnholt: Brepols, 1980.

Irenaeus. *Adversus Haereses*. Patrologiae Cursus Completus, Series Graeca 7. Paris, 1863.

———. *Against Heresies*. In *Ante-Nicene Fathers*. Vol. 2. Edited by A. Roberts and J. Donaldson. Grand Rapids: Eerdmans, 1989.

Origen. *De Principiis*. Die Grieschischen Christlichen Schriftsteller 5. Edited by P. Koetschau. Berlin: Berlin Academy, 1913.

———. *On First Principles.* In *Ante-Nicene Fathers.* Vol. 4. Edited by A. Roberts and J. Donaldson. Grand Rapids: Eerdmans, 1989.
Tertullian. *De Praescriptione Haereticorum.* Corpus Scriptorum Christianorum Orientalium 2. Edited by A. Kroymann. Vienna: Tempsky, 1942.
———. *The Prescription of Heretics.* In *Ante-Nicene Fathers.* Vol. 3. Edited by A. Roberts and J. Donaldson. Grand Rapids: Eerdmans, 1989.
Theodore of Mopsuestia. *Commentary on the Minor Epistles of St. Paul.* Edited by H. B. Swete. Cambridge: Cambridge University Press, 1880–1882.
———. *Theodri Mopsuestini Commentarius in Evangelium Johannis Apostoli.* Syriac Series, Corpus Scriptorum Christianorum Orientalium 4.3. Edited by J. M. Vosté. Louvain, 1940. (English translation of some fragments in Greer [*Captain of Our Salvation*; *Theodore of Mopsuestia*], Norris [*The Christological Controversy*]).

Secondary Sources and Literature

Ackroyd, P., and C. F. Evans. *The Cambridge History of the Bible.* Vol. 1. Cambridge: Cambridge University Press, 1970.
Aldama, José Antonio de. *Repertorium pseudochrysostomicum.* Paris: Centre national de la recherché scientifique, 1965.
Allen, Pauline. "The Homilist and the Congregation: A Case Study of Chrysostom's Homilies on Hebrews." *Augustinianum* 36 (1996) 397–421.
Allen, Pauline, and Wendy Mayer. "The Thirty-Four Homilies on Hebrews: The Last Series Delivered by Chrysostom in Constantinople?" *Journal of Theological Studies* 65 (1995) 309–48.
Ameriger, Thomas Edward. *The Stylistic Influence of the Second Sophistic on the Panegyrical Sermons of St. John Chrysostom.* Washington, DC: Catholic University of America Press, 1921.
Attrep, Abe. "The Teacher and His Teachings: Chrysostom's Homiletic Approach as Seen in Commentaries on the Gospel of John." *St. Vladimir's Theological Quarterly* 38 (1994) 293–301.
Attwater, Donald. *Saints of the East.* London: Harvill, 1963.
Aubineau, Michel, editor. *Codices Chrysostomici Graeci I: Britannae et Hiberniae.* Paris: Centre national de la recherche scientifique, 1968.
Aulén, Gustaf. *Christus Victor: An Historical Study of the Three Main Types of the Idea of Atonement.* Translated by A. G. Herbert. London: SPCK, 1970.
Barnabas. *Epistles.* Translated by K. Lake. The Loeb Classical Library. London: Heinemann, 1912.
Barnard, Lawrence R. "Christology and Soteriology in the Preaching of John Chrysostom." PhD diss., Southwestern Baptist Theological Seminary, 1974.
Bardenhewer, Otto. *Patrology: The Lives and Works of the Fathers of the Church.* Translated by Thomas J. Shahan. St. Louis: Herder, 1950.
Bate, H. N. "Some Technical Terms of Greek Exegesis." *Journal of Theological Studies* (1923) 59–66.
Baur, Chrysostomus. *John Chrysostom and His Time.* Translated by Sr. M. Gonzaga. 2 vols. 2nd ed. Gateshead on Tyne: Sands, 1959.

———. *S. Jean Chrysostome et ses oeuvres dans l'histoire littéraire*. Recueil des travaux; publiés par les membres des conférences d'histoire et de philology 18. Louvain: Université de Louvain, 1907.

Benin, Stephen D. "Sacrifice as Education in Augustine and Chrysostom." *Church History* 52 (1983) 7–20.

Bettenson, Henry. *The Early Christian Fathers*. London: Oxford University Press, 1956.

Blowers, Paul M., editor and translator. *The Bible in Greek Christian Antiquity*. Notre Dame: University of Notre Dame Press, 1997.

Bouyer, Louis. *The Spirituality of the New Testament and the Fathers*. Vol. 1 of *A History of Christian Spirituality*, 3 vols., by Louis Bouyer et al. London: Burns & Oates, 1963.

Bright, William. *The Age of the Fathers: Being Chapters in the History of the Church during the Fourth and Fifth Centuries*. Vol. 2. London: Longmans, Green, 1903.

Brightman, F. E. *Liturgies Eastern and Western*. Oxford: Clarendon, 1896.

Cameron, Averil. *Christianity and the Rhetoric of the Empire: The Development of Christian Discourse*. Berkeley: University of California Press, 1991.

Campenhausen, Hans von. *The Fathers of the Greek Church*. London: A. & C. Black, 1963.

Carson, D. A., and J. D. Woodbridge, editors. *Scripture and Truth*. Grand Rapids: Baker, 1995.

Carter, Robert, editor. *Codices Chrysostomici Graeci II: Germaniae*. Paris: Center national de la recherche scientifique, 1970.

———. "The Future of Chrysostom Studies." *Studia Patristica* 10 (1970) 14–21.

Chadwick, Henry. "Eucharist and Christology in the Nestorian Controversy." *Journal of Theological Studies* (1951) 145–64.

Chase, Frederic Henry. *Chrysostom: A Study in the History of Biblical Interpretation*. Cambridge: C. J. Clay, 1887.

Clark, Elizabeth A. "John Chrysostom and the Subintroductae." *Church History* 46 (1977) 171–85.

Coleman-Norton, P. R., editor. *Palladii Dialogus de Vita S. Joannis Chrysostomi*. Cambridge: Cambridge University Press, 1928.

———. "St. Chrysostom and the Greek Philosophers." *Classical Philology* 25 (1930) 305–17.

Cunningham, Mary B., and Pauline Allen, editors. *Preacher and Audience: Studies in Early Christian and Byzantine Homiletics*. Leiden: Brill, 1998.

Cyril of Jerusalem. *Cyril of Jerusalem and Nemesius of Emesa*. Edited by William Telfer. The Library of Christian Classics 4. London: SCM, 1955.

Daniélou, Jean. *From Shadows to Reality: Studies in Biblical Typology of the Fathers*. Translated by Wulstan Hibberd. London: Burns & Oates, 1960.

———. *Origen*. Translated by Walter Mitchell. London: Sheed & Ward, 1955.

Devréesse, R. *Le commentaire de Théodore de Mopsueste sur les Psaumes*. Studi e Testi 93. Vatican City, 1939.

Dewart, J. M. "The Notion of 'Person' Underlying the Christology of Theodore of Mopsuestia." *Texte und Untersuchungen* 116 (1975) 199–207.

Dockery, David S. *Biblical Interpretation Then and Now: Contemporary Hermeneutics in the Light of the Early Church*. Grand Rapids: Baker, 1992.

Dreyfus, Francois. "Divine Condescence as a Hermeneutic Principle of the Old Testament in Jewish and Christian Tradition." *Immanuel* 19 (1984–85) 74–86.

Fairbairn, Donald. *Grace and Christology in the Early Church*. Oxford Early Christian Studies. New York: Oxford University Press, 2003.

———. "Patristic Exegesis and Theology: The Cart and the Horse." *The Westminster Theological Journal* 69 (2007) 1–19.

Farrar, Frederic W. *History of Interpretation*. London: Macmillan, 1886.

Fee, Gordon, D. "The Text of John and Mark in the Writings of Chrysostom." *New Testament Studies* 26 (1980) 525–47.

Ferguson, Everett. "Preaching at Epiphany: Gregory of Nyssa and John Chrysostom on Baptism." *Church History* 66 (1997) 1–17.

Finn, Thomas M. *The Liturgy of Baptism in the Baptismal Instructions of St. John Chrysostom*. Washington, DC: Catholic University of America Press, 1967.

Florovsky, Georges. "The Lamb of God." *Scottish Journal of Theology* 4 (1951) 13–28.

Fotopoulos, John. "John Chrysostom: On Holy Pascha." *Greek Orthodox Theological Review* 37 (1992) 123–34.

Frank, Georgia. "'Taste and See': The Eucharist and the Eyes of Faith in the Fourth Century." *Church History* 70 (2001) 619–43.

Froehlich, Karlfried. *Biblical Interpretation in the Early Church*. Sources of Early Christian Thought. Philadelphia: Fortress, 1984.

Garrett, D. A. *An Analysis of the Hermeneutics of John Chrysostom's Commentary on Isaiah 1–8 with an English Translation*. Studies in the Bible and Early Christianity 12. Lewiston: Mellen, 1992.

Garroway, Joshua. "The Law-Observant Lord: John Chrysostom's Engagement with the Jewishness of Christ." *Journal of Early Christian Studies* 18 (2010) 591–615

Gorday, Peter. *Principles of Patristric Exegesis: Romans 9–11 in Origen, John Chrysostom, and Augustine*. New York: Mellen, 1983.

Grant, Robert M., and David Tracy, editors. *A Short History of the Interpretation of the Bible*. 2nd ed. London: SCM, 1984.

Greeley, Dolores. "The Church as the 'Body of Christ' according to the Teaching of John Chrysostom." PhD diss., University of Notre Dame, 1971.

Greer, Rowan A. "The Antiochene Christology of Diodore of Tarsus." *Journal of Theological Studies* 17 (1966) 327–41.

———. "The Antiochene Exegesis of Hebrews." PhD diss., Yale University, 1965.

———. *The Captain of Our Salvation: A Study in the Patristic Exegesis of Hebrews*. Beiträge zur Geschichte der biblischen Exegese 15. Tübingen: J. C. B. Mohr, 1973.

———. *Theodore of Mopsuestia: Exegete and Theologican*. Leigton Buzzard: Faith Press, 1961.

Gregg, Robert C., and Dennis E. Groh. *Early Arianism: A View of Salvation*. London: SCM, 1981.

Grillmeier, Aloys. *Christ in Christian Tradition: From the Apostolic Age to Chalcedon (451)*. Translated by John Bowden. 2nd ed. London: Mowbray, 1975.

Gwatkin, H. M. *Studies of Arianism*. 2nd ed. Cambridge: D. Bell, 1900.

Hall, Christopher A. *Reading Scripture with the Church Fathers*. Downers Grove: InterVarsity, 1998.

Hanson, R. P. C. *Allegory and Event: A Study of the Sources and Significance of Origen's Interpretation of Scripture*. London: SCM, 1959.

———. *Tradition in the Early Church*. London: SCM, 1962.

Hardy, E. R., and C. Richardson. *Christology of the Later Fathers*. The Library of Christian Classics. London: SCM, 1954.

Harkins, Paul W. "Pre-Baptismal Rites in Chrysostom's Baptismal Catecheses." *Texte und Untersuchungen* 93 (1966) 219–38.

———. "Text Tradition of Chrysostom's Commentary on John." *Theological Studies* 19 (1958) 404–12.

Harnack, Adolf von. *Bible Reading in the Early Church*. Translated by J. R. Wilkinson. London: Williams & Norgate, 1912.

Hatch, Edwin. *The Influence of Greek Ideas on Christianity*. Gloucester, MA: P. Smith, 1970.

Hauser, Alan J., and Duane F. Watson. *A History of Biblical Interpretation*. Vol. 1, *The Ancient Period*. Grand Rapids: Eerdmans, 2003.

Hay, Camillus. "Antiochene Exegesis and Christology of Theodore of Mopsuestia and John Chrysostom." *Australian Biblical Review* 12 (1964) 10–23.

———. "St. John Chrysostom and the Integrity of the Human Nature of Christ." *Franciscan Studies* 19 (1959) 298–317.

Hill, Robert C. "Akribeia: A Principle of Chrysostom's Exegesis." *Colloqium* 14 (1981) 32–36.

———. Introduction to *Commentary on the Psalms*, by John Chrysostom. 2 vols. Brookline, MA: Holy Cross Orthodox Press, 1998.

———. "A Pelagian Commentator on the Psalms?" *Irish Theological Quarterly* 63 (1998) 263–71.

———. "The Spirituality of Chrysostom's Commentary on the Psalms." *Journal of Early Christian Studies* 5 (1997) 569–79.

———. "St. John Chrysostom and the Incarnation of the Word in Scripture." *Compass Theological Review* 14 (1980) 34–38.

Hubbell, Harry M. "Chrysostom and Rhetoric." *Classical Philology* 19 (1924) 261–78.

Jaeger, Werner. *Paideia: The Ideals of Greek Culture*. Translated by Gilbert Highet. Vol. 2, *In Search of the Divine Centre*. Oxford: Blackwell, 1947.

Juzek, J. H. *Die Christologie des hl. Johannes Chrysostomus: Zugleich ein Beitrag zur Dogmatik der Antiochener*. Breslau, 1912.

Kannengiesser, Charles. "Athanasius of Alexandria and the Foundation of Traditional Christology." *Theological Studies* 34 (1973) 103–13.

Kelly, J. N. D. *Early Christian Creeds*. 3rd ed. London: Longman, 1972.

———. *Early Christian Doctrines*. 5th ed. London: A. & C. Black, 1977.

———. *Golden Mouth: The Story of John Chrysostom: Ascetic, Preacher, Bishop*. Trowbridge: Duckworth, 1995.

Kennedy, George A. *Greek Rhetoric under Christian Emperors*. History of Rhetoric 3. Princeton: Princeton University Press, 1983.

Kenny, Anthony. "Was St. Chrysostom a Semi-Pelagian?" *Irish Theological Quarterly* 27 (1960) 16–29.

Kerrigan, Alexander. *St. Cyril of Alexandria: Interpreter of the Old Testament*. Analecta Biblica 2. Rome: Pontificio Instituto Biblico, 1952.

Koen, Lars. *The Saving Passion: Incarnational and Soteriological Thought in Cyril of Alexandria's Commentary on the Gospel according to St. John*. Acta Universitatis Upsaliensis: Studia Doctrinae Christianae Upsaliensia 31. Uppsala: University of Uppsala, 1991.

Kopecek, Thomas A. *A History of Neo-Arianism*. 2 vols. Patristic Monograph Series 8. Philadelphia: Philadelphia Patristic Foundation, 1979.

Korbacher, J. *Ausserhalb der Kirche kein Heil? Eine dogmengeschichtliche Untersuchung über Kirche und Kirchenzugehörigkeit bei Johannes Chrysostomus.* Münchener Theologische Studien 27. Munich: Hueber, 1963.
Krupp, R. A. *Shepherding the Flock of God: The Pastoral Theology of John Chrysostom.* New York: P. Lang, 1991.
Kugel, James L., and R. A. Greer. *Early Biblical Interpretation.* Library of Early Christianity 3. Philadelpia: Westminster, 1986.
Laistner, M. L. W. *Christianity and Pagan Culture in the Later Roman Empire.* Ithaca: Cornell University Press, 1967.
Lampe, G . W. H., and K. J. Woolcombe. *Essays on Typology.* Studies in Biblical Theology. London: SCM, 1957.
Lawrenz, Melvin Edward. "The Christology of John Chrysostom." PhD diss., Marquette Univeristy, 1987.
Liebeschuetz, J. H. W. G. *Antioch: City and Imperial Administration in the Later Roman Empire.* Oxford: Clarendon, 1972.
―――. *Barbarians and Bishops: Army, Church, and State in the Age of Arcadius and Chrysostom.* Oxford: Clarendon, 1991.
Macgilvray, Walter. *John of the Golden Mouth: Preacher of Antioch, and Primate of Constantinople.* London: James Nisbet, 1871.
Mayer, Wendy, and Pauline Allen. *John Chrysostom.* The Early Church Fathers. London: Routledge, 2000.
McGuckin, John A. *St. Cyril of Alexandria: The Christological Controversy.* Vigiliae Christianae 23. Leiden: Brill, 1988.
McKenzie, J. L. "The Commentary of Theodore of Mopsuestia on John 1:46–51." *Theological Studies* 14 (1953) 73–84.
McKibbens, T. R. "The Exegesis of John Chrysostom: Homilies on the Gospels." *Expository Times* 93 (1982) 264–70.
McManners, John. *The Oxford History of Christianity.* Oxford: Oxford University Press, 1993.
Meeks, Wayne A., and Robert L. Wilken. *Jews and Christians in Antioch in the First Four Centuries of the Common Era.* Sources of Biblical Study 13. Missoula, MT: Scholars, 1978.
Meyendorff, John. *Christ in Eastern Christian Thought.* 2nd ed. Translated by Yves Dubois. New York: St. Vladimir's Seminary Press, 1975.
Meyer, Louis. *Saint Jean Chrysostome, Maître de Perfection Chrétienne.* Paris: Gabriel Beauchesne, 1933.
Michaud, E. "La christologie de St. Jean Chrysostome." *Revue Internationale de Theologie* 17 (1909) 275–91.
―――. "La soteriologie de St. Jean Chrysostome." *Revue Internationale de Theologie* 18 (1910) 35–49.
Mitchell, Margaret M. *The Heavenly Trumpet: John Chrysostom and the Art of Pauline Interpretation.* Hermeneutische Untersuchungen Zur Theologie 40. Tübingen: Mohr Siebeck, 2000.
―――. "'A Variable and Many-Sorted Man': John Chrysostom's Treatment of Pauline Inconsistency." *Journal of Early Christian Studies* 6 (1998) 93–111.
Murphy, F. X. "The Moral Doctrine of John Chrysostom." *Studia Patristica* 9 (1972) 52–57.

Nash, Henry S. "The Exegesis of the School of Antioch." *Journal of Biblical Literature* 11 (1892) 23–37.

Neander, August. *The Life of John Chrysostom*. 2nd ed. Translated by J. C. Stapleton. London: R. B. Seeley & W. Burnside, 1838.

Neill, Stephen. *Chrysostom and His Message*. World Christian Books 44, 2nd ser. London: Lutterworth, 1962.

Norris, R. A. *The Christological Controversy*. Sources of Early Christian Thought. Philadelphia: Fortress, 1980.

———. "Christological Models in Cyril of Alexandria." *Texte und Untersuchungen* 116 (1975) 255–68.

Oberman, Heiko A. *Forerunners of the Reformation: The Shape of Late Medieval Thought*. Translated by Paul L. Nyhus. London: Lutterworth, 1967.

O'Keefe, John J. "'A Letter that Killeth': Toward a Reassessment of Antiochene Exegesis of Diodore, Theodore, and Theodoret on the Psalms." *Journal of Early Christian Studies* 8 (2000) 83–104.

Old, Hughes O. *The Reading and Preaching of the Scriptures in the Worship of the Christian Church*. Vol. 2, *The Patristic Age*. Grand Rapids: Eerdmans, 1998.

Osborn, Eric. *Ethical Patterns in Early Christian Thought*. Cambridge: Cambridge University Press, 1976.

Packard, A. A. "Chrysostom's True Christian Philosophy." *Anglican Theological Review* 45 (1963) 396–406.

Pagels, Elaine. "The Politics of Paradise: Augustine's Exegesis of Genesis 1–3 versus That of John Chrysostom." *Harvard Theological Review* 78 (1985) 67–99.

Palladius. *Dialogue on the Life of St. John Chrysostom*. Translated and edited by Robert T. Meyer. Ancient Christian Writers 45. New York: Newman, 1985.

Paverd, Frans van de. *St. John Chrysostom, the Homilies on the Statues: An Introduction*. Rome: Pontificium Institutum Studiorum Orientalium, 1991.

Payne, Robert. *The Holy Fire: The Story of the Fathers of the Eastern Church*. London: Skeffington, 1958.

Pelikan, Jaroslav. *Credo: Historical and Theological Guide to Creeds and Confessions of Faith in the Christian Tradition*. New Haven: Yale University Press, 2003.

———. *Divine Rhetoric: The Sermon on the Mount as Message and as Model in Augustine, Chrysostom, and Luther*. Crestwood, NY: St. Vladimir's Seminary Press, 2001.

———. *The Preaching of John Chrysostom: Homilies on the Sermon on the Mount*. Philadelphia: Fortress, 1967.

Pittenger, Norman. *Christ for Us Today*. London: SCM, 1968.

Pleasants, Phyliss R. "Making Christian the Christians: The Baptismal Instructions of St. John Chrysostom." *Greek Othodox Theological Review* 34 (1989) 379–92.

Pressensé, Edmond de. *Christian Life and Practice in the Early Church*. Translated by Annie Harwood-Holmden. London: Hodder & Stoughton, 1877.

Prestige, G. L. *Fathers and Heretics*. London: SPCK, 1977.

———. *God in Patristic Thought*. London: SPCK, 1952.

Puech, Aime. *Saint John Chrysostom*. Translated by Mildred Partridge. London: Duckworth, 1902.

Quinn, Jerome D. "Saint John Chrysostom on History in the Synoptics." *Catholic Biblical Quarterly* 24 (1962) 140–47.

Ramsey, Boniface. *Begining to Read the Fathers*. London: Darton, Longman & Todd, 1986.

Riley, Hugh M. *Christian Initiation: A Comparative Study of the Interpretation of the Baptismal Liturgy in the Mystagogical Writings of Cyril of Jerusalem, John Chrysostom, Theodore of Mopsuestia, and Ambrose of Milan*. Studies in Christian Antiquity 17. Washington, DC: Catholic University of America Press, 1974.

Rufinus. *A Commentary on the Apostles' Creed*. Translated by J. N. D. Kelly. London: Longmans, Green, 1955.

Sawhill, John Alexander. "The Use of Athletic Metaphors in the Biblical Homilies of St. John Chrysostom." PhD diss., Princeton University, 1928.

Schaüblin, Christoph. *Untersuchungen zu Methode und Herkunft der antiochenischen Exegese*. Cologne: P. Hanstein, 1974.

Schoedel, William R., and Robert L. Wilken, editors. *Early Christian Literature and the Classical Intellectual Tradition*. Theologie Historique. Paris: Beauchesne, 1979.

Schulz, Hans-Joachim. *The Byzantine Liturgy: Symbolic Structure and Faith Expression*. New York: Pueblo, 1986.

Sellers, R. V. *The Council of Chalcedon: A Historical and Doctrinal Survey*. London: SPCK, 1961.

———. *Two Ancient Christologies*. London: SPCK, 1940.

Siddals, Ruth M. "Logic and Christology in Cyril of Alexandria." *Journal of Theological Studies* 38 (1987) 341–67.

Simonetti, Manlio. *Biblical Interpretation in the Early Church: A Historical Introduction to Patristic Exegesis*. Translated by John A. Hughes. Edinburgh: T. & T. Clark, 1994.

Stephens, W. R. W. *Saint Chrysostom: His Life and Times*. London: John Murray, 1872.

Studer, Basil. *Trinity and Incarnation: The Faith of the Early Church*. Translated by Matthias Westerhoff. Edinburgh: T. & T. Clark, 1993.

Swetnam, James. "Christology and the Eucharist in the Epistle to the Hebrews." *Biblica* 70 (1989) 74–95.

Taft, Robert. *Liturgy in Byzantium and Beyond*. Aldershot, UK: Variorum, 1995.

Tanner, R. G. "Chrysostom's Exegesis of Romans." *Studia Patristica* 17 (1982) 1185–97.

Telfer, W. "The Fourth-Century Greek Fathers as Exegetes." *Harvard Theological Review* 50 (1957) 91–105.

Thiselton, Anthony C. *New Horizons in Hermeneutics*. Grand Rapids: Zondervan, 1997.

Torjesen, Karen Jo. *Hermeneutical Procedure and Theological Method in Origen's Exegesis*. Berlin: de Gruyter, 1986.

Torrance, Iain R. *Christology after Chalcedon: Severus of Antioch and Sergius the Monophysite*. Norwich: Canterbury Press, 1988.

———. "'God the Physician': Ecclesiology, Sin and Forgiveness in the Preaching of St. John Chrysostom." *Greek Orthodox Theological Review* 44 (1999) 166–73.

Torrance, Thomas F. *The Christian Frame of Mind*. London: Handsel, 1985.

———. *Divine Meaning*. Edinburgh: T. & T. Clark, 1995.

———. *The Doctrine of Grace in the Apostolic Fathers*. Edinburgh: Oliver & Boyd, 1948.

———. *The Mediation of Christ*. Exeter: Paternoster, 1983.

———. *Theology in Reconciliation*. London: Geoffrey Chapman, 1975.

———. *The Trinitarian Faith*. Edinburgh: T. & T. Clark, 1988.

Trakatellis, Demetrios. "Being Transformed: Chrysostom's Exegesis of the Epistle to the Romans." *Greek Orthodox Theological Review* 36 (1991) 211–29.
Trigg, Joseph W. *Biblical Interpretation.* Message of the Fathers of the Church 9. Wilmington: M. Glazier, 1994.
———. *Origen: The Bible and Philosophy in the Third-Century Church.* Atlanta: John Knox, 1983.
Turner, H. E. W. *The Patristic Doctrine of Redemption.* London: Mowbray, 1952.
———. *The Pattern of Christian Truth: A Study in the Relations between Orthodoxy and Heresy in the Early Church.* Bampton Lectures 1954. New York: AMS, 1978.
Vaccari, A. "La 'Teoria' Esegetica Antiochena." *Biblica* 15 (1934) 94–101.
Vawter, Bruce. *Biblical Inspiration.* London: Hutchinson, 1972.
Walchenbach, John R. "John Calvin as Biblical Commentator: An Investigation into Calvin's Use of John Chrysostom as an Exegetical Tutor." PhD diss., University of Pittsburgh, 1974.
Waldrop, Charles T. *Karl Barth's Christology: Its Basic Alexandrian Character.* Religion and Reason 21. Berlin: Mouton, 1984.
Wallace-Hadrill, D. S. *Christian Antioch: A Study of Early Christian Thought in the East.* Cambridge: Cambridge University Press, 1982.
Warfield, Benjamin B. *The Person and Work of Christ.* Edited by Samuel G. Craig. Philadelphia: Presbyterian & Reformed, 1970.
Welch, Lawrence J. *Christology and Eucharist in the Early Thought of Cyril of Alexandria.* San Francisco: Catholic Scholars, 1994.
Wiles, Maurice. *The Christian Fathers.* Knowing Christianity. London: Hodder & Stoughton, 1966.
———. *The Spiritual Gospel: The Interpretation of the Fourth Gospel in the Early Church.* Cambridge: The University Press, 1960.
———. "Theodore of Mopsuestia as Representative of the Antiochene School." In *The Cambridge History of the Bible*, edited by P. Ackroyd and C. F. Evans, 1:489–510. Cambridge: Cambridge University Press, 1970.
Wiles, Maurice, and Mark Santer, editors. *Documents in Early Christian Thought.* Cambridge: Cambridge University Press, 1975.
Wilken, Robert L. "Exegesis and the History of Theology: Reflections on the Adam-Christ Typology in Cyril of Alexandria." *Church History* 35 (1966) 137–56.
———. *John Chrysostom and the Jews: Rhetoric and Reality in the Late Fourth Century.* Berkeley: University of California Press, 1983.
———. *Judaism and the Early Christian Mind: A Study of Cyril of Alexandria's Exegesis and Theology.* New Haven: Yale University Press, 1971.
———. "Tradition, Exegesis, and the Christological Controversies." *Church History* 34 (1965) 123–42.
Williams, Rowan. *Arius: Heresy and Tradition.* London: Darton, Longman & Todd, 1987.
———, editor. *The Making of Orthodoxy: Essays in Honour of Henry Chadwick.* Cambridge: Cambridge University Press, 1989.
Winslow, Donald, F. "Christology and Exegesis in the Cappadocians." *Church History* 40 (1971) 389–96.
Wolfson, Harry A. *The Philosophy of the Church Fathers: Faith, Trinity, Incarnation.* 3rd ed. Cambridge: Harvard University Press, 1976.

Woodbridge, John D. *Biblical Authority: A Critique of the Rogers/McKim Proposal.* Grand Rapids: Zondervan, 1982.

Yarnold, Edward. *The Awe-Inspiring Rites of Initiation: Baptismal Homilies of the Fourth Century.* Slough, UK: St. Paul, 1972.

Young, Frances. *Biblical Exegesis and the Formation of Christian Culture.* Cambridge: Cambridge University Press, 1997.

———. "Christological Ideas in the Greek Commentaries on the Epistle to the Hebrews." *Journal of Theological Studies* 20 (1969) 150–63.

———. *From Nicea to Chalcedon: A Guide to the Literature and Its Background.* London: SCM, 1983.

———. "A Reconsideration of Alexandrian Christology." *The Journal of Ecclesiastical History* 22 (1974) 103–14.

———. "They Speak to Us across the Centuries." *The Expository Times* 109 (1997) 38–41.

———. *The Use of Sacrificial Ideas in Greek Christian Writers from the New Testament to John Chrysostom.* Cambridge: Philadelphia Patristic Foundation, 1979.

Subject Index

Adoption as sons. *See* sons by grace
Akribeia, 70–71, 78
Alexandria
   city of, 1, 10
   episcopal see of, 13–14
   school of interpretation, xiv,
      28–47, 48, 49, 50, 51, 70
   tradition, 19–21, 85, 88, 247–59
Antioch
   City of, xiii, xiv, 1–10
   episcopal see of, 10–15
   school of Interpretation, xiv,
      18–21, 47–81
   tradition, xiv, 29
Apollinarius/Apollinarianism, xiii,
   66, 86, 87, 201
Arius/Arianism, Neo-Arianism,
   xiii, 7, 51, 94, 96, 119, 183,
   250
Askētērion, 3, 5, 16, 51
Assumed Man, 65–66, 169–70, 170,
   220, 245, 259
Athanasius, 20, 21, 23, 40, 42, 45,
   71, 87, 88, 90, 117, 200, 201,
   248, 258
Augustine, ix, 2, 10, 23, 150, 224
Aulén, Gustaf 120–21, 146

Baptism
   Christ's Baptism, 73, 94, 106–12
   and the Christian life, 93, 105,
      113–17, 122, 197, 225, 254,
      256
   and union with Christ, 117–18,
      133, 143–44, 198
   as renewal of the divine image,
      113–17, 227–29

Basil of Caesarea, 40
Baur, Chrysostomus, xvi, 4, 5, 6, 9,
   51, 53, 54, 78, 172–73

Chadwick, Henry, 138–39, 147
Chalcedon
   city of, 13
   Council of, xiii, 97, 251
   Christology, 86
Charity, 158, 159, 162, 163, 235,
   236–37, 242
   as *Eleēmosynē*, 159, 162, 236
Chase, Fredric Henry, 70
Christ (Jesus)
   consubstantiality with the
      Father, xiii, 8, 65, 93, 94, 104,
      117–18, 119, 125, 140, 145,
      147, 151, 165–66, 179, 182,
      183, 250–51, 256
   Incarnation, 101, 117, 118, 139,
      170, 180, 250
   preexistence, 38, 198, 243
   single subject, xv, 88, 93, 147,
      172, 199, 200, 258
   Son by nature, 87, 94–97, 104,
      119, 168, 178, 181
   Son of God, xv, 180, 187, 250,
      251–53
   suffering and death, 24, 168,
      170, 175, 178, 179–200, 204,
      232, 236, 240, 241, 243–44,
      250, 252, 253–54
Christology
   adoptionist, 106–7
   divisive, 171, 179, 219, 220, 245

Christology (*cont.*)
  union of natures, xiii, 86, 97, 99, 102, 180, 182
  unitive, xv, 94, 146–47, 167, 168, 172, 179, 200, 219, 232, 242–45, 256, 258, 260
Clement of Alexandria, 23, 29, 30–33, 34, 36, 37, 39, 80–81, 247
Constantinople
  city of, 1, 8, 11-14, 16
  episcopal see, xiii, xiv, 1, 3, 5, 7, 10–14, 40, 58, 172–73, 257–58
  First Council (AD 381), xiii, 5
  Second Council (AD 553), 62–63
Cyril of Alexandria, 10, 23, 40–47, 53, 71, 80–81, 87–88, 97, 107–9, 111–12, 117, 138, 139–40, 147, 170, 200–201, 220, 248, 258

Diodore of Tarsus, 3–4, 16, 28–29, 51–58, 59, 66, 72–73, 75–76, 78, 81, 86, 248
Divinization, 169

Ephesus, Council of, xiii
Eucharist, xv, 6, 7, 84, 118, 119, 128, 138–45, 146–47, 196, 215, 217, 255

Florovsky, Georges, 98
Froehlich, Karlfried, 19, 38, 48, 54

Gnostics, 24, 25–27, 30, 33, 36, 121, 171, 247
God the Father, xiii, 7, 8, 25, 26, 34, 36, 38, 44, 91, 93, 94–96, 98, 100–102, 104–7, 108, 111, 114, 115, 117–18, 119–24, 125–30, 134, 136, 140, 142, 145, 146–47, 149, 151, 156, 162, 163, 165, 166, 171, 181–89, 197–99, 205, 207–8, 210, 212–17, 229, 230–31, 236, 240, 250–51, 252, 253, 254, 256
God the Son. *See* Christ
God the Holy Spirit, 7, 8, 21, 22, 34, 35–36, 43, 55, 57, 61, 62, 63, 67, 69, 71, 73, 80, 91, 101, 103, 105, 106, 107–12, 113–17, 130, 133, 134, 140, 156, 162, 167, 211, 214, 215, 222, 226, 227, 229, 232, 233, 235, 240–43, 245, 247, 252, 254–57
Grace
  as assistance, 178, 219–20, 232–41, 242–43
  as *eudokia*, 97, 232
  as incorruption, 104, 112, 138
  Christ as the source of, 99, 116, 121, 122, 147, 202, 205–6, 216, 242, 244
  sons by grace, 93–94, 102–5, 110–11, 113–18, 189, 200, 219, 226, 242–43, 256–60
  transformation by, 148–67, 227–32, 242, 244, 245
  priority in salvation, 222–27, 242, 244
Grant, Robert M, 25, 27, 29, 39, 60
Greer, Rowan, 20, 25, 169–70, 171–72
Gregory of Nazianzus, 10, 16, 40, 90
Gregory of Nyssa, 40, 107
Grillmeier, Aloys, 21, 87

Harnack, Adolf von, 68
Holy Spirit. *See* God the Holy Spirit
Hypostasis, 250
Hypostatic union, xiii, 97, 183, 251

Incarnation. *See* Christ
Irenaeus, 21, 23, 25–26, 27, 28, 39, 80, 102, 121, 247

Katastasis, 220
Kelly, J. N. D, 4, 6, 7, 9, 11, 25, 88, 173

Logos-Son, the
    as the natural Son, 94–98
    as the personal subject in Christ, 87, 166, 179, 181, 199, 245, 253
    as the single subject in Christ, xv, 88, 93, 147, 172, 199, 200, 258
    as teacher and guide, 30
    distinct from the Father, 94–98
    equality with the Father, 94–98

Monasticism, 4, 51

Natural Communion
    of the Godhead, 95, 98, 147, 250,
    participation in, 98, 102, 121, 124, 137–40, 141, 145, 146, 147, 165–66, 213, 231, 235, 254, 259
Nestorius, 52, 58, 62, 87, 139
Nicea
    Creed, xiii, 66, 183,
    Council of, xiii, 251

Origen, 28, 34–40, 41, 46, 80, 81, 248

Pelagian Controversy, 224
Prestige, George, 50
Prosopon, 131,

Quasten, Johannes, 48, 50, 52, 172

Redemption, 47, 70, 75, 91, 93, 96, 98, 99, 100–102, 109, 112, 118, 134, 136–37, 139, 146, 147, 202, 211–13, 216, 218, 252, 254, 257

Salvation, 26, 38, 71, 91, 93, 98, 99, 100, 102, 120–24, 126, 131, 137, 139, 141, 155, 156, 161, 169, 170, 171, 176, 178, 188, 190–93, 195, 197, 198, 200, 208, 209, 220, 221, 224–27, 232, 242–45, 250, 252, 254, 256, 259
Schaff, Philip, 33, 77
Sunkatabasis, 70, 82, 249

Tertullian, 21, 23, 25, 27–28, 30, 31, 50, 80, 247
Theodore of Mopsuestia, 4, 28, 29, 49, 51, 52, 58–67, 72, 73, 75, 77, 78, 81, 86–88, 90, 97, 169, 170, 220, 245, 248, 259
Torrance, Thomas, 24, 31, 40, 200–201, 207

Virtuous Life, the, 117, 149, 150, 152–54, 157–65, 166, 167, 192, 240, 241, 243, 245, 249, 256–58

Wilken, Robert, 41, 43–45, 107–8

Young, Frances, 17, 28, 48, 85, 149, 170–72

www.ingramcontent.com/pod-product-compliance
Lightning Source LLC
Chambersburg PA
CBHW070238230426
43664CB00014B/2341